The Sink

Crime, Terror,

and Dirty Money

in the Offshore World

Jeffrey Robinson

M&S

National Library of Canada Cataloguing in Publication

Robinson, Jeffrey, 1945–
   The sink : crime, terror, and dirty money in the offshore world / Jeffrey Robinson.

Includes bibliographical references.
ISBN 0-7710-7584-7

1. Money laundering.   2. Banks and banking – Corrupt practices – Caribbean Area.   I. Title.

HV6768.R62 2003   364.16'8   C2003-903665-0

We acknowledge the financial support of the Government of Canada through the Book Publishing Industry Development Program and that of the Government of Ontario through the Ontario Media Development Corporation's Ontario Book Initiative. We further acknowledge the support of the Canada Council for the Arts and the Ontario Arts Council for our publishing program.

Typeset in Bembo by M&S, Toronto
Printed and bound in Canada

This book is printed on acid-free paper that is 100% recycled, ancient-forest friendly (40% post-consumer recycled).

McClelland & Stewart Ltd.
The Canadian Publishers
481 University Avenue
Toronto, Ontario
M5G 2E9
www.mcclelland.com

1 2 3 4 5   07 06 05 04 03

Please note: All dollar amounts cited in the text are United States dollars unless otherwise indicated.

CONTENTS

For my old pal
Mort Shuman
1936–1991
tu nous manques

GLOSSARY

back-to-back loans: loans that are guaranteed with money hidden, usually offshore

BCCI: Bank of Credit and Commerce International

bearer share: an anonymous company owned by whoever happens to have physical possession of the share certificate

BMPE: Black Market Peso Exchange

BoE: Bank of England

BoNY: Bank of New York

BSA: Bank Secrecy Act

CD: Certificate of Deposit

CFATF: Caribbean Financial Action Task Force

CI: confidential informant

CSE: Communications Security Establishment

CSIS: Canadian Security Intelligence Service

CTR: Currency Transaction Report

DEA: Drug Enforcement Administration (U.S.)

EC: European Community

ECHELON: U.S.-organized spy system operated by the National Security Agency in conjunction with Canada, the U.K., Australia, and New Zealand

FATF: Financial Action Task Force

FinCEN: Financial Crimes Enforcement Network (U.S.)

FinTRAC: Financial Transactions and Reports Analysis Centre (Can.)

FISAC: Financial Investigation and Special Access Unit (U.K.)

FIU: Financial Intelligence Unit

FRU: Financial Reporting Unit

FSA: Financial Services Authority (U.K.)

FSF: Financial Stability Forum

FTC: Federal Trade Commission

G8: the eight industrial nations grouped together under the auspices of the OECD

GCHQ: Government Communications Headquarters (U.K.)

hawallah: traditional Third World underground paperless banking system

IBC: international business corporation (shell company)

IFO: independent foreign owner

IPB: International Private Banking

IRS: Internal Revenue Service

KLA: Kosovo Liberation Army

KYC: Know Your Customer

LCN: La Cosa Nostra (another name for the Mafia)

MLCA: Money Laundering Control Act

MROS: Money Laundering Reporting Office (Switz.)

NASD: National Association of Securities Dealers

NCIS: National Criminal Intelligence Service (U.K.)

NORAID: IRA-backed charity

NSC: National Security Council (U.S.)

NTFIU: National Terrorist Financial Investigation Unit (U.K.)

OCC: Office of the Comptroller of the Currency (U.S.)

OECD: Organisation for Economic Co-operation and Development

PTA: pass-through account

Public Citizen: Washington-based government watchdog

PWC: PricewaterhouseCoopers

SAR: Suspicious Activity Report

SBA: Swiss Bankers Association

SEC: Securities and Exchange Commission

SHARE: Shareholders Association of Canada

shell bank: a company licensed to operate as a bank without having a physical presence anywhere

Smurf: named for the cartoon characters, these are armies of workers who deposit small amounts of cash in banks, as part of the money-laundering process, hoping to avoid reporting restrictions

SO-12: Special Operations – Intelligence (U.K.)

UAE: United Arab Emirates

PROLOGUE

When the government of Antigua granted an offshore licence to Hanover Bank Ltd., the deal was typical and straightforward. The company could operate as a bank anywhere in the world, except Antigua.

After all, that government had long ago predetermined, if any offshore bank licensed on the island was going to scam someone, it was not going to be an Antiguan. Which was fine with the owner of Hanover, an Irishman with absolutely no banking experience, because he never had any intention of scamming anyone in Antigua. A former public-relations adviser to Irish Prime Minister Charles Haughey, he didn't even plan on opening an office in Antigua. The reason he chartered his bank on the island was because he knew that no one there particularly cared about how he ran his business, as long as he didn't do it in Antigua.

Not that Hanover had a physical presence anywhere else. There was no building, there were no tellers, there were no drive-through cash machines. The bank was nothing more than a plaque on a wall in the office of a company-formation agent in the Caribbean and some files in a sitting room in Ireland. Its two clients were an international fraudster and a U.S.-based convicted money launderer. No one in Antigua audited Hanover's books. For that matter, neither did anyone in Ireland, where the Central Bank didn't have a clue that Hanover was in business.

Still, Hanover had a correspondent relationship with a bank in the Channel Islands, which, in turn, had a relationship with the New York branch of a Chicago bank, which had an office in Canada. Such is the nature of the offshore world that a bank that didn't exist could do business in North America.

Five thousand miles to the northeast of Antigua, in Moscow, the Soviet Union was little more than a bad memory. During the heyday of the Communist Party, there was only one bank in town – the State. When the Iron Curtain disintegrated, however, banks rose from the ashes. By the end of the 1990s, there were around two thousand banks in Moscow alone, 85 per cent to 90 per cent of them owned by, run by, or otherwise managed by organized criminal groups.

One of those new banks was controlled by speculators who were systematically raping the Russian economy by stealing funds from former Soviet industries. The money was funnelled out of the country to shell companies with bank accounts in the Channel Islands. From there, it was moved to New York. In the course of six months, no fewer than ten thousand transactions were lodged in a single account, amounting to $4.2 billion. Eventually $7 billion was moved out of Russia this way, laundered through those accounts and dropped into the Bank of New York.

The paramount lesson of Russian capitalism is clear. In the global business environment where there is such easy access to the offshore world, bad guys don't need to rob banks, they can buy them.

Twenty-eight hundred miles south of Moscow, a financial institution in Sudan was doing business according to the strict teachings of Islam. The Al Shamal Islamic Bank had its headquarters in the centre of Khartoum. At least until 1998, the bank had correspondent relationships with American Express, Citibank, the Arab American Bank, ING Bank in Indonesia, Commerzbank in Germany, Crédit Lyonnais in Switzerland, and Standard Bank in South Africa. Although some of those agreements were inactive by 9/11, each bank maintained correspondent accounts in the United States, Britain, Canada, Australia, New Zealand, and throughout the West.

Correspondent banking is an acknowledged necessity of global finance. Nevertheless, it allows institutions in dubious offshore jurisdictions to conduct business in countries where they are not licensed. Al Shamal opened in 1982 backed by Saudi money. The U.S. State

Department maintains that Osama bin Laden invested \$50 million in the bank. Al Shamal refutes that. In a written statement, the bank acknowledges that bin Laden held three accounts there from 1992 to 1997, but asserts that he was never a founder or a shareholder. Whether he was or he wasn't, it remains that Al Shamal's correspondent relationships gave bin Laden open access to western banking.

According to a U.S. Senate report, virtually every major bank in the world – especially the biggest in North America and Europe – holds accounts for offshore banks and/or banks in suspect jurisdictions. Even though recently passed laws make it more difficult for U.S. banks to hold accounts for "shell banks" such as Hanover, loopholes in the laws are gaping. The banking lobby in Washington made sure of that, fighting the various bills that would have restricted such relationships. In their eyes, it was vital to guarantee that the offshore world would survive and flourish. After all, business is business. And the business of moving money into and out of shady jurisdictions is so colossal, so hugely profitable for the banking industry, that most people outside the industry never saw it as anything but a money spinner, at least not until 9/11.

The cornerstone of twenty-first-century globalization was laid during the final decade of the twentieth century, which brought about the greatest quantum leap in technology since man invented the wheel. Satellites, faxes, cellphones, the Internet, and e-mail reduced the planet to the size of a PalmPilot.

Although national sovereignty was not yet dead, the concept that we've lived with since the seventeenth century has been administered last rites. Radical changes in transport and communications seriously impede governments' ability to exercise controls over the movement of goods, services, people, and ideas. Not just in the West, where change is often welcome, but in the closed societies of Asia and the Middle East, where change threatens the power base of dictatorial rule. The momentum is such that, inevitably, it is unstoppable. The rivers, mountain ranges, oceans, and imaginary lines that originally defined borders would always be there, but the national supremacy that those borders imply is swiftly evaporating.

Consider the Quebec independence movement. It's based entirely on the misconception that separation would create a country that could be governed. What was true in the 1970s is no longer so because there is nothing left to be governed, besides speed limits and stop signs that say "Arrêt." Real power no longer lies in Ottawa or Washington or London or Paris. Military might does. But real power is exercised in boardrooms. Real power is pharmaceutical companies and telecoms and insurance companies and banks, which are no longer Canadian or Québécois or, for that matter, American, British, or French. They are "beyond nationals." They are command and control. And in the globalized world of the twenty-first century, corporate command and control is *realpolitik*.

As corporations have replaced nation-states – serving markets that fuse like single-cell amoeba to form larger, more powerful, more intelligent creatures – globalization of the legal economy simultaneously globalized the underworld. As newly globalized exchanges found emancipation beyond territorial control, so did terrorism and organized crime. Money drives all of them, and while money has always been a political force, never before has it been so easy for people intent on committing crimes to harness that energy.

Burrowing inside the confusion created by the global flood of goods, services, people, ideas, and "megabyte bucks" – blips on computer screens that are not tethered to central banks or geography – transnational organized criminals and terrorist mobs like al-Qaeda emerged with the capacity to impose themselves way beyond their station.

In the globalized world of the twenty-first century, there is, at any given time, an estimated $600 billion to $700 billion in dirty money circling the planet looking to get clean. The lion's share is drug money. But, as crime and terrorism are twins, it is increasingly difficult to separate drug money from terrorist money. At times they look alike. At times they are the same. All too often, the link that binds them are weapons – handguns for assassinations, automatic rifles for insurrections, weapons of mass destruction to promote political ideals.

In the globalized world of the twenty-first century, drugs, arms, and dirty money are the Holy Trinity. They move like a malignant virus through the system, driving crime and terror, breeding unabated offshore in the murky heart of the legitimate, global financial world. Organized criminals and global terrorists work the same neighbourhoods, deal in the same "currencies" – drugs, diamonds, fissile materials – and bank with the same people.

Until 9/11, many European and North American politicians considered foreign-sponsored terrorism something that happened only in other countries, and believed that organized crime needed to be defined locally. The reasons are obvious: they couldn't do much about global terrorism anyway, except sit on committees, issue reports, and point fingers; and by insisting that crime was a local issue, they could convince themselves they were solving the problem. But law enforcement is a declaration of sovereignty. The state dictates: You may not comport yourself in a certain manner while inside this imaginary line. So, while the politicians passed laws and funded law enforcement to stop and punish those who did not comply, like old generals, they were sending their armies out to fight the last war. In this globalized world of twenty-first-century crime and terror, those who do not comply have created wealth and safety by purposely functioning beyond reach.

More cops on the beat may mean fewer little old ladies having their purses stolen, but it has no effect whatsoever on real crime and real terror. It simply gives politicians the right to boast that the crime rate is coming down – making them worthy of re-election – because diminishing crime rates is what's supposed to happen when politicians promise to tackle crime. Except that when the bottom line of the business of crime and terror jumps from where it was at the beginning of the 1990s – around $100 billion to $300 billion – to $600 billion to $700 billion at the end of that decade, there is reason to suggest that politicians don't know what they're talking about.

Which, until 9/11, most of them clearly didn't.

Just look at the way inattention, incompetence, and narrow "local issue" thinking has allowed money launderers, criminals, bankers, accountants, brokers, company-formation agents, financial advisers, and lawyers to get rich off the back of dirty money. That $600 billion to $700 billion represents a mere 10 per cent of the wealth that is today hidden offshore. In other words, there is $6 *trillion* to $7 *trillion* – that's twelve zeros – moving through the offshore world, beyond the reach of western laws and out of sight of western law enforcement. What's more, that money is protected from oversight by those same bankers, accountants, brokers, company-formation agents, financial advisers, and lawyers

– and with the conscious support of dozens of governments – by a system that has been deliberately designed to short-circuit oversight.

Out of 190 or so jurisdictions in the United Nations, at least 65 offer secret banking that, in some cases, is absolutely airtight. It has been estimated that four thousand banks operate in the offshore world, most of them with no physical presence anywhere. The Swiss, once famous for their numbered accounts, are no longer at the top of the league. Dozens of jurisdictions do it better than Switzerland, more efficiently and with a much lower risk of detection.

Most offshore centres have two things in common: unsustainable population growth and limited natural resources. Banking and company fees become an important source of income, derived from a non-polluting, employment-hungry industry. As long as banks and companies are restricted from doing business in the home jurisdiction, the population is safe from the frauds and felonies that might be associated with shell banks and international business corporations (IBCs).

Surrounding this are legitimate financial institutions, which charge handsome fees to provide special services, euphemistically called "private banking." Holding out the promise of tax-efficient investment, tax avoidance, and ultimate discretion, major banks offer these services to clients willing to pay those handsome fees. The fact that banking secrecy does not legally exist in Canada does not hinder Canadian banks from offering such services to their wealthiest clients. In some cases, those wealthiest clients are legitimate businesses that use the offshore world for both legitimate and illicit reasons. In that respect, there is no inherent difference between the Mafia's money, al-Qaeda's money, and Enron's money.

During the first few months of the Bush administration – a Texas-oil-connected White House – official U.S. policy was to turn a blind eye to money laundering as a tax-evasion tool in the Caribbean. It is perhaps no coincidence that this happened at the same time that the Texas-based energy company, Enron – with no fewer than three thousand shell companies offshore – was fighting to stay alive. Enron called its shell companies "corporate subsidiaries" and "partnerships." They were set up for two reasons: to avoid taxes, which the company successfully did in four of its final five years; and so that the regulators, analysts, and shareholders couldn't find out what Enron's management was doing with the company's money, which was stealing it.

That the offshore world is the financial equivalent of a black hole should not come as a surprise to anyone who looks at the basic economics of jurisdictions offering secret banking, totally opaque corporate duck-blinds, and economic citizenship. But this colossal force, sucking money into offshore banking and corporate secrecy, has reached the point where it poses a serious risk to western stability.

Within days of the World Trade Center and Pentagon atrocities, as the financial war on terrorism slowly gathered momentum, attention rightly turned to the offshore world. In response, foreign bankers in jurisdictions that had customarily been shut tight to outside scrutiny voluntarily announced that they would take the initiative to root out any terrorist money hidden there. Some accounts were, in fact, frozen. At the same time, certain jurisdictions simply gave themselves a clean bill of health – *terrorists have not been, nor will they ever be, welcome here* – in the obvious hope that such proclamations would allow them to return to business as usual.

The offshore world was saying, No one here will do business with terrorists as long as no one anywhere else worries about the way we do business with criminals of other persuasions, whether they're organized Russians or Enron.

This remains the anthem of the sink that is the offshore world.

As so much of that world is enveloped by the British Commonwealth, a fair question is: Why doesn't Britain do something about it? The answer is simple – and this holds true for Holland and France, two other nations with heavy investments in the offshore world – there are no votes in it. Direct intervention in the offshore world is too hard a sell. Shutting down an island somewhere offers no immediate political capital. Anyway, the cost is too high. There are no substitute crop programs for out-of-business offshore banks. There are no alternate jobs for out-of-work company-formation agents. Throughout the Eastern Caribbean, offshore money has become the mainstay of the local economy. In other areas, it has become the mainstay of political corruption. A draconian crackdown would not feed the poor or pave the roads. Instead, it would threaten the local economy, possibly destroy the tourist industry, and put natives on the breadlines.

Lamentably, dirty money is estimated to be as much as 2 per cent of the world's gross domestic product, making it so vital to the global economic system that a thorough purging would have severe economic ramifications throughout the First World. And yet:

From the Channel Islands, funds collected as supposed Islamic charities were laundered on their way to America to support al-Qaeda.

From Toronto, telephone-marketing fraudsters have managed to hold on to a large share of the $40-billion global industry they helped to create by defrauding foreigners, and then moving their money through the offshore world, depriving Canadian law enforcement of access to the victims and to the proceeds of crime.

In Cyprus, Russian criminal organizations control a huge percentage of the 48,000 shell companies registered there, 47,000 of which have no physical presence whatsoever – no roof, no phone number, not even a post box.

From Dubai, the offshore banking capital of the Gulf States, five times as much money moves back and forth to the Indian subcontinent through the *hawallah*, or underground, banking system than through legitimate banking channels. *Hawallah* bankers in Dubai – and in Afghanistan and in Pakistan, and in ethnic neighbourhoods across North America and Europe – assert their cultural right to do business in this traditional way. Which means no paperwork or money trail.

In four American cities, a Somalian-based wire remitter was shut down in dawn raids in November 2001 by U.S. Customs officers who suspected that the Al Barakaat network was funding terrorist cells. Among the evidence uncovered was a connection with an Islamic charity whose money was in the Channel Islands. The jury remains out on just how much money moved through these offices, but it took 9/11 for someone to act, even though Al Barakaat had been suspected of moving money illegally for at least two years prior to 9/11.

In the totally phony offshore jurisdiction of Niue, some two thousand people living on a rock in the middle of the Pacific earn an estimated $2 million a year in fees from licensing phony banks and dubious shell companies, representing 7 to 10 per cent of the national economy.

Relatively nearby, in the equally phony offshore jurisdiction of Nauru, ten thousand natives licensed four hundred offshore banks that at one point accounted for more than 5 per cent of government revenue.

In Puerto Vallarta, Mexico, police deported a former Edmonton real-estate agent named Alyn Richard Waage. They sent him to California, where he stands accused of bilking fifteen thousand people in fifty-seven countries out of $60 million through his fraudulent Tri-West Investment Club. The company was registered in Panama, maintained mail drops in Belize and the Bahamas, and laundered money through banks in Mexico, Costa Rica, and Latvia, before bringing it back to New York.

The offshore world is a place where money trails evaporate into thin air, where dirty money mingles with the financial traffic of the world's legitimate businesses, where connections smudge and are then erased, and where anyone looking for the truth is confronted by so many man-made barriers – many of them frequently cloaked in the guise of legality – that inquiries are, in the end, mostly futile. With so much at stake, the people best positioned to put a stop to this are the very same people making money from it – bankers, accountants, brokers, company-formation agents, financial advisers, and lawyers. It's hardly surprising that they don't have much incentive to do so.

Again, the Caribbean is the best example. The banks are there. The shell companies are there. The Colombians are nearby. The Italians are willing to meet there. And these days the Russians are there too, having turned the Caribbean into organized crime's version of the warm water port the Soviet military could never establish.

That bank secrecy is a service many people are willing to pay for goes without saying. But to claim, as many of these jurisdictions do, that selling such a service is their sovereign right as long as no laws are being violated in that sovereignty – with total disregard to laws being violated elsewhere – is more than just disingenuous. Most people who hide money are doing so for reasons that, at best, might be questionable and, at worst, are blatantly illegal somewhere.

By taking the moral high ground in their defence of secrecy, these jurisdictions ignore the fact that, as long as stealth is the product, no matter how it's disguised – an international business corporation, a numbered bank account, an insurance trust – two questions must be asked: Who is buying that product? And, Why are they paying for it?

Unless those questions are then satisfactorily answered, the offshore world will continue, intolerably, to be the sink that washes dirty money in direct support of crime and terror.

Money-laundering facilities evolved because there was enough money that needed to be laundered to create laundromats. At the same time, those laundromats generated enough cash flow and reinvestment for criminals and terrorists that greater sums needed to be laundered. Accordingly, by reducing the amount of money looking to get clean, you affect the laundromats. By abolishing the laundromats, you severely disrupt the cash flow and reinvestment of the business of crime and the business of terror. As long as drug traffickers, terrorists, fraudsters, tax evaders, and other criminals – both private and corporate – are permitted to use legitimate means to achieve illegitimate ends, then any attempt by any jurisdiction to corral money laundering and somehow interrupt the financial activities of these drug traffickers, terrorists, fraudsters, tax evaders, and other criminals is tantamount to pissing in the wind.

I

LIKE A THIEF
WITH A BLUEPRINT

"Show me an attaché case that can hold $2 million
and you can have the $2 million."

– Frank Sinatra

On a blustery Friday morning, March 13, 1931, a panel of twenty-three random citizens who'd never met before sat down on hard wooden chairs in a dingy, windowless room of the ancient federal courthouse in downtown Chicago and, with the door guarded by armed U.S. Marshals, listened to United States attorney George E.Q. Johnson – a tall, thin, stern man wearing gold-rimmed glasses – as he asked them to formally inculpate the most notorious gangster in the country for failing to pay $32,488.81 in income tax seven years earlier.

After several days of hearing evidence, the men and women of this grand jury returned an indictment that, the judge ordered, would be kept secret until further investigations were completed concerning Alphonse Capone's subsequent tax years 1925 to 1929. The same group met again on June 5 to return a second indictment, charging Capone with twenty-two counts of tax evasion totalling over $200,000. The following week, they indicted him again, along with sixty-eight members of his gang, this time on five thousand violations of the Volstead Act – the law that created Prohibition by banning the manufacture, transportation, and sale of beverages containing more than 0.5 per cent alcohol.

Facing a possible thirty-four years behind bars – for running a $2.5-million-a-year industry that was built on illegal booze, gambling, prostitution, and five hundred murders – Capone agreed to plead guilty in exchange for a short sentence. Johnson was willing to discuss it for several reasons: he was concerned with potential jury tampering; recognized the real possibility that witnesses might wind up dead; and feared that defence lawyers might successfully argue that the statute of limitations had run out on some of the charges. So after lengthy negotiations with Capone's attorneys, Johnson recommended a custodial sentence of two to five years. Believing it was a done deal, Capone started bragging that he'd be out in under thirty months. That incensed the judge, who accepted Capone's guilty plea but then handed down eleven years. Furious, Capone reneged on his plea and decided to take his chances with a jury. The trial didn't last long and on Saturday, October 17, he was found guilty on some, but not all, of the tax-evasion charges. The judge accepted the jury's decision and gave Capone eleven years anyway.

Watching this from the sidelines, a twenty-nine-year-old New·York bootlegger named Meyer Lansky couldn't believe that, where G-men with guns had failed, accountants with pencils had succeeded.

Capone's dim-witted brother Ralph – a.k.a. "Bottles" Capone – suffered a similar fate. The way Lansky viewed life, that should have been warning enough. Capone's lieutenants, Frank Nitti and Jake Guzik, were also charged with tax evasion. Ironically, four decades later, Lansky himself would have to face those charges. But now, in 1931 – the same year that gambling was relegalized in the State of Nevada – Lansky was shocked that Capone had fallen for "the rum-runner's myth."

Throughout Prohibition, bootleggers had convinced themselves that because booze was illegal, the money they made on it was not taxable. The same false impression was shared by gamblers taking illegal bets on horse racing. "The income tax law is a lot of bunk," Capone had insisted. "The government can't collect legal taxes from illegal money."

Lansky, aghast at how easily Capone's world had crumbled, was determined not to fall into that same wide trap. At first glance, he was staring at a no-win situation. Pay taxes and you admit your guilt. Don't pay taxes and you get done like Capone. Eventually, though, he realized there was a third possibility. The Internal Revenue Service (IRS) could only make a tax-evasion case if they could find the money. If the Feds couldn't find the money, he reasoned, then the money was, by default, not taxable. With this as his premise, he turned to the one place where secrecy was already a business – Switzerland.

Long before Holocaust money needed a place to hide, or James Bond gave secret Swiss banking a patina of cinema glitz, the gnomes of Zurich were selling stealth. Several banks offered anonymous banking to clients during the French Revolution. By the end of the nineteenth century, all of them were offering numbered accounts. But it took New Jersey, Delaware, and Great Britain to help the Swiss find their niche.

Facing a budgetary crisis in the mid-1880s, the governor of New Jersey passed a law permitting businesses located across the Hudson River in New York to incorporate in his state. For a small fee, New York businesses could pretend to be New Jersey businesses, which would save them from paying New York's higher taxes. Based on New Jersey's success, Delaware went one step further. Towards the end of the 1890s, that state offered incorporation to anyone looking to avoid taxes anywhere. Today, Delaware is America's foremost offshore centre.

The tax advantages built into a registered company somewhere else were further enhanced by British case law. Judges ruled that a company was resident for tax purposes in the jurisdiction where it was controlled. If the management was in Britain and the factory was in Germany, then the company was British. By that same principle, a company doing business in the U.K. was not subject to British tax as long as the business was entirely "controlled from outside" the U.K. To define that term, judges asked several questions: Where do the directors permanently reside? Where is the seal of the company? Where are the minutes of the meetings kept? Where are the books of accounts and transfer kept? And where are transfers approved?

As long as the answers to all those questions was "someplace besides Britain," the company was deemed to be non-resident for U.K. tax purposes. The significance of the ruling is that it applied to the entire British Empire, which opened the door for Bermuda and the Bahamas to sell companies resident in their jurisdiction but controlled from elsewhere and, therefore, not subject to tax in Bermuda or the Bahamas.

The Swiss got into the game when they realized they could use dummy companies to create a second barrier of secrecy. Lawyers formed shell companies for clients whose names never appeared on the incorporation documents. A numbered account was opened by the lawyer in the name of the shell, and those few bankers who knew about the shell's account never know who the beneficial owner was. Only the lawyer knew, and he could not be forced to reveal his client's name because it was protected by attorney-client privilege. The Swiss also allowed the shares of one dummy corporation to be held by a second shell.

In 1934, the Swiss added another ingredient, making it a criminal offence for anyone working in a bank to reveal any details whatsoever of any account, creating a system that was, in those days, impregnable.

Because there was money to be made in this, Liechtenstein invented trusts that were even more secret than anything the Swiss had for sale. Luxembourg went one better. Where Swiss banking rules dictated that two senior executives in each bank needed to know a client's identity, the Luxembourgois limited that to one. Not to be left out, the Austrians decided that no one in any bank needed to know anyone.

As new markets for corporate, financial, and individual protection grew – and competed with each other for business – some very wealthy men figured out how to use companies formed in the Bahamas to mask business transactions. Notable among them were the heirs of J.P. Morgan and American financier Andrew Mellon, a man who served Presidents Harding, Coolidge, and Hoover as secretary of the treasury. In this scenario, Bahamian companies purchased goods from all over the world destined for import into North America, marked-up on them, then sold the goods to their own companies in North America. Those companies showed little or no profit for tax purposes, sheltering them, instead, in the no-tax Bahamas.

From such humble beginnings, this highly profitable practice of "transfer pricing" came to affect as much as 60 per cent of the world's trade. That's how much is estimated to take place inside the confines of multinational enterprises. Although Revenue Canada can't come up with figures that would quantify tax avoidance through transfer pricing in Canada, a report in the United States suggests that the U.S. Treasury lost $53 billion in revenues to transfer pricing in 2001.

Transfer pricing was a fledgling industry in 1936, when bankers in the Bahamas were also working out the advantages of moving money through offshore trusts. Originally made available to wealthy Brits, then to wealthy Canadians, one of those first trusts, Bahamas General, was taken over by National Westminster Bank. Of course, as soon as one big bank got involved, others followed, and offshore trusts were soon widely offered in Canada. Essentially, this was the birth of "private banking." Canadian banks opened throughout the British overseas territories, including Anguilla, the British Virgin Islands (BVI), and, eventually, the Cayman Islands.

Yet, Switzerland was still the best bet for hiding cash. As this was an era when no one cared where cash came from, Meyer Lansky had no trouble hiding his there. However, stashing money in the faraway Alps, out of the taxman's reach, also put it beyond his reach. And therein lies the difference between capital flight (hiding assets to protect them) and money laundering (hiding assets to protect them, then repatriating those protected assets in a different guise in order to enjoy them).

The "Lansky Syllogism" became: If the Feds can't follow the money, they won't be able to find it; if the Feds can't find it, it's not taxable; consequently, if you can camouflage this untaxable money to make it look like taxable money, then the Feds won't recognize it when you show it to them, which means you can bring it home and use it.

That prompted the question: How do you bring your hidden money safely home from wherever it's been hidden?

And a few winters after Al Capone took up long-term residence on a rock in the middle of San Francisco Bay, Meyer Lansky, wintering in Florida, looked south and could almost see the answer.

—

Opium has played a role in the politics of the world for the past four thousand years. Its influence spread from the Mediterranean, where it was first used as a folk medicine, through Asia, and back to the Indian subcontinent, where it was first used recreationally. The commercialization of opium opened the trade routes and, along with coffee and tobacco, sustained European mercantilism for two hundred years. By the middle of the nineteenth century, opium was already one of the world's major commodities. In 1805, pharmacologists turned raw opium into the painkiller morphine, and in 1858 doctors decided that the speediest way to deliver it into the bloodstream was with a hypodermic needle. By then, the drug had already been misused for nearly forty years. For a while, the opium derivative heroin was an ingredient in commercial cough medicines. Thanks largely to opium, the European chemical industry became the European pharmaceutical industry.

But the downside effects of opium were so dangerous and abuse became so widespread that by the First World War most western governments began to outlaw it. The League of Nations imposed codes on opiates, the 1925 Geneva Convention restricted the manufacture and export of heroin, and the 1931 Limitation Convention attempted to confine heroin to medical use. To fill gaps in the market, Chinese criminal syndicates in Shanghai and Tientsin supplied European and North American criminal syndicates with product. Within a few years, organized criminal enterprises in the West were producing it in sufficient quantities to compete with the Asian suppliers. They met the demands of the market and assured huge profits for everyone along the supply chain.

The Second World War imposed controls on shipping that cut into the easy transport of opiates, creating a new market in North America for Mexican heroin. After the war, it was business as usual and addiction rates began to climb. Governments responded by escalating the drug wars. The sale and distribution of heroin became more dangerous for traffickers and, as a result, more profitable. Poppy fields expanded, refineries sprouted up, and Lucky Luciano rewrote his epitaph by inventing the French Connection.

While this was going on, the rise of Italian and French communism brought the newly formed U.S. Central Intelligence Agency (CIA) into the game. The CIA recruited local mobsters to take on the local communists and, heavy-handedly, tipped the balance in favour of the mobsters, who then used their new-found powers in the pursuit of illegal activities, notably drug trafficking. It is a scenario that would be repeated many more times over the next fifty years: from the Golden Triangle of Burma, Thailand, and Laos to the Golden Crescent of Iran, Afghanistan, and Pakistan; throughout Latin America stretching from Mexico all the way down through Panama, then across Venezuela, Colombia, Ecuador, and Peru; from unofficial support of the Nicaraguan Contras to official support of corrupt governments in Bogota fighting the Colombian terrorist organization FARC; from Luciano's labs in Marseilles to the establishment of the Corsican Mob in Afghanistan and the subsequent colonization of the poppy fields there by the Taliban. Wherever there was heroin, there was the CIA.

Heroin was king, and for organized crime the Eighteenth Amendment to the United States Constitution ushered in a sideshow. Prohibition created an era when everybody wanted booze and only some people wanted heroin, so the Mob concentrated on booze. But in 1933, when the Twenty-first Amendment put an end to bathtub gin, allowing the government to tax all that whisky coming down from Canada, drugs were once again the best game in town.

There is really only one reason why criminals work at the business of crime.

Putting psychopaths and people who commit crimes of passion to the side, most people commit crimes for money. That's why they rob banks. That's why they work extortion. That's why they hijack trucks. That's why they run numbers. That's why they invent frauds. That's why they traffic heroin. Criminals are criminals because they think crime pays.

For the really smart ones – like Maier Suchowljansky – it often does.

Born in Grodno, then Russia, now Poland, in 1902, he arrived in Brooklyn with his parents in 1911 and, after Americanizing his name to Meyer Lansky, dropped out of school at the age of fourteen. For a time, he worked as an apprentice toolmaker. But there was never going to be a lot of money in that, and this was a boy who wanted to have a lot of money. So he looked for it on the streets and took it when he saw it. Even though the diminutive Lansky needed thick-heeled shoes to hit five feet, four inches, he turned out to be tough enough that he never walked away from trouble.

One of the street kids who tried to give him trouble was Salvatore Lucania. But the tiny Jew stared back at the lanky Italian and a lifelong friendship was born.

The Lucania family had emigrated to the States in 1907 when Salvatore was just ten. Within a few years, he was a reluctant resident of a home for juvenile delinquents. He followed that, in 1916, with a spell in prison for possession of heroin. As soon as he got out, having Americanized his name to Charlie Luciano, he set about working his way up the ladder of organized crime and, before long, was a prime suspect in a series of gangland murders. By then, his pals Frank Costello, Albert

Anastasia, and Vito Genovese were calling him Lucky. He'd survived a brutal knife fight and legend had it that's where the nickname came from. The truth is less romantic. They dubbed him Lucky because he was extraordinarily successful at picking horses.

Lansky's other boyhood friend was a Jew named Benjamin Siegel. Born in Brooklyn in 1906, Siegel had a volatile temper and was said, by some of the other kids, to be "as crazy as a bedbug." The handle stuck, he came to be known as Bugsy, and got as crazy as a bedbug whenever anyone called him that. Lansky and Siegel started as small-time extortionists and street-level hoodlums, moving whatever heroin the Bug and Meyer Gang could handle. Like everyone else, they changed tack with Prohibition. They got good at what they did – which was street-level whisky sales – and it didn't take long before Lansky's smarts and Siegel's sheer nastiness got them noticed by a real player.

Arnold Rothstein was perhaps the most important criminal of the era. Today, he is best remembered as the gambler who fixed the 1919 World Series – baseball's famous Black Sox Scandal – which earned him a walk-on role in F. Scott Fitzgerald's *The Great Gatsby*. He is also, supposedly, the model for Nathan Detroit in the musical *Guys and Dolls* and Nicky Arnstein in *Funny Girl*.

One of the brightest men in the business history of crime, Rothstein realized early on that life as a criminal exposes you to personal risk. So, to minimize personal risk, he established himself as backer. He started in the heroin business, expanded into stolen diamonds and various black markets, and, eventually, became America's premier bootlegger. He also wrote the textbook on the care and feeding of politicians and judges, turning graft and corruption into an art form. He met Lansky somewhere around the start of Prohibition, liked him and brought him under his wing. Siegel came along as part of the deal. Rothstein backed their early ventures and, by example, taught Lansky a lesson that served him his entire life: stay in the background, don't trample on egos, and become indispensable to everyone else's business by carving out your own niche in their supply chain. Rothstein's niche was the finance of smuggling. Lansky's was the finance of dirty money.

Yet Rothstein's real contribution to twentieth-century crime must be the word *organized*. He wasn't like so many of his contemporaries, a thug who committed crimes. He was a criminal who comported himself like a businessman. At a time when almost everything was resolutely divided along ethnic lines, he crossed those lines to put diverse people together.

Sound business, it was also a mean trick because neighbourhoods had definable boundaries and most people stayed within them. It was that way with schools, clubs, and at work, especially in New York, where melting-pot immigrants spent a generation or two denying the melting-pot process. The Mob was no different. The Italians stuck with Italians, the Jews stuck with Jews. Rothstein's legacy is of a Jew who was accepted by them all. He was close to the Italians, notably Al Capone. He could hobnob with Irish gangsters like Owney Madden, who ran Manhattan's Hell's Kitchen, and with Irish millionaires in plush Back Bay Boston estates like John F. Kennedy's bootlegging father, Joe. He accepted Luciano as Lansky's friend and brought him into the clique. He saw to it that Luciano's friend Frank Costello – whose real name was Francesco Castiglia and who would come to be known as the Mafia's prime minister – accepted Lansky and Siegel as his friends. He showed them all how to forge bonds across tribal lines and how to establish "syndicates," which turned into "organized crime," which made Luciano and Lansky and the others men to be reckoned with.

Rothstein would be murdered by gamblers to whom he owed money in November 1928. But by then, his "syndicate" business model was firmly in place. Lansky and Siegel were operating several distilleries, supplying whisky to Italian, Irish, and Jewish distributors and speak-easies. And Luciano, who had a piece of the action with them, was now a made-member of Joe Masseria's crime family.

Not yet businessmen in the Rothstein mould – that would come with time – Luciano, Lansky, and Siegel were still thugs playing at business. But Rothstein left a huge void and these guys were smart enough to fill it. In April 1931, Luciano reshuffled the deck by conspiring with Masseria's sworn enemy, Salvatore Maranzano, to kill his boss. If Lansky and Siegel weren't actually in on the hit – and there is reason to believe they might have been – they certainly knew about it and helped Luciano arrange it. Maranzano then divided New York into five families and rewarded Luciano by naming him head of one of them. In turn, Luciano appointed Costello as his underboss and promoted Vito Genovese into a position of responsibility. Four months later, Luciano – and very likely Lansky and Siegel – struck again, this time eliminating Maranzano.

Luciano, Lansky, and Siegel were now the biggest players in the East. They ran businesses, jointly and separately, that employed tens of thousands of people and generated tens of millions of dollars. But it didn't last long because so much of it was based on whisky. When Congress made booze legal again, that was the end of that. Some of the Mob stayed in the whisky business. But the commodity was nothing special, competition was everywhere, and profits were a shadow of what they'd been. For men like Luciano, Lansky, and Siegel – and their cohorts Costello, Genovese, Joe Bonanno, Carlo Gambino, Johnny Torrio, Longy Zwillman, the Fischetti brothers, Santos Trafficante, Sr., Tony Accardo, Sam Giancana, Joe Adonis, Carlos Marcello, and all the others who whose names would become legendary in the history of twentieth-century crime – the fallback position was heroin.

Prostitution was still a thriving investment, but risks were too high for profits that seemed too low, as Luciano would find out. Extortion, fraud, and numbers rackets were much less risky, but the profits reflected that. Booze had been special because it had defied the ratio – it was a low-risk, high-profit commodity. The lament became, "If only they'd make whisky illegal again!"

Slowly, however, it began to dawn on some of these men that whisky might not have been quite so unique after all. It was illegal and therefore fruitful, but illegal only proved fruitful in this case because a wide section of the population wanted it enough that they would openly flout the law to have it. That's what increased profits and reduced the risks. It wasn't the whisky, it was the demand for whisky. The greater the public appeal, they realized, the easier it was to entice local politicians and cops to look the other way, which in turn reduced risk. That's when some of them – and Meyer Lansky was clearly at the forefront – wondered, What else does the public want enough to break law for?

The answer was gambling.

It was illegal everywhere, except Nevada. Yet anyone who wanted to shoot craps or play roulette could always find a roadhouse somewhere with tables. Anyone who wanted to place a bet on a race or a ball game could go to their barbershop because barbershops across the country were tied into a bookies' wire.

By 1932, the national bookies' wire was controlled by Moe Annenberg. He's the father of Walter, who owned Triangle Publications, published

TV *Guide*, the *Philadelphia Inquirer*, and *Seventeen Magazine*. He owned radio and TV stations and, during Nixon's reign in the White House, served as U.S. ambassador to the Court of St. James.

Annenberg, Sr., fought with, and eventually made peace with, the Mob to control the national wire. He already owned the daily racing form, which, with gangster money and muscle, gave him a virtual monopoly on information coming out of the nation's racetracks. To suggest that either Moe or Walter Annenberg allowed that information to be misused is pure speculation. To suggest that criminals with access to that information wouldn't use it to their advantage flies in the face of reason.

As everything was already in place, all the Mob had to do was upgrade the product. Speakeasies traded booze for craps tables and roulette wheels. Roadhouses became "carpet joints" – sawdust was no longer the floor covering of choice – and the business prospered for the next twenty years. From the end of Prohibition through the 1940s, the public wanted to gamble and the Mob did what the Mob does best – supply illegal demand.

Typically kitted out with a dozen roulette wheels, half a dozen craps tables, and half a dozen card tables, there was the Piping Rock and the Arrowhead Inn, next to the racetrack in Saratoga, New York; the Agua Caliente in Tijuana, Mexico, an afternoon's drive from Los Angeles; the Beverly Club in Louisiana; the Riviera across the bridge from Manhattan in New Jersey. There were gambling barges in southern California taking punters beyond the three-mile limit where laws against gambling didn't apply; and wall-to-wall carpet joints in Hot Springs, Arkansas; Galveston, Texas; and Cleveland, Ohio, too. Entire cities were transformed by illicit gaming, much the way Branson, Missouri, today is a city of supper clubs and show palaces.

This was the heyday of Montreal as a nightclub and gambling town.

As competition increased, the product improved. Carpet joints offered food and dancing and big-name entertainers like Jimmy Durante, Sophie Tucker, Joe E. Lewis, and an up-and-coming kid from Hoboken, New Jersey, named Sinatra. There were carpet joints wherever there was room for one. But it was in Hallandale, Florida, where Lansky made his mark on this era.

It began with a small-time Chicago operator named Julian "Potatoes" Kaufman, who'd been on the run and fallen under the paid protection of a Genovese family lieutenant named Vincent "Jimmy Blue Eyes" Alo.

In those days, Hallandale was nothing more than a way-station for itin-erant fruit pickers. Kaufman opened a bookies' shop in a fruit packing shed and, because the itinerant workers had cash on payday to spend, he added a roulette wheel and a craps table. He called it The Plantation.

Luciano had introduced Alo to Lansky some years before and those two had become mates. Alo was only a year older than Lansky, equally short and equally shy. Where Lansky had the brains to devise a scheme, Alo had the backup muscle to guarantee that it worked. Eventually Alo would be the watchdog positioned between Lansky and the Mob. He would keep one eye on Lansky, to make sure that Lansky played straight with the boys, and the other eye on the boys, to make sure that none of them ever muscled in on Lansky. In turn, both Lansky and the boys took care of Alo.

So now, when Alo told Lansky that some locals had shut down The Plantation, Lansky concocted a plan to reopen it next door. Potatoes unexpectedly found himself with more partners than he'd ever imag-ined, including Lansky, Alo, Luciano, Costello, and Siegel. Lansky dubbed the place The Farm, and put his brother Jake in charge of doling out bribes to local politicians to keep it open. On the back of The Farm, this group – minus Potatoes – opened the much more grand Colonial Inn right next door to Gulfstream racetrack. From Hallandale, their carpet joints spread south into Dade County and Miami, and north to Palm Beach. The public wanted to play, the locals grew rich on the gam-blers, and the cops were paid to worry more about traffic than the mob-sters who were bringing economic prosperity to south Florida.

By design, carpet joints, like all casinos, were profitable because the odds are always with the house. What made them extremely lucrative – and the reason why the Mob has always revered casinos – was "the skim." A basic "fingers in the till" game, it's about helping yourself to a share of the winnings after the money moves from the tables and before it gets to the accountant's office. If there's $100,000 at the roulette wheel and you only hand $80,000 to the accountant – which is what the taxman and your partners get to see – the $20,000 difference is yours, free and clear. All you have to do is make it disappear. But Lansky came to see the carpet joints as more than mere cash cows. They were a near-perfect washing machine. By adding heroin money to the daily take, street cash could be disguised as house profits.

Gambling money was pouring in, and the skim was making a lot of people very rich. But there was also so much heroin money coming in that the Mob in Hallandale needed to do something with it. The carpet joints couldn't absorb it fast enough. That's why Siegel headed west to build the biggest, most spectacular carpet joint ever. Financed by his friends, he would invent the Las Vegas Strip, construct The Flamingo hotel and casino, sustain huge cost overruns, open it disastrously, infuriate his partners by stealing from them, and, eventually, suffer the ultimate fate for his betrayal.

Lansky, in the meantime, was still haunted by Capone's mistake. With more cash than he'd ever seen as a bootlegger, he was more anxious than ever to keep the IRS from finding it. He theorized that if he could put a casino outside the jurisdiction of the IRS, sitting between his cash businesses — especially heroin trafficking — in the States and his secret bank accounts in Switzerland, he'd have the perfect cogwheel to turn his two money engines in tandem.

And the place to do that, he decided, was Cuba.

Only ninety miles away, and easily accessible by boat and plane from Florida, the island was a popular vacation spot. In 1933, a thirty-one-year-old army sergeant named Fulgencio Batista y Zaldívar had rallied the military to overthrow the government of Gerardo Machado. He'd installed himself as chief of the armed forces, had seized control of the country, and had inaugurated a reign of massive political corruption. He'd also put out the welcome mat for organized crime.

It's not entirely clear when Lansky first visited Cuba, but by 1937 he'd acquired a franchise on some gaming tables in the casino at Havana's Hotel Nacional. A chaotic place, with different people owning different table rights in the same room, the casino provided Lansky with the opportunity to move money from Florida to the safety of Havana and also move money hidden in Switzerland through Havana and back to Florida. The taxman wouldn't know about the money leaving the country, but he'd be welcome to count whatever was coming in, as that was a "legal" return on an overseas investment.

Two years after Lansky set up in Cuba, Batista decided to do something about the disarray in the gambling industry. He hired a New England racetrack owner to modernize Oriental Park racetrack and asked Lansky to reorganize Havana's casinos. Accordingly, one of the first things Lansky did was to take over the racetrack casino so that he could launder money through there too.

The operative verb being *to launder*.

It's called what it is not because Al Capone had a string of launderettes that he used to hide his income – that's a bedtime fable – but because it aptly describes the process. Dirty money, being the proceeds of illegal activity, is fed into legitimate businesses and through them into the legitimate financial system, washed through a strategy to obscure the money trail – moved in and out of shell companies, secret bank accounts, and multiple jurisdictions so that law enforcement can't follow it – and then brought out the other end scrubbed and shiny, looking exactly like legitimately earned income.

Some crooks in those days did use jukeboxes, pinball machines, and slot machines to explain away the cash they were generating from their traditional trades of extortion, protection, bootlegging, and narcotics. But Lansky never called it money laundering and there's certainly no reference to anyone calling it juxing, pinballing, or slotting. In fact, the term *money laundering* didn't come into the English language until the Watergate scandal in 1973. In Lansky's mind, he was merely taking capital flight to the next level. But there's no doubt that he laid the groundwork for what would come, and that first giant step for mankind left its footprints in Cuba.

Seven years after seizing power, Batista decided to validate his dictatorship by running for president. He won the 1940 election, but somehow mismanaged the rigged election four years later and got voted out. He retired to a well-feathered nest in Florida. By then, Lansky and his chums had taken over a substantial part of the action at the Nacional and were settling into casinos all over town. Lansky was fast becoming the single most powerful foreign investor in Havana.

Along the way, Lucky's luck ran out. Manhattan District Attorney Thomas Dewey busted Luciano in June 1936 on sixty-two counts of compulsory prostitution and shipped him off to serve two fifteen-year terms at Dannemora Prison in Clinton, New York. Referred to by fellow inmates as "Siberia" because of its remote and harsh conditions, Luciano spent six years there before his lawyers and Lansky worked out a way to get him moved.

With the war in Europe and the Pacific in full swing, Lansky sent out feelers through lawyers suggesting that Luciano could be of real assistance to the Pentagon. There's no doubt that the government seriously considered enlisting his help. Luciano claimed that he could – and later swore that he did – exert his influence with the longshoremen to keep Italian stevedores working in the ports of New York when the U.S. declared war on Italy. He also maintained that, during the planning stages for the invasion of Sicily, he personally supplied American intelligence with underground contacts on the island.

Records do indeed show that the U.S. Navy was concerned about sabotage at the docks in Brooklyn, and that the Office of Naval Intelligence (ONI) in Manhattan looked to the Mafia for help. Sometime around 1942, officers contacted Joseph Lanza, a mobster with ties to the longshoremen. There is serious doubt, however, about Luciano's role.

When he applied for a suspension of his sentence on February 8, 1943, Luciano cited some vague assistance he'd rendered to the navy. Although there's no hard evidence to show that his collaboration with the government ever transpired, that didn't stop Luciano from applying for a reprieve. On January 3, 1946, it was granted on the condition that Luciano agree to deportation and promise never to return. On February 10, 1946, Luciano sailed out of New York Harbor on the SS *Laura Keene*, bound for Italy. Knowing that the press would be at the pier reporting on mobsters waving goodbye, Lansky stayed away.

Luciano settled in a villa on the Via Lucillo in Montemario, a quiet residential neighbourhood just to the north of Vatican City in Rome. He was there eight months before he took the first step in reneging on his pledge not to come back.

On October 29, 1946, this time without any press coverage, Meyer Lansky was waiting on the tarmac at Camaguey Airport to welcome Lucky to Cuba.

Lansky installed his old pal in the presidential suite at the Nacional. A few weeks later, Luciano took up more permanent residence at No. 29, Calle 30, in the fashionable Miramar district of Havana. He spent days at Oriental Park playing the horses with Lansky and, later in the evenings, they gambled together at the Nacional. Like the celebrity he'd become, Luciano held court with American tourists and wealthy Cubans who'd previously known him only by reputation, and met often with old friends and associates who arrived from the States to pay homage. Shadowed by the FBI, Luciano was overheard telling people that while he had no present business connections in Cuba, he planned to remain there for a long time and was "hoping to establish himself in some legitimate business in the near future."

Around the same time that Al Capone died in Florida, in January 1947, Luciano put out the word that he wanted "the boys" to come to Cuba for a summit. He didn't say as much, but he intended to enthrone himself as *capo di tutti capi*, the boss of bosses of the American Mafia. Attendance was mandatory, as was "a little something" to welcome Lucky back. That translated to cash. The legitimate business in which he was hoping to establish himself was the Nacional's casino. The $150,000 that he expected to collect was to pay for his share of it.

On February 11, two Chicago gangsters – Joe and Rocco Fischetti – flew to Havana from Florida for the meeting that was to begin the following day. They brought along with them their friend, Frank Sinatra. Years later, Sinatra's FBI file would suggest that he had an obscure family tie to Al Capone. The three Fischetti brothers – Charlie was the third one – operated carpet joints in Chicago and Miami and were also related to Capone. Not that this explains Sinatra's lifelong fascination for wiseguys, simply that the Sinatra-Fischetti friendship might somehow be part of the confused Mafia concept of family. Certainly the friendship lasted a long time. Perhaps more importantly, through that friendship, Sinatra forged what has to be his most significant Mob association – one he often denied but one that would have very serious repercussions – with the Fischettis' boss in Chicago, Sam Giancana.

Many years later, Sinatra's presence at the so-called Havana Conference would assume mythical proportions as tales of the meeting grew with each telling. In one version, Sinatra had been invited along as a bag man for the Fischettis, who worried that if they carried money to Luciano they might be stopped, but reckoned that if Sinatra carried the cash it would be safe because no one would bother to check him. In 1963, when the Nevada Gaming Commission held licensing hearings on Sinatra's Cal-Neva Lodge hotel and casino – where Giancana was, illegally, his secret partner – they asked him about that meeting. Sinatra confirmed that he'd gone to Cuba in early 1947, but insisted that he was there on vacation and swore under oath that he did not have anything to do with gangsters.

One of the commissioners fired point-blank, "Did you fly to Havana with $2 million in an attaché case?"

That's when Sinatra retorted, "Show me an attaché case that can hold $2 million and you can have the $2 million." He wasn't asked if he was carrying any money for the Fischettis, so he never had to answer that one. Nor did he ever bother to explain how or why, when the Italian police raided Luciano's home, they found a gold cigarette case inscribed, *To my dear pal Lucky, from his friend, Frank Sinatra.*

The oft-repeated version of this story has it that Luciano was discovered living in Cuba only when the Havana Conference ended with a Christmas party in Sinatra's honour. But FBI records reveal that isn't so. The U.S. embassy in Rome had been informed in October 1946 that Luciano – travelling on an Italian passport in the name of Salvatore Lucania – had left Italy, and the U.S. embassy in Havana had been informed a few days later by the Cuban intelligence service that he'd arrived. FBI records also indicate that Luciano was kept under constant surveillance by both the Cubans and the Americans. There was no Mafia Christmas bash and his discovery there had nothing to do with Sinatra. The Cuban press had already stumbled across Luciano at the racetrack several days before Sinatra arrived with the Fischettis. An article appeared in *Tiempo En Cuba* on February 9, 1947, noting Luciano's presence on the island. That article tipped the American press to the story. When Sinatra's name got thrown into the mix, coupled with Luciano's, the story stayed in front of the public for weeks.

Both governments suddenly faced the dilemma of what to do with Luciano. An official American report labelled Luciano's presence in Cuba "sufficiently dangerous," and on February 21, Washington issued an ultimatum. Either Cuba deport Luciano or shipments of much-needed American pharmaceuticals would be halted. The Cubans arrested Luciano the following day and declared him an undesirable. They held him at the Tiscornia Immigration Camp until March 20, when, despite last-ditch legal wrangling by Luciano's friends in high places, the Cubans stuck him on a Turkish freighter bound for the Canary Islands and Genoa, Italy.

While that event changed Luciano's life, it didn't alter much, if anything, for Lansky. He continued commuting between Florida and Cuba, representing his own interests, and also the interests of his partners, especially Luciano. Although that same year, when some locals in Hallandale moved to shut down the Colonial Inn, Lansky began selling out. It was just in time because, what did change things, materially, for Lansky, were the lofty ambitions of a Democrat from Chattanooga, Tennessee, and an out-of-work Cuban president in Daytona Beach, Florida.

In May 1950, Senator Estes Kefauver launched a fifteen-month-long, fifteen-city pilgrimage to challenge the Mob. His "Special Committee to Investigate Organized Crime in Interstate Commerce" was uniquely armed with an executive order from President Harry Truman that gave Kefauver the right to examine the tax returns of anyone the committee chose to subpoena as a witness. Television was becoming America's most powerful medium, and Kefauver understood that by putting every known crook in the country in front of the cameras and forcing them to testify about gambling and racketeering, even if they evaded his questions – which most of them did – the glare of publicity would take its toll. In all, he and his four committee members called 600 witnesses, compiled 12,000 pages of testimony, and delivered hundreds of hours of public hearings into more than 25 million living rooms.

Although Kefauver never actually proved the existence of a formal mobster alliance, he concluded, "There is a nation-wide crime syndicate known as the Mafia, whose tentacles are found in most large cities." He even described it as, "The cement that helps to bind the Costello-Adonis-Lansky syndicate of New York and the Accardo-Guzik-Fischetti syndicate of Chicago."

Gambling, he decided, was the root of this evil. "Gambling profits are the principal support of big-time racketeering and gangsterism. These profits provide the financial resources whereby ordinary criminals are converted into big-time racketeers, political bosses, pseudo-businessmen and alleged philanthropists. Thus the $2 horse player and the 5-cent numbers player are not only suckers because they are gambling against hopeless odds, but they also provide the moneys which enable underworld characters to undermine our institutions."

The "Kefauver Hearings" popularized the word *Mafia*, demonstrated clearly the power of organized criminals – especially their ability to corrupt the political system – launched a national assault on the Mob, and set the tone for congressional hearings for the next twenty years, which probed further into the business of organized crime in America. Among the people subpoenaed to testify were Tampa Mob boss Santos Trafficante, Sr., who would be ruined by these hearings; "Murder Incorporated" boss Albert Anastasia, who would be killed before the decade was out; "Prime Minister" Frank Costello, who became famous overnight for shielding his face from the cameras, which then focused on his trembling hands; and the naturally shy Meyer Lansky, whose demeanour made him look as dangerous as your average bank teller. The hearings also helped to popularize the Fifth Amendment of the Constitution, as over and over again, questions were answered with "I plead the Fifth" and "I refuse to answer the question on the grounds that it may tend to incriminate me."

Kefauver set his sights on Florida. Although he never actually went to Hallandale, he described it as "the sin city capital of the South." That didn't please Lansky, who, following one of his three appearances before Kefauver, got into a now-much-quoted conversation with him. Knowing that Kefauver was a gambler, Lansky asked, "What's wrong with gambling? You like it yourself. I know you've gambled a lot."

The senator acknowledged that was true. "But I don't want you people to control it."

Lansky assumed that by "you people" Kefauver was referring to Jews. He snapped, "I will not allow you to persecute me because I am a Jew."

Kefauver's response was to get a federal grand jury to return a twenty-one-count indictment against Lansky. The charges were mostly for "corrupting racetrack gambling." Lansky pled guilty to five counts, was fined $2,500, and given a three-month suspended sentence. Even though his conviction would be overturned twenty years later, this slap on the wrist reminded Lansky that his carpet-joint innings were over.

What Kefauver never counted on when he began his hearings were two very specific after-effects. First, the Mob's ardour for Las Vegas intensified, which, consequently, touched off a building boom there. Second, by shutting down cities like Hallandale, he greatly enhanced the attraction of Cuba.

As for the out-of-work president in Daytona Beach, Batista's ego ultimately got the best of him. He headed home to Cuba, snatched back power two months before the 1952 elections, and, having learned his lesson in 1944, shamelessly rigged the ballot so that this time he could not be defeated. By now, the gambling Mecca he'd helped to create was being run by crooks who were acting like crooks – everyone was stealing from everyone else. Batista believed that if the punters were being robbed they'd go somewhere else, so he decided to replace those crooks with his own crooks.

The crook he trusted the most was his old chum Meyer Lansky.

Having recently taken over Havana's Montmartre Club, Lansky also understood that high-stakes gambling was most profitable when it was run honestly. He accepted Batista's invitation to become Cuba's unofficial "minister of gambling," which came with a $25,000 yearly salary. For Lansky, it was a licence to print money.

In turn, at Lansky's behest, Batista's police ran the worst of the crooks off the island, meaning Lansky's major competitors. Lansky then convinced Batista to subsidize his clean-up of the gambling industry with government grants, and to enact Hotel Law 2074. That awarded tax exemptions plus a casino licence to foreigners investing more than $1 million. Taking full advantage of both, Lansky wound up controlling the Nacional for less than fifty cents on the dollar. He installed his brother Jake as manager of the Nacional and the Montmartre Club, then acquired a stake in the Tropicana. Lansky's sometime associate, Santos Trafficante, Jr., – who'd lived on the island for more than twenty years and was de facto head of the Tampa Mob – was allowed to take over operations of the Sans Souci, the Sevilla-Biltmore, the Commodoro, and the Deauville. The two were part-owners of the Capri, where another Lansky friend, actor George Raft, had a share. The only hotel and casino that even came close to a Mob-free zone was the Havana Hilton, because the chain's founder, Conrad Hilton, promised to keep it honest. But Batista sold the casino licence to a consortium of Lansky's friends for a $1-million cash kickback and that effectively neutered Mr. Hilton.

It goes without saying that everyone had to kickback Batista and his entourage at every turn. That included a nightly share of the gambling tables, in addition to what he was taking for the rights to control prostitution and, in Trafficante's case, to transship heroin. It meant that, for all intents and purposes, the Mob was running its own country.

Now, Lansky decided to furnish it better. In partnership with Luciano and Costello, Lansky arranged for the Batista government to fund the jewel in Havana's crown – the Riviera Hotel. A 440-room, 21-storey extravaganza, it would be the largest, most luxurious purpose-built casino-hotel outside of Las Vegas.

Bizarrely, as this was Lansky's monument to himself, he would not allow his name to appear on any of the official documents. Not even the casino licence. That was held by Eddie Levinson, a Lansky crony from New York. Nor would Lansky put his name on the books of the corporation that would own the hotel. That was fronted by Ben and Harry Smith, out of Toronto. The only place where Lansky's name appeared was as director of the kitchens.

For the man who supposedly once said, "Crime is bigger than U.S. Steel," the pieces had fallen neatly into place. Even if Lansky didn't actually say it, and there is some doubt that he did, comparing crime to U.S. Steel wouldn't have been too far from the truth. Each casino maintained bank accounts in Miami. Cheques and cash were couriered from Cuba to those banks daily, and from Florida the funds were wired elsewhere. Some money went to legitimate businesses in the States. Some just disappeared into the night. Money also moved from Cuba to Switzerland, then came back to Mob accounts in the States as legitimate earnings from businesses in Cuba. By the time the Riviera opened for business, just before Christmas 1956, so much heroin money was pouring into Cuba that Lansky's laundromat – an anti-Disneyland – had become the most decadent spot on the planet.

Havana was "America's whorehouse."

By now, too, the Batista regime had grown so wildly corrupt that unrest was spilling onto the streets and, more importantly, about to come down from the Sierra Maestra mountains. A former baseball player, law student, and political prisoner named Fidel, together with his brother Raul, their comrade Che, and 128 other malcontents, were making ready to take the island.

Batista had secured promises from Washington that, should he have to leave Cuba in the dead of night, he'd be permitted to enjoy unhindered asylum in Daytona Beach. But there's not a lot of evidence that Lansky had an exit strategy. For a man as bright as him, it's unthinkable that Lansky didn't see the writing on the wall. Perhaps he figured that the kickbacks to Batista – which had climbed to a high of 30 per cent of the Riviera's gaming table receipts – were some sort of insurance policy to guarantee safe harbour no matter what happened.

Perhaps he was, as some historians have recently asserted, hedging his bet by getting money to Castro. Or, perhaps, he was simply blinded by his own success. After all, like a thief with a blueprint, he'd just invented the world's first offshore financial centre.

2

THE NEXT CUBA

"Winning isn't the most important thing, it's second to breathing."

– New York Yankees owner George Steinbrenner

Meyer Lansky's dream of a world beyond the reach of the IRS suffered a rude awakening when the rebels came down from the mountains and, with the help of guns provided by American gangsters – notably Lansky's own associate, Santos Trafficante, Jr. – seized control of the island. Che Guevara took Havana on New Year's Day, 1959. Batista had escaped on New Year's Eve, carrying $40 million. Castro marched in on January 8. Lansky had fled the night before, leaving $17 million behind. A few days later, as if to say thank you for coming to my insurrection, Castro shoved Trafficante into jail and left him there for a year.

For a while, Washington played the anxious suitor and, for a while, it appeared as if Castro was available for the courting. But the fleeting romance succumbed to protracted acrimony. Castro tossed out the Americans, claimed control of the casinos, and saved his goodnight kisses for the Russians. Lansky put a $1-million bounty on Castro's head, payable to anyone upon his return to Havana, although deep down, he must have known it was a lost cause.

Nursing his wounds back in Miami, Lansky had lived to play again another day. He'd also learned some valuable lessons about "the next Cuba." It would have to be small and close enough to the U.S. mainland to get tourists and gamblers in and out easily. In that respect, it would look a lot like the last Cuba. It, too, would have to come furnished with a thoroughly corrupt political regime, held together by a despot greedy enough to welcome the Mob. But unlike Batista, that tyrant would have to be so firmly in place that the political environment would remain stable no matter what. And the Mob's money would have to be spread so thick and so wide that, if some other tyrant seized power, he'd need them to maintain his own stability.

At first glance, the Dominican Republic seemed to fit the bill. The man in charge was General Rafael Léonidas Trujillo, one of the bloodiest autocrats in Latin American history. With Trujillo's blessings, mobster Joe Bonanno was already moving heroin through the Dominican Republic to the United States. So clearly, Trujillo was someone the Mob could deal with. But because Lansky and his friends did not necessarily trust Bonanno, they looked for a different way to get to Trujillo. The key became his ex-son-in-law, Porfirio Rubirosa.

Forever described as a "playboy" – as if that was his job description – when Rubirosa wasn't chasing women around Palm Beach and New York, or marrying Trujillo's daughter, or marrying French actress Danielle Darrieux, or marrying tobacco heiress Doris Duke, or marrying Woolworth heiress Barbara Hutton, or just sleeping with actress Zsa Zsa Gabor, he was working as the general's bagman. It was Rubirosa who collected the various fees and commissions that Trujillo claimed from deals his government arranged with American businesses. Along the way, he got to know Frank Sinatra, who introduced him to John Kennedy – birds of a feather – who in turn took an interest in the Dominican Republic.

Kennedy feared that the Russians might try to move in on yet another Caribbean island. That worry, together with his distaste for Trujillo, was shared with Allen Dulles, the CIA chief he'd inherited from President Eisenhower. What Kennedy didn't know until Dulles told him was that Bonanno and Trujillo were trading drugs for weapons. Eisenhower had been furious and, consequently, the CIA approved a plot by seven Trujillo colleagues to kill the Dominican ruler. At the end of May 1961, barely four months into the Kennedy presidency, JFK refused to pull the plug on Trujillo's assassination.

Unknowingly, Kennedy was now on a collision course with the Mafia boss of Chicago's Outfit, Sam Giancana.

The Outfit and the Kennedys had history. Like many of America's major gangsters in the early 1960s, Giancana and his pals had run booze with Kennedy's father, Joe, during Prohibition. Some of the money Kennedy, Sr., made as a whisky smuggler was reinvested in Chicago when, in 1945, Joe bought the Merchandise Mart. Supposedly the largest commercial establishment in the world, it remained the bedrock of the Kennedy family fortune for fifty years. Needless to say, no business that size could function in Chicago in those days without certain people being taken care of. Workers were supplied by the city's Democratic machine. Where "jobs for the boys" went, so went the Teamsters Union. Along with the Teamsters came the Outfit.

In 1960, Giancana played his part in JFK's presidential campaign. He not only delivered cash to the Kennedys – using Sinatra as his intermediary – but sat back and watched as one of his girlfriends, Judith Campbell, was introduced to Kennedy by Sinatra, and quickly became a Kennedy girlfriend too. Giancana used Campbell as a conduit for more campaign cash.

For the November election, Giancana and the Outfit were in the shadows of the Cook County "cemetery vote," helping to stuff Chicago's ballot boxes with votes from dead people. Some historians contend that those were the votes that carried Illinois for Kennedy, which swung the election away from the Republican candidate, Richard Nixon. The Democratic Party political machine of Mayor Richard Daley, with the Outfit in the background, are the indisputable chief suspects. And while other historians argue that the votes stolen for Kennedy in Illinois were nullified by votes stolen for Nixon in other states and, therefore, did not play such a momentous a role, it doesn't alter the fact that Giancana felt Kennedy owed him.

The assassination of Trujillo upset Giancana's plans. He'd staked a hefty share of his Outfit's financial future on Las Vegas and was now looking to move offshore. As a corporate entity in Vegas, the Outfit controlled the Sands, the Sahara, and the Riviera. But Las Vegas, like Cuba, had been declared an "open" city, in effect, a free-trade zone where any Mob family could work gambling or hookers or drugs or extortion for as long as it could hold on to the business. And everybody was there. Lansky had part of the Thunderbird; the Cleveland Mob ran the Desert Inn and the Stardust; New England's Patriarca family had the

Dunes; and a Lansky–Costello partnership was behind the Tropicana. The Teamsters were mixed into this as well, at Caesar's Palace, the Dunes, and the Fremont. Although there was plenty of money to be skimmed, there were a lot of fingers dipping into the pot. Giancana wanted someplace that would belong to Chicago and he'd set his sites on the Dominican Republic

His scheme revolved around Bobby Baker, a very powerful man whom Giancana had slipped into his own pocket. In the days when Lyndon Johnson was the omnipotent Democrat in the Senate, Baker – Johnson's closest and most trusted confident – was referred to as "The 101st Senator" and "Little Lyndon." Now, with Johnson as vice-president, Baker's corrupt influence was such that he was being paid by Trujillo to be his lobbyist on Capitol Hill, and was being paid by Giancana to seduce legitimate hotel chains (mainly Intercontinental) and airlines (mainly Pan Am, which owned Intercontinental) into a Dominican investment.

While Giancana was manoeuvring the Outfit's takeover of Santo Domingo, Allen Dulles and the CIA were busy cooking up Operation Mongoose. A series of conspiracies to overthrow Castro, one of the plots included hiring the Mafia to kill him. When word reached Giancana that he might be called on to show his patriotism, he made certain that Kennedy knew he'd signed on. But the Attorney General, John's brother Bobby, had other ideas about Giancana. Bobby had already annoyed Giancana by labelling him a dangerous gangster in his 1960 book, *The Enemy Within*. Now, learning that Giancana was eyeing the Dominican Republic, Bobby moved against the Outfit and, at the same time, extracted John from his friendship with Giancana's pal, Frank Sinatra.

A financial scandal took Bobby Baker out of circulation, killing Giancana's offshore plans. For good measure, Bobby ordered the FBI to get into Giancana's face. Agents hounded the Chicago mobster at every turn, harassing him when he could least afford to find himself targeted by law enforcement and severely hampering his ability to earn a living. Bobby also set off in hot pursuit of the Teamsters Union.

FBI records reveal that Giancana took this as a personal affront. They leave no doubt that he was fed up with Bobby's Justice Department and their bellicose harassment of him. He was aggravated when the Kennedys abandoned Sinatra. And he was exasperated by Bobby's relentless targeting of the Teamsters. In Giancana's eyes, the brothers were disloyal, and infidelity was not something he could accept gracefully. Which is why, if you believe in conspiracy theories – especially the one that suggests the Mafia murdered John F. Kennedy – it's easy to give credence to claims that the Kennedys' "betrayal" of Giancana lies somewhere at the heart of it.

The Dominican Republic would have suited the Mob, at least in the short term. But that was gone. So Lansky, still in search of the next Cuba, needed to find somewhere else. By this time, casinos were happening all over the Caribbean, notably in the Netherlands Antilles – Aruba, Bonaire, Curaçao, and Sint Maarten – and in Haiti. Some were legit, most were not, Haiti being the worst of the bunch. But after taking a good look around, none of those places seemed quite as enticing to Lansky as the seven hundred islands and cays that made up a British colony just thirty minutes by air from Miami. Communications were good, real estate was cheap, access was easy, the political system was stable enough, and the politicians were corrupt enough that the place was ripe for plucking.

Best of all, the route into the Bahamas was already paved.

⟶

In July 1944, representatives from forty-four nations gathered at Bretton Woods, New Hampshire, to put the final touches on an agreement to stabilize the world's postwar economy. They established the International Monetary Fund (IMF), fixed the price of gold at $35 an ounce, tied the U.S. dollar to gold, then tied the exchange rate of other convertible currencies to the dollar. The theory behind Bretton Woods was that, by imposing monetary stability, the western powers could guarantee money supply, stabilize interest rates, and slow recession.

Everyone recognized the benefits of this, especially Joseph Stalin.

The Russian ruble, in its non-convertible state, might have been a symbol of fiscal sovereignty for the Soviet dictator, but the truth of the matter was that when it came to imported goods and services, he was dependent on the stability of western economies in general and the strength of the U.S. dollar in particular. And while dollar dependency might have looked like an obstacle to the Soviets on their road to world dominance, it was hardly insurmountable because Russia is an oil producer, oil is a dollar commodity, and Stalin had dollar revenues. What he didn't have was someplace safe to bed down his dollars until he spent them. In those days, the only banks holding dollar deposits were American, which put the Communist Party of the U.S.S.R. in the odd position of being a commercial client of their avowed capitalist enemies.

Stalin was uncomfortable about that, for two very practical, decidedly non-ideological, reasons.

The first was the Tsar's IOUs. Three decades after the October Revolution, the world was still awash with Russian bonds. For all intents and purposes, the bonds were worthless because the Communists said they were. These were the Tsar's debts and as long as Stalin had no intention of honouring them, bond holders had no way of collecting on them. But that could change if someone discovered Soviet dollars sitting in New York. Bond values would soar before the ink was dry on the first lawsuit.

The second reason was the Cold War. Stalin feared that, as friction between the two superpowers increased, Washington might be tempted to hold the Soviets to ransom by seizing Russian money in the States.

Now, it may be apocryphal, but there's a story told about the ruler of Abu Dhabi, who was keeping all his money stacked in the basement of the royal palace. One day, his finance minister came to him to announce that rats were eating the bank notes and warned that if he didn't get his money out of the basement immediately, there wouldn't be any left. When the ruler of Abu Dhabi confessed that he had no place else to put his money, the finance minister suggested he deposit it in a bank. So, the ruler ordered that his money be removed from the basement, piled into oxen carts, and driven to a bank. A week later, the ruler called for his finance minister and commanded, Take me to the bank, I want to see my money. Needless to say, banks don't stash money, they loan it out to people, businesses, and even other banks. Now, an embarrassed finance minister had the awkward task of explaining to the ruler why his money wasn't actually at the bank, even though it was in the bank.

When a bank doesn't have enough money immediately available – if cash reserves are inadequate and someone wants to see his money –

the bank has a liquidity problem. To get around it, the bank asks the government to print more money and lend it to them through the discount window. In Stalin's day, the Federal Reserve – America's version of a central bank – did that for American banks but was not inclined to do it for foreign banks. Theoretically, Washington allowed banks outside the States to hold dollars as long as they could jump through some very narrow hoops. Among other things, foreign banks were required to maintain liquidity levels much steeper than most of them could afford.

What Stalin couldn't foresee, and what the Americans never counted on when they signed Bretton Woods, was that by pinning the world's currencies to the dollar, Washington was creating a monster with an enormous appetite for dollars. The Marshall Plan injected a gigantic $13 billion into Europe between 1948 and 1951, and European central banks were buying substantial amounts to bolster their own depreciating currencies. Suddenly, a colossal quantity of dollars was housed outside the United States. Those dollars needed someplace to go, and two banks that slipped quietly into the business of housing them were the Moscow Narodny Bank in London and the Banque Commerciale Pour l'Europe du Nord in Paris. Both just happened to be Soviet-owned and both just happened to be served by British financial advisers.

In the aftermath of the 1956 Russian invasion of Hungary, the Kremlin's British financial advisers – who were in touch with the two banks' British financial advisers – agreed that it would be especially prudent to move Russia's dollars out of America's clutches and into Paris. Their timing was good because the following year, when the Moscow Narodny Bank in London faced a crisis – triggered by a British balance of payments emergency, which itself had been brought on by the Suez Crisis – Banque Commerciale could loan Moscow Narodny enough dollars to assure liquidity. The cable address of Banque Commerciale was "Eurobank" and the loan was described as "Eurobankdollars," which was eventually shortened to "Eurodollars."

Seeing how liquidity could be assured through dollar loans negotiated outside the United States, several international banks piled onto the bandwagon. At the same time, responding angrily to the international crisis in Suez – which Washington had bluntly warned the British not to precipitate – the Americans seized dollar assets held in the States by all the participants. The freeze didn't last long, but it infuriated the

Arabs, and once it was over, Arab governments moved their money out of U.S. banks and into this brand-new Eurodollar market. That meant bedding down dollars in London – ironically, the enemy from Suez – which was the heart of this brand-new market.

Without realizing it, the Russians had stuck a dagger into Bretton Woods and unwittingly provided nutriment at a critical moment in the gestation of the modern offshore world.

Rich North Americans had wintered in the Bahamas and sport fishermen had plied the waters there for years. But in the mid-1950s, tourism in the islands was a far cry from what it is today. For tourism to flourish, there had to be an infrastructure. And the story of how that infrastructure evolved – how the pieces got put into place for the Mob – is filled with a cast of screwballs and eccentrics, any one of whom could have come straight off the pages of a Damon Runyan story.

A swindler from Baltimore named Wallace Groves first showed up during the Great Depression and lived in the Bahamas on and off – the notable off period being 1941 to 1944, when his residence was a U.S. federal prison – for most of his adult life. He was forever dreaming up schemes that entailed bilking the local treasury. His partner in crime was Sir Stafford Sands, a Bahamian attorney and power-broker who maintained tight relations with white minority "Bay Street Boys" government. Conveniently, Sands was also chairman of the Development Board, which, effectively, made him the minister for tourism.

More than just "vaguely villainous," as some Bahamians remember him today, Sands was thoroughly corrupt. He was also a bigot who would leave his country when black majority rule was introduced to die in stubborn exile in 1972 at London's Dorchester Hotel. And yet, his legacy as the architect of the island's modern economy is such that his oval, spectacled face stares back from the Bahamian ten-dollar bill.

Sands's strategy to bring the islands into the twentieth century – while all the time ensuring his own financial security – saw Groves play the front man. In 1955, the two men applied for a government grant of fifty thousand acres, all sorts of tax breaks plus the promise of more land, to create the Grand Bahama Port Authority. Needless to say, the scheme was approved. But when Sands admitted that this was far too substantial a project to pull off on their own, he and Groves fast-talked the enigmatic Daniel K. Ludwig into backing them.

A postwar financier who showed up on everybody's "richest men in captivity" list, Ludwig owned the world's largest merchant shipping fleet and therefore had the wherewithal to guarantee the project's success. He dug the harbour while Groves and Sands developed the land. The result was Freeport, the Caribbean's first significant industrial centre and purpose-built parking lot for cruise ships. Groves and Sands's next step was to transform Freeport into a tourist resort. For that, Groves brought in a Canadian con man, Lou Chesler.

Known as "Moose" because he weighed nearly three hundred pounds and looked like one, Ontario-born Chesler made his first million in 1946, at the age of thirty-three, flogging dodgy Canadian mining stocks. He took his money to Florida, sold swamps to the gullible, bought dry land for himself, and by 1960 had multiplied his fortune fifty-fold. Along the way, he went out to Hollywood, bought Associated Artists, named himself chairman, and, through various share manipulations, turned one company into another to become chairman of Seven Arts. Chesler had learned the art of duplicity back in the early 1940s from a skilful fraudster named John Pullman.

Born in Russia, Pullman spent his early years in Canada, emigrated to the States, and, after serving in the U.S. Army, wound up in Chicago bootlegging whisky. In 1931, he was convicted for violations of the Volstead Act and served six months. While in jail, Pullman met a rum-runner from Minneapolis named Yiddy Bloom. When they both got out, Bloom introduced his new friend Pullman to his old friend Meyer Lansky and, some years later, Pullman introduced his new friend Lansky to his old friend Lou Chesler.

Chesler and Lansky hit it off and worked several scams together, most notably injecting Mob money into the 1958 redevelopment of Miami International Airport. So now, when Groves brought Chesler into the Freeport project, Chesler arrived holding hands with Lansky.

In the meantime, Pullman concluded that he didn't like being an American criminal any more, so he gave up his citizenship to become a Canadian criminal. Except he didn't like the Canadian weather, so he moved to Switzerland, where he hooked up with the intensely mysterious Tibor Rosenbaum.

A Holocaust survivor, Rosenbaum was either an agent for the Israeli intelligence service Mossad or a businessman whom Mossad could call on for favours. The extent of his service has never been made clear and probably never will be. It is known that, between the end of the Second World War in 1945 and mid-1948, Rosenbaum ran guns from Czechoslovakia to Palestine. He is remembered today as one of those men who helped forge Israeli statehood. It is also known that, at some point over the following ten years, Rosenbaum spent a great deal of time in – of all bizarre places – Liberia. After doing whatever it was he did there, by the time he moved to Geneva, Rosenbaum was carrying a black diplomatic passport as an honorary counsel for Liberia.

In 1959, almost certainly with Mossad backing, Rosenbaum created the Banque International de Credit (BIC), which was to become a legendary laundry. Liberian diplomatic passports would also, in their own way, become part of the offshore world's myth.

So Pullman joined Rosenbaum in Geneva while Chesler, in the Bahamas, formed a company called Devco, which acquired land from Groves and Sands's port authority in exchange for Devco shares. Chesler then folded Devco into a pair of bogus Canadian shell companies and announced plans to build the deluxe Lacayan Beach Hotel. Incongruously, included in the blueprints for a hotel where people would be spending most of their time outside on the beach in perfect weather were several large indoor squash courts.

Despite having failed to attract enough tourists to support Chesler's resort, Sands formed a company with Chesler and Groves called Bahamas Amusement. The ink was still wet on the incorporation documents when the government granted Bahamas Amusement – part owned by the man in charge of tourism – an exclusive ten-year licence to operate casinos on the island. Seconds later, miraculously, by connecting a few dots on the Lacayan's blueprints, the squash courts became the Monte Carlo casino.

It was opened in January 1964, several weeks before the hotel itself was completed. Lansky bankrolled it and put in his own guy, Dino Cellini, to supervise it. When the deceit, conflicts, and corruption became too obvious even by Bahamian standards, when Sands's puppets in government "suddenly realized" that the country was overflowing with mobsters, Premier Roland Symonette ordered out a handful of the most prominent goons, with Cellini heading the list. But the extradition paperwork conveniently got lost in the bureaucratic maze and everyone, except Cellini, was allowed to stay for up to four years. Lansky sent Cellini to England, where he joined his brother Eddie in the background of the Colony Club, one of London's most notorious casinos. Fronted by actor George Raft, Dino and Raft were eventually declared undesirables and tossed out of the U.K.

No sooner was the Monte Carlo up and running when John Pullman moved from Geneva to Freeport to open the Bank of World Commerce (BWC). Years later, the New Jersey Casino Control Commission would describe BWC as a sink for some of the nation's top gangsters where "millions of dollars passed through the door and were reinvested in syndicate controlled projects in the United States."

The casino skim from Vegas now mingled with casino skim from the Bahamas and moved through BWC on its way to BIC in Switzerland. To oil the works, Rosenbaum opened a local subsidiary of BIC in Freeport called Atlas Bank. He then turned to Africa, to help despots there bring stolen booty into the West, laundering it through BIC and Atlas and, from the Bahamas, investing it for them in North America. Not to be left out in his own backyard, Stafford Sands opened a bank in Nassau called Intra Bahamas Trust Ltd., which was tied to Intra Bank of Beirut, headquartered in Lebanon, which is one of the world's most underrated drug-money-laundering centres.

Enter here the hapless George Huntington Hartford II.

A man born with a $90-million silver spoon in his mouth, he was heir to the A&P grocery store empire. Hartford was also a man struggling to make his own dreams come true. By the time he'd graduated Harvard in 1934, he'd dropped the George and replaced the II with tags such as art collector, museum benefactor, magazine publisher, author, and property developer. The problem was that, most of the time, he lost money and by the end of his life he'd gone through a sizeable amount of his fortune.

In the early 1950s, Hartford had "discovered" a seven-hundred-acre beach ten minutes by boat from Nassau called Hog Island. Measuring four miles by two-thirds of a mile, it got its name because it was overrun with pigs. Hartford bought it the same day he spotted it, never thinking it might be a good idea if his lawyers came down first to read the small print on his $11-million purchase. Hartford intended to develop the place into one of the world's great tourist resorts. He renamed it Paradise Island and, over the next several years, dropped another $19 million trying to make it look like its new namesake.

At the heart of his plans was a hotel and casino complex. At the heart of his downfall was the fact that he chose the wrong law firm to advise him. Instead of going with Stafford Sands, he opted for honest lawyers and was, therefore, never able to acquire the necessary gaming licence. Compounding the sin, Hartford sank money into the underdog, black power Progressive Liberal Party, which was tantamount to treason in the eyes of Sands and his white United Bahamians.

That Hartford soon ran into cash-flow troubles simply exposed his carcass to the circling vultures. He was forced to sell part of his interest for $750,000. Inexplicably, Hartford then turned around and lent $2 million to the man who'd bought that part interest, accepting repayment in unregistered stock, which he quickly discovered he couldn't sell to anyone. So his new partner – the same fellow who still owed him $2 million – offered to help out with a $1-million loan, which wound up being secured with another hefty chunk of Paradise Island shares. The original guarantees were quickly pulled and the loan was called in. Hartford's stake was sold and the net result was that his $30-million investment in Paradise Island produced a $28-million tax loss.

The group that moved in on Paradise Island was called Mary Carter Paint. They'd already tied up with Groves and Chesler in Freeport and would, in time, evolve into Resorts International. With Sands help, it was Mary Carter Paint that secured the casino licence and saw Paradise Island rise out of Hartford's ashes.

Lansky, in the meantime, was feeling the all-too familiar chill of political change. So he followed Hartford's lead by quietly backing the Progressive Liberals. By the time the black Bahamian opposition just barely squeaked into power in 1967, Sands was on his way into exile and the island's new leader – Lynden Pindling – was on his way into the pocket of the great survivor, Meyer Lansky.

⌐

Besides Chesler and the newly Canadian Pullman, Lucien Rivard was around in those days too. He showed up in Cuba in the late 1950s and got connected with the now-famous French Connection heroin supply.

That was Luciano's business. He smuggled Turkish opium into Lebanon, where Italian chemists turned it into heroin. They handed it off to Corsican smugglers who shipped it to Montreal. There, the Cotroni family moved it by truck through Buffalo and Detroit and into New York, where the Bonanno family distributed it onto the streets.

Rivard began running some of that heroin around Montreal and Vancouver. He merged his trafficking with the Cotronis' and on the back of that started trading heroin for firearms, which he smuggled into Canada. When Castro took over in Cuba, Rivard was arrested and sentenced to death. It was only through an intervention by the then minister of external affairs in Ottawa that got him deported back to Montreal.

By the early 1960s, Rivard was the man that Vic "The Egg" Cotroni put in charge of the family's heroin importation. But by then the cops had targeted Rivard. He was arrested, held in prison, escaped, and went on the run. When he was captured again, he wound up in a Texas courtroom and was sentenced to twenty years. He served just about half that time. Paroled in 1975, he lived the rest of his life quietly in Montreal, although police suspect he was still dabbling in the business until his death in February 2002.

Another Canadian who made a name for himself in those days was Willie Obie, whose real name was William Obront, and who is sometimes referred to as Canada's Meyer Lansky.

A Montrealer born in 1924, he hooked up with Cotroni and became the family's chief laundrymen. As the money man behind what was, in effect, the Bonanno family's Canadian subsidiary, Obront spent most of his life in the background, deftly sidestepping the kind of publicity that would haunt his partners in crime. Like Lansky, he also understood the need to hide illicit activities inside otherwise legitimate businesses, and at one point was running nearly forty of them. But the days of wide-open Montreal – where gangsters thrived on gambling, nightclubs, prostitutes, and abortion clinics – were left to legend.

And drugs eventually became the Cotronis' downfall.

While Obront moved money through legitimate companies – at Expo 67, for instance, he controlled all the vending machines – and while he was overseeing all of the Mob's bookmaking activities in Ottawa and Hull, the Cotronis were getting very rich with heroin. The problem was that some of the Cotroni mob wanted to get richer. A split developed between the Sicilian and Calabrian factions of the family. The Sicilians wanted to expand their drug trafficking. The Calabrians wanted to keep life simple. Vic Cotroni tried to calm the waters by naming a younger man, Paulo Violi, as his successor. But Violi was a Calabrian and Carmine "Lilo" Galante – underboss of the Bonanno family and the man in charge of the family's Canadian interests – naturally sided with his fellow Sicilians.

The family's troubles hit the fan in 1977, when the Quebec Crime Probe forced Galante's hand. The government had bugged Violi's office and were able to listen to him explain his crime connections with the Bonannos. Then Frank Cotroni, Vic's younger brother, got busted. Violi now suggested to Galante that the Sicilians were dealing behind his back. So Galante called time on Violi and ordered him eliminated. In his place, Galante installed Nicolo Rizzuto. A Sicilian with ties to the Caruana-Cuntrera clan, Rizzuto agreed with Galante that drugs was where the money was and quickly expanded that side of the business.

Obront had also been named in that Quebec Crime Probe. The panel accused him of washing nearly $90 million of the Mob's gambling, narcotics, and extortion money in just two years through a series of companies, empty shells, and offshore banks. But by then, Obront had moved to Florida and was insisting that he was now just another retired Canadian businessman living in the sunshine.

As heroin poured into Canada for the American market, new gangsters arrived to challenge the old order. One of them was Marcel Salvail, then in his mid-thirties, who ran operations on Montreal's south shore. Summoned to testify for that 1977 probe, he, too, decided that the peaceful life of a retried businessman in Florida was more attractive than constant harassment by the Sûreté de Québec and the Montreal Police.

Not surprisingly, Obront and some of his fellow French Canadians – who colonized Hollywood, Florida, in such numbers that the city came to be called "Petit Quebec" – soon hooked up with Obront. It took the cops six years, but in 1983 a joint operation of the RCMP, FBI, and DEA busted Obront, Salvail, and Nick Cotroni for running a $50-million-a-year Quaalude ring. Along with a couple of dozen other Canadians, a couple of dozen other Americans, and some Colombians, this bunch had cornered nearly three-quarters of North America's Quaalude market. On the back of that, they were also bringing cocaine into Canada.

Bizarrely, Obront testified in his own defence that he didn't know Salvail, who was described at the trial as the world's number-three drug trafficker. But the evidence – including wiretaps – was overwhelming and the jury found them guilty on all twenty-eight counts. Then in his early sixties, Obront was sent away for twenty years.

⁓

As younger men moved into the business, they brought with them younger ideas.

The infighting that the Cotronis suffered was nothing new. But the mammoth influx of money that came with heroin exacerbated differences and jealousies. Even the all-powerful Luciano was unable to maintain control and, from the mid-1950s until his death in 1962, infighting jeopardized the Sicilians' ability to do business.

Almost as soon as Luciano was gone, the younger generation moved against the older leaders and seriously weakened the Mafia's authority around the world. Gangland murders increased. Law enforcement took advantage of the confusion and began to break up old alliances. At the same time, the Americans coerced the Turks to crack down on opium production, which created a source of supply crisis for the French Connection labs in Marseilles.

Their fallback position became Southeast Asia. The French colonized the region and, until they got thrown out in 1954, French and Corsican gangs had smuggled vast quantities of gold, currency, and heroin back to the Mediterranean. Now, with more than 70 per cent of the world's opium grown in the Golden Triangle countries of Thailand, Laos, and Cambodia, those same French and Corsican gangs reignited old friendships and reopened the Saigon-Marseilles smuggling routes.

In 1965, John Pullman travelled to Hong Kong to check out gambling, banking, and the narcotics business. The war in Vietnam was bringing tens of thousands of drug-hungry American GIs into the region, creating a brand-new customer base. That the Mob intended to exploit this goes without saying. That the Mob showed this kind of market vision is testimony to their capacity for freewheeling capitalism.

Santos Trafficante, Jr., had, by then, inherited what was left of Luciano's heroin interests. The same year that Pullman went to Hong Kong, Trafficante – looking to maintain market share – sent one of his young

lieutenants to Vietnam. Frank Furci opened clubs in Saigon, and infil-
trated others on military bases, using them to move black-market money
and drugs. Though stiff competition soon forced the inexperienced
Furci to retreat, Trafficante himself showed up in 1968 to underwrite
both his concerns for and increasing investment in the region.

The following year a summit took place at the Continental Palace
Hotel in Saigon. With the war in full swing, French and Corsican syndicates looked to opium producers in the Golden Triangle to assure their
own supply. Within two years, Golden Triangle heroin was moving
through Chinese labs in Hong Kong, on to Chile, across the border into
Paraguay, then north and into the Caribbean.

The Bahamas were geographically ideal for transshipping drugs into
the U.S., and had been used for that since the 1950s. Starting with
Jamaican marijuana and Paraguayan cocaine, it escalated with the arrival
of Southeast Asian heroin and Colombian cocaine. Not only did all
those islands and cays offer thousands of hiding places, but the traffickers
were also protected by Pindling – premier for seven years before independence and prime minister for nineteen years after independence. In
1984, Pindling was implicated in a corruption and drug scandal that,
predictably, went nowhere. An inquiry exonerated him after hearing his
explanation for spending eight times more on his personal life than his
official salary. According to Pindling, legitimate business associates gave
him cash presents because they liked him.

His regime ended with a plea for a laundering of his character. In
Pindling's farewell speech, he asked, "I hope that future generations will
not find me sorely wanting." Many didn't, still don't, and yet he was.
His legacy is one of popular liberation and education for the masses,
underpinned by corruption, cocaine, and criminals.

⬤

Pindling was a manipulator who sold out to dirty money. He set a
tawdry example for the rest of the offshore world, opening a door –
that still isn't shut – to a multitude of crooks and con men. Yet few of
those crooks and con men have ever been able to equal the panache of
the original eccentric who now appeared in the doorway.

Born in Turkey in 1927, Benno Cornfield was raised and educated in
Brooklyn, where his family changed their last name to Cornfeld and he

changed his first name to Bernard, except that everybody always called him Bernie.

Short, stocky, bearded, and bald, he was extremely intelligent, incredibly funny, almost always unconditionally charming, and almost always wonderful company. He had a ferocious temper, which he lost occasionally, and a total lack of respect for time, which he hardly ever kept. Making a date with him for lunch didn't guarantee he'd even be there for dinner. He was also, always, distracted by two overwhelming obsessions that took demonic control of his life: money and women.

Different ways of keeping the same score, one fed off the other, giving him the air of a man incredibly good at both. But when you saw him up close, when you knew him well enough to get past the paraphernalia of image, it became apparent – especially at the end of his life – that he wasn't extraordinarily adept at either. Although he surrounded himself with the trappings of success, which more often than not included dozens of totally gorgeous women, it was as if he was wearing boutonnières because he liked the message, not because he appreciated flowers. Once he'd lost the accoutrements of serious wealth, when the planes, the yachts, the mansions, the cars, the famous hangers-on, and his own model agency were all gone – toys locked away forever – it was not just the quantity of his ladies that dried up.

An incessant hustler, Bernie never stopped working a room, never stopped stalking an opportunity – financial or female – and many women felt uncomfortable in his presence. If he liked you, he might not hit on your wife, but there was usually a moment when you suspected he was pondering her underwear. For the same reason, men occasionally found his company disconcerting. It wasn't easy to have a serious, lengthy conversation with him if there was a short skirt within two hundred yards.

That said, he was an absolute original and, if you happen to like absolute originals, it was impossible not to like Bernie.

Throughout his life, people were always saying that he was a born salesman and therein lay his genius. Had that been true, had his talent been that simple to define, he might be remembered today as the best mutual-funds salesman ever. But having known him well and having listened to him tell stories of how it used to be, it's evident that his real genius was his capacity to isolate problems and then go about solving them in a unique way. His cunning was unequalled.

After graduating from Brooklyn College, he spent a year or so as a Trotskyite intent on changing the world. Once he discovered that radical socialists don't eat as well as old-fashioned capitalists, he hooked up with a young mutual-funds manager just out on his own named Jack Dreyfus.

Bernie decided that American GIs in Europe had money to spend, so with Dreyfus's blessing, he moved to France to flog mutual funds to soldiers. This was the mid-1950s. His territory included bases across Europe, but his bachelor lifestyle revolved around Paris. There he concocted a one-room operation called Investors Overseas Services (IOS) and collected a staff of otherwise-out-of-work ex-pats. Under his tutelage, this bunch of semi-misfits got extremely good at high-pressure selling and, before long, they were all making a lot of money.

Before long, too, Bernie was coming to realize that IOS could be more than just a cash cow, that he'd created an infrastructure that could be put to better use than churning out clients for Dreyfus. To make real money he needed management fees, not commissions, so instead of selling Dreyfus funds, he decided to sell his own. In 1960, he created International Investors Trust, followed shortly by a mutual fund that held shares in other mutual funds, called the Fund of Funds. He pitched these investments, many of them registered in Canada, with the unmistakable question, "Do you sincerely want to be rich?" And so many people answered yes that he found himself inundated with their money.

Needless to say, there was considerably more to IOS than he allowed outsiders to see. Bernie was making himself seriously rich by tapping into middle-class anxieties. Until he and IOS came along, only the wealthy could call on personal banking connections. The middle classes in many countries, who were just as worried about asset protection, didn't have those connections or the necessary funding to buy fiscal refuge. That's what Bernie sold them. Together with a Harvard lawyer named Edward Cowett – who was the legal mastermind behind all this – IOS structured itself and its funds to exploit tax breaks, secret banking, legal loopholes, and the paucity of offshore oversight.

Which is what brought Bernie to the Bahamas. He nested his funds there, in shell companies designed to prevent scrutiny. His army of salesmen spread out around the world, smuggling trunks of cash out of Latin America, Asia, and the currency controlled nations of Europe, and flew them into the Bahamas, where Bernie deposited them in Tibor Rosenbaum's Atlas Bank.

While Bernie advertised IOS as an investment, and wrapped IOS in a shawl of integrity – peppering his board of directors with the former governor of California Pat Brown, with FDR's son James Roosevelt, and with advisers to the governor of the Bank of England – his real business was capital flight and tax evasion.

From the Bahamas, Rosenbaum moved IOS's money to Geneva, where Bernie arranged to lend it back to his investors so they could purchase IOS shares. It meant that someone in, say, Brazil, who wanted to protect his assets, had access to a smuggling service to get money out of the country, and paperwork from a Swiss bank to show his taxman that the IOS shares he was holding – which he'd actually paid for – were only mortgaged.

This concept of back-to-back loans quickly became the flavour-of-the-month money-laundering ploy by Colombian drug traffickers. Following Bernie's lead, they spent all of the 1970s, 1980s, and most of the 1990s dumping drug cash offshore, borrowing their own money to buy real estate, and declaring the income from the real estate to the taxman in Bogota in order to justify their wealthy lifestyles.

Unquestionably, this basic laundering system served Bernie well for five or six years, permitting him to enjoy the fruits of global empire building. By the mid-1960s, he was reportedly worth $1.5 billion, enough to buy a lot of fruit. It also bought him the Overseas Development Bank (ODB). His friend Rosenbaum objected, contending that Atlas in the Bahamas and BIC in Switzerland could handle whatever it was he needed. But owning a bank was one of the ultimate toys and while IOS was riding high, Bernie bought a lot of toys. For good measure, Rosenbaum went partners with him and owned 20 per cent of ODB.

What most people didn't realize about Bernie, until it was much too late, was that his toys lived inside a house of cards. And the house that Bernie built took a serious knock in 1966. The Brazilians cottoned on to what he was doing, arrested thirteen IOS salesmen, and seized records for more than ten thousand clients. Bernie hired his own SAS-like commando team to get his salesmen out of Brazil – which they did – but not before the government charged IOS with smuggling $100 million out of the country.

The following year, the Swiss decided they didn't like the way he was running his business either. IOS was offshore in the Bahamas and, before long, in Panama too. But Bernie, now living in Switzerland, was trying to make people believe that IOS had a Swiss pedigree. The Swiss reckoned it didn't matter where he lived because the Bahamian and Panamanian incorporation documents stipulated that the companies were managed offshore. Although they couldn't yet make a criminal case against him, they put enough pressure on him that Bernie moved across the border to France. Hardly forced to slum, he owned a castle in France stocked with antique furniture, gourmet food, vintage wine, and centrefold playmates. For good measure, he also had the similarly equipped, forty-room Douglas Fairbanks mansion in Beverly Hills.

Many years later, Bernie would say that the Swiss hounded him not because he pretended that IOS was Swiss but because the bankers didn't like how he'd made offshore funds popular, in direct competition to secret Swiss banking. There might be some truth in that because by 1967 the offshore world was awash with several hundred funds – IOS imitations and wannabes – holding assets of close to $4 billion.

The Bahamas was booming. So was Panama, which was aggressively turning itself into a sink of such distinction that someone would later remark, "Panama isn't a country, it's a business." Other jurisdictions were also cottoning on to the idea that they could sell shell companies to help people hide assets, or allow foreigners to incorporate banks as long as those foreigners didn't take deposits from any locals.

As laundering facilities grew more plentiful, ensuring cash flow and reinvestment for illicit activities, crime and intrigue kicked up a gear. Honduras turned itself into a cocaine bridge. Guatemala offered mobsters sanctuary by selling passports. Costa Rica and Nicaragua sold out to the CIA. Paraguay set out its stall, with anything and everything for sale in the wide-open frontier town that was then called Ciudad del Stroessner and is today called Ciudad del Este. Argentina responded by becoming a major drug transshipment point, moving cocaine from Colombia east to Africa and Europe, and moving heroin from the Mediterranean north to the Caribbean, the U.S., and Canada. As drug trafficking and illicit activities increased, creating more cash, laundromats multiplied. More laundromats meant more room for dirty money, which in turn brought about more laundromats.

Allen Jones Lefferdink, a man who once said, "I have only two kinds of days, happy and hysterically happy," was a fraudster from Nebraska who bilked investors in Colorado, came to the islands, started Mutual Funds of America, used investors' money to buy himself an insurance company and two banks offshore, then disappeared with $15 million.

Jerome Hoffman started a Liberian company called International Investors, turned that into a pair of mutual funds in Bermuda, and disappeared with $12 million.

Lansky's pal Ed Levinson, together with another friend, Ben Siegelbaum, opened the Exchange Bank of Geneva, bringing along with them Yiddy Bloom and John Pullman, to create yet another extension of Pullman's and Rosenbaum's operations in the Bahamas.

A fraudster named Clovis McAlpin liked the loan-back scheme so much he bought his own Swiss bank to make it work. He invited one of his friends in on the deal – a stock-manipulating crook from Detroit named Robert Vesco – and together they bought Standard Commerz of Lucerne. Although that partnership didn't turn out to be as successful as McAlpin had promised, it opened Vesco's eyes to the offshore world and IOS.

All this time, Lansky himself was more active than ever, running his own bank. Purchased secretly in 1958, Miami National was not only the national collection centre for silver dollars used in Las Vegas's slot machines, it was the conduit for dirty money coming back from the Bahamas and Teamster money heading offshore. The bank financed the Mob's move into south Florida real estate and connected with other local banks of dubious pedigree, especially the highly suspect Bank of Perrine, which turned out to be a sink used by the CIA in various covert operations. Investigations later revealed that Miami National was an important link between the Teamsters and Charles "Bebe" Rebozo, the Cuban American who owned Key Biscayne Bank, was tied into the Cleveland Mob, and is best remembered as Richard Nixon's bagman.

Rebozo and Miami National underwrote the purchase of Nixon's "winter White House" in Key Biscayne. They managed it through a company called Keyes Realty, which had previously been identified in the Kefauver hearings for its links to organized crime. The property passed through the hands of a Cuban "investment" group, the Teamsters and Miami National, before being sold by Keyes to Nixon at substantially less than market value. Furthermore, Keyes ties into the Bay of Pigs invasion – some of its Cuban exile employees were directly involved – and to some of the men who took part in the Watergate break-in. It was also used to launder money for Nixon's re-election campaign funds. Following the money trail through Keyes, you can connect Rebozo to Lansky, to casinos in the Bahamas, and from there to Resorts International. For good measure, Bernie Cornfeld was a shareholder in Resorts International.

In his heyday, Bernie had IOS offices in one hundred countries, a sales force of fifteen thousand, and funds valued at $2.5 billion. But he couldn't make it work forever, and wasn't the kind of man to quit while he was ahead. Facing a two-pronged attack by the Brazilians and the Swiss, Bernie was unable to sustain his Latin American capital-flight business, which seriously cut into his cash flow. He couldn't carry his monstrous overheads and was unwilling to cut back on his own lifestyle. He believed the answer was to go public. But that turned out to be too wild a ride, with IOS shares bouncing all over the place, from $5 to $19 then sinking to under $3. The Securities and Exchange Commission refused to buy into Bernie's claim that a mutual fund holding shares in a dozen other mutual funds was a dozen times better than any one of the funds it was holding, and moved against him for securities' violations. The IOS board turned against Bernie and pressure mounted on him to stand down. He held on as long as he could, which was much too long.

If Bernie was a likable scoundrel, then the vulture who now came sweeping out of the sky was a detestable sleazebag.

When Robert Vesco's interest waned in Standard Commerz of Lucerne, he looked around and spotted IOS. The board was in the market for a bailout and he somehow conned them into letting him do just that. Once inside the company, instead of saving it, he simply stole the assets. Some $260 million to $300 million disappeared into offshore shells.

By then, Vesco was under indictment in New York for illegal contributions to Nixon's 1972 presidential campaign. He couldn't go back to the States, so he headed for the safety of Costa Rica, where he lived under the protection of presidents José "Pepe" Figueres and Daniel Oduber. He invested $13 million in radio and television stations, a newspaper, and a hotel. He also acquired tens of millions of dollars' worth of Costa Rican bearer bonds, enough that he purportedly had it within his power to create an instant financial crisis. Such was Vesco's way of ensuring he'd always have someplace safe to sleep.

In 1976, he was indicted again in the U.S., this time for the theft of $224 million of IOS funds. Two years later, a new president in Costa Rica withdrew the welcome mat. Vesco settled in the Bahamas, where he opened a bank and assured his continued residency by offering various members of the Pindling government a rare kind of account – one that featured perpetual withdrawals without the pain of ever having to make a deposit. His generosity was rewarded with a Bahamian diplomatic passport.

Immunity was a handy thing to have, especially now, because Vesco was embarking on a business venture that would really piss off the Americans. Installed on his own non-extraditable Bahamian island, Cistern Cay, Vesco went into business with his neighbour, who lived on the private island of Norman's Cay. Carlos Lehder was then an associate of cocaine trafficker Pablo Escobar. Vesco helped Lehder turn the Bahamas into the primary transshipment point for cocaine going to North America. Finding a niche for himself as their *consiglieri*, Vesco's corporate skills lifted Lehder and Escobar from second-rate smugglers to entrepreneurs running the vertically integrated Medellín cartel.

When Vesco ultimately became such an embarrassment to the Bahamians that even Pindling took notice, Vesco fled to Nicaragua. He'd been courting some influential Panamanians, including Manuel Noriega, who might have given him shelter there, except that Noriega had his own troubles. From Nicaragua, Vesco headed for Antigua, where the government of Vere Bird sold him sanctuary and a passport with a false name. Bird resisted American pressure to hand over Vesco long enough for Vesco to phone Pepe Figueres in Costa Rica and beg a favour. On Vesco's behalf, Figueres negotiated safe haven for him in Cuba. Castro agreed, not as a courtesy to Figueres but because Vesco was willing to pay a gigantic premium for the privilege. Legend puts the figure at $1 billion, but it's doubtful that Vesco had that much to play with. Then, too, even if the payment was only 10 per cent of a billion – which Vesco did have – it's hardly chump change.

So Castro installed Vesco in a guest villa in La Coronela, the most exclusive district of Havana, and assigned a detachment of security guards, as much to protect him as to keep him leashed in. Vesco was permitted to mingle with the diplomatic set at the country's most fashionable golf club, to send his children to the International School, to throw lavish parties, to invest in sugar and tobacco, to build a series of beachfront homes, to deal in coffee futures, and to run a huge money-laundering operation out of Cayo Largo in southern Cuba. He used his Colombian connections to turn Cuba into a cocaine transshipment point – generating "rent" for the Castro brothers – and to call on his Panamanian connections to help Fidel beat the U.S. embargo on Cuban goods. To manage that, Vesco designed a system where sugar was shipped from Havana to Panama, relabelled and reinvoiced there as Panamanian sugar, then brought into the States. The same tactic worked for Cuban lobster. Conversely, Vesco arranged for American goods, which could not legally go to Cuba, to be laundered through Panama, where invoices showed them heading one way when they were actually on a ship bound for Havana. The best the Americans could do was indict Vesco yet again, this time for conspiring to smuggle cocaine into the United States.

Inevitably, the Swiss reopened their file on Bernie Cornfeld. While they scrutinized IOS, they locked him up for eleven months. Unable to summon help from the commandos who'd once freed his salesmen in Brazil, Bernie hired the finest restaurants in Geneva to cater his meals inside. He was charged with embezzling $7 million, but the Swiss couldn't make the charges stick and he was acquitted. Bernie spent much of the rest of his life living in a small mews house in London, still hustling. In 1995, on a visit to Israel, he suffered a stroke and friends had to chip in to bring him back to the U.K. He died a few weeks later.

That same year, Castro charged Vesco as an *agent provocateur* for unnamed foreign governments. Vesco had embarked on a scheme with Richard Nixon's nephew Donald to develop a wonder-drug that would cure cancer and arthritis. It turned out to be less than wonderful. The U.S. State Department was put on notice that Cuba might be prepared to hand him over, but that didn't happen.

Bernie had once predicted that the day would come when Vesco would simply outlive his usefulness, that Castro would unceremoniously turn his back on Vesco. Which is exactly what happened. Castro sent Robert Vesco to jail for thirteen years.

Somewhere, Bernie was having a posthumous last laugh.

3

THE RULES OF NOWHERE

"Faith is believing in something you know can't be so."

– Huckleberry Finn

In the early 1960s, the pool of dollars beyond the control of U.S. authorities finally reached the point where the value of dollars held in foreign hands actually exceeded the value of America's gold reserves. For the first time in American history, the risk of a "ruler of Abu Dhabi scenario" was very real.

Not having enough gold at Fort Knox directly threatened the international monetary system, the dollar's standing as the world's primary currency, and the economic might of the United States. The situation was further aggravated by America's increasing involvement in Vietnam, which added considerable sums to the amount of currency flowing overseas. The balance of trade became widely disproportionate and draconian measures seemed inevitable.

Starting with the Kennedy administration in mid-1963 and going through Lyndon Johnson's term, which ended in January 1969, the Americans attempted to tighten financial regulations and institute capital controls, in the vain hope of restricting the flow of dollars overseas. But the war in Vietnam wreaked havoc on the balance of payments. Johnson made the controls voluntary until they failed, then made them mandatory, which also failed. Major international banks viewed these interventions as unnatural restraints on the natural flow of money, and invented ways around them. Johnson argued that the measures were political necessity, but to pacify big business, he permitted companies operating overseas to keep those profits outside of the country. The question for those companies was, Where do we put those profits? The obvious answer was in our own backyard – the Bahamas.

The new gold rush was on. American banks opened offshore branches, companies followed those banks offshore, and more banks followed those companies. Gangsters had shown big business the way, and by the time Richard Nixon replaced Lyndon Johnson in the Oval Office, the Bahamas had become one of the world's foremost money centres.

As money accumulated beyond the reach of those governments where that money was originally issued, the concept of sovereignty suffered yet another blow. Once upon a time, rule was defined by a mountain range or a river; or by a beach plus three miles of ocean, which happens to have been the distance a cannon ball could travel; or in the sky, to the altitude that a hot air balloon could fly. While the three-mile limit was later extended to twelve miles to give fishing fleets a monopoly on catches that would otherwise have been in international waters; and while altitude was later extended to 50.55 miles because of jet planes; much of what sovereignty used to mean now lay in tatters because the offshore world is, by definition, beyond sovereignty.

Nation-states could dictate supply, and finance ministers could tinker with interest rates, but governments were ultimately losing control over their own currency. It was being waylaid by countries with no real international influence, except their ability to sweep great sums of money away from those nation-states that backed the money. The power vacuum left in-between was filled by banks and corporations. As a result, all these years later, any government that thinks it controls its own financial destiny has failed to understand the political might that has been seized by businesses – both legitimate and illicit – through their offshore holdings.

History makes that abundantly clear.

In the late 1960s, mirroring Lyndon Johnson's concerns, finance ministers and Central Banks across Europe were equally worried about their currencies. Increased speculation was creating too much volatility in the markets, which destabilized political agendas. Equating control of their currency to control of their destiny, several governments teamed up to bully banks with legislation aimed at limiting currency trading.

The Brits, French, Swiss, and Germans all said to the banks, If you trade the pound, the two francs, and the deutschmark, you have to play by our rules, and if you don't play by our rules, if you create too much misery for our currency, we're going to throw you out of the country. That sounded like a good idea to the politicians, but bankers knew it was never going to work. The horse hadn't merely bolted, it was living in a beachfront condo in the Caribbean.

A trader at Citibank came up with a scheme to beat the finance ministers. Instead of booking trades in London or Paris, Zurich or Frankfurt – where the ministers could monitor them – he booked trades out of sight and beyond the horizon at the bank's "Nassau Desk." And he got away with it for quite a while, until someone in Switzerland discovered that the trades were not being booked in the Bahamas. They were going through New York, to a desk in Citi's trading room where the bank flew a cardboard sign that read *Nassau*. Eventually, after the trades were booked there, a clerk in the Bahamas copied them into a second set of books, just in case someone ever showed up to see them.

The Swiss screamed foul, the other European governments complained, and the Securities and Exchange Commission (SEC) launched its own investigation. In the meantime, Citibank brought a new computer system on-stream that allowed them to book trades made anywhere in the world, instantaneously, somewhere else. So now, a trade made in London or Paris could be legitimately booked in the Bahamas, which eliminated the need for the cardboard sign in Manhattan and, effectively, rendered the case moot. Anyway, by then, almost all of the major U.S. banks had cottoned on to the trick and were running their European trades through the Bahamas.

Seeing so much money heading south, the State of New York came up with offshore banking in the heart of Manhattan. The Bahamians were imposing strict secret banking laws and reinforcing a commitment to shelter money from foreign tax authorities. In response, the New Yorkers created International Banking Facilities (IBFs), which loosened fiscal restrictions, made capital markets more user friendly, and offered tax advantages to foreign banks. Some dollars flowed back onshore, but nowhere near as many as the Americans were hoping for, because New York couldn't get into the most important business of all – capital flight. To do that, the state would have had to put the two big-ticket items on the menu: secret banking and shell companies to facilitate tax evasion. And that was out of the question.

New York's inability to compete with the Bahamas highlighted the great divide between onshore and offshore. It all boiled down to "regulatory risk." Where is your money most likely to get found? In onshore New York, regulatory risk was very high. In offshore Nassau, it was very low.

Put another way, people with money to hide sent it to banks offshore, because they worked for their customers, and not to banks onshore, because they worked for the taxman.

———

Bernie Cornfeld pioneered the way, demonstrating how the offshore world was designer-made for capital flight and tax evasion. By using IOS to move money from Brazil through the Islands, into Switzerland, and sometimes back again, he established one the most important rules of offshore commerce: create confusion through multiple jurisdictions.

The more borders you put between yourself and the authorities, the less likely it is that those authorities will get across all the borders. It was one thing for the Brazilian police – or the Argentine police or the Swiss authorities – to investigate Cornfeld locally. But the moment they stepped across the border, they faced intertwining shells in multiple jurisdictions where foreign cops had no authority. That formula remains the bedrock of the offshore philosophy of several industries, most notably shipping.

As far back as the 1950s, Aristotle Onassis and his brother-in-law Stavros Niarchos decided they were paying too much tax to the Greek government on their merchant shipping fleets. To save money, they bought "flags of convenience." Registering each ship as an IBC in the Bahamas, they then listed the shell company as a vessel on Panama's shipping register. It meant that their Greek fleets, which were now Bahamian, could pretend to be Panamanian. Onassis and Niarchos not only avoided Greek taxes but, as each ship was an anonymous company, they could hide behind those shells to protect their personal wealth.

Today, Liberia and Panama are the most important maritime registries of convenience, accounting for somewhere around 75 to 80 per cent of the world's merchant tonnage. Not by coincidence, Liberia and Panama are also among the world's most prominent dirty-money sinks.

Liberian shell companies are de facto suspect, especially since Liberia became a leading force in Africa's illicit arms market. A recent United Nations (UN) report singled out Liberia for funnelling revenues from ship registration to weapons purchasing and smuggling, in direct violation of UN embargoes. Meanwhile, Panama remains a pivotal player in drug-money laundering.

The reason why flags of convenience are popular becomes obvious every time an oil tanker breaks up on rocks and destroys hundreds of miles of coastline. The Panamanian ship is owned by a Bahamian shell, which is insured through a shell in Bermuda, which has reinsured the policy with a shell in Antigua, which turns out to be nothing more than a plaque on an office door and an answering machine. Some people call it smoke and mirrors. Others label it a fiction.

The most commonly made case for offshore banking and shell companies revolves around three areas: private investment, so that you can minimize your tax liabilities while maximizing privacy; asset protection, so that you can safeguard your holdings from political, fiscal, and legal attempts to confiscate them; and estate planning, so that you can leave your property to whomever you choose without having legal restraints and conditions imposed on your wishes. It is no coincidence that offshore banking, offshore insurance, and offshore ship registration – which make up the three main money spinners – are all heavily regulated in the rest of the world.

Walter Wriston, former chairman and CEO of Citicorp, confirms that "capital goes where it is wanted, and stays where it is well treated. It will flee onerous regulation and unstable politics. . . . No amount of rhetoric or spin control can fool capital for long."

By the 1970s, transfer pricing and trade between companies tied together in cross-border alliances were big enough money spinners to assure prosperity for the offshore world. Capital flight was right up there with them. Offshore banks were now holding more Latin American money than U.S. banks were sending to Latin America to keep those countries afloat. But a new money spinner was entering the equation and, in both volume and velocity, it would quickly dwarf the others.

It was drugs.

The explosion of demand, and the production that geared up to meet it, multiplied exponentially both the supply of and the demand for offshore banking and shell companies. It happened because the offshore world was there to help it happen, and the offshore world was there to help it happen because it was happening.

"The significance of this," says Washington lawyer Jack Blum, a world-class expert on money laundering and the offshore world, "was lost on the vast majority of people. In the main, they believed, it wasn't important. It hadn't reached the scale of, 'If you don't pay attention to this you're going to get clobbered.' We hadn't yet been through all the successive mergers that produced mega-corporations. Executives weren't yet making hundreds of millions a year. Being multinational was relatively new. Things hadn't yet got out of kilter. It wouldn't be until communications improved and transportation improved and money became totally portable, exchangeable, and interchangeable that anyone would sit up and scream, 'What the hell's going on here?'"

For some jurisdictions, it was confirmation of the prophesy that the meek shall inherit the earth. For others, it was good business. For many, it was both. The U.S. State Department estimates that 40 per cent of all the cocaine and 30 per cent of all the heroin that shows up on North American streets transits through the Caribbean. As drug trafficking increases offshore, so does offshore banking. In a country as poor as Haiti, for example, as drug transshipment has noticeably increased, the number of banks on the island has quadrupled.

Selling stealth and deception is non-polluting. Safeguarding someone's assets from whatever civil or criminal liabilities he or she would otherwise encounter at home doesn't require significant capital investment. Nor does it require a skilled workforce. You become a haven by declaring yourself a haven. You legislate secrecy, hang out your shingle, and, just like that, you're in business.

As Blum confirms, "You're in the United States, you're under American law. You cross the border, it's Mexican law or Canadian law. Traditionally, law has always gone hand in hand with the territory. But when you're dealing with money moving around the world, when it can move anywhere, when it can be booked anywhere, then where's the law? In this instance, the law is wherever you chose to make it."

Sovereignty was finally dead.

Paul Helliwell understood that better than most.

So did Manuel Noriega.

Helliwell was an intelligence operative in the Second World War who never got out of the game. A lawyer by trade, he set up his Miami practice to work like a CIA cut-out.

Noriega was chief henchman to Panama's dictator, Omar Torrijos. He was also the man who eventually unseated the men who murdered Torrijos to seize power.

As an attorney, Helliwell helped the Disney Corporation disguise a thirty-seven-thousand-acre interest in Orlando – which would become Disney World – by running purchases through shells in Panama and the Cayman Islands. He counted among his other clients the Grand Bahama Port Authority. He was head of the Republican Party in Florida and a confidant of Bebe Rebozo. As a part-time spook, Helliwell set up shells throughout the offshore world to hide funding for CIA gun running and the Bay of Pigs invasion. He also put together a holding company called Florida Shares, which owned several small financial institutions, including the CIA cut-out Perrine Bank. But his masterpiece was his 1964 creation of Castle Bank and Trust. Born out of a shell in Panama – part owned by Daniel K. Ludwig – Helliwell housed the bank in Nassau, opened a branch in the Caymans, and established correspondent relationships around the world. On the surface, the bank was selling tax evasion to wealthy Americans. Below the waterline, Helliwell was laundering money to pay for the CIA's expeditions into drug trafficking.

Unaware of the CIA connection, the FBI and DEA stumbled across Castle Bank while looking at a trafficking ring. They brought the IRS in to peruse the bank's clients. But, just as the taxmen discovered some wealthy Americans hiding money, their investigation was abruptly wound down. That's because the CIA pulled strings to get it wound down.

The moment Castle was exposed, the CIA decided it had outlived its usefulness and the bank quickly collapsed. As soon as it was gone, a tiny bank opened in Australia, mirroring Castle's operation. The Nugan Hand Bank picked up many of the pieces left on the floor by Castle, became a player in the Pacific, and opened in the Caribbean too. Its directors were mostly retired Americans, high-placed spooks and former military intelligence officers. Nugan Hand suffered the same fate as Castle, and sank just as quickly. What records were left showed that fraud, extortion, money laundering, and drug trafficking were what this bank was all about. The difference between the two banks, however, was starkly seen in the difference between the fate of the men fronting it. Paul Helliwell died in his own bed. Frank Nugan was found dead with a bullet hole in his head, an apparent suicide, and Michael John Hand just disappeared, never to be seen again.

Manuel Noriega fared much better in his offshore adventures by living to tell the tale, but only just. He'd been Torrijos's intermediary with the Colombian cocaine cartels and had arranged several lucrative deals with Robert Vesco's partner and neighbour in the Bahamas, Carlos Lehder. In exchange for a piece of the action, Panama provided Lehder with storage and transshipment points for his cocaine, and with banking facilities to launder his money. Panama's secret banking laws, first established in 1927 and considerably tightened over time, make Switzerland's appear almost transparent.

By the time he'd taken rule of the country in 1983, Noriega had embarked on a spectacular series of deals with both the Colombians – to help traffic their drugs and launder their money – and also with the DEA. As their guy in Panama, the DEA were paying Noriega up to $200,000 a month to tip them off to drug trafficking and money laundering. He was also earning $10 million a month from Lehder.

Playing both ends against the middle, Noriega handed Lehder's competitors to the DEA, which kept them both happy. Although, in one case, he shut down a bank belonging to the Cali cartel, which didn't exactly endear him to the Orejuela brothers, who owned the cartel. Legend has it, they put out a contract on Noriega that only got lifted through the direct intervention of Fidel Castro, who was also paying Noriega to help Cuba break U.S. sanctions.

To hide his own money, Noriega first used Panamanian banks, then diversified around the world – both onshore and offshore – opening accounts at BCCI, Banque National de Paris, First American Bank, and the Algemene Bank Nederland. He moved money through the Caribbean, sometimes in his own name, at other times in the name of the Panamanian Defense Force, at still other times in the names of offshore shells he'd set up to hide the true ownership of his money. When he was finally taken down – kidnapped in Panama, brought to Florida, and thrown into prison for forty-three years – the nation he left behind had mixed emotions about his departure. He was an ugly dictator and many democratic-loving Panamanians were glad to see the back of him. But he'd also helped create a laundromat that has made many Panamanians very rich.

Thanks, in large part, to Noriega, Panama's Colon Free Trade Zone is a home away from home for the drug cartels and other transnational organized criminal groups. It is the second-largest free-trade zone in the world – after Hong Kong – and the largest cash business on the planet. It is a magnate for drug trafficking, contraband, and money laundering. Thanks, almost entirely, to the Colon Free Trade Zone, dirty money is today the backbone of the Panamanian economy.

With 350,000 shell companies and 150 banks thriving in its shadow, it's not surprising why one U.S. Customs official notes, "The country is filled with dishonest lawyers, dishonest bankers, dishonest company-formation agents, and dishonest companies registered there by those dishonest lawyers so that they can deposit dirty money into their dishonest banks. The Free Trade Zone is the black hole through which Panama has become one of the filthiest money-laundering sinks in the world."

—

Whereas Noriega is still a hero to certain folks in Panama, someday there will be statues of Harold Wilson, James Callaghan, and Denis Healey all over the offshore world, a sign of gratitude to two British prime ministers and one chancellor of the exchequer for singularly having failed to understand the realities of economics.

In October 1973, the Organization of Petroleum Exporting Countries (OPEC) oil embargo quadrupled the price of a barrel in a mere few weeks, creating colossal wealth for the producing nations, especially the Gulf States. Those "petro-dollars" had to go somewhere and their natural home was London's Euromarket. So tens of billions of dollars gushed into Britain. It could have been boom-time for everyone, except that Labour governments, under Wilson, Callaghan, and Healey, decided to screw it up by instituting currency controls. Misguidedly, they believed that the way to guarantee Britain's financial prosperity was to limit free trade by stopping the mass exportation of the national currency. They didn't realize that money had become stateless, that it was beyond the control of any government, that the market for money was bigger than many governments put together, and that several banks were bigger than those governments as well.

These days, no politician could afford to be so foolish. As business guru Peter Drucker puts it, "Money has slipped the leash."

Even then, Wilson, Callaghan, and Healey never stood a chance. The big banks sidestepped controls. So did big business. So did the wealthy. Smaller banks, the ones that couldn't afford to stay at the table, also headed offshore. The islands were cheaper, welcomed large dollar deposits, and spoke English. Most of them were more or less politically stable. Most of them had reasonable communications and transportation facilities. None of them had exchange controls or imposed interest-rate ceilings.

By dramatically raising the cost of doing business in the U.K., the Labour regime penalized the poor, empowered the rich, and created new-found wealth offshore. At the same time, Lynden Pindling was liberating the Bahamas from British control.

As a result of Bahamian independence in 1974, some bankers had second thoughts about the financial sector there. With Britain in charge, the island seemed safe. But the WASP banking world didn't have a high opinion of native politicians, most of whom seemed to have been cut from the same cloth as Pindling. Some of those WASP bankers decided it might be time to start looking for someplace else to go.

That racism played a part in the development of the offshore world is undeniable. As one person put it, "White bankers wouldn't trust a black crook. White crooks, okay. But not black crooks." Which is also why nearby ports of call in the Eastern Caribbean didn't land the business. Instead, money headed westward, past Jamaica to a British crown colony – which meant it was still acceptable to the white world – called the Cayman Islands.

Some 480 miles southeast of Miami, the Caymans consists of three islands, 525 banks, 900 mutual funds, 400 insurance companies, 40,000 IBCs, and about the same number of residents. As there are no direct taxes on income, profits, wealth, or capital gains, the government must make its money on indirect taxes, which include sales tax, import duties, stamp duty, plus the sale of banks, mutual-funds insurance companies, and IBCs.

Commercial finance came slowly. In 1953, Barclays opened the island's first foreign branch. Ten years later, a second bank arrived – the Royal

Bank of Canada – being the opening salvo in a campaign by Canadian money managers to colonize the Caribbean. The island's third foreign bank, a year after that, was the Canadian Imperial Bank of Commerce. As more and more money left the Bahamas, the pace in the Caymans picked up and, within twenty years, the Caymans could boast one bank for every forty-nine residents. Abuse brought embarrassment and several banks have since been shut. So now there's only one bank for every seventy-six residents, which still isn't bad considering that by holding assets of nearly $900 billion – more than twice the amount on deposit in all the banks in New York – it works out to $22.5 million per resident.

Not that every resident has that much. For that matter, you won't find $900 billion on the island. A few years ago, a local businessman needed to raise a lowly $1 million in cash to pay for a banknotes-on-the-table deal, and it took him several weeks to manage it. Unlike financial centres in Europe where vaults are filled with the stuff, the water table in the Caymans is so high that there are no basements.

No basements, no underground vaults, no cash.

Even if they had vaults, you still wouldn't find $900 billion there because it's never been there and there's no reason for it to go there. Most of the money is in New York. Whatever transactions are booked in the Caymans have nothing to do with moving that money. It's only blips on a computer screen pretending to be the location of the money.

"What is all this money doing offshore?" New York's legendary District Attorney Robert Morgenthau answers his own question. "It is not there because of the sunshine and the beaches. To be blunt, it is there because those who put it there want a free ride, depositors, investors, banks, and businessmen want to avoid or evade laws, regulations, and taxes."

Morgenthau is unrelenting in his aversion to the Cayman Islands and the way they do business. "Tax havens which rely on bank and corporate secrecy are knowingly assisting customers of theirs to commit tax fraud. Unlawful tax shelters do not need to be kept secret."

One of the engines that drove this long period of prosperity was drug money. It poured in from the 1970s well into the 1990s. Then the Russians arrived on the wings of capital flight. Since 1992, it is estimated that as much as $300 billion to $400 billion has bled out of the Russian economy. Some of it stayed in Europe – London, Frankfurt, and Vienna, and less obvious financial centres such as Cyprus, Latvia, and Turkey. Some if it went to Dubai. Some of it wound up being invested in the United States. But at one point, a lot of it either moved through the Caribbean or was bedded down there for a while. And in a few cases it still lives there. In the Caymans, at least in the beginning, they welcomed the Russians with open arms.

Russian money was followed by money that used to be in Hong Kong. Fearing the Chinese takeover of the colony, investors shipped out a great deal to be bedded down in the Caymans for safekeeping. Some of it was legitimate money. Some of it was owned by Asian organized criminals. But by the time it got to the Caribbean, it all looked sparkling clean. What's more, just because it now lived in the Caymans, that didn't mean the money wasn't still being managed from Hong Kong.

These days when you mention money laundering in the Caymans, you get the same answer, almost verbatim, from everyone you speak with: no one here wants money launderers; we systematically reject dirty money; we've cleaned up our act; the Caymans is no longer a sink for the world's drug cash.

When it comes to drug cash, there may be some truth in their avowals. It's a lot tougher for a Colombian cocaine trafficker to hide his money there. Although it's not beyond the realm of belief that the trafficker might have a lawyer in Switzerland who manages a Luxembourg company that is financing a huge land development project in Haiti, which is being financed with a back-to-back loan out of the Caymans. They also insist there is no terrorist money there either. And, it must be said that, over the past few years, the Caymanians have got better at looking for both drug cash and terror dollars. But that's not the same as saying there's no dirty money regularly coming into the Caymans. UPS and Fedex 737s arrive daily, filled to the brim with express envelopes for banks and trusts and mutual funds and IBCs registered on the island. It's hard to imagine so many flights a week, filled with that many "documents," flying into any other jurisdiction of forty thousand people.

Throughout the history of the Caymans as a financial centre, there has been tax evasion. People tell you there, too, that tax evasion – like drug money and capital flight – is not what the Caymans is all about. They're fast to point out that, in 2000, the government negotiated a treaty with the U.S. ending, once and for all, ambiguities in tax-evasion cases. The island agreed to provide American prosecutors with some banking and corporate information. And, for a while, it seemed as if one former Caymanian banker's rebuke – "the Cayman Island government is knowingly aiding and abetting tax evasion" – was a thing of the past.

That is, until the Caymanians announced in 2002 that maybe it wouldn't sign the treaty after all.

That there is a legitimate place for offshore banking and offshore companies is an accepted fact of global finance. That there is legitimate room for confidentiality – especially where business dealings and personal finance are concerned – is also a given. But necessary confidentiality and ultimate secrecy are two different things, and that distinction is not often made when there is profit to be had by confusing the two.

Jean-Pierre Roth, chairman of the governing board of the Swiss National Bank, typified the offshore banker's stance in a recent speech in Basel. "The beneficiary of banking secrecy is the client, not the bank."

While that may ring true, without strict banking secrecy, the money goes elsewhere. As some jurisdictions have "liberalized" and begun to co-operate with foreign authorities, there's been an observable shift of funds to jurisdictions that don't co-operate. In the Caymans, for example, when the government announced that they would sign that tax treaty, money moved away. When they reneged on the deal, money came back. So despite Roth's claims, secrecy is a product for sale that does, indeed, benefit banks.

"In Switzerland," Roth continued, "privacy rules are not limited to the banking sector, but they apply with equal vigor to professions such as doctors, lawyers, solicitors, and the clergy."

That's true in Switzerland, as it is throughout much of the world. But if you live in say, Calgary, the fact that a doctor in Geneva won't publicize your medical condition is of little consequence. Neither would a doctor in Calgary. Anyway, you don't go to Geneva because a doctor there keeps your secrets. You go because, by law, a banker must.

Roth then insisted, "Swiss people would not comprehend, and indeed they would not support, any initiative aimed at throwing out financial privacy principles simply because some dishonest people have taken advantage of them, any more than they would accept giving up medical secrecy because of a few cases of health insurance fraud. Nor could the Swiss understand, or accept, that the foreign clients of our banks be treated any differently, i.e., without the same amount of due trust and respect."

Of course not. It would cost them too much money.

Sharing Roth's agenda, the Swiss Bankers Association (SBA) talks an equally good, equally disingenuous game. A pamphlet published in 2001 called *Dirty Money? No, Thanks!* tries to create a morally responsible face of secret banking. "The Swiss financial center has many assets, but its sound reputation is surely the most important . . . every attempt at money laundering is considered a risk to its reputation."

The pamphlet cites a report from the G8's money-laundering oversight group, the Financial Action Task Force (FATF), which credits Switzerland with "extremely effective measures to combat criminal activities." Pointing to the 1998 law, the SBA stresses how it obliges everyone active in the financial sector, not just bankers, to identify clients and establish the beneficial owners of assets. Notes the SBA, this law comes on the back of more than twenty years of the strictest codes enforcing due diligence.

If that's so, if twenty years of the strictest codes had successfully enforced due diligence, how come they needed yet another law in 1998?

The answer is obvious: because the codes didn't work. Just look at twenty years' worth of Swiss embarrassment after they got caught red-handed, hiding money for crooks named Abacha, Marcos, Noriega, Bhutto, Mobutu, and Duvalier, plus the Cali cartel, the Medellín cartel, the traditional Sicilian Mafia, the 'Ndrangheta, the Camorra, the Russian Maffiya, and enough fraudsters and tax evaders to fill a small stadium. How long does the list have to be to prove the SBA wrong?

Nor does the 1998 law work all that well. Granted, it puts increased responsibilities on the private sector, through mandatory reporting where corruption or criminality is suspected, and expands reporting responsibilities from banks to "financial intermediaries." But co-operation has been so minimal that, two years after the law came onto the statute books, the head of Switzerland's Money Laundering Reporting Office (MROS) quit. So did the rest of his office, all five of them. They left because, despite the law, the government flatly refused to put its money where its laws were and give the office real powers to do something about money laundering. The 1998 law is filled with loopholes through which "financial intermediaries" can claim that reporting is not required. As a result, the MROS has been receiving fewer than one report of suspected criminal activity per bank per year!

To give the dog its due, secrecy in Switzerland is not what it used to be. But that's not because the gnomes got religion, it's because pressure from European governments over transparency in tax matters, and from the U.S. in the fight against money laundering, rudely muscled the Swiss into a corner.

When Seagram magnate Edgar Bronfman, Jr., and others led groups in search of Holocaust money, stringent denials came from Switzerland, categorically refusing the notion that this money was hidden there. Swiss bankers assumed their best air of utter indignation, furious that anyone would even insinuate they were party to such heinous behaviour. That is, until Holocaust money was found in Switzerland, and those bankers were shown to be outright liars. They next responded with rage that anyone would suggest that the presence of Holocaust money automatically meant they were harbouring dirty money.

Having reputational risk shoved down their throats left the Swiss with no alternative but to become better global citizens. That's not to say they're good. Just better. Underneath it all, the gnomes seem less concerned with being accused of brokering dirty money than they are with how forced changes benefit other jurisdictions.

If you can't hide it in Switzerland, you can walk it across the border to Liechtenstein.

In 2000, the tiny principality found itself included in an OECD list of thirty-five countries that had laws or policies deemed to be obstructive for foreign tax authorities. Fearing an effect on business, the good people of Vaduz – Liechtenstein's only city – redressed the windows by changing the law that otherwise guaranteed secrecy for certain classes of criminals. But they refused to k ill the goose. In the end, they couldn't even fool the characteristically gullible OECD into thinking that real change was afoot. Two years after finding themselves on that list, the Liechtensteiners were still on it.

Looking for a scapegoat, they conveniently blamed the Swiss. The prime minister's office announced that Switzerland was behind attempts to change the banking regulations in Liechtenstein, in order to secure an unfair competitive commercial advantage.

Hardly a revelation of earth-shattering proportions, when the United Nations looked into Swiss banking, they found the gnomes desperately worried that erosion of client confidentiality diminished the nation's competitive advantage. One Swiss banker told the UN, "The time has come to take a stance and defend, in a lucid and resolute manner, an asset of which the country may be proud and which it cannot do without."

Hoping to occupy the moral ground, Niklaus Blattner, chief executive of the SBA, suggested his members would opt for doing what's right. "In the scramble for a share of the global wealth management market, the long-term prize will go to those financial centres with the highest regulatory standards." This flies in the face of conventional wisdom, which dictates that the prize belongs to those bankers who, under the guise of self-regulation, don't self-regulate, giving themselves a competitive advantage over those who do.

The fallacy of self-regulation lies at the heart of the matter for offshore bankers. That money hidden in an account may contribute to crime, violence, and corruption outside the jurisdiction where the bank is registered is not their concern. And laws in most offshore centres reflect that. It's only a crime if it's a crime in the jurisdiction, except sometimes, when the jurisdiction simply can't avoid it, like with terrorism.

No, what really worries folks in offshore jurisdictions goes back to that SBA pamphlet and reputational risk. But it's not reputational risk the way the SBA put it. It's the risk that comes from first having to deny you're involved, then getting caught at it, then having to retract your denials. It's the reputational risk that the Swiss suffered when they denied holding Holocaust money, got caught with it, were exposed as liars, and were then forced to admit they'd had it all along.

In other words, getting caught is bad for business.

"The offshore world was created as an answer to a simple question," lawyer Jack Blum is fast to conclude. "That is, How do we step out of our responsibility for our actions in the place where we live? The idea is to remove legal responsibility from our own society so that we can say, We don't have any responsibility here. So that we can say, We're governed by the rules of nowhere. And a lot of people, for a lot of different reasons, like the rules of nowhere. You don't want to pay taxes? You don't want some government to insist that an investment is truly an investment and not just a scam? You want to run a hedge fund and put other people's money in fairy dust and cotton candy? Then you need a place where there are no rules, where you can do everything, where there is no accountability. It's the rules of nowhere that built the offshore world."

4

CANADA OFFSHORE

"Canada was one of the last industrialized countries to introduce a system of mandatory reporting of suspicious transactions."

– Auditor General of Canada, 2003

Canada and the United States share the world's largest trade partnership. Every day, nearly $1 billion crosses the longest, unarmed border in the world. But because of that cross-border traffic – which includes drugs, currency, and monetary instruments – and because of Canada's highly sophisticated financial services sector, where Canadian money laundering is concerned, the Americans have assumed a slightly cynical posture. Sort of like the way some wealthy people warmly welcome their fondest cousins to a Sunday barbecue, then spend the whole time thinking, They can't be as rich as us so how come they're driving such a fancy brand-new car?

In this case, after setting the tone for the fight against money laundering, the United States looked north and wondered, Why aren't they following our lead?

"Canada remains vulnerable to money laundering and terrorist financing," the U.S. State Department has maintained for years, and repeated yet again in the 2003 International Narcotics Control Strategy Report. And while the State Department concedes that successive Canadian governments have shown particular concern about the criminal abuse of cross-border currency movements, the word *vulnerable* comes up a second time in that report. "Canada's financial institutions are vulnerable to currency transactions involving international narcotics-trafficking proceeds that include significant amounts of U.S. currency or currency derived from illegal drug sales in the United States."

Put another way, one former State Department official wants to know, "What the hell took Canada so long to get on the money-laundering bandwagon?"

Singling out Canada is a bit artful. It took most everyone else too long, and some places still haven't managed it. True, the United States has driven the fight, but it took Washington sixteen years – from 1970 to 1986 – to convince the rest of the world that the rules of nowhere connected dirty money, organized crime, and, eventually, global terrorism. And then it took several banks, a bunch of crooks, and a lot of tears to underscore the point.

The first step in what would prove to be a very steep and costly learning curve was the United States' Financial Recordkeeping and Reporting of Currency and Foreign Transactions Act, otherwise known as the 1970 Bank Secrecy Act (BSA). It recognized the necessity to identify dirty money at the earliest stage of the laundering process, that is, when cash is fed into the banking system. Primarily, the BSA required banks to file Currency Transaction Reports (CTRs) for cash deposits over $10,000.

The next step came in 1984, when Ronald Reagan's Commission on Organized Crime issued its watershed report, *The Cash Connection*. It was the first time that any government anywhere officially acknowledged the links between organized crime, financial institutions, and money laundering. That report was followed by two more from the commission: *America's Habit: Drug Abuse, Drug Trafficking and Organized Crime* and *The Impact: Organized Crime Today*.

Combined, the three successfully laid the groundwork for passage of the 1986 Money Laundering Control Act (MLCA), which set criminal penalties for washing the proceeds of "unlawful activities." The use of those two words widened the offence of money laundering away from drug trafficking to include all sorts of criminal conduct. In effect, this helped to make the charge of money laundering similar to the charge of conspiracy, a kind of catch-all offence that prosecutors could use in conjunction with other charges. Simply put, as long as money was involved with the crime – which it almost always is – and as long as that money was somehow disguised to avoid detection, then money laundering could be charged.

While this was going on in the States, the rest of the world did nothing. There were stirrings in Canada, Australia, and Britain, suggesting that money laundering was an area that needed to be dealt with. But it would take several more years before anything was done, and then, in the case of Canada and Britain, the route would be that of "suspicious cash transactions." A lame system, it is based on the erroneous belief that the people most likely to launder money should decide what's suspicious.

It wasn't until 1989 that Canada made money laundering a criminal offence and provided that the proceeds of certain crimes could be seized. Two years later, the Proceeds of Crime (Money Laundering) Act set down requirements for financial institutions to keep records of certain cash transactions, notably those over CAD$10,000. But in those days, money laundering was considered to be a function of the drug business. Which is why, when the RCMP set up their first proceeds of crime unit that year, they focused entirely on drugs.

Needless to say, there simply weren't enough traffickers convicted or enough traffickers' assets seized to make the act a best-seller. During the first twelve months that the Mounties pursued criminal assets, they got their hands on CAD$221 million. Considering that Canada was, in those days, a world-class drug-money-laundering sink – with tens of billions passing through the financial sector – CAD$221 million isn't a lot of money. That said, it was a start and better than most of the rest of the world, which was doing nothing. That said, it would take another five years before other forces across Canada established similar proceeds of crime units.

However, there was a growing community of law enforcement people who understood money laundering and were beginning to be heard in Ottawa. The government responded, eventually, by establishing the Advisory Committee on Money Laundering. Despite senior bureaucrats who had their own agendas, and a strong private-sector lobby intent on stopping the government from interfering with the banking and finance sectors, the committee recommended that a revised approach was needed to deal with money laundering.

A year later, the government introduced Bill C-9 – An Act to Facilitate Combating the Laundering of Proceeds of Crime. Becoming law in 1993, it required Canada's financial services sector to assume an anti-money-laundering posture.

The law was aimed at everyone dealing in cash as part of their business, profession, or activity. It stipulated that any cash payment over $10,000 required a specific record of the transaction, including identification of the person who paid in cash. But it stopped short of obligatory reporting. Mirroring the act of 1991, records only needed to be maintained, which gave financial institutions a way around what they viewed as an intrusion into their affairs. If a competent authority asked to see any records, there was time to make some up. However, the government still expected suspicious transactions to be reported.

Along with that came the principle of Know Your Customer (KYC). The thinking was that KYC would oblige financial institutions and businesses to pay attention to the people who were spending large amounts of cash. But at the very heart of voluntary KYC lies a paramount fallacy – if you're in cahoots with a drug trafficker and helping him launder money through your business, you do know your customer and, because you also know the source of the money, you have no suspicions. So honest people complied as they best they could – to varying degrees – while drug money continued to be washed by crooks who never had any intention of complying.

Unfortunately, it's one thing to pass a law, another to get people to obey it. The financial industry was angry with the added expenses that compliance was going to cost. Luckily for them, however, there were enough loopholes to allow banks, investment houses, and money remitters to skirt around the side of the act. The FATF watched that happen and decided, "The suspicious transaction reporting regime does not appear to be working effectively."

For a while, it was business as usual, prompting one American commentator to note that Canada was "the Maytag of the north."

A few years after that, at a regular FATF meeting, with a blacklist of non-compliant countries on the agenda, Britain pointed a finger at Canada and suggested that it be added to the blacklist. The Brits reasoned that Canada did not have a system for evaluating suspicious cash transactions and therefore was in non-compliance with FATF recommendations. The Brits insisted that Canada is no better than Antigua. Returning the compliment, Canada demanded that Britain be added to the blacklist for allowing Jersey, Guernsey, and the Isle of Man to operate, almost without interference. In that respect, came the allegation, the United Kingdom has become Antigua.

In the end, the family spat was resolved with a family compromise. The children promised to do better and the parents punished neither. Both countries escaped the blacklist – although Antigua didn't – and Canada made good on its promise to do better.

Bill C-81 – An Act to Facilitate Combating the Laundering of Proceeds of Crime and to Establish the Financial Transactions and Reports Analysis Centre of Canada – was a good idea at the time, but Parliament recessed and the bill disappeared. It was rewritten and showed up six months later, in June 2000, as Bill C-22 – The Proceeds of Crime (Money Laundering) Act.

This new law brought with it real change. The scope of money laundering widened to make KYC, record-keeping, and reporting much stricter. All financial institutions – not just banks, but money remitters, casinos, accountants, and real estate agents, to name a few – are required to report all cash transactions over $10,000 and all international electronic fund transfers over that amount as well. They are required to report suspicious transactions, regardless of the amount, and they are now obliged to know the beneficial owner of shell companies wishing to open an account. Most importantly, the act established a Financial Intelligence Unit (FIU) and the Financial Transactions and Reports Analysis Centre, otherwise known as FinTRAC.

With a four-year budget of only CAD$139 million – considerably less than what the Mounties seized during the first year of the proceeds of crime unit – FinTRAC was placed under the ultimate control of the minister of finance and did, effectively, bring Canada that much closer to the FATF's idea of full compliance with money-laundering requirements. Wildly underbudgeted, its mission is to collect and analyze information to detect and deter money laundering.

At the end of 2001, in response to the 9/11 attacks, terrorist financing was criminalized and the new act, incorporating the last one, was renamed The Proceeds of Crime (Money Laundering) and Terrorist Financing Act. Under what is now called Bill C-17, FinTRAC's budget remained the same but its responsibilities were expanded to include terrorist financing.

As the designated repository of all cash and suspicious transaction reports, FinTRAC combines them with open source material and other information to create a database of money-laundering intelligence. But unlike its American cousin – the Financial Crimes Enforcement Network (FinCEN), which not only offers information to law enforcement but welcomes inquiries from law enforcement – the effectiveness of FinTRAC has been seriously handcuffed by those members of Parliament who see FinTRAC as a type of Big Brother. Accordingly, FinTRAC is not a law enforcement agency. Instead, it is an independent government agency with a mandate to "collect, analyze, assess and, where appropriate, disclose financial intelligence in order to assist in the detection, prevention and deterrence of money laundering and the financing of terrorist activities."

Its effectiveness gets down to those words *where appropriate* because it's not law enforcement that's allowed to decide what's appropriate.

"To protect the privacy of Canadians who are completing legitimate financial transactions," explained the Auditor General of Canada in her 2003 report to Parliament, "several safeguards and limitations were built into the centre's mandate. These include: keeping the centre itself independent and at arm's length from law enforcement agencies, such as the RCMP and other police forces; restricting the amount of information that can be disclosed to law enforcement agencies; limiting the length of time that data can be kept."

In practice, that means a cop looking to follow the money of a drug-trafficking ring, or a securities fraudster, cannot ask FinTRAC what information exists. He must request specific information by applying to a judge for what is called "a designated disclosure." In essence, he must follow a search warrant procedure to establish reasonable grounds for his access to the information. That, of course, presupposes the fact that he knows what he's looking for.

By its very nature, a financial investigation is not always about what you see, it's often about what you don't see. For example, a drug trafficker has just come back from a holiday in France, but the investigator can't find any receipts. He suspects that the trip might have been paid for with funds outside Canada, which suggests that the trafficker has an offshore bank somewhere. But when the investigator turns for help to FinTRAC, if he doesn't know what information they're holding on the trafficker – say, a reference to the purchase of insurance instruments in the Isle of Man – he's not going to get whatever they've got because he won't know to ask for it.

Notes one senior FinTRAC executive, "If our analysis reveals something that is consistent with money-laundering behavior, then there are provisions by which we can disclose that information to law enforcement without them needing to get a court order to see it. The system may be a little cumbersome, but the idea is not to withhold information, it is to share information."

One estimate suggests that FinTRAC is now fully geared up to deal with three million financial transaction reports a year. By statute, after it analyzes everything it's got, if money laundering or terrorist financing is suspected, FinTRAC must disclose some of the information it's holding to the relevant law enforcement agency. But it is forbidden by law from telling the cops the whole story. Under those circumstances, it can only reveal the target's addresses, banks, and specific account numbers. FinTRAC is prevented from going into the nature of the transactions that have taken place at those banks or to elaborate on what analysis was done to reach the conclusion that law enforcement should look into this. It's then up to law enforcement, flying on a wing and a prayer, to figure out the rest.

In the end, FinTRAC has been designed to be a grown-up version of the kid's party game, hot and cold. *Turn left, cold. Turn right, hot. This way, getting hotter. That way, getting colder.*

Oddly, it is less cumbersome if law enforcement decides to send information to FinTRAC. If an officer has identified specific targets in a money-laundering case, he can pass that along to FinTRAC. At that point, if an analyst at FinTRAC looks at the data and does a work-up on those people, and if the analyst finds behaviour consistent with money laundering, FinTRAC is permitted to do a disclosure back to the officer. And yes, if an analyst at FinTRAC happens to spot some money exchanges in Vancouver and notices that the following day the same person did the same thing in Montreal and notices, again, that a week later there are wire transfers to Hong Kong – if an analyst can lay out the laundering map like that – the information he might eventually be permitted to provide law enforcement could be valuable.

But all of that is contingent on FinTRAC having sufficient information to pass along. They should know it when they see it. FinTRAC is

staffed, at the senior level, by many highly experienced financial investigators. Although, apparently, they're not allowed to see the information FinTRAC holds either. Access is limited to the analysts. So, the
people best qualified to judge the quality of information are excluded
from the process. And anyway, the gathering process stops at the very
point where the information becomes most valuable – the border. The
moment money laundering moves offshore, as almost all money laundering does, FinTRAC is out of business. The way it stands now, there's
no extraterritorial jurisdiction that goes with the legislation. In other
words, if a Canadian bank in the Caribbean takes cash from an arriving
foreigner, the local authorities might want to know about it. But if it's
not "suspicious," and the bank employee who's in on the laundering
also has the authority to make the decision about what's suspicious, the
local authority will never know. Nor will FinTRAC.

That's one colossal loophole in the law.

Unfortunately, there is another, even bigger.

Originally, the justice minister ruled that lawyers would be required
to report, just like other non-financial service businesses through which
large sums of money move. There is a standard belief in law enforcement that no lawyer ever needs to put cash through a client account.
That legitimate attorneys take cheques and that the appearance of cash
is congenitally suspicious. There can be no argument that a lawyer's
client account is as good a method as there is to launder money because
the lawyer can always claim client-attorney privilege to cover this
opening stage of the money-laundering cycle.

Many lawyers take a different view and when they saw that they were
included in the reporting requirements, they raised hell. There had been
a similar situation in the States some years before. When the American
Bar Association was reminded that even attorneys had to file transactions reports for cash payments over $10,000, one group decided to
protest. It was the ABA subcommittee for criminal defence attorneys.
Their argument was, if a defendant on a money-laundering charge pays
his lawyer more than $10,000 in cash, the lawyer will have to report on
his own client. That, they argued, becomes a violation of client-attorney
privilege because it risks turning the defence lawyer into a witness against
his own client. The matter has been tested and the U.S. courts have held
their ground, insisting that lawyers comply. There are cases winding their

way through the system that will eventually allow the Supreme Court to make the final decision, but in the meantime, U.S. attorneys file cash transaction reports.

Canadian attorneys don't.

The government originally insisted they would have to obey the law. But push came to shove and Canada's eighty thousand lawyers argued, successfully, that the requirements forced them to spy on their clients by secretly reporting to an agency of government. So they got their exemption, which means client accounts are still a viable way to wash dirty money. Lawyers do have to report suspicious cash transactions like everyone else, except that, like everyone else, it's up to them to decide what's suspicious.

It's hardly a surprise that most cops are less than thrilled about it.

"That exclusion is far more reaching than Ottawa understands," comments one officer who is now working terrorism out of Toronto. "If I go to a lawyer and say I think you're holding some terrorist money, it's illegal for them to tell me if they are or not. Under the old system, I could ask them about someone and under the old law there was a disclosure possibility. Now they can't tell me even if they want to. Money-laundering investigations now stop as soon as they hit a lawyer's office. Is it any wonder that Canada is becoming a hub for terrorist financing? Think about it, if you're a terrorist and you know that lawyers are exempt, where's the first place you're going to start looking?"

When a senior executive at FinTRAC hears that, he shakes his head and shrugs. "I can't promise we'll catch that, because when money laundering is done intelligently, it's very hard to spot. And even harder to stop. But we're trying. And we will catch a lot of stuff that used to go right past us. Listen, it's not a perfect system, but at least it's not like it was ten years ago in Canada when people walked into banks carrying two bags of cash because they only had two hands."

<hr />

Steven Kaiser didn't need a lawyer to do his money laundering because, for all intents and purposes, he was a legitimate businessman and exactly the kind of client any financial institution would want to have.

He easily passed everyone's KYC requirements. The six-foot-two, fair-haired "international business consultant" had an office with a secretary and employed his wife to work there too. He paid their social security and their health benefits, and he paid all his taxes. He maintained good business records, wore suits to work, drove an upmarket BMW, lived in one of Toronto's right neighbourhoods, heli-skied in the Rockies every winter, took his wife to Europe twice a year, and spent two weeks with her every year, as well, at their condo in the Caribbean.

The rest of the time he was Canada's most successful independent hydroponic marijuana farmer.

One of the country's fastest-growing enterprises, hydroponic marijuana is a hidden hothouse crop, and these clandestine grow operations have reached epidemic proportions throughout Canada. For the most part, it is run by organized Vietnamese criminal groups, in a joint venture with outlaw motorcycle gangs, like Hells Angels, who handle transportation and some distribution.

"The grows are killing us," comments Ontario Provincial Police (OPP) Detective Rod Carscallen. "We're looking in the greater Toronto area alone at a minimum of 10,000 grow houses, and could be as many as 15,000 to 20,000. Greater Vancouver has at least 20,000. Northeast of Montreal, the police took down an entire subdivision. There are easily 20,000 grows in Quebec. Canada-wide? It's anybody's guess, but 100,000 wouldn't surprise me. I'd even say that 100,000 is a conservative guess."

The grow houses are just that, regular homes in regular suburban neighbourhoods that have been gutted to accommodate hundreds of marijuana plants. Many of the houses are rented. But the ones that are sold almost always follow the same scenario. A young Vietnamese man convinces a real-estate broker that he can pay for a house he wants to buy. He puts down as little as possible – ordinarily 5 per cent of the price – in the form of a bank draft that's been purchased somewhere with cash. He then arranges a mortgage, and mortgage fraud is rampant.

The police wonder how some twenty-year-old Vietnamese fellow who's been in Canada for two years and doesn't yet have citizenship can secure a $300,000 mortgage. The suggestion is that lawyers, real-estate agents, and some mortgage lenders are in on it. No one ever reports suspicious transactions and the names registered on the deeds either don't exist or they're nominees.

Carscallen mentions one case where a fellow took over three houses this way and doesn't hesitate to say, "The real-estate agent was in on it.

Up to his eyeballs. Damn right he knew what was going on. How could he not? He probably went out looking for marijuana growers."

In another recent case, a husband-and-wife team used stolen identities to show a credit history for which they obtained a $220,000 mortgage over the Internet. They met with a lawyer once and he facilitated the deal. Later, when the lawyer was asked to pick them out of a lineup, he couldn't. The couple kept up the mortgage payments for a year or so, then walked away. Once they were gone, there was no one for the mortgage lender to find.

What they left behind is a totally ruined house.

To run a grow, the gangs gut the basement and the top floor, leaving the ground floor to look as if it's being lived in. They put in a couch and other furniture, and use timers to turn the living-room lights on and off. If anyone peeks inside, everything appears to be normal. They also mow the lawn regularly, so that no one suspects the house is not lived in.

But the basement and top-floor windows are covered so that no one can see from the outside that huge grow lamps are burning twenty-four hours a day. Inside temperatures can range from 75°F up to 95°F, and remain constant all day, all week, all month. There is also plenty of water streaming through the cultivation, creating a greenhouse in a building not built to be a greenhouse. It gets so humid inside that the houses sweat right through the bricks to the outside.

Each plant gets it own pot, and there are enough pots to completely cover the floor space. It's not uncommon to find as many as eight hundred plants growing in a medium-sized grow house.

The electricity that feeds the lamps might cost as much as $20,000 a year, except the gangs don't pay for it. They bypass the meter by drilling into the foundation, slice into the electricity supply, and reroute it. For the hydro company, that's unrecoverable income. But oddly enough, according to various police agencies, very few of Canada's hydro companies openly acknowledge this as a big problem. Some of them confess that up to 2 per cent of their output is stolen every year, but don't seem anxious to admit that perhaps as much as 80 per cent of that 2 per cent is stolen by these grow houses.

Worse still, because of the way the gangs have rerouted the electricity, around one in ten grow houses end up having a fire.

"Everything that's associated with these houses is absolutely wrong," Carscallen insists. "There's mould everywhere. Gyprock starts falling off the drywalls. The gangs take out stairwells, destroy the foundation to set up the bypass, and vent everything through the chimney. Whatever they need to do to accommodate the growth, they do. So you look at a house worth, say, $300,000, and get two or three of them on a street of fifty or sixty houses. The grow houses are destroyed to the point where they have to bulldozed. What do you think that does to property values on the rest of the street?"

Drug police say that finding these houses, when you know what to look for, is easy. They use handheld thermal imagers to get a heat signature, which becomes grounds for a search warrant. But there is so much heat venting out of the chimney that you can usually smell pot all over the street. There are plenty of other telltale signs, as well. The earth around the electricity meter is disturbed. In the winter, everybody has snow on their roof, except these places. Upstairs and basement windows are all blacked out. The farmers only come and go at night, and then they never park in the driveways, they pull right into the garage and shut the door behind them.

What the cops get when they finally take down a house is the farmer, who's been paid to tend the crop for a year. It's not unheard of that, after working there for a year, whoever owns the house just gives it to the farmer.

So the police arrest the farmer, but they're usually kids and they hardly ever talk. They won't give up their boss because they know what will happen to themselves and their family if they do. That makes a financial investigation – to get behind the people who are behind the grows – difficult, if not impossible.

"We would love to go after the financial side of this," Carscallen continues, "because there is so much money involved and that's the way to really put a dent in it. If each house can harvest a four-hundred-plant growth four times a year, and a conservative estimate values each plant at $1,000 per crop, you're looking at $1.6 million a year per house. Now think about houses where they're growing six hundred plants and eight hundred plants and even more. And think about streets with three or four or five houses on them. It's no wonder they can afford to walk away after a year."

One house hit by the OPP netted thirty tons. The growers were moving ten-pound bags of B.C. Bud. That's the hot-ticket item. A highly potent variety, the THC1 content ranges from 15 to 25 per cent. The THC content of homegrown marijuana during San Francisco's hippie 1970s was a mere 2 per cent. Historically, the police used to figure that a one-pound bag of Bud was worth $3,000. But these guys were shipping ten-pound bags across the border into the States. One guy they eventually popped told them he was taking fifty-five pounds per trip and sometimes made two trips a day, six days a week. Naturally, the OPP tried to find out who was paying this guy. But all he'd say was, it was an Oriental fellow who was giving him $15,000 per trip.

The OPP believes that a lot of this marijuana is going into New York City and from there is possibly transported across to Holland. According to other law enforcement agencies in Ontario, there is so much marijuana coming out of Canada that even if everyone in the country smoked an ounce a day, the entire population could not consume the product produced. What cash stays in Canada gets laundered through casinos, Oriental restaurants, and grocery stores. But even that soon leaves the country, laundered through offshore companies, before disappearing into thin air.

Every so often the Americans get a big hit, stop a couple of hundred pounds coming into the States, and sometimes they seize money too. But for Canadian police, once the marijuana and the money has crossed the border, it's gone. With provincial drug squads working 24/7 just going after the grows, no one's got the budget or the manpower to follow the money.

Notes one Toronto drug squad officer, "Even if we could get the funding, where would we start? In Scarborough, our guys are spending all their time working gangs and crackheads. You say to them, Go after grow houses and they say, Great, but who's going to look after the gangs when they start shooting each other? And I know for a fact that Scarborough is lit up like a Christmas tree."

It's hardly surprising, considering that marijuana and cannabis products are the most widely available drugs in Canada and greater amounts than ever before are being grown indoors. A multibillion-dollar industry, it has become Canada's third-largest agricultural cash crop. One government estimate suggests that B.C. Bud at 15 per cent potency can sell on the streets of Vancouver for $1,500 to $2,000 per pound, $3,000 to $4,000 per pound just across the U.S. border in Bellingham, Washington, and $6,000 to $8,000 per pound farther south in California. On the East Coast, the DEA reports that B.C. Bud starts at around $8,000 per pound. Ontario and Quebec variations are only slightly cheaper, due to less-expensive transportation costs.

With that kind of money to be had, it's no wonder that the Vietnamese' partners, Hells Angels, have discovered that hydroponic marijuana can be used as a currency in the United States to buy cocaine, meth, and ecstasy, which they then smuggle back across the border into Canada.

So, the Vietnamese and Hells Angels control Canada's hydroponic marijuana industry – and do so with vengeance – meaning that there isn't any room for anyone else to elbow their way in. Which makes Steven Kaiser's business all the more remarkable. He operated without any interference, largely because he was smart enough to stay low-key. Very few people knew he was in the game. Those growers who brag or try to go big time off the backs of the Vietnamese gangs – the ones who wear their wealth on their sleeves and flash their money all the time – are the ones who soon find their houses torched, their Porsches trashed, and their own lives at risk. Kaiser simply went about his business with the quiet of a businessman who didn't want to attract any attention. He supplied only one distributor. Very deliberately, Kaiser made sure that he didn't threaten anyone else's operation.

His houses were jammed with as many as two thousand plants and he harvested four crops a year. At one point, he was running as many as five houses at the same time. Multiply all that by a simple $1,000 – the round figure yield per plant – and you're looking at a $40-million-a-year business.

And he was in business for at least ten years.

Paid in cash, Kaiser did his own smurfing. He would walk into dozens of banks and buy drafts or money orders, always staying below the $10,000 reporting limit. In Greater Toronto, where there are banks on just about every street corner, he could launder the money from a month's harvest in a couple of days. Apparently, on those rare occasions when someone in a bank bothered to ask, he would explain that he needed the draft for his account in the Caymans. And that seemed to be a good-enough answer that no further questions were asked.

The accumulated drafts and money orders were forward to the Caymans by Fedex or Purolator and deposited into one of several shell company accounts he'd established there. Eventually that money was reinvested in villas and condos that he rented out to generate a further income.

He maintained an office under the name Lansing Consulting in a sub-urban strip mall. Using that for his bookkeeping, he would fax invoices every month to a company called Juniper International in Dublin, Ireland. Except the fax number that he dialled didn't ring in Dublin, it was answered at a management services company in London, England.

The people in Britain were under instructions that whenever they received an invoice from Lansing in Toronto addressed to Juniper in Dublin, they were to forward it to another fax machine, this one in the Netherlands. That fax was received by a man who had instructions to change the invoice heading from Juniper International to one of Kaiser's shell companies, and fax that to the Caymans.

It was a pretty neat trick. In the Caymans, a management company paid the invoice to Barclays Bank in London. That money would then be wired back to Kaiser with an invoice marked "consulting fees – paid" from Juniper International in Dublin.

Kaiser's existence was now justified.

I'm a consultant. I send invoices. I receive payment for the consultant fees. I pay my taxes and my employment insurance and health benefits for himself, my wife, my secretary, and the nanny.

If Revenue Canada had ever bothered to stop by, all they'd ever see were invoices out, money in, and taxes paid.

Unlike the Vietnamese who purchased houses, Kaiser rented his, for up to three years at a time. He rationalized that if he bought a house and the location was found, he'd lose his investment in it. As long as he leased, his risk was diminished.

Landlords rarely checked on him. But then, why should they. He appeared to be an upstanding individual who wore nice clothes and drove a fancy car. He would tell the landlords that his business was nearby and that he'd just separated from his wife. He'd then hand them thirty-six postdated cheques for the rent, which ran $1,500 to $1,800 a month. If the landlord ever bothered to drive by, he'd see that his house was being maintained. If the landlord ever asked the neighbours about Kaiser, they'd tell him that everything was quiet. He only gave landlords his cellphone number, so if they ever bothered to ring up, he'd explain that he was out of town and couldn't meet. Anyway, there wasn't much reason to meet because his cheques keep clearing.

Also unlike the Vietnamese, Kaiser didn't steal electricity. He understood that added to the risks of being caught, so he paid for his hydro, which sometimes ran more than $1,500 a month.

Ironically, it was his honesty that brought about his downfall. While no one at Ontario Hydro asked questions about his electricity consumption – because the bills were paid on time every month and also because there was no program at that time on their computer to spot such heavy usage – it wasn't until he paid two hydro bills at the same time that anyone took notice.

For whatever reason, instead of doing this separately, he handed over hydro payments on two separate residences, in two separate names, both for high amounts. Sometime in 1998 someone got suspicious and eventually the hydro company contacted the police. York Regional set up surveillance on the two residences and, of course, recognized a grow operation immediately.

They established reasonable grounds for a search warrant, went inside, grabbed the marijuana, located Kaiser, shut down his other houses, and effectively put him out of business. He was so important and his operation so unique that they even issued a press release, which prompted a news story about the busts on television.

One of the people who saw that story on the news was Kevin Burk. An RCMP officer working proceeds of crime, he rang York Regional and asked if they were planning on pursuing Kaiser's assets. His contact there explained that they didn't have the personnel to do that, and suggested that if Burk wanted to do that, he'd be very welcome.

Burk did want to do that and set out in search of Kaiser's assets.

"When you're dealing with proceeds of crime," Burk explains, "you have to establish a starting point and a finish line. We settled on a solid ten years. That's how long we decided he was in business. The key to the investigation was establishing a record of his business dealings in Canada, and then hoping to get enough international co-operation to find the money once it left Canada."

In that regard, Burk was lucky because Kaiser kept meticulous records. "When we searched his house we found just about everything we needed. Each month he put all of his receipts and invoices into an envelope and there was one envelope for every month. If he bought magazines, he threw the receipt in the envelope. All of his Visa receipts and all of his American Express receipts and all of his airline tickets went into the envelopes. He was writing off as much as he could as a tax deduction, so he kept everything he needed in order to claim an expenses against his business. That's how we were able to calculate what he spent over the course of ten years. We could see, for example, when he drew $10,000 on his American Express card and how, at the end of the month, he paid it all off. We could see where the money was coming from."

Burk could also see all those invoices going back and forth to Dublin, and spent two and a half years putting all the pieces together. He was able to establish that the Dublin fax number was in England and had seen wires coming in from Barclays in London, so he sent a request to Britain for assistance, and figured he'd eventually hear back someday. But a City of London detective named Doug Reeman picked up the request and – being a real pro who understands financial crimes – surprised everybody in Canada by coming back to them with a mountain of stuff.

"Most of the time, you send your international request through head-quarters, and it goes through lawyers, over to England, through their lawyers, to some chief somewhere who filters it down. If you're lucky, you eventually get back just about what you asked for. With Reeman, he knew what we needed. He went after what we'd requested and when he saw what he'd acquired with the first batch of warrants, he took that extra step and went for a second batch. He had the foresight to see the case, and got us everything in one package."

Based on what Reeman supplied, Burk realized there was no reason to bother with the Dutch side of the story. Holland was only a mail drop for shelf companies and, anyway, everything he needed to know about them was in the files supplied by Reeman. But Burk did pursue Kaiser in the Caymans. And there, too, he was pleasantly surprised.

"They were exceptionally co-operative. This was the time when they were trying to get off the FATF list, so maybe that's why. But they helped us with Kaiser, and with another target that we believe might have been affiliated with Kaiser. This other fellow has exactly the same MO when it comes to money winding up in the Caymans."

Kaiser had started in the Caymans with accounts at Guardian Bank and Trust, a now-infamous money-laundering and tax-evasion bank. Guardian afforded him access to Canada through correspondent relationships with Credit Suisse in Toronto, the Royal Bank of Canada in the Caymans, and Toronto-Dominion. When Guardian was closed as a result of the FBI's Operation Cabletrap (see Chapter 10), Kaiser moved his assets to another bank that also provided access through Canadian correspondents.

Burk was able to seize $2.8 million. While York Regional was preparing the case for court and Burk was getting his paperwork together for the asset seizures, Kaiser decided to enrol in Western University's Richard Ivy School of Business.

That troubles Burk to this day. "It tells me we didn't get all his assets. In fact, I know we didn't. While he was at business school, he put his wife and children up in a condominium. We obviously missed something because he was able to pay for that. He paid what, $20,000 a year tuition, plus maintained his family while he was going to school all day. His wife didn't work. No, we didn't get it all. Who knows, maybe we missed a large safety deposit box with cash somewhere. I even asked him, What did I miss? He assured me, You got it all."

Kaiser not only got his MBA, and made the dean's list, but got his sentencing hearing postponed so that he could attend graduation. Once that was out of the way, the judge gave him a twenty-month conditional sentence.

As one of the officers who worked the case puts it, "Just the cost of doing business."

When Kaiser finished his MBA, he contacted Burk to ask for a letter of recommendation. Because convicted criminals are otherwise barred from travel to the United States, Kaiser knew that he had a better shot at a better job if he could tell his employer that he wasn't under any travel restrictions. He wanted Burk to put in writing what a great guy he was and note that he'd co-operated fully with the police.

Even today, Burk shakes his head in amazement. "That was not going to happen!"

If this case had taken place in the States, some people suggest, Kaiser might have been looking at ten years hard time. But the Canadian judge didn't see it that way. The United Nations International Narcotics Board did, however, when they criticized Canada for its "lax attitude toward illegal growers of cannabis."

As for the assets seized, there are people who believe that proceeds of crime should mean assets still available, plus assets spent, becoming a tax, if you will, on the lifestyle lived through criminal means.

Here, too, Canada doesn't see it that way.

"It's sometimes difficult for everybody to see the big picture," Carscallen explains. "We produce this marijuana in Canada using Canadian dollars and sell it in the States for American dollars, which is an immediate 50 per cent markup. You don't see the grow guys complaining to the Bank of Canada about the low value of our dollar."

Nor do the police often see the banks readily making themselves available to do their part in putting a stop to this.

"They're in no hurry to do anything for us," one financial investigator gripes. "Getting information out of them can take years. We put in a request for information in March and maybe the bank will come up with it in May the following year. That's not unusual. Six months is good."

It often works out that the case has gone to court before the documents arrive from the banks. It puts the cops in the awkward position of having to entertain a guilty plea without knowing how much money is involved and where it is. Prosecutors are happy to get a conviction, but without the documents, the cops can't go after the proceeds.

Which is why some officers are now saying that Canada needs a law that says, for certain types of crimes, the police are automatically entitled to a person's banking records, a company's financial records, and the records of the company's subsidiaries.

"For a lot of banks," Carscallen explains, "it's a matter of calling it up, pressing Print, and there's the information. Currently, we've got to have a warrant to do that. But the warrant can wind up in a big pile of requests. It's not that the banks and their lawyers fight it, the problem is the time it takes to process everything because I'm just one officer with one case, and all the other cases pile up."

"The banks," another officer adds, "could be a lot more helpful than they are. Makes you wonder why they're not."

In 2002, the Association for the Protection of Quebec Savers and Investors, a bank watchdog headquartered in Montreal, petitioned the then Big-Six Canadian banks to do something about their offshore activities. Concerned that this side of their business had gotten out of hand – that offshore profits were overriding offshore due diligence – the association used each banks' chartered shareholders' proposal provisions to force this vote:

"It is proposed that the board of directors of (bank name), in collaboration with the Canadian Bankers Association and the federal government, examine whether their subsidiaries should remain in tax havens and report back to the shareholders at the latest five months prior to the 2003 general meeting. Tax havens are the evil of world economy: tax evasion, money laundering, terrorism, crime, unlawful transactions, shelters for proceeds of crime, etc. It is a constant threat to legal economy. American author Jeffrey Robinson revealed how fiscal havens corrupt the world and specifically Canada which he describes as being viewed a 'candy store' by criminal organizations. Banks are one of the transit areas, if not the main one, for the fruits of illegal economy. They would be 'good corporate citizens,' acting in the best interest of shareholders, if they would take the initiative of adopting proper countermeasures to the perverse and harmful effects of the global plague of tax havens."

The association found a ready ally in SHARE (Shareholders Association of Canada), a B.C.-based corporate governance watchdog. SHARE's response to the proposal was simple and to the point: "Issues arising from 'tax havens' pose a significant reputational risk to Canada's leading banks. The profile of illicit banking transactions has increased significantly in the wake of the World Trade Towers attack. The international debate about the consequences of downward pressure on national tax rates is also growing."

But SHARE's recommended approval of the proposal was a lone voice in the wilderness. Institutional Shareholder Services (ISS), a provider of proxy voting and corporate governance services, stated the case for the banks: "It is not within the scope of shareholder oversight to subject banks to the type of study and report required by the proposal."

Not that the banks needed anyone in the corner. As stated in their respective management proxy circulars: they already operate responsibly within the framework of existing laws; they already have responsible measures in place to deal with illegal activity; and the proposal does not distinguish between legal and illegal activity.

At National Bank of Canada, the reasoning went, "The Bank and its subsidiaries co-operate with the various authorities to ensure that the free flow of capital is not used for undesirable ends such as money laundering."

There's no doubt that all of the nation's banks, with hand on heart, would repeat the same claim. But not all of them did it quite so precisely. Scotiabank suggested, "While the proposal raises a general question about the appropriateness of tax havens, its explanation focuses solely on illegal activities around money laundering. The two issues are not related." An odd thing for a company like that to say, considering its not-too-distant past. In those days, under the name Bank of Nova Scotia, it was the bank of choice in numerous money-laundering cases. Furthermore, tax evasion is almost always an ancillary criminal act as a result of money laundering. After all, if you've got criminally obtained funds offshore, you're not going to declare them to Revenue Canada. By the same token, if you're looking to evade taxes by going offshore, you need to obliterate the money trail, which is part of the money-laundering process. So the two issues are not only related, they're joined at the hip.

But then the management obviously wasn't thinking of that, or of the not-too-distant past, when they insisted, "Scotiabank has always been very aggressive in establishing rigorous policies and procedures for both our domestic and international operations to address these illegal activities."

Perhaps the best reason for voting down the proposal came from Toronto-Dominion: "'Tax haven' is a vague term that is difficult to define."

Again, to be fair to the banks, they have all come a long way in the past few years, putting into place anti-money-laundering controls to stay compliant with the Canadian law. It is also necessary to state, categorically, that none of the banks would, in any way, shape, or form, knowingly participate in criminal money laundering as defined by Canadian law. The problem is that they have only arrived at this point, having been dragged there, kicking and screaming, by law enforcement and those politicians who have proved immune to the various banking lobbies.

While Toronto-Dominion – which has the smallest offshore presence of the Big Six – also had the smallest No vote, they defeated the proposal with 91.8 per cent of the bank's shares. Royal Bank of Canada posted the largest No vote, with 95.9 per cent. The other four fell in between.

Had the six voted unanimously for the association's proposal, it would have cost them nothing and, at the same time, been a resounding endorsement of their much-stated purpose in the fight against money laundering. But when it comes to questions that delve too deep into their business activities – particularly offshore money laundering and tax avoidance/tax evasion – banks openly exhibit a "them against us" chip on the shoulder.

In the end, doing what they are required to do by law, and going that extra mile because it's the right thing to do, are not the same thing.

According to the non-governmental anti-corruption organization Transparency International – now looking at just the Big Five – Scotiabank has the largest Canadian presence offshore. They operate in twenty-six tax-haven jurisdictions, including five that have appeared on the FATF blacklist for falling short of international standards. Those were Dominica, Grenada, the Philippines, St. Kitts, and St. Vincent. The bank has also operated in other highly suspect jurisdictions like Labuan and Panama. Of all North American banks, only New York's Citibank operates in more offshore jurisdictions.

Royal Bank of Canada came next on the Canadian list with seventeen offices offshore, among them FATF-blacklisted Dominica, Lebanon, and St. Kitts. Additionally, Royal Bank had a presence in highly suspect Montserrat. CIBC, with twelve offshore branches, was in St. Vincent; Bank of Montreal with seven and Toronto-Dominion with three were not in any FATF-blacklisted jurisdiction.

All five have a presence in Singapore, and PricewaterhouseCoopers (PWC), auditors to some of the Big Five, has expressed reservations about that country. The PWC Web site offers the translation of an article published in Singapore, obviously as a warning to their clients. "Despite the tight regulatory and supervisory environment, Singapore remains an attractive location for criminals to launder their illegal proceeds."

Citing a 2002 U.S. State Department report that categorized Singapore as country where there is a high risk of money-laundering activities, the article on the Web site explains, "A person carrying a stash of notes does not have to declare them at the customs checkpoint when entering Singapore. After passing through customs, this person could launder his money by colluding with a business which has a high cash transaction volume. . . ."

But then, you don't have to go all the way to Singapore to find someplace that requires a long look. A poll conducted in 2002 by Canada's provincial securities regulators concluded that as many as thirteen thousand investment-house client accounts were being held offshore. Although the Investment Dealers Association of Canada insists that represents a mere 1 per cent of all the client accounts in the country, the amount of money involved is said to be staggering. Accounts were found throughout the Caribbean in addition to Egypt, Lebanon, and Russia.

Obviously, it is not illegal to hold money or assets offshore and there are provisions in the Canadian tax codes that, under specific conditions, make offshore accounts advantageous. But when you look at fraud, tax evasion, insider trading, trafficking, and other criminal acts, the percentage of offshore accounts becomes astronomically high. Those offshore accounts almost always feed back to Canada's anti-money-laundering-active banks through correspondents that might not automatically share the banks' anti-money-laundering agenda.

A further study, this one by the Financial Stability Forum, noted that there were obvious inadequacies – they referred to them as "black holes" – when it came to financial supervision in certain offshore jurisdictions. Named in that survey were Aruba, Belize, the Caymans, Costa Rica, Liechtenstein, Panama, and the Bahamas. The Big-Five Canadian banks either operate there themselves or they have correspondent relationships there or, in some cases, they do both.

Without meaning to pick on Toronto-Dominion, one of that bank's offshore relationships serves a good example of how potentially dangerous this sector can be. Toronto-Dominion is listed as the Canadian correspondent for an Antiguan bank that maintains accounts with locally incorporated offshore gaming and Internet gambling companies.

This is not to cast aspersions at any particular Antiguan bank or company, but the nature of Internet gambling business and the reputation of that island cannot be ignored. Especially by a Canadian bank indirectly involved with that business. It is currently illegal for anyone in the United States to take part in Internet gambling. By definition, if money involved in an illegal activity within the U.S. is moved out of the country in order to disguise participation in that illegal activity, it can be construed as money laundering. Under U.S. law, foreign banks that participate in the movement of laundered funds can be exposed to criminal proceedings.

The question then becomes, Is Toronto-Dominion's management – or is the management of any serious and responsible Canadian financial institution – really going to depend on the regulatory authorities in Antigua to make certain that no U.S. residents move money through Canada in order to place illegal bets?

Irregardless of how vague the term *tax haven* is, banks that have in the past relied on offshore authorities to regulate themselves now litter the landscape.

And onshore regulators who rely on offshore regulators to be vigilant wind up staring at disaster.

That's one of the ways that BCCI happened.

5

SINKS 'R' US

"You never know what you can get away with unless you try."

– General Colin Powell

The Bank of Credit and Commerce International (BCCI) is the textbook model of offshore money laundering. But it didn't just happen in a test tube. It took a few good people to do nothing in order to create catastrophe.

For sixteen years, from 1970 to 1986, drugs bombarded the United States, coming at the country from every direction: cocaine from Colombia; cocaine and heroin from Mexico; marijuana and heroin from the Orient; heroin from Turkey and Nigeria via Europe; marijuana, cocaine, and amphetamines from Canada.

As drugs saturated the streets, money from those drug sales was dumped into the banking system. As law enforcement geared up to go after individual bankers, traffickers diversified to wire remitters and businesses, like supermarkets, where they could feed cash into the system. As the cops got wise to that, the traffickers began bulking cash out of the country. The money headed for Canada, or was shipped south into the Caribbean. Just like the drugs that arrived by boat, plane, on the backs of mules, in steamer trunks, in refrigerators, in sacks of coffee, and in car bumpers, cash left the same way the drugs had come in.

It was easy getting cash across the northern border, where Canadian banks and wire remitters operated oblivious to U.S. laws and without much interference from Canadian laws. It wasn't any more difficult getting cash across the southern border, where Mexican banks, wire remitters, and currency exchanges set up on the banks of the Rio Grande to handle the influx. But it was easiest of all once the cash reached the Caribbean, where nations like Antigua deliberately turned themselves into laundromats. There was even an in-transit bank at the airport to handle cash from arriving couriers, managing it so efficiently that the courier could deposit the money and get back onto the same plane for the flight home.

In Anguilla, a wooden shack at the end of the runway had the word *Bank* painted on the front of it so that pilots could taxi up and not have to shut down their engines.

In Montserrat, hundreds of banks were chartered by a government desperate for money, with total disregard to the people chartering those banks or to the fact that absolutely none of the banks had a physical presence on the island.

In the British Virgin Islands, Irish-born accountant Shaun Murphy sat in a shack on a beach sticking pins in a huge map of the world, registering forty shells and opening ninety different bank accounts for just one client in forty different places around the world. That client later dropped a Samsonite suitcase to him from a passing airplane, with $2.3 million stuffed inside. It took two days just to count it.

Money flashed around the world, across borders, in and out of shell companies, through banks in the Channel Islands and Switzerland, through shell companies registered in Luxembourg and Liechtenstein, and somehow arrived, finally, back into the hands of Colombians and Mexicans, Turks and Nigerians, Chinese, Japanese, and traffickers from all over Southeast Asia. It wasn't stopped, because the people who could stop it were getting rich: dealers on street corners in Philadelphia and Edmonton; bankers in Miami, Geneva, London, and the Bahamas; wire remitters in Montreal; lawyers in Panama; company-formation agents in the Caymans and the Isle of Man; and, of course, the traffickers themselves. They all raked in unbelievable heaps of money. At one point, the Cali cartel had annual profits of $7 billion, three times greater than General Motors.

But during those sixteen years, law enforcement came to understand that the way to stop it was by going after the money, and little by little, that's what they learned how to do.

The first of the big "follow the money" cases was the famous Pizza Connection. An offshoot of Lucky Luciano's French Connection, morphine base from Turkey was shipped to Sicily, where it was refined, then moved through Canada and into the States. From 1979 to 1984, nearly $1.6 billion worth of heroin was distributed through a franchised network of pizzerias that stretched across the industrial Northeast and into the Midwest. The Mafia's original intention was to wash cash from the drug sales through the tills with the pizza sales. But all too soon there was far too much money for the restaurants to launder, so the traffickers turned to Wall Street. The various money trails led through major financial institutions including Merrill Lynch, Chemical Bank, E.F. Hutton, Handelsbank, and Credit Suisse. The case was prosecuted by the brash young U.S. attorney for Manhattan, Rudy Guiliani.

While the Pizza Connection was in full swing, the DEA was working a two-year undercover that saw agents posing as bankers to expose a $150-million money-laundering operation through Panama for a Colombian trafficker named Eduardo Orozco-Prada. In a similar case, the Feds targeted the financial dealings of a trafficker named Oscar Cuevas, who smuggled $123 million out of Los Angeles and into Britain and from there had it transferred into Swiss banks.

Other operations followed. In Greenback, federal agents posing as launderers moved money through a bank in Miami to the Cayman Islands branch of the Costa Rican bank BAC International. In Pisces, the DEA washed drug cash straight into Panama. In Expressway, the FBI moved $16 million for the Medellín cartel through U.S. banks and into Panama. In Polar Cap, the government exposed a multibillion-dollar laundering network that indicted Pablo Escobar, head of the Medellín cartel. His money was washed through jewellery stores in Los Angeles and, with the use of offshore shells plus banks in Canada, Switzerland, Italy, Germany, and Uruguay, wound up in the Panamanian subsidiary of Colombia's Banco de Occidente. A second phase of Polar Cap saw $121 million seized in the U.K., Switzerland, Luxembourg, Austria, Panama, and in 1,035 U.S.-based bank accounts. In Dinero, the DEA established the RHM Bank in Anguilla, through which agents laundered $12 million in forty days for six Cali cartel–connected clients. Dinero was important for many reasons: it exposed links between the cartel and the traditional Sicilian Mafia; uncovered a drugs-for-arms swap, demonstrating how drugs, money, and arms all function together; and showed how legitimate businesses, such as supermarkets and car-rental agencies, could be used to launder money.

But it was Operation C-Chase in Florida – the *C* standing for *cash* – that really made the case for following the money. Customs agents working an undercover sting of the Medellín bunch collected drug cash in Los Angeles, Miami, and New York, then dumped it in the Tampa branch of the Bank of Credit and Commerce International (BCCI), at the time one of the ten largest banks in the world.

This hugely complicated and costly five-year operation – which moved $34 million through BCCI Tampa – produced more than twelve hundred secretly recorded conversations and four hundred hours of clandestinely recorded videotape, which exposed offshore networks running through Britain, France, Italy, and Panama. In 1990, the evidence that the agents had amassed led to dozens of convictions, including BCCI bankers.

The significance of C-Chase was in what followed.

When they began, the undercover agents and their handlers believed that the laundromat they were targeting – the biggest they'd ever seen – was inside BCCI. By the time they finished, they realized that the laundromat wasn't inside BCCI – it was BCCI.

———

Created in 1972 by a fifty-year-old Indian-born banker named Agha Hasan Abedi, BCCI was originally backed by the ruler of Abu Dhabi, Sheikh Zayed bin Sultan Al Nahyan, members of the Saudi royal family, and the Bank of America. It was capitalized at $2.5 million. Five years later, Abedi was boasting 146 branches in 32 countries and claiming to control assets of $2.2 billion. Only the Bank of America sussed that something wasn't right and pulled out. The rest of the world fell for Abedi's scam, especially the British.

Abedi had registered the holding company that owned BCCI in Luxembourg, a jurisdiction with strict banking secrecy. However, what he really wanted was the credibility that being a British bank could give him, so he opened branches in Asian neighbourhoods across the U.K. He registered BCCI a second time, now in the Cayman Islands, then moved his top management to London. Over the next fifteen years, the

Bank of England (BoE) gave Abedi and BCCI a clean bill of health. With hindsight, it's easy to see why: Abedi made certain that there wasn't much for anyone to see; the British government had its own agenda; and the Bank of England was generally incompetent.

Oddly, the BoE did show some concern at the very beginning, because it refused to charter BCCI as a bank. Instead, it handed Abedi the less weighty title of "licensed deposit taker." Abedi later claimed it was because BCCI operated "outside the club," suggesting a racist motive for refusing to accept his bank as the real thing. And there might have been a grain of truth in that, except that his bank wasn't the real thing. Not that it mattered to the public if BCCI wasn't officially a bank, because they didn't know the difference between a bank and a licensed deposit taker. BCCI had forty-five offices in Britain that looked like banks and operated like banks and, for all intents and purposes, were banks. Except in the minds of a few folk along Threadneedle Street.

That BCCI was chartered in Luxembourg and the Caymans, deliberately placing it beyond BoE regulation, should have set off alarm bells. Instead, the BoE turned up its highfalutin nose and left it to the Luxembourgois and the Caymanians to regulate BCCI. Except the Luxembourgois and Caymanians were counting on the Bank of England to do it. What they all would have seen, had anyone bothered to look, was massive fraud at every level. Abedi was creating capital accounts in the Caymans by using the bank's money in Luxembourg, then creating capital accounts in Luxembourg by using the bank's money in the Caymans. Abedi hired different auditors for every jurisdiction. As long as they didn't compare notes – which there was no reason to believe they would – no one would find out that the banks were capitalized by thin air.

In 1976, Abedi tried to buy the Chelsea National Bank in New York, but state regulators nixed that deal. Among other things, they objected to the B in BCCI standing for *bank*. As a licensed deposit taker, it was not legally allowed to call itself a bank. The BoE failed to stop it.

Thwarted in New York, Abedi went south to Atlanta, hired Jimmy Carter's pal and disgraced former budget director Bert Lance, and through him surreptitiously acquired the National Bank of Georgia. It was one of Abedi's mates, Saudi businessman Gaith Pharaon, who officially bought that bank, and the Independence Bank of Encino,

California, too. He paid for them with a $500-million loan from Abedi, secured with the shares of the two banks. Abedi then sold National Bank of Georgia to Financial General, a holding company in Washington secretly owned by more of his friends. And just like that, Abedi illegally gained control of three U.S. banks.

When the Securities and Exchange Commission (SEC) figured out what was going on, it threatened to take action against Abedi and his backers. There was even talk of a criminal case. So Abedi worked out a deal to pull the wool over the SEC's eyes. Financial General was renamed First American Bankshares and, he said, would be independent of BCCI. In reality, it was always Abedi's. To give First American a pedigree, Abedi installed two prominent Americans on the board. Clark Clifford, an exalted D.C. attorney and elder statesman who'd served as an adviser and friend to almost every president since Harry Truman, was named chairman. His law partner Robert Altman, husband of TV's Wonder Woman Lynda Carter, was named president.

By then, Abedi had opened BCCI offices in Panama, where Manuel Noriega was his largest single depositor. Middle Eastern terrorist Abu Nidal was soon channelling funds through BCCI, followed quickly by the Medellín cartel. By 1988, Abedi's laundromat had 417 branches in 73 countries and reported assets of $20 billion. And, all this time, the Bank of England maintained that everything was just dandy.

The drug money pouring into BCCI Tampa turned out to be the tip of a gigantic iceberg. Massive amounts of cash were also coming into BCCI Miami. From there, the money would be flown by private jet to Panama and the Caymans, wired onto BCCI Luxembourg, then transferred to the traffickers' BCCI accounts anywhere in the world, but especially Colombia. BCCI opened seven branches there, five of them in Medellín.

To cover the cash deposited in Florida and confound anyone looking for a money trail, Abedi invented a ghost bank. His computers were programmed to show the Florida cash as having been deposited first in BCCI Bahamas – which didn't exist – and then bulked to Miami as part of a normal internal bank transfer. BCCI Miami even fulfilled the requirements of the Bank Secrecy Act by filing the proper forms with U.S. Customs to account for the concocted importation of cash.

Diversifying further afield, Abedi sent some of BCCI's laundry work to Canada and expanded throughout the Caribbean, opening in marijuana-rich Jamaica, Barbados, Curaçao, and Trinidad. He also set up in the United Arab Emirates (UAE) to serve the heroin trade in the Golden Crescent of Pakistan, Iran, and Afghanistan. And he set up in Hong Kong to serve the heroin trade in the Gold Triangle of Laos, Burma, and Thailand. Ultimately Abedi even opened in the Bahamas, where hundreds of shell companies were formed to disguise the movement of dirty money back and forth with BCCI Miami.

However, Abedi was chasing shadows. His balance sheet was fiction. Although many of his liabilities were real, most of his assets weren't. The faster he opened banks, the faster the system sprang leaks. To plug holes, he stole $150 million from a staff pension fund. Eventually, Abedi would steal $10 billion of depositors' funds. International banking supervisors in Basel had grown increasingly concerned with his management of BCCI's assets, and reported this to the BoE. But auditors there failed to see Abedi's frauds.

Fearing that the British might one day cotton on to him, Abedi moved the treasury out of the U.K. to Abu Dhabi. By then BCCI was the object of investigations in Switzerland, Canada, France, Luxembourg, Brazil, Singapore, Bermuda, the Caymans, Cyprus, and even Nigeria.

In the States, indictments came down from C-Chase. Senator John Kerry, presiding over the Subcommittee on Narcotics Terrorism and International Operations – under the auspices of the Senate Foreign Relations Committee – opened hearings on BCCI's association with Noriega. Under oath, two convicted drug dealers claimed they'd laundered funds through BCCI Panama and that their introduction to the bank had come from Noriega. A further Senate inquiry would reveal that Noriega had used BCCI to wash tens of millions of dollars.

Kerry's chief investigator on the subcommittee, Jack Blum, realized right away that BCCI might be the biggest laundromat of all time and tried to interest the C-Chase investigators in the wider picture. They were too busy with their own case. So Blum went to the IRS and the Justice Department to bring them in. Neither shared his enthusiasm. Finally, he went to see the New York district attorney. And Robert Morgenthau was very interested. Able to claim jurisdiction because First American Bankshares had offices in New York, Morgenthau's tenacious assistant John Moscow led the charge.

A sturdily built native New Yorker now in his mid-fifties, Moscow is deceptively friendly. Everyone who likes him – and after thirty years of chasing financial crooks there are plenty of cops and prosecutors and government officials who like him – really likes him a lot. When you mention his name to people who have been on the same side of the courtroom, you always get a broad smile and are reminded, "John's my friend." He is hospitable, witty, and seriously bright. Very few people know the ins-and-outs of financial crime better than John Moscow. But the people who run up against him in his role as the D.A.'s deputy chief of the investigations division – those people who find themselves on the wrong side of the courtroom – soon discover that bonhomie doesn't count and that tangling with him can end in tears. He is relentless when he investigates crimes, resolute when he pursues people who perpetrate them, and ruthless when he prosecutes people who need to be prosecuted.

Although it embarrasses him to hear it, John Moscow is a star.

He set his sites on BCCI, Abedi, and everyone involved with BCCI's takeover of First American, including Clifford and Altman. But when Moscow turned to the BoE for help, folks there became obstructive.

In March 1990, the BoE's governors were informed by the intelligence services that Abu Nidal controlled forty-two accounts at BCCI branches around London. Eight months later, they were handed two reports, one from the City of London Fraud Squad, the other from a Middle Eastern accountant, outlining massive frauds at BCCI. Two months after that, the governors learned that BCCI had amassed some $600 million in unrecorded deposits.

Refusing to let the BoE off the hook, Morgenthau and Moscow showed their files to Deputy Governor Eddie George. In no uncertain terms, they threatened to raise public hell if the Bank of England didn't do something about BCCI. Eddie George returned from that meeting in New York to warn the bank's governor, Robyn Leigh-Pemberton, that the New Yorkers were on the warpath. In March 1991, Leigh-Pemberton ordered an audit. When it was finished, in July of that year, the BoE was out of excuses and BCCI was shut down.

Morgenthau and Moscow indicted Clifford, Altman, Abedi, and the number-two man at BCCI, Swaleh Naqvi. Clifford and Altman were ordered to stand trial, although the case against them subsequently fizzled out. Naqvi was arrested in Abu Dhabi, extradited to the United

States, charged with conspiracy, wire fraud, and racketeering, pled guilty, and was sentenced to eleven years. In Abu Dhabi, a court convicted twelve BCCI officials in absentia – including Abedi and Naqvi – and sentenced them all to lengthy prison terms. But Abedi never saw the inside of a courtroom. He became the subject of an extradition battle with the Pakistanis, which the Americans lost. By then, he was ill and bedridden. He died in Karachi in August 1995. He was seventy-three.

It is now known that there were several parties interested in keeping BCCI's pipeline open through the offshore world. Among them: the BoE, which had been told to keep its distance by the British security services as they were using BCCI to monitor several people, including Saddam Hussein; the CIA, which was using BCCI to launder funds for the Iran-Contra affair and also washing money for Afghan rebels; the U.S. Defense Intelligence Agency, which maintained a slush fund at BCCI; and MI-6, which had a relationship with Abedi frontman Kamal Adham – the former chief of Saudi intelligence – that provided a convenient channel to the Gulf States. Furthermore, BCCI had been involved in financing the transfer of North Korean Scud-B missiles to Syria; had helped to broker and finance the sale of Chinese Silkworm missiles to Saudi Arabia; and had acted as financial middleman when the Saudis needed Israeli guidance systems for those missiles.

When the BCCI affair ended in crocodile tears for the innocent depositors who'd entrusted Abedi with their life savings, Leigh-Pemberton testified to a House of Commons Select Committee that he had never been "particularly happy" with BCCI's presence in the U.K. Which is as close as anyone at the bank has ever come to admitting a mistake.

To this day, still impervious to criticism and despite a mountain of evidence to the contrary, officials at the BoE arrogantly insist that the bank did nothing wrong.

Astonishingly, Leigh-Pemberton actually told that committee, "If we closed down a bank every time we found an incidence of fraud, we would have rather fewer banks than we do at the moment."

There's no reason to believe that the lessons of BCCI have been indelibly stamped on the brains of banking regulators around the world. However, they were definitely learned by some Russians looking to do the same thing, but better.

In the old days under the Soviets, unless you were one of the chosen few, bilking the system was what you did to stay alive. When the fraud of communism disintegrated and a fledgling, kind-of-capitalistic Russia tried to extract itself from the quicksand, the people carried with them into this new world their cynicism, their deep-seeded distrust of all things official, and their well-honed instincts for self-preservation.

The government opted for privatization of the old Soviet industrial complex, but that was strictly a western concept. Corruption was what the people understood. They'd learned their lesson in the rigid world of the forced economy. Standing in line for hours to buy whatever might be at the end of that line was how they'd paid their dues.

Now, in the sudden freedom that was 1990s, it was as if the rules had vanished with their rulers, and their right to steal was inalienable. Everything was for sale, and anything that couldn't be bought could be filched. Companies, over-taxed and over-burdened by extortion, produced documents to show that they were importing something – it hardly mattered what – and so to pay for the goods, they transferred money out of the country. Like contrails in the sky marking the paths of high-flying jets, throughout the past decade, tens of thousands of money trails have come out of Russia. That the corresponding goods never arrive back in the country surprises no one.

One popular destination for this mass capital flight is Britain. In addition to modern financial facilities provided throughout the City of London, there are fashionable properties to live in, expensive private schools for Russian children, art and antiques to be bought at auction, elite shopping, and, until recently, money-laundering laws lax enough to be almost non-existent. For the Russians, London is a hub with easy access to other western financial centres, especially the Channel Islands and the Caribbean. A few years ago the Moscow-based financial newspaper *Kommersant* noted, "Tens of millions of dollars have left the former Soviet Union, specifically bound for Britain." Today, the figure is into the tens of billions. And a chunk of that came from a group of Russians who set up a circuit through Britain and the Channel Islands that turned out to be the Bank of New York (BoNY) scandal.

At the heart of it were two young women.

Lyudmila Pritzker was born in Leningrad in 1958. At the age of nineteen she married an American named Brad Edwards and moved with him to the States. She Americanized her name to Lucy, had a child, divorced her husband, and wound up working as a teller for the Bank of New York. In 1988, BoNY bought Irving Trust, an old, established Manhattan-based financial institution that had been actively pursuing business in Eastern Europe. Edwards soon found herself working in BoNY's newly acquired Eastern European Division.

Her manager there, Natasha Gurfinkel, was also Russian-born. Three years older than Edwards, Gurfinkel was married to Konstantin Kagalovsky, Russia's representative to the International Monetary Fund (IMF). Kagalovsky and his financier chum Mikhail Khodorkovsky shared business interests in a Russian bank called Menatep. That bank is believed to have had an interest in the totally crooked European Union Bank of Antigua (EUB). Records show that EUB was owned by a Bahamian shell company called Swiss Investment Association. A major shareholder appears to have been Alexandre Konanykhine, who, at the time that EUB was chartered in July 1994, was in jail in the States for violating his visa conditions. According to the *Washington Post*, Konanykhine was also wanted in Russia for embezzling $8.1 million from another Moscow bank in 1992.

In September 1995, EUB opened its doors or, more accurately, turned on its computer. Because the bank didn't exist in Antigua, or anywhere else for that matter, except in cyberspace. It's only presence was on the Internet. The bank's Web site read, "Since there are no government withholding or reporting requirements on accounts, the burdensome and expensive accounting requirements are reduced for you and the bank."

Within nine months, EUB was claiming to have assets of $2.8 million and 144 accounts in 43 countries. Naturally, EUB was also claiming to maintain the strictest standards of banking privacy, reinforced by the claim – somehow made with a straight face – that Antigua was a serious financial centre with serious penalties for anyone violating its serious banking secrecy laws. Shortly after EUB went on-line, the Bank of England warned the U.S. Federal Reserve Bank that while Menatep was denying any involvement in EUB, Konanykhine had asked the Antiguans to keep Menatep's involvement in EUB a secret.

Among many things not publicly disclosed was that EUB's computer server – which was, effectively, the bank – was located in Washington, D.C. And that the man operating the computer server, who was effectively the banker, was in Canada. How much money was ultimately funnelled through the bank – washed by Russians for other Russians and, as well, for some of their Latin American drug-trafficking friends – is not known. Nor will it ever be. Because one day in mid-1997, just like that, someone unplugged the computer. That was the last anyone ever heard of the depositors' money. Upwards of $12 million is said to have disappeared.

There are links between EUB and Menatep and further links between Menatep and the scandal-plagued, now-defunct Moscow-based financial institution, Inkombank. Both Menatep and Inkombank had relationships with BoNY. Inkombank was one of several clients brought to BoNY by Natasha Gurfinkel, who'd wrenched it away from rival Republic Bank. A much-heralded coup, by 1995 Inkombank was BoNY's largest generator of fee income, making BoNY the most important clearing bank in Russia for domestic transactions. Only later did anyone learn that Republic had filed suspicious activity reports about Inkombank with federal regulators and was glad to see Inkombank take its business elsewhere.

About a year after going to work under Gurfinkel, Edwards remarried. Peter Berlin was a molecular chemical physicist from Moscow who'd recently arrived in the States. The couple lived in New Jersey and Berlin worked out of their flat, which was the registered address for his company, Benex. Before long, Berlin was brokering sales of electronic goods to Russia. And it was while running this phase of his business that he was asked by some of his clients to provide false invoices on the back of which they could ship money out of Russia. Berlin had the means of facilitating the movement of funds and his wife had access to a bank they could use. So in 1996, Benex International opened an account at BoNY's Wall Street headquarters. Six months later, a company called Becs International also opened an account at the same BoNY branch. Lucy Edwards was listed as a Becs employee and had a signature authority on the account.

Unaware of Edwards's involvement with Benex and Becs, BoNY promoted her to vice-president and assigned her to their London offices, specifically to seek out new Russian business. By this time, Berlin had moved into a one-room office at 118-21 Queens Boulevard, in Forest Hills, New York. And that's where Peter Berlin and his wife, Lucy Edwards, might be today – commuting between London and New York – had it not been for a scam in Canada and a kidnapping ransom in San Francisco.

Britain's National Criminal Intelligence Service (NCIS) was investigating the YBM Magnex scandal, a fraud perpetrated on the Toronto Stock Exchange. The man behind it was Semion Mogilevitch, an alleged Russian Maffiya boss. One of many shell companies NCIS stumbled across in that investigation was Benex. At first glance, it looked like just another empty shell through which money flowed. That Benex was using an account at the Bank of New York didn't seem out of the ordinary either, because shell accounts pop up all the time at legitimate banks. But when the NCIS officers took a really close look at Benex, they were dumfounded by the amount of money moving through a Benex account in Jersey, Channel Islands, and into BoNY. During a single six-month period, ten thousand transactions shifted $4.2 billion!

NCIS passed the intelligence along to the Americans.

Around the same time, the Russian police asked the FBI for help in a kidnapping case. A $300,000 ransom had been paid to secure the release of a man named Edouard Olevinsky. The bureau traced the payment from the victim's bank in San Francisco through BoNY and an offshore account in the Channel Islands to the Sobin Bank in Moscow. The offshore account belonged to Benex.

The NCIS file wound up at the New York D.A.'s office. The FBI file wound up at the U.S. Attorney's Office in Manhattan. Suddenly, two U.S.-based investigations plus the NCIS investigation in Britain were all looking at Benex and BoNY. Unbeknownst to those three, the National Crime Squad in London had also stumbled across Benex and Becs in their pursuit of a separate case dealing with drug money laundered through the Channel Islands.

When the four investigations finally converged, they turned into the largest international money-laundering inquiry in history. It entailed eighty-seven-thousand electronic transfers to move $15 billion. Some of those transfers involved Russian companies evading taxes. Some of them linked Benex and Becs with Russian organized criminals. The New

York Police Department, the Federal Reserve Board, and the Comptroller of Currency all took an interest in this. Before long, investigators had widened the case to include banks and financial relationships in more than fifty jurisdictions.

Blissfully unaware of law enforcement's interest in their business, the Gurfinkel-Edwards team mined sources that other foreign banks left untapped. By summer 1999, they were dealing with Russian clients that other foreign banks had turned down. That's when the *New York Times* broke the story of the enormous sums being washed through BoNY.

For more than a month, from the middle of August until early October, this was a fast-moving, front-page news story. Denials, shock, and horror by BoNY officials were followed by Edwards's dismissal. Then Gurfinkel resigned. Her husband, Konstantin Kagalovsky, denied any wrongdoing – everybody involved with this denied wrongdoing throughout most of it – and the IMF grew concerned. Press reports suggested that some of the money funnelled through Benex and BoNY might have been IMF funds originally intended to keep the Russian economy afloat.

Edwards's and Gurfinkel's offices at BoNY were searched, documents were removed and sealed, and their homes were searched as well. When British police raided the Edwardses' London flat they found business stationery imprinted with both Benex and Bank of New York logos. When Berlin's office in Forest Hills was raided, four new companies came to light. Two of them had banking relationships with BoNY. And one of them was registered at an address that tied it to a network of companies, including an offshore bank, licensed by Russians in the highly suspect offshore Pacific Island jurisdiction of Nauru.

At this point, the chief culprit appeared to be Mogilevitch. While he was based in Budapest during the YBM Magnex scandal, the U.S. State Department had pressured the Hungarians into doing something about his presence there and he'd been given the bums rush back to Russia in July 1999. In April 2003, the U.S. Justice Department unsealed an 86-page, 45-count indictment relating to the YBM Magnex case, charging Mogilevitch and three others with racketeering, wire fraud, mail fraud, securities fraud, and money laundering. The FBI issued a warrant for his arrest. Money was moved through dozens of banks, including Royal Bank of Scotland, Barclays, Royal Bank of Canada, CIBC, Mellon Bank, and

Chase Manhattan; and some twenty countries, including Britain, Canada, the U.S., the Caymans, Nevis, Cyprus, and Nauru. Mogilevitch's name also continues to pop up in connection with the BoNY matter. The FBI believes that some of the $15 billion that went through the Benex account in the Channel Islands was proceeds of the YBM Magnex scam.

But not all of that money came from YBM. Enter here a new and even more worrying connection.

While investigating a Russian mobster named Yuri Essine and his Italian-based export business, authorities in Italy took an interest in the growing Russian presence along the Adriatic coast. In particular, they wanted to know more about Russian organized crime links in the city of Rimini.

A typical beach resort with a pleasure-boat port, hotels, and fish restaurants, Rimini is also filled with nightclubs and travel agencies where the signs out front are written in Cyrillic. It's a city that lost its way in the tourist battle against more fashionable resorts, went in search of new markets, and discovered the Russians. Planeloads of them now show up every week. But these aren't tourists who sit on the beach and eat ice cream. Instead, they step off their chartered flights and are bussed directly to a wholesale leather-goods market just outside of town. Carrying wads of brand-new $100 bills, they buy up whatever they can, sending their purchases back home by the planeload. Some of these Russians may be legitimately working for an import/export business. Most of them are not.

The Russians invading Rimini are believed, by the Italian police, to be part of a huge money-laundering circle. It starts with drugs sold in Russia. That street cash is washed through Rimini's leather wholesalers, who, it must be said, are more than happy to have this influx, which they then bank in nearby San Marino, safely out of reach of Italian tax inspectors. The goods shipped back to Russia are sold in the new markets there and the profits generated are reinvested in drugs.

The Italians only stumbled across this while looking at Yuri Essine. He led them to Rimini and while looking at Rimini, they discovered Benex. A major investigation was launched, dubbed Operation Spider-web, which rounded up fifty people and indicted one hundred others. The investigation continues in Italy, France, Switzerland, and Germany, where more than three hundred bank accounts have been seized. According to the Italian police, by tracing money moved through Benex, one offshoot leads to Boris Yeltsin's family. Others point to several important Russians suspected of money laundering, fraud, and, in one case, arms smuggling. Most worrying of all, there are financial connections through Benex that suggest links exist between Russians in Italy and Chechen rebels in the former Soviet Union, who, in turn, have financial ties to al-Qaeda.

When the BoNY scandal shook out, Gurfinkel was not charged. She sued BoNY in Moscow for $270 million, alleging illegal suspension from her job and libel. In September 2001, the Russian court threw out most of her case. What remained was settled two months later, when BoNY paid her $5 million, including $300,000 to cover her legal fees. The Yeltsin family has immunity from prosecution, although BoNY has announced that two accounts held by a family member at BoNY's Cayman Islands branch contains $2.7 million. Edwards and Berlin pled guilty to various felonies, including conspiracy to commit money laundering. As of mid-2003, neither had been sentenced because they were actively co-operating with the authorities. The information that led to Spiderweb is said to be the first of several leads that could keep Edwards and Berlin out of jail for the foreseeable future.

That leaves BoNY.

The bank got its wrists slapped for sloppy bookkeeping, so the board put its best face forward and came up with double-talk. A press release was issued saying that the board had full confidence in the chairman and chief executive officer, Thomas Renyi, noting that Renyi had "no direct responsibility for the events." But then the board felt the need to add that the chairman and chief executive officer has ultimate responsibility for the bank. Consequently, the board lowered Renyi's annual compensation for 1999 by around 11 per cent to $6.58 million. His total package the year before had been $7.38 million, which, on the face of it, seemed to be saying that Renyi's parking ticket for the fiasco was going to cost him $800,000.

Except, the following year, Thomas Renyi made it all back in spades, pocketing a whopping increase, for a combined salary and compensation package of nearly $21 million.

6

POTENTATES IN THE CITI

*"Much that we had done to keep private banking private becomes
'wrong' in the current environment. The business itself is very highly
attractive, and there is no reason why we cannot pursue it in a sound way,
but it will take an adjustment."*

– John Reed, then CEO of Citicorp

For the chairman of a public company like Thomas Renyi to pocket a $21-million thank you from the board when his bank, during his watch, had just gone down in history as the centrepiece of the largest-ever money-laundering scandal is, even by American corporate standards, fairly bad taste.

That said, corporate America's version of fairly bad taste pales by comparison with what goes on in the rest of the world when it comes to people in positions of trust helping themselves to money. Just look at what's been going on for decades in Latin America, the Indian subcontinent, Asia, and throughout Africa. Even then, there are few places on the planet where corruption and political criminality has reached the unimaginable heights that it has in Nigeria.

Since independence in 1960, it's estimated that as much as $120 billion has been siphoned out of the Nigerian treasury and moved into the offshore world for safekeeping by dishonest politicians. Nigeria today is a monument to the former heads of state and the gaggle of crooks surrounding them who ravished the nation and jettisoned their own people to destitution. Among the accused stands Ibrahim Babangida, president from 1985 to 1993, whose entourage allegedly left the country $20 billion poorer.

If it's true that in confusion there is profit, then the sheer complexity of Nigeria is one reason for this swamp of political depravity. Nigeria became a British colony late in the colonial era only because Germany was threatening to colonize it. What the British left behind is not so much a nation as it is a confederation of tribal states with unnatural boundaries drawn up simply to suit the whims of the colonial masters.

Twice the size of California, it's assumed that around 130 million people live there, but no one can be certain because the usual state of affairs in Nigeria is utter confusion and census taking is a practical impossibility. There are 250 ethnic groups and nearly as many different dialects spoken. About 30 per cent of the population is Hausa-Fulani, living in the northern half of the country. The Yoruba make up a little over 20 per cent and populate the southwest corner, which includes Lagos. The Ibo are just shy of 20 per cent and are found mainly in the southeast. The rest are minority groups like Ijaw, Kanuri, Ibibio, and Tiv. Religiously, the country breaks down into Muslim, Christian, and indigenous beliefs.

During the days of British rule, it was said that the Hausa-Fulani ran the army, the Ibo ran the government, and the Yoruba were the entrepreneurs. But that would suggest that the Hausa-Fulani and the Ibo aren't as opportunistic as the Yoruba, which they are. Historically, Nigerians have always been the best traders in Africa. They have created a well-documented transshipment hub for heroin and cocaine, moving drugs in all directions: north to Europe; south to South Africa; and either directly across the Atlantic or through Latin America for the U.S. and Canadian markets. Nigerians also oversee a significant money-laundering centre. At the same time Nigerians are Africa's most talented, freewheeling fraudsters. Their reputation is well deserved, having set loose a plague on the world known as 419 Fraud.

Named after the Nigerian law that made this particular scam illegal, millions of letters and e-mails are sent around the world from Nigerian criminal enterprises offering large cuts for helping someone get money out of one country and into another. The only thing you have to do is allow that person to deposit a large sum into your bank account. Once

the funds clear, you agree to forward some of that money to your bene-
factor, and get to keep the rest for your troubles.

In the past, the Nigerians used the post office to deliver their 419
letters, counterfeiting stamps for bulk mailings. But postal authorities
got wise to that and began pulling millions of letters out of the system
instead of delivering them. Anyway, snail mail is a risky and expensive
way of doing businesses. So they turned to e-mail. And while some
people have been accused of overhyping the business potential of the
Net, there's no denying that it has worked wonders for fraud. Using
e-mail not only diminishes the possibilities of getting caught – hiding
in cyberspace is akin to being invisible – but greatly reduces operating
expenses to near negligible. It costs around $50 to buy one million e-mail
addresses and almost nothing to spam letters across the globe.

A recent example, a gem filled with spelling and grammatical errors,
comes from someone calling himself Mr. Day:

> Dear Sir: This may reach you as a surprise, I am sending you this mail
> due to my present urgent position.
>
> I am Mr. Deoff Day, the officer in charge of special projects to Mr. John
> Mendelson who recently resigned as a member of the board of directors of
> Enron Energy Corporation, a multibillion-dollar energy corporation in the
> United States of America.
>
> My Job description amongst others is auditing, verification and recom-
> mending for payment, funds for our overseas operations and projects for
> work done by our Europe and Far East countries clients.
>
> Just before Enron filed for bankruptcy, we were in the process of paying
> out huge funds to some of our foreign clients, this was however suspended
> after the federal agents stepped in following the discovery that our account-
> ing firm Arthur Anderson was carrying out some accounting irregularities.
>
> Incedentaly [sic], before the company was sealed, I succeeded in securing
> some vital classified documents in collaboration with my boss who ordered
> that the documents be destroyed. These documents shows [sic] how funds
> meant for overseas payment are lodged abroad. These funds are safely in
> offshore bank accounts.
>
> Presently, I am in the island of Haiti and need a reliable friend that
> can assist in standing in as a client of Enron, of which payment for work
> done is long overdue.

If you agree to work with me in this venture, I will provide all information and details in respect of the funds deposited, that will empower and enable you to collect the funds on my behalf.

I would provide you with more details as soon as you acknowledge receipt of this mail.

Please note that this venture is completely safe as we shredded all documents concerning the whereabout [sic] of our offshore accounts before the company folded up and the funds can not be traced anywhere in the world.

I expect your prompt response. And please respond only to this my confidential mail address. Kind regards, Deoff Day.

Once you provide Mr. Day with all your banking details, if there's enough in your account, he will empty it. If not, he'll slip into advance fee fraud mode and explain that, in order to get your share of the money, you'll need to pay certain bank charges. Or he'll ask you to put up some money at the last minute to bribe an official. Or you'll have to pay an unexpected legal fee. Whatever his excuse, once the money is paid, he'll come back for more and keep coming until you stop paying him. And that's the last you'll see or hear about your promised millions.

Sometimes the author of the letter is a government official, or a senior adviser to a political leader of another country, or a family member of an important Nigerian official: The Ministry of Petroleum of Nigeria is due a payment of $23.5 million that has been held up by government currency controls and you can take a quarter of that if you'll help them launder it through your account; An aide to the late Mobutu Sese Seko of Zaire wants to get his hands on $22 million that's been stashed in a secret offshore bank account and will allow you to have 25 per cent of it if you will allow him to transfer the entire sum into your bank account; The widow of His Excellency, the late President, is due $45 million, but the money is being blocked by corrupt tax officials who are trying to steal it and you can have a big cut of this money simply for helping her get it away from them and out of Nigeria.

To create a scenario that sounds real, current events are often used. In one letter that followed the World Trade Center and Pentagon attacks, the author claimed to be representing the families of Nigerians killed on 9/11, whose money has been blocked because bank records were also destroyed that day. In another, a Nigerian government employee named Richard Moore was listed as one of the victims of the attacks. The bank manager holding his $10-million account put the money in escrow. But miraculously, Moore survived and now wants his money. Unfortunately, the courts won't release it to him because he was proclaimed legally dead. So the bank manager is looking to run the monies through someone else's account, and for that service Moore will happily allow the person to keep $3 million.

Like all frauds, 419 plays directly on greed. Many people simply can't resist the opportunity to make a fast $10 million, even when their better judgment tells them this is too good to be true. Which, of course, it is. Around 1 to 2 per cent of the people who receive the 419 letters fall for the scam, and the average loss is in the $200,000 range per victim.

Making the scam additionally dangerous, some people are foolish enough to show up in Lagos and demand their money back. They risk getting killed, or beaten up and put on the first plane home, or sold yet another scam on the back of the first one, which winds up costing them even more.

In addition to spamming e-mails to anyone and everyone, the criminals behind these letters also frequently hone in on specific groups. They often prey on charities. They also like to go after bankers. One bunch of Nigerian fraudsters, including a man pretending to be Chief Paul Ogwuma, governor of the Nigerian Central Bank, hit on a director of the Banco Noereste Brazil. They convinced him that they were brokering a massive energy deal and he duly forwarded funds to offshore shell companies with bank accounts in Switzerland, China, the U.K., Nigeria, and the U.S. It turned out to be the biggest 419 swindle to date, as the Nigerians walked away with $181.6 million.

Leading the charge against the con men is the United States Secret Service. They maintain a mammoth database of letters and e-mails, coordinate investigations with law enforcement around the world, and recently opened an office in Lagos specifically to pursue 419 fraud. The problem is that attempting to use western law enforcement techniques in a nation that is, for all intents and purposes, lawless can prove frustrating. To begin with, you're never sure with whom you're dealing.

Bureaucracy in Nigeria is a series of overlapping systems — tribal, feudal, regional, federal — based on nepotism, favours, bribes, plus a myriad of contradictory alliances and allegiances. There are hundreds of elected tribal chiefs with fealty to the kings of different regions. Conflicting agendas are the norm, to the point where rule in Nigeria is a room full of people all talking at the same time in different languages. It's tough to get heard. Rationally, the whole process is irrational. There's no way to run this country. There's no way to police it. And there is certainly no way to catch bandits if you've come from the outside.

A nation of massive oil wealth, the king of the hill is the man who knows how best to distribute the booty. Following a fairly standard model, the man in charge is expected to divvy the oil revenues with the people below him. Those people must then share their take with the people below them. The money flows down through the immediate circle of advisers and to the military commanders. If the king of the hill gets too greedy or allows the system to run amuck, he's toppled and someone else takes over the distribution system. It goes without saying that none of this money ever trickles down to the average guy, which is why just over half of Nigeria's population is living today on less than a dollar a day.

The civilian government that the British left in place on independence fell to a military coup in 1966. Generals held on to power for the next thirteen years before handing the reins back to civilians.

In 1979, the price of oil had skyrocketed and the country should have prospered. But elected president Shehu Shagari and his mates were so incompetent and so corrupt that they plunged the country into near bankruptcy. They ran up foreign debts of $18 billion, while hustling $15 billion out of the country for themselves. They bought all sorts of goods and services no one needed at prices four times above the market, helping themselves to kickbacks at every stage. One of the commodities they overbought was cement. And at one point, Lagos harbour was so overcrowded with hundreds of cement ships waiting for months to unload that, eventually, the cement in the holds hardened and the ships had to be scuttled. The military finally said enough is enough and General Muhammadu Buhari sent the president packing. Two years of severe repression later, General Ibrahim Babangida ousted Buhari.

Under Babangida's rule, in 1989, a North American oil company tried to try to put a deal together with the government. Refineries in Nigeria were operating at 40 per cent capacity and Babangida was importing oil to meet the country's needs. This at a time when Nigeria was a major OPEC oil-producing nation. So the North Americans suggested a swap. In exchange for crude oil, plus drilling concessions and royalties on any oil discovered, they would repair the refineries and guarantee to get them running at 90 per cent capacity, eliminating the need to import. Negotiations went on for months, and wound their way up to the minister of petroleum, which is where the deal got killed. Unbeknownst to the North Americans, key Babangida supporters owned interests in oil refineries in the Ivory Coast and Benin. They were making a fortune refining Nigerian oil, then selling it back to Nigeria. There was no way the government was going to change that.

Eventually Babangida declared that he would hand the country back to civilian rule and organized elections for 1993. But when his former business partner Chief Moshood Abiola won, Babangida cancelled the results. He hung on only long enough to create an interim civilian government, which was quickly overthrown by General Zachary Sani Abacha.

By comparison, the man who now became king of the hill made all the others look virtuous.

⌐

The 1980s saw the world economy lose its balance.

Oil prices shot sky-high and interest rates spiralled, topping 20 per cent. The industrial world toppled into recession and the Third World was swamped with mega-debts. Many developing countries that had borrowed beyond their means when rates were low were unable even to meet interest payments. Poland defaulted in 1980, so western banks pulled the plug on several Eastern bloc countries. Two years later, Mexico defaulted. And suddenly the crisis was full blown.

For the major western banks, ever in search of profits, throwing more money at Latin America was out of the question. But as the Third World sank in the mire, wealthy Latinos rushed to get their funds into safer places, willing to pay handsome fees to ship money by the ton from Argentina, Brazil, and Venezuela. Bernie Cornfeld was only one tour leader taking them to the offshore world. The big banks couldn't fill their sightseeing buses fast enough. There was plenty to be made servicing anyone in search of asset protection. In many cases, the people who were now trying to escape the confusion and mismanagement of their governments were the same ones who'd helped create the plight by ripping off the loans that the banks originally made to keep the countries afloat. Not that this was going to stop any major bank from getting its share of this burgeoning new market. So they created banks inside their own banks – private banking – as an enclave for a select group of wealthy clients willing to pay steep fees for the privilege of organized capital flight.

Higher returns and tax avoidance might have been the agenda when private banking was still a fledgling idea in the 1970s. But when demand for capital flight was highlighted by the debt crisis, many wealthy individuals concluded that capital flight was their best chance for survival. Responding to that, the big banks opened offices for their private banks in all those places where the wealthy were threatened. An obvious end of the road for this money was Zurich or Geneva, where non-Swiss private banking groups – especially British, Canadian, and American – could effectively sell Swiss banking secrecy. But Switzerland wasn't the only destination on offer. The trick was to spread accounts over several jurisdictions because the more borders you put between the money and someone looking for it, the less chance there is that anyone will be able to go the full route and find it. So private banking was about selling Cayman Island trusts and Bahamas shell companies that could open bank accounts in Luxembourg and Liechtenstein. It was about selling Uruguayan bank secrecy to nearby Argentines, Caribbean anonymity to Canadians, Venezuela banking to Brazilians, and Channel Island banking to Venezuelans.

One estimate suggests that perhaps as much as 80 per cent of the loans made by commercial banks to governments in Latin America during those crisis years of the 1980s never reached their destined countries, remaining instead in western bank accounts. In Latin America, two-thirds of total debt is thought to have been deposited in western banks.

For public consumption, the major banks have always made it appear as though private banking was just another name for personalized asset management, investment, trust and estate planning. But people with serious money always had those services available to them. In reality, private banking during the debt crisis was mainly about capital flight. And not that much has changed today. Each client is assigned a private banker whose job is, simply put, to make sure that the client doesn't take his money somewhere else. One way a private banker does that is by helping clients get better returns on their money. Another way is by keeping clients' money out of the reach of other people who might want a share of it, such as governments, ex-spouses, and creditors.

In 2001, when the U.S. Senate's Permanent Subcommittee for Investigations opened a lengthy and very thorough look at private banking and the offshore world, one banker admitted under oath that his superiors forbade him from keeping any records in the U.S. that could link shells to their owners. At any given time, he said he dealt with thirty to forty clients, some of whom maintained as many as fifteen shells. To remember which was which and who owned what, he used "cheat sheets," which he kept secret from bank officers who actually made surprise inspections to assure themselves that if law enforcement ever raided their offices, they would never find evidence that could incriminate their clients.

Just three years previous, the U.S. Federal Reserve had queried Bankers Trust on exactly this issue. The bank agreed to establish a database that they would consult should a subpoena order them to identify which shells belonged to which clients. And Bankers Trust did create that database. But they deliberately housed it in the Channel Island of Jersey, where U.S. subpoenas had no standing.

Needless to say, fees for such services have never come cheap, and are usually pegged to the client's net worth. It's not uncommon to find fees exceeding $1 million a year. Which is how private banking came to be the industry's major growth area. The lure of big profits brought more banks into the arena. Heightened competition meant more services on offer. The next logical step from tax avoidance is tax evasion, and the next logical step from capital flight is money laundering. Which is how drug money and funds pilfered by people in high office got mixed into this.

From Jean-Bédel Bokassa, the flesh-eating emperor of the Central African Republic, to Romania's first family, Nicolae and Elena Ceausescu, despots everywhere rushed into private banking.

In Haiti, the Duvalier "Dos" – Papa and Baby – helped themselves to $16 million of a $22-million grant from the IMF. Much of it was washed through Canada and hidden in private banking in the Channel Islands. An additional $400 million was stashed in offshore companies and private Swiss banks.

During their reign in the Philippines, Ferdinand and Imelda Marcos made the Duvaliers look like amateurs. Those two were so crude in their greed that even the Swiss were embarrassed by them. When Ferdinand died in exile in Hawaii in 1989 and Imelda stuck him in a refrigerated box to await burial at home, Swiss bankers refused to comment on the rumours that the family had stashed $15 billion in private banking vaults. The Marcoses' horde was said to include 1,241 tons of gold in storage at Zurich's Kloten Airport. Swiss officials searched the customs-free storage area at the airport – or at least they said they did – and announced that no gold was found. It turned out that the $13.2 billion worth was a hundred yards away in the UBS bank's private airport vault. However, by the time Ferdinand's fridge was turned off and he was buried in the Philippines, the gnomes had miraculously found, and agreed to return, $500 million of pilfered assets. They obviously didn't look very hard because before long another $356 million showed up in numbered accounts at Credit Suisse and Swiss Bank Corporation. Marcos money has also since been located in four Liechtenstein foundations and one Panamanian shell company. Ten years after Marcos's death, the government of the Philippines was still trying to freeze some Swiss accounts and had only accounted for around $2 billion of the supposed $5 billion that Marcos stole.

Then there was Indonesia's President Suharto. Forced out of office at the age of seventy-seven, after thirty-two years, his family had also bilked the country out of billions of dollars. The old man positioned himself, his family, and his friends to share on a near 50-50 basis with Indonesia's economic prosperity. Foreigners invited in to mine gold or to build toll roads were required to have local partners. Those Indonesian companies, which provided no capital, were owned by the Suhartos and their friends. For example, Suharto's oldest daughter built power plants and owned toll roads. His son, Bambang, owned a bank. Another son, Hutomo – known as Tommy – built cars under special dispensation from the government that exempted him from tariffs and taxes, raising costs for his competitors by 60 per cent. Tommy also controlled the sugar, paper, cement, and flour industries.

The World Bank believes that as much as 30 per cent of the money lent to Indonesia disappeared without a trace, most of it going into the private banking accounts of the Suharto family and their chums.

Forbes Magazine estimates the family is worth $16 billion. The CIA says $40 billion.

It was much the same story with Mobutu Sese Seko, the last of Africa's old-time potentates and the ruler of Zaire. He'd run the country into the ground with an iron hand for three decades and, during that time, acquired a personal fortune worth $5 billion. Said to be the only world leader who could pay off his country's national debt from his own pocket, Mobutu's style was to treat the national treasury as his own bank account. When the U.S. sent him $1.4 million to help his troops fight a civil war, he simply pocketed the entire amount. Despite his enormous wealth and Zaire's huge natural resources, he never seemed especially troubled by the fact that his country was the fifth poorest in Africa. Nor did it seem to bother him that one out of every six children in Zaire died before the age of five from malnutrition. His money disappeared into private banking.

One of the dominant institutions in private banking throughout this period was Citibank. Under Walter Wriston's chairmanship, capital flight became the bank's single most profitable business. Citi set up outposts – they called it International Private Banking (IPB) – in various countries specifically to bring in new business. Wriston emphasized Citi's role in the Third World and his successor, John Reed, was Argentine-born and innately understood Latin America. So Citi easily took the lead.

But competition for the Latin American market was rough and aggressive. Chase and Swiss Banking Corp. were players there too, as were UBS, Bank of Boston, and Bankers Trust. American Express Bank got into the private banking game in Panama, then expanded to Miami – by then fast becoming the financial capital of Latin America – and also opened in London, Paris, Geneva, and Singapore. Brokers rushed in as well. Merrill Lynch International, Shearson, Bear Stearns, E.F. Hutton, Bache, Morgan Stanley, First Boston, and Goldman Sachs all became private bankers to some degree. Not to be left out Royal Bank of Canada, Bank of Montreal, Lloyd's, Marine Midland, Natwest, and Deutsch Sudamerikanische all jumped on this bandwagon. By 1986, the world's top-twelve banks had grabbed 40 per cent of the capital flight market. The top fifty controlled 75 per cent.

Mexico quickly became a significant battleground. In 1988, Harvard-educated Carlos Salinas de Gotari was elected president. Four years later,

Mexican billionaire Carlos Hank Rhon – a Citibank IPB client – introduced his private banker to his friend Raul Salinas, the president's brother. That private banker was Cuban-born Amelia Grovas Elliott, known to everyone as Amy. A native Spanish speaker, she was IPB's lead officer in New York for the bank's business in Mexico.

Interestingly enough, a couple of years later, Elliott would be called as a witness in the Texas money-laundering trial of an American Express banker who'd laundered funds for Mexican trafficker Juan Garcia Abrego. At the time, she didn't have a clue that Raul Salinas was tied into this. Nor could she guess that Abrego was the source of some of the Salinas funds she was helping to hide in Switzerland and the Caymans. During that trial, Elliott was asked how she saw her job. She responded, "Private banking is the area of the bank that deals with clients with more money than the general public, that does it on a more white gloved kind of environment."

A white-gloved environment was exactly what she provided for Salinas. IPB set him up with accounts in New York, London, and Switzerland, which, in and of itself, would not otherwise have been suspect. But the way Elliott did it and the amount of money that went through the bank – $87 million, most of it in Mexican cashier's cheques – should have raised very loud alarm bells at Citi. That they didn't made the case noteworthy.

To begin with, Elliott listed Raul Salinas as Confidential Client #2. Carlos Hank Rhon was already CC#1. IPB then opened five accounts for CC#2 in New York. Another account, in the name of a shell company, was opened at the bank's trust company in Switzerland. The account itself was called Bonapart. Cititrust Cayman Islands then formed a shell called Trocca, which was listed as the owner of all CC#2's private bank accounts. Three additional shells were listed as Trocca's shareholders and three more shells were listed as Trocca's board of directors. A Trocca account was also opened at IPB London.

The name Salinas was deliberately omitted from all IPB files, and never appeared in connection with anything. The one piece of paper that showed Raul Salinas was the beneficial owner of Trocca, and therefore of all this money, was purposely kept in the Caymans, where bank secrecy laws forbid anyone from divulging its existence and no foreign country could subpoena it.

IPB loaned CC#2 some $3 million, which they invested for him. They also gave him credit cards for his accounts in the names of the shells so that whatever charges he made would never be associated with him directly, or ever appear in Mexico, thus allowing him to use his money without paying taxes on it. Furthermore, IPB helped obscure any money trails by moving some funds deposited by CC#2 through concentration accounts.

That's one of the tricks of private banking.

Sometimes called "settlement accounts," they're temporary homes for money without a home, monies that are waiting to be claimed or monies that have not yet been properly designated to an account. For example, funds arrive for J. Smith with the account number 12345, and someone realizes that while there is a client named J. Smith, his account number is 54321. That money is left in a concentration account until the confusion over J. Smith's money is straightened out. By putting CC#2's money through the concentration account, Citi allowed it to comingle with other funds, clouding the money trails both inbound and outbound. Since then, Citi has prohibited the use of concentration accounts for client transactions. But other private banks still regularly use them.

What no one at Citi realized when Carlos Hank Rhon brought Raul Salinas to the bank was that Salinas was carrying a lot of baggage. He led Elliott and her bosses to believe that the bulk of his money came from the sale of his construction company and family wealth. In truth, it came from Abrego, and also from political corruption during his brother's presidency. IPB had accepted Salinas as a client without bothering to investigate his background or his financial situation. Elliott also waived the requirement for several references, accepting the word of Hank Rhon that Salinas was who he said he was. But the initial $2-million deposit that opened his account did not come from Salinas. It was transferred from one of Hank Rhon's accounts, on the grounds that Hank Rhon owed Salinas the money for a deal that hadn't gone through. So IPB violated its own rules right from the start by not knowing its customer or the source of his funds. Had IPB done the due diligence that Citi normally should have required, the bank would never have taken Salinas as a client, and would never have wound up being associated with a murderer.

At the time of Carlos Salinas de Gotari's election as president of Mexico, Francisco Ruiz Massieu was secretary-general of the country's ruling Institutional Revolutionary Party. But he was no fan of the Salinas family and at one point he posed a real threat to Carlos's political career. In turn, Raul understood, that threatened his own livelihood. So Raul did what any loving brother would do – he assassinated Ruiz Massieu.

He got away with it for several years, but justice finally caught up with him once his brother left office in 1994. An investigation was opened into the Ruiz murder and in February 1995 Raul was arrested for it. The next day, an officer at IPB London suggested they should quickly move Salinas's $20 million out of the country and into Switzerland so that law enforcement couldn't find it. When it was decided that they couldn't manage it without leaving a money trail, IPB decided to cover its own butt and call in Salinas's $3-million loan.

Towards the end of that year, Raul's wife, Paulina Castanon, left Mexico for Switzerland to withdraw $84 million from one of Raul's accounts at Banque Pictet, where it was deposited under the false name Juan Guillermo Gomez Gutierrez. The Swiss arrested her. At one point, the officers who interrogated her said he couldn't understand why she tried to take $84 million, which attracted attention. He asked, "Why didn't you just take out a little bit every time?" She answered, "That's what I was doing."

The Swiss froze that account and others in six cantons that they believed were owned by Raul. The total came to $132 million, including $27 million at IPB Switzerland. The investigators also located the $20 million in London. Raul was found guilty of Ruiz's murder and is currently in prison. Carlos Salinas de Gotari left Mexico for exile in Ireland. Which is where the Salinas family saga ends. But for IPB – which, over a four-year period, earned around $2 million on the Salinas account – worse was yet to come.

This client's name was Asif Ali Zardari. A Pakistani legislator and former government official, Zardari also happened to have been married to Pakistan's prime minister, Benazir Bhutto.

Ignoring the fact that Bhutto had been dismissed as prime minister in 1990 for alleged corruption – she was re-elected in 1993 and would be dismissed a second time in 1996 – and also ignoring the fact that

Zardari himself had spent more than a year in jail on charges of corruption, IPB nevertheless opened three private accounts for him in Switzerland, and allowed him to maintain one in Dubai, with an initial deposit of $18 million. Just as they had for Salinas, IPB formed shells for Zardari through which he could move money, in this instance basing two of them in the British Virgin Islands. Using those shells, over the next three years, Zardari laundered $10 million in kickbacks on a gold scheme he was running.

The government of Pakistan finally shut Zardari down, indicting both him and his wife. A Swiss court then froze his accounts and indicted him for money laundering. A court in Pakistan then convicted him of accepting the kickbacks.

Citicorp chairman John Reed summed up the Zardari business for his board of directors by saying, "I do not yet understand the facts, but I am inclined to think that we made a mistake."

More mistakes were to follow.

El Hadj Omar Bongo had been Gabon's president since 1967. A former public servant who'd never earned more than a few thousand dollars, Bongo opened his first account with IPB in Bahrain in 1970, making an initial deposit of $52 million. IPB subsequently opened accounts for Bongo and members of his family in London, Paris, Luxembourg, Switzerland, Jersey, Bahrain, and New York. Gabon is the richest country in sub-Sahara Africa, with a per capita GDP of $6,300. Bongo's Citibank private bank accounts held as much as $130 million. Following the usual pattern, IPB established shell companies in the Bahamas and gave Bongo a coded account name. They loaned him $50 million, issued credit cards to him and his family, and helped invest his money for him. His fees at IPB were running over $1 million a year. At no point did Bongo ever give IPB a clear explanation of where his funds came from. Although it was later discovered that IPB listed Bongo's wealth as coming from government funds.

In spring 1997, the press reported that Bongo was under investigation by French authorities in conjunction with a corruption scandal at the French oil company, Elf Aquitaine. Certain officers at Elf were believed to have bribed certain officials in Gabon. The Swiss authorities responded to a French request to freeze bank accounts, and some of them included funds belonging to Bongo. A Swiss court reportedly described Bongo as "the head of an association of criminals." The case is still ongoing.

The Office of the Comptroller of the Currency in Washington, D.C., was also unhappy about Bongo holding accounts with Citibank and wanted to know more about the source of his funds. Explanations were slow in forthcoming, but when the accounts came up for regular review, IPB decided they would close them. The official reason they came up with was that the accounts had caused too many questions to be asked, required too much paperwork, and had incurred too many incremental costs.

A more believable excuse might have been that someone at IPB was suddenly afraid of getting caught. Still, closing accounts is unusual in the private banking industry, where business as usual means doing whatever you have to in order to keep clients.

It was business as usual for IPB when Nigeria's General Abacha showed up with government funds in his pocket.

A career soldier and civil servant all his life, in 1988 Abacha had dispatched his oldest sons, Ibrahim and Mohammed, to begin a relationship with IPB New York. A shell was created, called Morgan Procurement, and three accounts were opened in code names. Among them were Gelsobella for the account in New York and Navarrio for the account in London.

Oddly, the IPB "relationship manager" who handled the accounts later claimed that he didn't have any idea that Ibrahim and Mohammed were related to General Abacha – a man recognized on the world stage for his audacious brutality – and wouldn't become aware of that fact for nearly three years. It was only after the Abacha family relationship with IPB ended that documentation came to light suggesting that at least one IPB officer knew who his clients were. The bank's paperwork read: "Father of Ibrahim and Mohammed, General Sani Abacha, is the current military ruler of Nigeria, where there is a lot of corruption."

Seizing power, Abacha dissolved all political parties in Nigeria, forbade demonstrations against the new regime, censored the media, and locked up people who opposed him. Instead of cancelling the account then and there, IPB did business with the Abachas for eleven years and helped them move $110 million through accounts in New York, London, and Jersey.

It must be said that Citibank was not the Abachas' only bank. Twenty different banks in Switzerland held more than 140 Abacha accounts. A substantial portion of the funds located there arrived after the 1998 Swiss money-laundering codes were put into law. Those codes had been held up to the rest of the world by the Swiss themselves as proof positive that the bad old days of dirty money were over, that money stolen by dictators was no longer welcome in Switzerland.

Sani Abacha died in June 1998, apparently of a heart attack. He was fifty-four. A best estimate has it that he stole $4.3 billion, some $2.3 billion of it directly from the national treasury. The remaining $2 billion came in from government contracts he put through his own shell companies and bribes from foreign contractors. Shortly after his death, his widow, Mariam, was stopped at Lagos airport trying to leave for Saudi Arabia. She said she was going to the Hajj. Her thirty-eight suitcases were filled with cash. Reports vary on the amounts involved, ranging from $50 million to $100 million.

Around the same time, Mohammed Abacha contacted IPB in London and asked that $39 million held in his account there be sent to three different accounts outside the U.K. But that money was on time deposit and wouldn't come due for another two weeks. Mohammed clearly sensed the urgency of the matter and urged Citibank London to find a way around the time lock. IPB responded favourably by offering Mohammed an interest-free overdraft of $39 million. IPB had it secured against the money on deposit, and Mohammed Abacha got his $39 million out of the country. Unfortunately for him, when Mohammed returned home he was arrested and charged with murder in connection with the death of the wife of one of his father's political opponents. He was promptly locked up.

The man who succeeded Sani Abacha, General Abdulsalami Abubakar, now went to all of his predecessor's cronies and demanded that they return whatever money they'd got from him. He collected $770 million and confiscated some property. He made good on his promise to call elections and another former general, Olusegun Obasanjo – who'd been a political prisoner under Abacha – became president in May 1999.

It was Obasanjo who intensified the international efforts to reclaim Abacha money.

By then, Credit Suisse private banking had discovered Abacha accounts holding $232 million. The Swiss Federal Banking Commission (SFBC) ordered a search of all banks in the country and in October put a freeze on Abacha accounts at five other banks.

In January 2000, the Swiss police announced that a total of $645 million had now been identified and frozen. Although a Swiss judge would later unblock $115 million of that. Six banks were reprimanded by the SFBC for serious omissions and individual failures in handling the Abacha accounts. Another six were castigated for discernible weaknesses in their controls. And six Swiss bank personnel were actually convicted for money laundering and other offences over the Abacha money. By sheer coincidence, the gnomes at UBS suddenly discovered they, too, were holding Abacha accounts funds. And another $60 million was frozen there.

Authorities in Luxembourg froze $670 million in eight separate accounts for seven offshore shell companies that the Abacha brothers held in that country. And authorities in Liechtenstein froze $109 million sitting in one shell company account and another DM100 million in another.

The Nigerians had turned to the U.K. for help, but no banks in Britain or Jersey seemed particularly anxious to co-operate. When asked to freeze accounts, they refused on the grounds that no criminal proceedings were underway in Nigeria. However, in spring 2001, Britain's Financial Services Authority (FSA) announced the discovery of $300 million sitting in forty-two Abacha accounts held in twenty-three different banks. The turnover of these accounts for the period of 1996 to 2000 was nearly £1 billion (then about $1.3 billion). But instead of pressing for prosecution against the banks and bankers in violation of U.K. money-laundering laws – if nothing else, they were dealing in stolen funds – the FSA suffered an enormous loss in credibility by simply slapping the wrists of fifteen banks for "significant weaknesses" in money-laundering controls.

In July 2002, Nigeria's Supreme Court ruled there was insufficient evidence to prosecute Mohammed on the murder charge, leaving him still facing 111 counts of laundering and corruption. While the court decision mystified some people, President Olusegun Obasanjo ordered negotiations to begin with the Abacha family for the return of Nigeria's money.

The two sides worked out a deal, brokered by the Swiss, wherein the Abachas agreed to hand back $1.35 billion in exchange for the government agreeing to free Mohammed from the cell where he'd been for the past three years. Under the terms of the agreement, the Abacha family would be permitted to keep around $100 million, which they somehow convinced the Swiss they'd acquired prior to Sani Abacha taking over as president. That a career soldier and public servant could amass such a fortune legally belies belief. But the Swiss fell for it and Obasanjo agreed to the deal, hoping to put the matter behind his government. When Mohammed agreed to the settlement, Obasanjo ordered him released. As soon as he got out, Mohammed denied agreeing to return the family's billion and the settlement collapsed.

There is a P.S. to the Citibank story.

Shoddy stewardship of IPB took its toll. Careers were ruined and reputations suffered, notable among them, Citi's.

Senator Carl Levin publicly chastised the IPB directors for getting involved with the Abacha family. "They weren't just asleep at the switch, they were in a deep sleep on this one."

Not everyone was quite so diplomatic. "There was a time," one New York prosecutor says, "when you heard the words *money laundering* and *private banking* and the first bank you thought of was Citi."

In 1998, Sandy Weill, then chairman of Travelers Group – a brokerage and insurance conglomerate – orchestrated a $70-billion takeover of Citigroup, then America's third-largest bank. Among the many problems he inherited was Citi's reputation. But very early on in his stewardship of the company, Weill undertook a massive cleanup of private banking, and ordered that controls and due diligence be severely tightened. His clean-out, and the changes he instituted of what he called "old bank," were so dramatic that these days Weill's era at Citi is known as "new bank."

Heads of state and former heads of state – referred to as "politically exposed persons" (PEPs) – are no longer welcome and, in fact, openly discouraged. Every client is now thoroughly vetted. Multi-layered controls put in place to monitor business are, Citi believes, the most severe in the industry.

One senior executive insists that people with dirty money to hide belong to "old bank." So much so that even if an extremely well-disguised potentate, trafficker, fraudster, or laundrymen foolishly bothered to show up, a relationship with "new bank" would be "virtually impossible."

Ironically, that executive says, the change has not only affected the people they deal with – radically so – it's boosted profits. He contends that Citi's private banking makes more money these days by deliberately keeping the wrong customers out than it did when "old bank" deliberately went looking for them.

7

CARIBBEAN WASH

"The big hurricane destroyed those documents."

– Lester Bird, prime minister of Antigua and Barbuda

For a couple of years in the mid-1980s, a fellow in Boston named John Fitzgerald worked as the principal laundryman for a well-organized marijuana-smuggling cartel run by the Murray family.

The head of the clan was Joseph Murray, late of Charlestown, Massachusetts, an avid Irish Republican Army (IRA) supporter totally dedicated to the British defeat in Ulster. His Irish roots gave him a natural affiliation with another IRA sympathizer, James "Whitey" Bulger, then leader of Boston's Winter Hill crime gang. In turn, Bulger was connected to New England's most important La Cosa Nostra (LCN) family, the Patriarcas.

It was only a matter of time before the groups joined forces. When they did, the result was an archetypal drugs, arms, and dirty-money connection. The Murrays brought marijuana in on fishing boats. Bulger financed the purchases and took a share in the distribution. Drug money was mixed with monies collected by NORAID, the IRA-backed charity. It was washed through the Bank of Boston, then used to pay for illegal arms, supplied by the Patriarcas. The guns were shipped to the IRA on the same boats that brought in the drugs.

Fitzgerald was the man in charge of the Murrays' finances. He began with Halcyon Days Investments, an IBC registered in St. Lucia. Using that, he opened a $3-million account at the Canadian Imperial Bank of Commerce. Two months later, he emptied the account and carried a cheque for the full amount to the Caymans, where he deposited it in the Guinness and Mahon Bank. He topped up the account there, and when it reached $5 million, he wired it out to a bank in Philadelphia. From there it went to Manufacturers Hanover Bank in New York, to the Bank of Bermuda, and finally to the Swiss American Bank (SAB) of Antigua. The money was held in the names of two IBCs, Rosebud Investments and White Rose Investments, until Fitzgerald transferred it out of the companies' accounts and into an SAB account in the name of a shell bank registered in Anguilla. By then, $5 million had become $7 million.

While this was going on, Murray got busted. He was sent away for ten years, served three, went home, and got involved in a domestic dispute with his estranged wife. He lost the argument when she shot him.

Eventually, Fitzgerald was also arrested. Deciding that co-operation was a better option than life behind bars, he did whatever the Feds asked, which included signing over the $7 million in Antigua. Unfortunately, before anyone could get to the money, Fitzgerald died. It then took the Americans until 1994 to file the necessary paperwork to claim the money. Once that was done, the Justice Department's Asset Forfeiture and Money Laundering Section wrote to the appropriate office in Antigua effectively saying, Please send us $7 million. As no one in Antigua was anxious to do that, it was two years later when they happened to mention that, just before the American request was received, SAB transferred $5 million to a government account. The bank then wrote off the remaining $2 million against fees incurred and, regretfully, nothing's left.

Several stern "give us back our money" demands followed, all to no avail. Ultimately, the Justice Department sued Swiss American Bank, Swiss American National Bank, Swiss American Holding Company of Panama, and the Bank of New York-InterMaritime Bank of Geneva, which had affiliations with Swiss American through a mysterious character named Bruce Rappaport. To press the case, certain documents were necessary, but repeated requests for them also fell on deaf ears. After all, it wasn't in Antigua's interest to hand over this money. So, the State Department dispatched Jon Winer to Antigua to collect it. He was, at the time, deputy assistant secretary for international law enforcement affairs. As such, he got all the way up to the prime minister.

Winer explained the case to Lester Bird, and politely reminded the prime minister, It's our money and we want it back, so please give us the documents.

That's when Bird asked if he'd heard about the big hurricane.

Winer didn't understand and asked what big hurricane?

Bird explained that there'd been a big hurricane in the Caribbean the previous week and bank records had been destroyed.

Winer wondered if a bank had been destroyed.

No, Bird told him, "the big hurricane destroyed those documents."

Winer was dumbfounded. "You're telling me, there was a big hurricane which destroyed the records pertaining to a single account? Everybody else's accounts are fine, except this one? A big hurricane destroyed the documents we want? Just those documents?"

And the Americans never got their money.

———

The twin-island nation of Antigua and Barbuda was first visited by Christopher Columbus in 1493. Ruled briefly by the Spanish, then the French, it became a British colony in 1632.

The creation of a thirteen-member legislative body in 1951 was the first step towards independence, and brought to power a local union activist named Vere Cornwall Bird. As first minister, he negotiated increased autonomy in 1959 and renegotiated for more autonomy in 1967. Although he was unseated by the opposition in 1971, he returned to power five years later, and became Antigua's first prime minister on independence in 1981. He ruled as the last of the great old-style Caribbean autocrats until 1994, when he stepped down and his son Lester succeeded him.

The year following independence, Antigua passed the International Business Corporation Act, turning itself into an offshore financial centre. It allowed the creation of IBCs, offshore banks, trust and insurance companies, and gave them a fifty-year tax-exempt status. It also gave the anonymous owners free reign in just about anything wanted they to do. There were no capital requirements, no exchange controls, and no statutory audit requirements.

For the payment of a fee, the government of Antigua was now in the business of selling licences to steal. And over the next decade and a half, they didn't even pretend that banks chartered there were legitimate. During the early to mid-1990s, at least a dozen Russian banks were licensed, many of which proved to be largely fraudulent. In just two years, 1994 to 1996, Antigua authorized the formation of twenty-seven offshore banks, four of them Russian-owned, one Ukrainian-owned. This at a time when the government was steadfastly denying that it was encouraging or otherwise tolerating money laundering.

Such claims had been falling on deaf ears in Washington and London for years, but decidedly came back to haunt Lester Bird when, in 1994, Antigua chartered the world's first cyberspace financial institution, European Union Bank (EUB). Like Hanover Bank, and most of those Russian banks, EUB wound up on the scrapheap, making a joke out of Antigua's offshore financial services sector. After all, an offshore bank chartered to do business in cyberspace raises several questions: Where is cyberspace? And, Which jurisdiction has the authority to investigate wrongdoings there? What's more, the reported theft of the bank's assets were not, under laws then in force, a crime in Antigua.

The Bird government talked a good game about cleaning up the mess, but if they did anything in direct response to the EUB scandal, it was merely to change the window dressing.

"It is not certain," a United Nations panel determined, "that there have been any fundamental changes. The authorities in Antigua have attempted to play down the European Union Bank case while also suggesting that they have taken measures to prevent future occurrence of this kind. What they have not explained adequately, however, is how a country with a population of between 65,000 and 70,000 can develop the capacity for adequate supervision of the myriad and complex financial services and institutions available on the island. Until there is such a capacity, the changes in Antigua will be merely cosmetic."

A similar warning came from Washington attorney Jack Blum, a severe critic of the island's record on financial due diligence. When Antigua announced it was investigating the EUB affair, Blum reminded the world, "The last time the government was involved in this kind of investigation – an investigation of weapons going to the Colombian drug cartels on an Antiguan end user certificate – no one was caught, no one was punished, and the American lawyer hired to do the investigation was never paid for his services. In short, do not expect much."

Around the same time that EUB made headlines, Swiss American Bank of Antigua came under suspicion as part of the Bank of New York fiasco. That's the same Swiss American Bank that once held and then dispersed John Fitzgerald's $7 million worth of marijuana money.

That bank was founded by the Swiss-based entrepreneur Bruce Rappaport. Owner of Antigua's influential West Indian Oil Company, he was once described by the *New York Times* as "a Swiss banker who has had brushes with governmental investigators." Born in Haifa in 1923, Rappaport surfaced in the press during the Iran-Contra affair of the 1980s. He was said to have been linked to a $10-million payment from the Sultan of Brunei to Colonel Oliver North, which North later insisted he never received. Rappaport sternly denied any involvement in the missing money. His name popped up again during the BCCI scandal over his alleged business relationship with a Middle Eastern shipping magnate who'd been financed by BCCI. Rappaport, who has never been charged or prosecuted for any crime, was a golfing partner of the late CIA director William Casey. His friendship with the Bird family earned him the status of Antigua's honorary consul for Russia.

When the BoNY scandal broke, Rappaport's name came up in connection with Inter-Maritime Bank in Switzerland, which he'd owned and had sold, in part, to BoNY. A statement issued by his office denied any involvement in the BoNY-Russian relationship. It noted that BoNY had held a 28 per cent stake in Inter-Maritime since 1996 and that Rappaport, who at one point owned 8 per cent of BoNY, then held less than 5 per cent. His position in BoNY-InterMaritime was that of non-executive chairman. The statement emphasized that Rappaport did not refer clients to the bank, had never brought any business to BoNY, was not involved in the day-to-day affairs of the bank, and had nothing to do with Russian money laundering. Rappaport insisted he had no personal or professional dealings with any of the people or any of the companies named in reports of the affair.

Three years later, the U.S. House of Representative Banking Committee called hearings on the BoNY scandal. Among the people asked to testify – because the committee believed he had "material knowledge of these matters" – was Bruce Rappaport. A man who has spent most of his life arduously staying away from any sort of publicity, he declined.

Rappaport no longer has anything to do with Antigua's financial services sector. His holdings there – the offshore Swiss American Bank, the onshore Swiss American National Bank, and the Antigua International Trust – have all been sold to local interests. Confusing the issue, however, is that when his entities were licensed by Antigua, SAB and SANB were both owned by Swiss American Holding Company, a Panamanian company. Furthermore, Swiss American Holding Company appears to have been owned by a Bermuda IBC, which in turn is owned by a charitable trust that is said to be controlled by Rappaport. So, he may no longer have nothing more to do with Antigua's financial sector or, perhaps, he does. This is not a place where total transparency is encouraged. Rappaport's Panamanian and Bermuda interests, sources in Antigua say, are Mr. Rappaport's own business and not related to anything in Antigua. He is no longer the island's honorary consul for Russia, and apparently hasn't been on the island in quite a while.

A U.S. Senate report critical of Antigua and aware of Rappaport's interests found that "throughout their (Antigua's) history, these banks have been troubled by controversial leadership, questionable practices by bank officials, and accounts that were repositories of funds from major financial frauds and other illegal activities."

Senate investigators went on to allege "Swiss American Banking Group has a history of involvement in controversial and questionable financial dealings and banking activities." In addition to accounts that held funds from frauds and other illicit activities, those investigators reported Antigua's reluctance to co-operate with law enforcement looking to seize proceeds of crime. "More recently, SAB has serviced accounts that are related to Internet gambling, an activity that is vulnerable to money laundering."

Despite such accusations, and a series of scandals that mangled the island's reputation, the Bird government kept doing business as usual. For more than fifty years, their power has turned the twin islands into, what one critic describes as, "a family estate." They largely control the media and, through wealthy and loyal friends, have real power over many of the most important businesses in the country. Family members have survived claims of corruption, accusations of involvement in drug trafficking, and a scandal involving covert gun shipments to the Cali cartel. One Bird family political critic claimed, in the mid-1990s, that without narcodollars, the economy would be in trouble. The government maintains that wasn't true then, and is not true now.

Still, so much money has washed through Antigua over the years that whatever credibility the financial sector there can lay claim to, in reality, most of it long ago went down the drain with the dirty water.

One man who found himself at the centre of the island's ruined reputation was William Cooper. A Californian who'd relocated there, he'd helped Rappaport organize Swiss American's interests by signing SAB's licence application as vice-president of Rappaport's Panamanian holding company. A member of SAB's board of directors, Cooper was general manager of the banking group from 1981 to 1984.

He turned up in 1990 running American International Bank (AIB). Registered by him for some people in Florida, when the original owners decided they no longer needed or wanted the bank, Cooper purchased it. He capitalized the bank at the minimum required $1 million by forming a company called AMT. That company borrowed $1 million from AIB, allowing Cooper to use the $1 million in paid-up shares of AMT to back his bank. Next, he formed AMT Management, AMT Trust, and a company called Ship Registry Services, uniting them with the bank under the umbrella of American International Banking Group. Eventually he added American International Bank and Trust, which was registered in Dominica.

Within five years, Cooper would claim, his banking group had eight thousand clients and held assets of $100 million. What really happened during those five years was that AIB laundered millions through correspondent accounts in the U.S. New clients were brought into the bank by way of a shell company, emphasizing confidentiality. The group also incorporated offshore banks for clients and AIB served as the correspondent for more than thirty of them, none of which had any physical presence anywhere. Included among the banks that AIB represented were Caribbean American Bank, Hanover Bank, and Overseas Development Bank and Trust.

Cooper was able to link those banks and the fraudulent activities of their clients to AIB's own correspondents, among them Jamaica Citizens

Bank Ltd. (now Union Bank of Jamaica) in Miami, the Toronto-Dominion Bank in New York, Bank of America, Popular Bank of Florida (now BAC Florida Bank), Chase Manhattan Bank, Norwest Bank in Minnesota, and Barnett Bank in Florida. The banks Cooper formed also had correspondent relationships with Privat Kredit Bank in Switzerland, Toronto-Dominion Bank in Canada, Midland Bank in Britain, and Berenberg Bank in Germany. On top of that, AIB had a relationship with Antigua Overseas Bank, which in turn had correspondent accounts at Bank of America, Chase Manhattan Bank, and Bank of New York.

He'd built himself a complex, but very competent, laundromat. At the same time, he ran a suspect investment scheme called The Forum. Described by the SEC as a glorified chain letter, investors were lured in with the promise of huge returns on highly speculative investments, most of which never got off the ground. A lot of his investors' money was funnelled through Antigua to a highly suspect operator, then operating out of Panama, named Marc Harris.

An accountant by profession, the twenty-five-year-old American-born Harris had his licence revoked in 1990 after he audited a mutual fund and failed to disclose that he both owned and ran it. He left the States shortly after that. Eight years later, his Harris Organization claimed to operate banks, insurance companies, a trust, and a brokerage. Harris said he employed 150 people, was the largest offshore service provider in the world, and managed over $1 billion in assets. Although, it appears that Harris never bothered to get proper licences for many of these services and was managing only around $40 million. At the same time, he was carrying huge liabilities.

In March 1998, articles published in the newsletter *Offshore Alert* accused Harris of stealing clients' funds, of laundering money, and of being broke. Harris sued publisher/journalist David Marchant for libel, claiming damages of $30 million. The British-born, Miami-based Marchant stood his ground. The trial took place in Miami, in July 1999. Harris did not appear, possibly fearing that his arrival in Florida would be met with subpoenas from the SEC, who'd already served two Harris employees with them. Harris lost the case, appealed, and then lost the appeal. Three years later, Harris was evicted from his offices in Panama, supposedly for non-payment of rent. He left for Nicaragua, where he changed the name of his business to avoid any association with his own reputation. That firm, Mitchell Astor Gilbert Trust, was registered on the island of Nevis, where the word *trust* can be used in a company name even if it isn't a trust.

According to people who attended seminars Harris held for prospective clients looking to evade taxes, his plan was called The Octopus. At the heart of it was a Panamanian shell. Branching out from there was a series of seemingly unrelated trading companies, banks, insurance companies, trusts, and leasing firms registered throughout the offshore world. The sole purpose of those IBCs was to generate tax-deductible expenses. The monies paid to them accumulated in the Panamanian shell. Secrecy laws in the various offshore jurisdictions made it impossible for anyone to link the various companies to the Panamanian shell and from there to the person evading taxes. Over an eighteen-month period, investigators estimate, the Forum-Cooper-AIB-Harris circuit moved $100 million for 30,000 clients through 1,600 banks and IBCs in the Bahamas, Antigua, Nevis, Panama, and St. Vincent. In May 2003, Harris was arrested in Nicaragua and sent back to Miami, where he sits in jail – bail denied – awaiting trial on all sorts of charges, including fraud and money laundering.

While this was going on, Cooper was also at the centre of another money-laundering scam, this one dubbed Risky Business by the U.S. Customs officers who investigated it.

Over a six-year period, from 1991 to 1997, eight hardened criminals working in Florida, Canada, and Britain – including a convicted murderer who'd once been sentenced to life in prison – duped more than four hundred people around the world out of more than $60 million. Using advertisements in the *New York Times*, the *Wall Street Journal*, *USA Today*, and the *International Herald Tribune*, the gang offered venture capital loans to finance businesses. Entrepreneurs, lawyers, doctors, sports' stars, and entertainment figures – including singer Dionne Warwick and *Star Trek*'s William Shatner – were lured into the scheme with the bait of seductively attractive interest rates. Warwick signed on and reportedly lost $100,000. Shatner wisely backed off.

Anyone answering the ads was invited to a series of interviews over the course of many months. By creating what appeared to be a selection process, the victims' desire to be chosen for the loan heightened.

At each meeting, the "executive" handling the matter was higher up the chain. Ostensibly, the meetings were to establish the victim's needs, to determine access to available funds, and to set out a payment plan for the "processing fees." At each step, victims were told they were getting closer to obtaining their venture capital. By the time they reached the contract stage, they'd been so expertly set up that they willingly handed over cashier's cheques to settle the fees. Signed contracts set into motion the next stage. A clause obliged them to obtain a letter of credit or bank guarantee – ranging from $2 million to $20 million – which was required by the "board of investors."

Obviously, no bank would guarantee that kind of money without collateral. If the victims had enough collateral to raise that kind of money, then they wouldn't need to deal with these crooks. So, at the end of the deliberately brief period allowed for acquiring a bank guarantee – usually five to seven days – the victims would have to admit that they'd failed to raise the money. At that point, someone in the syndicate would explain how, regrettably, they were now in breach of the contract, that the deal was cancelled, and that their processing fee would be forfeited to cover expenses.

Some victims got angry and went away. Others believed the person they were dealing with when he said there might be a way around the problem. The victim would then be introduced to various "facilitators" and "underwriters" – other gang members – who professed to be in a position to help them get the necessary guarantees. That, of course, entailed additional upfront fees, usually $10,000 to $35,000. When that inevitably ran into problems, more facilitators and underwriters were brought in, incurring more fees. The most stubborn victims wound up paying as many as six fees, a few losing as much as $2 million.

Their money ended up in the Caribbean American Bank (CAB) or the Caribbean International Bank (CIB), both formed by Cooper under the umbrella of AIB. At one point, he was looking after as many as sixteen brass-plate banks. The story is all the more perverse because shortly after Cooper set up CAB and CIB, Russian criminals arrived with funds to wash.

To accommodate his Risky Business clients, Cooper established shells for each of them, then issued gold Visa cards through CAB in the names of those shells. That allowed the gang members to spend money freely, without being associated with it. One gang member ran up bills of

$23,000 a month, using his Visa card to pay for plastic surgery, gambling junkets, and lingerie from Victoria's Secret. He also bought a car for a woman he'd met the night before in the Bahamas.

A federal grand jury in Gainsville, Florida, indicted eight people in March 1998 for their part in Risky Business. Customs officers arrested members of the gang and successfully froze several accounts at Caribbean American. In a last-ditch effort to save his stake, one gang member tried to hire lawyer Vere Bird, Jr., the prime minister's brother. According to court records, he offered Bird, Jr., 20 per cent of the frozen funds if he could unfreeze them. Bird, Jr., backed away from the case when that gang member was arrested.

Within three years, everyone associated with Risky Business was doing time in a federal penitentiary. Except Cooper. He was alive and well and safe in Antigua. The Americans tried to extradite him, but Cooper denied involvement in the matter and fought extradition. By this time he was a citizen of Antigua, which meant that in order for the Americans to get him onto a plane, his crime in the States had to be a crime in Antigua too. Local attorneys acting for the Americans tried various tactics, only to fail. The court ruled that based on the Extradition Treaty with the U.S. signed in 1996, the crime of money laundering – for which Cooper stands charged in the States – was not a crime in Antigua at the time of the requested extradition. Antigua's Parliament only outlawed money laundering in 1998.

Before they can resubmit the extradition request, the Americans need to link Cooper to an offence recognized by the Antiguans during a specific time period. Supposedly to help them do that, in early 2003, Antigua's director of public prosecutions arranged to have certain documents handed to the Americans and invited them to sit down with Antigua's attorney general to review what the islanders now recognize as "the Cooper problem."

━━━

Halfway through U.S. President Bill Clinton's second term, the idea began to brew that new anti-money-laundering banking regulations were necessary.

Specifically, the Federal Reserve Board and the Office of the Comptroller of the Currency wanted to impose much stiffer "Know Your

Customer" (KYC) requirements. They were looking to oblige banks to categorize customers and report irregular activities. For example, anyone who did not normally make large cash deposits or withdrawals would be reported if they did; anyone who'd never wired money overseas would be asked for an explanation if they attempted to. Proponents argued the regulations were a necessary step in keeping dirty money out of the U.S. financial system. Opponents said such regulations would add to the cost of doing banking while, at the same time, turning financial institutions into policemen.

The all-powerful Senate Banking Committee, led by Texas Republican Phil Gramm, promised that the new regulations would never be passed.

Around the same time, Representative Jim Leach, a fairly moderate Republican from Iowa who oversaw the House Banking Committee, cosponsored the Money Laundering and Financial Crimes Strategy Act. It gave the president the authority to implement a national strategy to combat money laundering and related financial crimes. The House passed it and, because it was fairly benign, the Senate passed it too. On the back of that, Leach championed the House version of a much stricter anti-money-laundering law. His intention was to put the trafficking of dirty money into the same league as the trafficking of drugs. One result would have been to make it almost impossible for U.S. banks to deal with offshore havens where secrecy was one of the products on sale.

The offshore world could not afford to let this happen, so their lapdog in the Senate – Gramm – was dispatched. That he's from Texas is no coincidence. The most vociferous critics of legislation aimed at penalizing banks for handling dirty money come from George W. Bush's home state. Banks there are a favourite repository for Mexican fortunes, both clean and dirty. Texas money and Texas mouthpieces were not going to allow some northerner from Iowa to change that.

Representative Ron Paul, another Texas Republican – and, like Gramm, a full-fledged stooge of the Texas banking lobby – rallied the dissenters: "This is basically twenty-first-century gunboat diplomacy. Because they're never going to use it against a major trading partner, they're only going to pick on small states."

His opposition was supported by words and money from several concerned parties, including officers and directors of two powerful border banks – the International Bank of Commerce of Laredo and the Laredo

National Bank – plus the Stanford Financial Group, a $14-billion Houston-based company with serious interests in Antigua.

The CEO of Stanford Financial is R. Allen Stanford, a dual national holding American and Antiguan passports. He owns the onshore Bank of Antigua and the offshore Stanford International Bank, which is the country's largest offshore bank. He also owns a local newspaper, a local airline, and the island's largest property development company.

According to the watchdog group Public Citizen, Stanford Financial, which had never made a federal campaign contribution prior to this, now dumped money into political action groups on both sides of the aisle. Between February 2000 and June 2001, Stanford gave Republicans $208,000 and Democrats $145,000. But he didn't stop there. As is his right, another $95,000 was sent to the political action committees (PACs) of Democrat Senate Majority Leader Tom Daschle, Democrat House Caucus Chairman Martin Frost, and Republican Senate Minority Leader – and fellow Texan – Trent Lott. That Stanford opposed these bills is understandable, as they would have severely damaged Antigua's ability to operate as a tax haven.

At no time has anyone suggested that this is unlawful. It is not. Stanford's contributions are perfectly within his rights as a citizen. Anyway, Stanford was hardly alone. The Texas banking lobby had no intention of letting this bill pass, and soft money poured in to stop it. Some of the money came "laundered" through the lobby from offshore jurisdictions intent on protecting their own interests. British and Canadian banks also contributed. As did major U.S. financial institutions with offshore interests, such as J.P. Morgan Chase, which has a big presence in Texas and a strong lobbying arm on Capitol Hill.

In the end, Gramm pleased his masters by shamelessly refusing to take up the Senate version of the bill, which eradicated any chance of it becoming law. There was some talk of trying to get a full House vote on the bill, which would have put pressure on Gramm, but he and his Texas Republican cronies – Richard Armey and Tom DeLay – made certain that never happened. Later, Gramm would, disgracefully, brag that he'd killed it "single-handedly."

What the public did not yet realize was that Gramm had a hidden agenda due to his connections with Enron. The public did not yet know the extent to which Enron was dependent on the offshore world to defraud investors and the IRS; that Enron was pouring money into this fight too; or that Phil Gramm's wife, Wendy, had been a member of Enron's board of directors for eight years.

She sat on the very same audit and compliance committee that was supposed to have exercised oversight of Enron's offshore frauds. Public Citizen reports that Wendy Gramm earned $915,000 to $1.8 million a year in salary, fees, dividends, and stock options over an eight-year period.

Her husband was a recipient of $97,350 in campaign and soft-money contributions from Enron from 1989 to 2001.

Antigua dove head first into the offshore business in 1982, and for much of the next nineteen years, it remained wildly unregulated. For three years in the 1990s, Allen Stanford held a seat on the island's financial services regulatory authority, where he tried to fortify the offshore sector against assaults by foreign tax authorities. He was acutely concerned with the island's standing as a financial centre, and there's no denying that he worked hard to bring Antigua up to his standards. But certain people close to Lester Bird believed they had too much to lose if the government cleaned up the industry. In 1997, powerful forces inside Antigua passed amendments to the existing money-laundering and company-formation laws, limiting law enforcement's ability to police the sector, strengthening bank secrecy, and impeding international co-operation.

Officials at the U.S. Treasury chastised "a prominent U.S. offshore banker" for "using financial and political clout" to take over the financial services regulatory agency.

Jon Winer, at the State Department, described the situation as "a leveraged buyout of Antiguan regulation by a private-sector person."

The Americans repeatedly warned Antigua that it would not tolerate an expansion of the country's haven status, but the amendments displayed Antigua's intentions to go its own way. After fruitless negotiations with Antigua, the Americans and the British issued official warnings to view with suspicion all transactions to, through, and from Antigua, or involving any of its nationals. Even the French, whose own Caribbean interests included St. Martin – a centre of increasing transnational organized criminal activity – voiced concern about Antigua.

So did the G8 finance ministers by convening the Financial Stability Forum (FSF) and, inside that, the Working Group on Offshore Financial Centers. They divided the offshore world into three categories: Group I (deemed to be co-operative in anti-money-laundering activities and well supervised) included Switzerland, Hong Kong, Luxembourg, and the Channel Islands; Group II (potentially co-operative but with low-quality supervision) featured Bahrain, Bermuda, Gibraltar, Malta, and Monaco; Group III (non-cooperative and with low-quality supervision) took in Liechtenstein, Nauru, Niue, Vanuatu, and most of the usual suspects in the Caribbean, including Antigua.

That was followed by an FATF review that named, and tried to shame, fifteen jurisdictions that were to be considered non-co-operative in the fight against money laundering. They were the Bahamas, the Cayman Islands, the Cook Islands, Dominica, Israel, Lebanon, Liechtenstein, the Marshall Islands, Nauru, Niue, Panama, the Philippines, Russia, St. Kitts and Nevis, and St. Vincent and the Grenadines. Although Antigua escaped that list, the FATF included fourteen other jurisdictions under the heading of "deficient": Belize, Bermuda, British Virgin Islands, Cyprus, Gibraltar, Guernsey, the Isle of Man, Jersey, Malta, Mauritius, Monaco, Samoa, St. Lucia, and Antigua.

To be removed from the various lists, Antigua was required to implement forty recommendations from the FATF, plus nineteen recommendations from the FATF's regional offshoot, the Caribbean Financial Action Task Force (CFATF). Combined, they outlined the role of a supervisory authority plus minimum standards for record-keeping and co-operation with law enforcement. They helped to create an environment in which a serious attempt to deter money laundering can thrive. But fulfilling the recommendations, and getting serious about money laundering, are often two different things.

The world lined up against Antigua, limiting the island's options, and the Bird government had little choice but to give in. Legislation was proposed and passed, nullifying most of the objectionable amendments of the 1997 law. Banking licences were revoked. Owners of IBCs were put on notice. Bilateral and multilateral co-operation in law enforcement was increased. And two new treaties – Extradition and Mutual Legal Assistance – were implemented with the United States.

Then came 9/11.

Within a month of the atrocities, no fewer than thirty nations conceded that it was time to get serious about the offshore world, at least in relation to terrorist funds. The Bush administration had already answered the call of the Texas banking lobby by announcing earlier that year that it would take a blind-eye approach to tax havens. But 9/11 had such profound effects on every aspect of life in the West that Bush simply could not ignore certain offshore realities.

The greatest fear of every money-laundering sink in the Caribbean was that, somehow, somewhere, al-Qaeda money would pop up. Lester Bird didn't need to be reminded what would happen if it did, and chose to make a first strike. Within weeks of the terrorist attacks, he pushed through an anti-terrorism finance bill, making Antigua the first country to respond that way to 9/11. Bird ordered every bank on the island to review the U.S. and U.K. lists of suspected terrorist-related organizations and individuals, warning that any bank making a false declaration would have its licence revoked and its principals sent to jail. When the reports came back, Bird was able to assure the Americans and the British that none of the listed terrorist-related organizations or individuals had a presence in Antigua.

The Americans responded by pointing out that charities and non-profit entities were still a problem, so Bird moved to close that loophole. In 2002, Antigua created a new office, the Financial Services Regulatory Commission (FSRC), with overall authority to regulate offshore banks, IBCs, insurance and trusts, plus Internet gambling.

Antigua insists that it's serious about cleaning up dirty money. Though actual prosecutions are almost non-existent, the country has made at least one very public stand. They charged former Ukrainian prime minister Pavlo Lazarenko with money laundering, froze $83 million that he allegedly stashed in the offshore European Federal Credit Bank (Eurofed), ordered it forfeited, then shut down the bank.

Lazarenko, who'd served his country from 1996 to 1997, was accused by his own government of stealing $2 million and stripped of his parliamentary immunity. He fled to the States, hoping for political asylum. Instead, he got arrested on charges of laundering $114 million, of which $70 million was supposedly washed through Antigua. According to the indictments, the money came from bribery, kickbacks, and illegal oil and gas sales. Ironically, these days, Eurofed's old Web site transfers automatically to an on-line casino.

That's an area where, despite their claims, Antigua still lacks credibility. They dove head first into Internet gaming, much the way they did with banks and IBCs all those years ago. On-line casinos and sports betting have been placed in a virtual free-trade zone. And where offshore on-line sports betting is probably no different than any onshore variety – as long as you can trust the offshore version to pay out – there have to be serious doubts about all on-line casinos.

Putting aside the obvious question – Why would anyone in their right mind trust a roulette wheel that he can't see except on a monitor? – some law enforcement officers who track on-line casinos suggest that none of them are legitimate. They say that not only is there a 100 per cent possibility that they cheat by rigging games, there is an almost equally high probability that any given on-line casino is involved in some form of money laundering.

"I have maintained from day one," says Detective Sergeant Dave Taylor of the Ontario Province Police (OPP), "that Internet gambling is nothing but money laundering. There are some people who actually get on and play. But during numerous investigations, we've found that on-line casinos almost always lead to organized crime."

A recognized expert on Internet gambling, Taylor has logged on to hundreds of on-line casinos in an undercover capacity. He says some are not set up to pay out, many don't have legitimate bank accounts, and some actually run their finances through convenience stores.

"We've watched money from street-level operations funnelled offshore, moved through the islands, then brought back as winnings. It's supposed to look like honest gambling, but we know full well that they've not established anything of the kind."

It's not uncommon, Taylor says, for casinos to offer new players a credit as an incentive to sign on. Some of those credits can be as high as $500. But, he suggests, those credits can be just another form of laundering.

"What's to prevent them from creating thirty thousand players? They can get lists of names from anywhere in the world. They buy a mass mailing list, or get credit card generators, and put down a name saying he's gambled $250. But that person never touched a computer and doesn't know that his name is being used. Or they can get on a hacker's site, and within five minutes download lists of valid Visa and MasterCard numbers. They put them on a database of clients, credit/debit the cards on their database, and move the money back and forth. Now the casino has a set of business records that shows all these people have played. It looks like a legitimate paper trail. What's a regulatory authority going to do, ask every name on the list whether or not he lost $250? I doubt it."

He notes that every gambling licence he's ever investigated leads to a lawyer's office on some island. "We have instances where one of the company's lawyers is the attorney general of the island. These groups connect to the islands simply to avoid jurisdictional problems. When they get found out, they jump to another island. They go to wherever they get the least hassle."

Included in the list of islands he sees most often are Antigua and St. Kitts and Nevis. Australia and New Zealand also show up fairly frequently, as do Niue and Nauru. The more obscure the place, the more difficult it becomes to follow a money trail. A tortuous process, even at the best of times, it relies on Mutual Legal Assistance Treaties (MLATs), which depend, in large part, on the goodwill of any given jurisdiction.

"Typically," Taylor explains, "that can add three years to the process. Antigua and the Caymans are infamous. There are piles of MLATs waiting to be processed. We send an MLAT asking for help, and pray. We're never sure if, at the end of the day, we'll ever get anything back. In the meantime, the bad guys have switched banks and jurisdictions four times."

In February 2003, the CFATF awarded Antigua a Grade-A rating for its anti-money-laundering initiatives. The island had been lobbying for the upgrade for some time. It was earned, they say, because Antigua is now fully compliant with all the recommendations of the FATF and the CFATF.

Sir Ronald Sanders is Antigua's representative to the CFATF, a long-time friend of Lester Bird, and the government's High Commissioner to the U.K. He is also the choirmaster in charge of singing the island's praise.

While the CFATF upgrade came out at a time when Sanders was vice-chairman of the group, and about to be named chairman, he does not see a conflict of interest. "Absolutely not. My taking over the chairmanship, in itself, should tell you something about the way in which the thirty countries which are members of it regard Antigua. Had they not thought that we were serious, I don't think I would have been elected to that position."

Nor does he see fulfillment of the FATF and CFATF recommendations as mere window dressing. "I don't think that's true. We've changed everything. You can't bring a dollar into Antigua and get it into a bank."

All too well aware of Antigua's reputation – he corrects, "former reputation" – Sanders says he was ashamed of accusations, like those levied in 1996 by *U.S. News and World Report*. The magazine said Antigua was a unique money-laundering sink, and noted that no other jurisdiction extended as warm a welcome to dirty money, having constructed a virtually unregulated banking industry built on secrecy and no reporting requirements. But Sanders insists, "The situation has changed radically. The island is on its way to becoming spotlessly clean. I'm not saying we've got all the answers, but we are trying every day to do better."

Significantly, bearer-share IBCs are no longer for sale. The idea that a company belonged to whoever physically possessed the share certificates was a concept that dated back to an era in European history when religious doctrine dictated that discretion in financial affairs was virtuous. In modern finance, there is absolutely no legitimate use for bearer shares. The only reason anyone ever bought a bearer-share IBC was to keep beneficial ownership of the IBC from being discovered.

They've been banned by the Bahamas (where there are around 47,000 IBCs), Jersey (30,000), and Hong Kong (500,000). The jurisdictions that still allowed them as of 2003 were Panama (370,000), Liechtenstein (75,000), and Luxembourg (68,000).

The Isle of Man (24,300) announced its intention to abolish bearer shares, while the Caymans (45,000) and BVI (360,000) came up with a way to "immobilize" them. They require bearer shares to be held by a registered third party. Ownership can be transferred, but not secretly. Gibraltar (8,300) also went with the flow, allowing bearer shares to be issued but requiring the beneficial owner to be registered. The shares must then be deposited in a Gibraltar bank. Transfer of ownership cannot occur without permission from Gibraltar's financial and development secretary, effectively nullifying any advantages.

In Antigua, where bearer shares were involved in just about every money-laundering scandal the island ever saw, anyone purchasing an IBC now must register the names and addresses of the beneficial owners and directors with the authorities. But like so many things in Antigua's history of money laundering, what you see is not always what you get.

One problem lies in the 13,500 IBCs already licensed. Beneficial owners and directors were required by law to register their names. Any IBC not compliant – perhaps because the beneficial owner doesn't want his identity known – has been struck off. But the actual number of cancelled licences is small. For the remaining IBCs, there's nothing more than hope that the beneficial owners and directors have complied honestly. If a scandal breaks and the registered names are not real, the law provides for criminal charges. But, by that time, the crooks will be long gone and Antigua will never knew who they were.

It's different with bank accounts. Antigua now provides that banks must know the true identity of account holders, must verify the nature of the account holder's business, and must identify the source of the account holder's funds. Because the banks' directors are known, if the banks don't fully comply, the directors will pay the price. And where there were once nearly sixty banks on the island, there are now only fifteen.

"The number has been so severely reduced," Sanders says, "because the government closed some and others simply could not meet the new criteria, which includes physical presence. Banks must now have an address, books, and records at the address, and mind and management there as well. The people who are managing the operation have to be physically present there."

Could Hanover or EUB happen again? Sanders hopes not. "Anything is possible in any jurisdiction, but if it happens now in Antigua, people go to jail."

That would include, he says, Mr. Cooper. "Certainly. And anybody else who operates in that way."

He acknowledges that the country got itself into a mess, and puts it down to laxity. "When offshore banking services began in Antigua, there was no real regulation. There was one man who was the supervisory authority. People applied to him and he issued a licence. In fact, issuing licences was all he did. Nothing changed until people like me began to say, We've got to make sure that this reputation which we've earned doesn't continue."

Internet gambling, however, is another problem that hasn't gone away. Besides being illegal in the United States, and the subject of legislation that could seriously affect all offshore jurisdictions offering on-line casinos, there is the matter of washing dirty money through the sites.

Here, Sanders takes the standard view. "Our regulations on Internet gambling are stronger than anybody else's in the world. That's a fact."

Granted, where there used to be more than one hundred registered Internet gambling sites operating out of Antigua, by mid-2003 there were only thirty-two. But saying you are policing an industry that is, at best, mostly dishonest, and actually being able to police it – especially when that industry only exists in cyberspace – are two different things. Antigua already went down that route with EUB.

Perhaps, not surprisingly, Sanders doesn't see it that way. He says Antigua is taking a long-term view. "I'm for putting an end to money laundering in any form that it exists. I'm for Antigua's reputation being strong. We are cleaning up our act, not because of what the offshore sector is worth today, but what it could be worth."

What the offshore sector is worth today is easily calculable. The fifteen banks pay Antigua a licence fee of $15,000. That's $225,000. The 13,500 IBCs pay $300. That's $4.05 million. Double that for the trusts, insurance companies, and on-line gaming sites, and you're in the neighbourhood of $10 million. Most of that, he notes, goes to the cost of regulation.

"So what else do we get? Employment. Rental of buildings? After that, you're scratching. But my contention has always been that there is more money to be made by building it legitimately. You cannot sustain employment, or your country's development, or anything on dirty money. It may come for a time, it may have a boom, but after that it's going to bust, and when it busts you're going to have people unemployed. You're going to have revenue disappear. Your economy is going to sink. It's not sustainable. The only thing that is sustainable is honest, clean, hard-working money. And that is what Antigua must go after."

At the time Sanders made those remarks in 2003, Antigua was still on the U.S. State Department list as "a Jurisdiction of Primary Concern" for money laundering. That assessment was not based on co-operation in the fight against money laundering, but rather on an evaluation of financial institutions engaging in "transactions involving significant amounts of proceeds from serious crime."

So, whatever Antigua's good intentions, it takes more than that to put an end to dirty money.

The nation may be in line with the FATF and CFATF recommendations, but it has also turned itself into a free-trade zone of deception on the Internet.

In this case, full compliance with those recommendations might do little more than to prove the old adage. You can indeed fool some of the people some of the time.

8

SMOKE AND MIRRORS

"Only the little people pay taxes."

– Leona Helmsley, tax felon

Some twenty-seven miles south-west of Antigua, the island of Montserrat is twelve miles long, seven miles wide, and suffers from the nasty temper of an active volcano.

In July 1995, Soufriere Hills erupted for the first time in recorded history. Seismic activity continued for several years, culminating in 1997 in a major disaster. Entire villages were destroyed, plumes of ash reached heights of forty thousand feet, and nearly 80 per cent of the buildings in the capital city of Plymouth were destroyed or badly damaged. More than six thousand people – out of a total population of ten thousand – fled the island. Many never returned.

Before the volcano erupted, Montserrat boasted a gaggle of 350 banks. Some of them had vaguely familiar names – Prudential Bank and Trust, Deutsche Bank (Suisse), Chase Overseas – and there was even one called World Bank. Of course, none of them had walls or a roof. They were merely brass plaques on the door of some company-formation agent. Although the owner of one called Zurich Overseas bragged that his bank did have a physical presence, of sorts. He held court every day at a local bar.

Such was the demand for banks on the island that a thriving cottage industry of wholesalers developed. They advertised Montserrat as a "bulletproof jurisdiction," offering folks the chance to "make exorbitant profits absolutely legally." They issued credit cards "in the name of the offshore bank, to give you the peace of mind you want." And invited clients to "place your assets out of reach of greedy tax collectors and governments, IRS, FBI, CIA, ex-wives, vicious relatives, or anyone wishing you bad. Your own offshore bank will have various overseas properties, investments, and assets while you are maintaining your anonymity."

For an additional fee, they provided a mail-drop address in major cities to make your offshore bank appear to be domiciled onshore in, say, London or Hong Kong, giving your bank an added patina of respectability.

Not that anybody on Montserrat cared who you were or what you did with your bank. It was yours to play with, as long as you submitted what looked like a legitimate business plan – wholesalers provided a template where you merely filled in the blanks – pretended that you were capitalized at $500,000, could come up with a formation fee of $3,000, and paid the annual fee of $8,000. Once you did that, as one wholesaler boasted, "You have arrived at the invisible world where secrecy, privacy, and freedom are of the greatest concern."

The secrecy, privacy, and freedom of Montserrat were what Panamanian laundrymen wanted when they came ashore to wash funds for the drug cartels and Manuel Noriega. Same thing for Israeli Mossad agents in the mid-1980s, who used their bank on that island to launder money in a weapons deal with Colombian drug barons. Montserrat was also the island of choice of Robert Graven. He called himself Brother Eduardo of the Circles of Light Church, and somehow convinced thirty thousand North Americans to send $3 million to the island's First American Bank to help him feed the poor. When it turned out that he was the only poor guy being fed, the FBI convicted him of fraud.

The situation eventually got so out of control on Montserrat that Britain could no longer delude itself into thinking problems didn't exist. Parliament was forced into the unprecedented step of amending Montserrat's constitution, removing responsibility for the financial sector from local control, and placing it under the authority of the British-appointed governor general.

Given those powers, the first thing the governor general did was to revoke 311 banking licences.

No discussion of Montserrat would be complete without a hearty mention of the self-proclaimed world's greatest living authority on offshore banking. Because Jerome Schneider – an American who, for the past several years, operated out of Vancouver, British Columbia – is the man who sold many of those 311 now-defunct banking licences.

Sometime in the mid-1970s, as the offshore banking boom gathered momentum, Schneider hit on a neat money-making idea: help people avoid taxes by selling them their own bank. He wrote a bunch of books explaining the concept and organized thousands of high-priced seminars promising "information that only an elite few enjoy."

His seminars became the prototype for dozens of competing "protect your assets" and "create wealth" conventions that are held regularly throughout the offshore world. Typically, they're constructed around the notion that people looking to cheat on their taxes will pay large fees to hucksters who tell them what they want to hear: It's easy to swindle the government if you know how to do it. Such seminars often take place in conjunction with meetings of medical and dental associations. It seems high-income clients have proven especially susceptible to the erroneous assumption that by owning an offshore bank you aren't tax liable on any income the bank generates, even though you're the bank's only customer.

Schneider relentlessly played off that and, in those early days, flogged more than two hundred banks in Montserrat. One of his clients was Marc Harris in Panama, who operated several banks there, including Fidelity Overseas, which took fees from clients without performing any services; First City, which doctored its own financial statements; and Allied Reserve, which operated in the United States without a banking licence.

Not surprisingly, given his relationship with Harris, Schneider's name came up during Harris's unsuccessful 1999 libel suit against David Marchant and *Offshore Alert*. In testimony for the defence, John Shockey – doyen of the U.S. Office of the Comptroller of the Currency, having served there for fifty-three years – revealed that Schneider had once served time in prison for a computer-related crime. Oddly, his conviction has since been sealed.

That Schneider's past was unknown to his clients is one thing. That the concept on which Schneider based the sale of those banks was fallacious is more serious.

There are, perhaps, as many as seventy-five jurisdictions around the world with offshore banks for sale. But using them to defraud the taxman – or to launder money – isn't as easy as promoters like Schneider make it sound. To begin with, some offshore jurisdictions have no credibility whatsoever. Besides Montserrat, banks in Nauru, Niue, Vanuatu, Bodrum (a Spanish-Moroccan haven), Campione d'Italia (on the eastern Turkish border), Tbilisi, and Montenegro aren't going to impress many people. Then, all the paperwork, bizarre trust structures, and layers of shell companies, which you must buy from the people peddling these offshore banks, do not automatically offer protection for tax purposes. In the States, for example, the IRS takes the view that banks formed in jurisdictions where effective regulation is non-existent, or banks that do not perform regular banking business, or banks where the owner is the only client, are not considered banks for the purpose of tax law. Other countries share those views, labelling them "Controlled Foreign Corporations," which nullify tax advantages.

It took the taxman a while to work out Schneider's tricks, especially the most sophisticated of all, "decontrol."

Describing himself as the "senior financial consultant" for Premier Corporate Services in Vancouver, Schneider touted a scheme to sidestep the "controlled foreign corporation" trap. For a fee of $15,000 to $60,000, he'd buy an offshore bank for you. In recent years, he mostly chartered them in Nauru, but occasionally purchased them in Tonga, Vanuatu, and the Marshall Islands. For an additional fee of $15,000, Schneider's partner – California attorney Eric Witmeyer – would detach the bank from your control by selling 51 per cent of it to what is called an independent foreign owner (IFO). In principle, that's a neutral third party. More often than not, the Schneider-Witmeyer neutral third party came complete with a mail-drop address in Hong Kong.

Except, there never was a sale and there never was a neutral third party. Witmeyer supplied paperwork that merely created the semblance of that. Nor did any money change hands. Instead of receiving a cheque for the sale of your bank by the non-existent IFO, you'd get a promissory note for a substantial sum of money that Schneider and Witmeyer simply made up. The remaining 49 per cent of your bank would be converted into a Shareholder Purpose Trust. That, Schneider claimed, meant you didn't have to declare your ownership of the bank. Therefore, any monies earned by the bank had nothing to do with you for tax purposes.

Next, the foreign bank, which was supposedly no longer in your control, would open an account at a major bank in Canada so that you could conduct all of your banking business through Canada. In most cases, that meant obtaining a loan for anything you wished to buy – boats, planes, houses, country club membership, art, jewels, etc. – which was secured against the funds held by your decontrolled foreign bank.

Schneider and Witmeyer sold the scheme to their seminar clients as being foolproof. But the U.S. tax authorities weren't so sure. And after ABC Television sent its newsmagazine show *20/20* to cover a Schneider seminar in Cancun, Mexico, in 1997, Schneider and Witmeyer's world started to come unstuck.

Using a hidden camera, *20/20* extracted an admission from one of the seminar speakers, "If you don't have a big mouth and are smart, your chances of getting caught are next to none." They caught Witmeyer in a lie about the banks in Nauru, and caught Schneider in a quasi-admission that decontrol didn't mean a thing.

Over the next five years, the IRS made several undercover contacts with Schneider, and put agents into his seminars. In 1999, they got themselves inside a deal with Schneider for the purchase of a bank. During those negotiations, Witmeyer repeated to the undercover agents something that Schneider liked to say: "We put all the documents in place. Then we turn the lights out. We create it in the full light and then just disappear into the background."

In February 2001, the IRS raided Witmeyer's home and office, taking away files and computers. At the same time, at the request of the U.S. under the mutual legal assistance treaty, the RCMP raided the Vancouver office of Schneider's twin companies, Premier Corporate Services and Premier Management Services. The Mounties conducted the search with two IRS agents as "observers." Under Canadian law, after a warrant is executed, it's up to the court to decide what evidence, if any, can be released to satisfy the treaty. Schneider's lawyer argued that the Americans had not been mere observers, that they'd helped to direct the search and that they'd illegally inspected documents on-site. One of the IRS agents admitted he'd copied some documents before the court gave its permission. Schneider's lawyer petitioned the court, Washington refused to allow the IRS agent to testify, and the British Columbia Supreme Court ruled that, under those circumstances, they would not allow the Americans access to the documents.

Schneider's win in Canada wasn't enough, however, to stop him from being charged in the States. In 2003, he and Witmeyer were indicted on one count of conspiracy to defraud the IRS, fourteen counts of wire fraud, and eight counts of mail fraud. The fifty-one-year-old Schneider pled not guilty. But the forty-eight-year-old Witmeyer, facing the possibility of going away for 115 years, gave up. After explaining to the court how Schneider promised taxpayers that their purchase of a bank, and the decontrol process that followed, was sufficient to protect their assets from the taxman, Witmeyer pled guilty to conspiracy to defraud the IRS and agreed to testify against Schneider.

It's fair to say that the firewalls put up by offshore banks and shell companies – the stealth sold by men like Schneider, Witmeyer, and Harris – serve no legitimate purpose. And where insurance fraud is concerned, the smoke and mirrors of the offshore world are custom-made for crime. Consider, for example, a group of Mexican politicians who, while Schneider and Witmeyer were working their "decontrol" gimmick, were working one called "the Dutch sandwich."

Money from bribes was laundered through an offshore trust set up in the Netherlands Antilles, hence the "Dutch" part of the sandwich. Those funds, moved through a shell bank, were used to purchase three savings and loans (S&Ls) in Texas, which had fallen on hard times. The S&Ls were on the block because their loan portfolios were overburdened with non-performing mortgages.

No sooner had the Mexicans taken over the three S&Ls than they bought a small domestic insurance company in Arizona that they paid for with loans from the S&Ls. Next, they took the non-performing mortgages from the S&Ls and swapped them for good bonds held by the insurance company. That meant the S&Ls were now collateralized with profitable paper, making them very attractive, and the insurance company was sitting on a portfolio of non-performing mortgages.

To get their money out of the insurance company, the group formed an offshore reinsurance company. The Arizona operation wrote off 94 per cent of their premiums to the reinsurer, which went straight back to the offshore trust. The S&Ls were sold for a handsome profit – that money also went into the trust – while the insurance company was allowed to go belly up. The Mexicans walked away with $300 million to $400 million.

Many entrepreneurs look at money as merely a way of keeping score. By that definition, the Mexicans won bigger than a Connecticut-based geek named Martin Frankel. But size isn't everything, and Frankel's $200-million theft earned him a place in the history of offshore fraud.

Between 1990 and 1999, Frankel siphoned funds from seven American insurance companies in five states. With the help of a disbarred lawyer, who had several convictions for securities fraud and money laundering, Frankel laid out an elaborate scheme that centred on a Luxembourg shell – through which he bought those seven insurers – and several other offshore shells that looked like reinsurance companies. Whatever money Frankel didn't spend on his own bizarre lifestyle – cloistering himself in a huge Connecticut mansion with women he met through ads in sex magazines – was wired through those offshore reinsurers to Switzerland.

Some people now believe that Frankel's use of the reinsurance shells was skilful enough to get away with the money, and he would have, had it not been for two things: there was too much money in the game; and Frankel was too greedy. Had he stolen a mere 10 per cent of what he did, it's conceivable he'd have walked away with a life of luxury. Instead, he was arrested in Germany in 1999 and, three years later, pled guilty to racketeering, conspiracy, wire fraud, and securities fraud.

Often, the same greed that brings victims into a scam traps the scammers. It happened to Frankel. It happened to Alan Teale.

A British con man who'd once been secretary of the Lloyd's Insurance Brokers Association, Teale was running the now-defunct Miami Insurance Exchange when he came up with a scheme that would eventually defraud 5,500 people out of $50 million.

He constructed a network of offshore shells that he fraudulently capitalized with non-existent properties and worthless shares. Known as the Teale Network, he then enlisted ninety co-conspirators to obtain reinsurance contracts. The companies that signed up with him believed they were protected. In reality, they were putting their own financial stability – and that of their clients – in severe jeopardy, because there was nothing behind any of Teale's reinsurance policies. By moving money through the Caribbean, Belgium, and Ireland, he merely created the semblance of a thriving network. Unpaid premiums piled up quickly, families were ruined, and eventually the cops moved in. The sixty-one-year-old Teale was found guilty of forty-one counts of various types of fraud, was sentenced to seventeen years, and died in prison after serving only two months.

The ramifications of the Teale Network are still being felt. A substantial portion of the world's insurance business – especially the reinsurance side of it – finds its way to jurisdictions with questionable regulation. The cycle may start at Lloyd's of London and legitimately go through Bermuda, an insurance tax haven with relatively strict guidelines. But insurers and reinsurers are forever reinsuring – spreading their risk as widely as possible – and that business quickly seeks out less well-regulated islands.

If due diligence has not taken place at every step along the way, if some reinsurance company in one of the islands doesn't have the assets and backing it claims to, should that company be permitted to sell reinsurance? History says no. But those smaller, less well-regulated islands don't have the resources to carry out extensive due diligence. And the bigger, better regulated jurisdictions – London and Bermuda – don't necessarily have any way of knowing what's really going on at the bottom of the food chain.

In Los Angeles in 1993, during the riots that followed the beating of a black man, Rodney King, by white policemen, a number of Korean groceries were destroyed by fire. They were insured by a company sitting in the unregulated British Virgin Islands. When they tried to collect on their policies, there was no money to pay out. The nature of the offshore world is such that no legitimate insurer can ever be totally certain that there is, in fact, enough money down the line to back the original risk. Even before the ink on the Teale matter was dry, one of his disciples used precisely the same scheme to rip-off $31 million in insurance premiums.

Still, when it comes to sheer nastiness and lives being ruined, not even Teale comes close to the Bramson family. Their insurance scam is pretty much a textbook case of how to use the offshore world to commit long-term fraud and ruin the maximum number of lives.

Norman Bramson, a foul-looking character born in the Midwest in 1923, was a dentist by trade who, instead of filling cavities, ran a drugstore in Skokie, Illinois. The father of five children, two of his sons – Leonard and Marty – followed him into the business. Except, by that time, his business wasn't running a drugstore, it was insurance fraud on a gigantic scale. Both sons were lawyers. The six-foot-five-inch Leonard was a gruesome fellow. Marty was a little smaller, and looked something like Groucho Marx.

The family first appeared on radar screens in 1980 when regulators in Illinois discovered they were selling policies to podiatrists, a particularly lucrative source for medical malpractice insurance due to the number of operations they perform. The State felt they were not providing adequate protection, ruled the Bramsons delinquent, and issued a cease-and-desist order.

Six years later, the family popped up again. The Mounties had observed Norman on several occasions going into the U.S. carrying suitcases filled with cash. They decided he was a Canadian drug-money launderer. So a specialized drug unit set up a sting operation, intending to grab him with the cash. But the surveillance team got compromised – Norman somehow found out about them – and the smuggling stopped. At least it stopped long enough that the Mounties concluded this was not a drug case, and moved the dossier over to a fraud team. That group tipped off U.S. Customs, who waited until Norman was moving cash again, then grabbed him at the border red-handed.

What neither the Americans nor the Canadians realized at the time was that Norman had simply moved his illicit medical malpractice insurance scam beyond the reach of Illinois regulators. He'd set up a boiler-room operation in Toronto and was still targeting podiatrists. He'd established International Bahamian Insurance (IBI) and was running ads in newspapers and professional journals offering medical malpractice coverage at 20 to 30 per cent below the market rate. The way he could afford to do that was by never paying out any claims.

Norman was using P.O. boxes and phone numbers in Chicago that automatically forwarded mail and calls to Canada. To create jurisdictional confusion, money collected there was deposited in the Royal

Bank of Canada in Toronto and another bank in Windsor, then wired to Citizen Bank in Miami. That bank had a correspondent relationship with the New World Bank in Anguilla, which Norman owned, and was nothing more than a storefront in a strip mall. A young woman manning the New World Bank phone cleared funds coming in by moving them through a correspondent account at the Caribbean Commercial Bank in St. Martin. The funds were then wired from St. Martin to the Cantrade Bank in Zurich, Switzerland.

When the Illinois insurance regulators finally cottoned on to Norman's newest rip-off, they issued injunctions against him. As usual, Norman stayed one step ahead by setting up new insurance companies with different names in different islands.

All this time, Marty was running Norman's pharmacy in Skokie. But he'd got his father's licence revoked by dispensing drugs without prescriptions. When that happened, Marty applied for a job as a Chicago police officer. He enrolled in the academy and, a few days before being sworn in, got arrested for having sex with underage girls. He moved to the Washington, D.C., area, opened another pharmacy, got arrested again – for selling controlled drugs – and was sent to prison. When he got out, he went to law school. Meanwhile, Leonard had just graduated law school and was working in the State Attorney's Office in Chicago. Only later was it discovered that, while Leonard was an assistant state's attorney, he was also president of Norman's fraudulent insurance company.

A few of the state's insurance investigators believed that Norman was using the insurance scam to launder Chicago Mob money, but could never get the local U.S. Attorney's Office interested in the case. As far as the Justice Department was concerned, this was a matter for the Canadians. In Toronto, the cops saw it as a case that really needed to be dealt with in Chicago. By then, Norman and the family had moved to Baltimore to work their scam there. That's when a pair of seriously determined FBI agents set out to stop them.

Jim Vaules and Don Wadsworth are now both retired and have teamed up again to run the National Fraud Center outside of Philadelphia. But in those days they were operating out of Atlantic City, where Vaules was special-agent-in-charge. Being a gambling town meant that Vaules, Wadsworth, and the other agents kept busy trying to sort out the Mob's influence in the hotels and at the gaming tables.

Insurance fraud had a fairly low priority. The way the Feds usually looked at it, the industry is regulated by the state, so fraud within the industry is a state matter. And insurance fraudsters play off that. They work one state until they get into trouble, skip across the line, and set up in another state. When they're ordered to cease and desist in the second state, they move on to a third. The problem often is that by the time the Feds get into the game, if they bother at all, it's late. The damage has been done and the smart crooks are long gone.

What made Vaules and Wadsworth unique was they didn't see it that way. Both of them had a strong background in white-collar crime, and both of them understood the kind of damage that white-collar criminals can inflict on unsuspecting citizens. So, when the deputy attorney general (DAG) for the State of New Jersey – who headed the insurance fraud group – brought the Bramson case to them, they jumped on it.

A dormant company, Preferred Indemnity Insurance (PII), had just been bought out. Normally, that wouldn't raise any suspicions. But PII was licensed to provide property and casualty coverage and, instead, was selling unauthorized high-risk coverage in asbestos removal and oil tank cleaning. What worried the DAG was that the people running it were moving premium money out of the country as fast as it came in, which meant their coverage was not backed by sufficient reserves.

Vaules and Wadsworth quickly linked PII to an address in Colombia, Maryland, and learned that the people running this company had once run an insurance scam in Chicago. Following those leads, they learned that seven companies were involved, and that all of them pointed to Norman, Leonard, and Marty Bramson.

In addition to Maryland, two companies operated out of Canada, one was in New Jersey, one was in Indiana, and, bizarrely, two in Guam. Looking more closely at those, Vaules and Wadsworth were able to identify four more offshore shells that also led back to the Bramsons.

The office and phone number for PII was an address of convenience. Call forwarding redirected calls to the Associated Insurance Company in Colombia, Maryland. A courier stopped by twice a week to pick up mail, delivering it to a company called Metropolitan Support Services in Greenbelt, Maryland. One of the people working at the rent-an-office admitted to the agents that whenever a state insurance regulator made an appointment to stop by, they hung a PII plaque on the front door so that the regulator would think he was visiting a legitimate office.

Looking at what they knew was manifest deceit, Vaules and Wadsworth now found several other companies tied to the Bramsons, including one called Legal Defense Support Services Ltd., which was registered in the Federated States of Micronesia (FSM). That's a four-nation alliance sitting out in the middle of nowhere in the Pacific Ocean.

Notes Vaules, "If you're running a big fraud and want to beat the taxman, you set up offshore shell companies so that you can bill your own companies for the operating costs. A lot of the shells the Bramsons created were done specifically to bill themselves for services. They were attorneys, so they had to have legal defence support services, they needed to send invoices to their companies and show a cost of operation. By the time we'd located sixteen companies, we could begin to recreate the paper trail."

When the agents were able to determine who served in what capacity with which company, Marty's name didn't appear on any documents. But Hans Martin and B.M. Martin turned up frequently. The agents soon found logs from meetings with state insurance regulators that Hans Martin had attended, and were able to established that both Hans Martin and B.M. Martin were, of course, Marty. As a convicted criminal, he was otherwise ineligible to be licensed by any state as a beneficial owner of an insurance company. So he invented aliases.

Another company they stumbled across was called Trans-Pacific Insurance, which caused Vaules and Wadsworth to do a double-take because there happens to be a legitimate company operating with that name. But the legitimate company is spelled Transpacific, no hyphen, and this one had a hyphen. It was based in the FSM. As Wadsworth later explained, "They tried to stay as close as they could to legitimate names. It's a trick all fraudsters use. They need to be able to pass the smell test."

By now, the Bramsons had branched out from podiatrists to the entire medical profession, shifting a lot of this new business to Trans-Pacific, making the money trail much harder to follow. One of their new clients was the American Organization of Healthcare Professionals (AOHP), through which the Bramsons were pretending to insure sixty-eight thousand nurses. As long as premiums were coming in, everything worked fine. But when a claim was filed, AOHP's members soon discovered that the Bramsons had built several escape hatches to avoid paying out.

Whenever they sent a policy to a newly insured client, it was deliberately one-page short. The missing page contained a clause that said, if you don't pay your premium within thirty days, you don't have coverage. So every claim that came in triggered a letter going out, quoting that clause on page 15 – the missing page. As the company hadn't received the premium within that time frame, the letter continued, the company had no choice but to consider the policy as lapsed.

The insured person would write back that he or she didn't have a page 15. So the Bramsons would send them the master policy, which now included that page. If the insured person didn't give up there, the next step would be to acknowledge the error. The Bramsons would say, All right, we believe you paid on time, it's obviously an oversight. All you have to do now is send us $2,000 and we will reinstate you. If the person continued to argue about it, the Bramsons would simply shut the door. If the person sent the money, the Bramsons would use it as a retainer to hire an attorney to fight the claim against the insured person, which gave the appearance of covering the policy.

With so many innocent lives and livelihoods now at risk, Vaules and Wadsworth hatched a sting to stop the Bramsons. The FBI maintained a terrific apartment – wired for sound and video – overlooking the ocean in Atlantic City. But to lure one of the Bramsons to the apartment, they would need a story.

Through the New Jersey insurance regulator's office, they were introduced to a legitimate insurance executive who'd been approached by the Bramsons. The family had been trying to sell him a much-too-low discounted product and he'd reported his suspicions. This man agreed to put the agents together with Marty. The story was that Vaules needed a legitimate company behind him in order to dump some phony insurance on an association of physical therapists. Marty wanted to know more and came to Atlantic City for a night on the town. There, with what Vaules describes as "all the props" – food, booze, and the casinos – Vaules explained his scam.

And Marty loved it. Vaules says, "He figured me for a guy running a scam and he was going to run a scam on the scammer. He smelled our money and figured he could get it and then move it offshore."

While still working Marty, the agents turned a former Bramson employee into an informant. He told them that the Bramsons' entire banking operation was run by Lenny, and that everything was on a hand-held Casio computer that never left Lenny's side.

The informant also helped them lure Lenny to a meeting at Fort Lauderdale Airport. As soon as Lenny was spotted, and the agents decided they could take him, word went back to an FBI command post to hit the other targets. One group of agents went through the doors at the Bramsons' offices in Maryland. Another group arrested Marty at home. A third missed Norman. He was nowhere to be found. But the agents at the airport took Lenny and, most importantly, grabbed his hand-held Casio.

The FBI lab was able to break Lenny's codes and, as a result, Vaules and Wadsworth got the Bramsons' entire banking network. It consisted of 314 accounts held in Canada, Japan, the Cayman Islands, Anguilla, Panama, Denmark, Switzerland, Liechtenstein, Luxembourg, Germany, the Netherlands, Israel, Greece, the Federated States of Micronesia, the Commonwealth Nations of the Marian Islands (CNMI), the Solomon Islands, and Saipan. Surrounding those accounts were at least fifty-three different shell companies, registered throughout the offshore world.

Marty and Lenny were charged and released on bail, but subjected to an electronic monitoring device. The court ordered that neither were to move any money from any of their accounts. Yet within a matter of days, a call came in that Marty was looking to get his hands on some offshore money. Vaules and Wadsworth rushed back to court and had the brothers' bail revoked. Marty cut his electronic ankle bracelet and made it out of town. Lenny tried, but he was too slow and spent the next nine years sitting in a cell.

Hoping to get a lead on the father-and-son fugitives, Wadsworth approached television's *America's Most Wanted*. The producers liked the idea and ran a big feature on the family.

A little old lady in San Diego was watching the program when she recognized a man she liked to dance with. She couldn't believe it. There was a social club at the apartment complex where she lived, and the fellow she now saw on television was the best dancer. She picked up the phone and within an hour the best dancer at the social club was in custody. In his room, police found currency taped under drawers and an indication that Marty was in Mexico.

Following that lead, Vaules and Wadsworth learned that Marty had arranged with a former prison cellmate to ship a boat – called *The Escape Clause* – from Buffalo, New York, across the country by truck, to Monterrey, California, where it would be put into the water and sailed to Mexico. Money was hidden inside the boat. The bureau intercepted it and confiscated the money. But Marty still had a stash somewhere, because when they finally located his whereabouts, he'd bought a nightclub. The FBI asked the Mexicans for help, but by the time the cops showed up at the nightclub, Marty was off to Europe.

An Interpol warrant was issued for his arrest. Several months later, a border guard in Liechtenstein pulled over a shiny new Mercedes on its way from Austria into Vaduz. It was just a routine stop because he didn't like the look of the two guys in the car. Opening the trunk he found a duffel bag filled with sixteen one-kilo bars of gold bullion and neatly wrapped stacks of yen, pounds, dollars, and Swiss francs. The total came to $5.6 million. Along with it were records indicating the location of several safety deposit boxes.

Marty was one of the two men. The other was his brother Carl, who'd flown to Europe to help gather up the family's hidden cash.

The United States wanted the Bramsons sent back home and applied for their extradition. Marty counted on staying in Liechtenstein and spent two and a half years fighting deportation. His attorney was a member of parliament who was close to the prince, and the government refused to honour its extradition treaty with the U.S. The State Department accused Liechtenstein of not playing by the rules, and a minor diplomatic row ensued. Wadsworth flew over to see what he could do. One night, after Marty's attorney left Marty's cell, some local cops shoved him into a car, drove him to the Swiss border, and unceremoniously turned him over to the police there. Within three weeks, Marty was back in the States.

Receivers, put into the various Bramson companies, uncovered 1,212 outstanding claims, amounting to $66.5 million. Assets came to about $11 million. Some doctors who'd insured with the Bramsons were forced into bankruptcy. One attorney who'd worked for them committed suicide.

"These guys ruined a lot of lives," Wadsworth says. "Lenny got nine years. Marty got ten. Norman served very little. We seized what assets we could, but the correspondent banking relationships and the offshore shell companies made it very difficult. We got a lot of bank accounts in all those countries, but don't know how many accounts we didn't find. We don't know what other assets we missed. Without the correspondent banking relationships and the offshore shell companies they never would have made it as far as they did. Without the offshore connections, they never could have made it work."

9

PONZI'S GHOST

"All scams are basically the same, and the people running them are typically not very bright, but they're brighter than their victims, which is all they need to be."

– David Marchant, investigative journalist

Carlos Bianchi left Italy in the waning hours of the nineteenth century, arriving in the New World to change his name from Carlos to Charles and from Bianchi to Ponsi. By the end of the First World War, he'd not only served time in a Montreal jail for cheque forging, he'd changed his name again, this time from Ponsi to Ponzi.

Around 1919, looking for greener pastures, Ponzi left Canada for Boston, where one day he received a letter from someone in Italy containing an international postal-reply coupon. It's a simple method of paying for postage in one country with the currency of another – sort of the global answer to self-addressed stamped envelopes. Because someone in, say, Scotland can't buy stamps to pay for return postage for his correspondent in, say, Vancouver, he buys one of these coupons from his local post office. The fellow in Scotland sends it to his correspondent in Vancouver, who exchanges it at his local post office for a stamp that covers the postage back to Scotland.

What caught Ponzi's eye was that the coupon he received from Italy had been purchased in Spain. He soon learned that while international postal-reply coupons were priced at a fixed rate of exchange, currency rates fluctuated to the point where this particular coupon had cost only

15 per cent of the value of the U.S. stamps he could buy with it. In other words, coupons bought in Spain and cashed in the States represented an instant profit of nearly 660 per cent. So Charles Ponzi promptly announced his entry into the international postal-reply coupon business.

However, instead of funding the venture himself, which might have been legal and would have been profitable, he invited investors to join him. As he outlined in the plan, he would personally travel to Spain to buy tens of thousands of coupons, bring them back to the States, where he would exchange them for stamps, and then wholesale the stamps to businesses. Promising 40 per cent profits in just ninety days, he reinforced investor confidence with the old trick of forming a corporation with a legitimate-sounding name: The Securities and Exchange Company, which, of course, abbreviated to SEC.

For the first few months, money trickled in slowly but steadily. It's when he upped the promise to 100 per cent profits that the floodgates opened and, on good days, hundreds of thousands of dollars arrived at his SEC. He got so rich so quickly that, within six months, he purchased a large stake in a New York bank and a Boston import-export firm. The only problem was, his fortune wasn't based on postal-reply coupons, he was simply spending his investors' money.

Towards the middle of 1920, the *Boston Post* newspaper canvassed post offices all over town, to discover that Ponzi couldn't be buying as many coupons as he claimed because that many coupons hadn't been cashed in. The paper's exposé brought investors to Ponzi's front door demanding their money back. He obligingly paid, with interest, using money he'd received from new investors.

Robbing Peter to pay Paul worked for a while, but by August the *Boston Post* was claiming that Ponzi was millions of dollars in debt.

Maintaining a calm and reassuring exterior, Ponzi did what con men typically do when faced with the truth – he sued the messenger. He filed a $5-million claim for damages from the *Post* and then, in the next breath, announced a $100-million international investment syndicate. Before he could get it off the ground, the Massachusetts State Banking Commission closed down his bank. Newspapers across the country jumped on the bandwagon, reminding the public of Ponzi's earlier scuffles with the Canadian authorities, while auditors went over his SEC's books with a fine-tooth comb. They quickly discovered that legitimate transactions were negligible. The grand total was a mere $30. Ponzi never even both-ered to put his international postal-reply coupon idea into effect.

His house of cards crumbled to the tune of $3 million. Ponzi went to jail for a few years in Massachusetts, was allowed out on parole, skipped and headed for Florida, where he set up a real-estate scam that earned him another trip to prison. At the time he admitted, "Only a fool would have a trusted a crook like me." Around 1930 or 1931, he was deported home to Italy. From there he made his way to Brazil, where, eventually, he died penniless.

His legacy is the "Ponzi scheme," and his ghost blithely lives on.

Gilbert Allen Ziegler, whose legacy is the misery and financial ruin he's inflicted on thousands of people who trusted him with their life savings, did Ponzi proud.

Born in Seattle in 1951, the heavy-set and balding Ziegler tells people he grew up in the Pacific Northwest, but is deliberately vague about much of his background. He claims to be a university graduate, but doesn't easily cough up the name of the school. It turns out that he attended Green River Community College in Auburn, Washington. He claims that in the 1970s he was the president of a business college, but doesn't name that school either. It turns out to be defunct. He also claims to be an ordained minister, and while he admits he never attended any sort of theological seminary or had any formal training, he doesn't go into the specifics of who ordained him. His c.v. also lists a master's of business degree and a doctorate, both unsourced.

By the 1980s, Ziegler was living in Hillsboro, Oregon, employed in "religious activities," his reference to a short period as a church admin-istrator. At various times, he says, he was a precinct committeeman for a local Democratic Party, a ballot status adviser for a local Libertarian Party, and a precinct committeeman for a local Republican Party. He claims to have taught economics, history of economic philosophy, advertising, and journalism. He says he was a partner in a Mexican fast-food restaurant, the founder and creative director of an advertising agency, a concert promoter, and the founder/president of a non-denominational organization of Christian fellowships.

He was also the architect of what the State of Oregon suspected was securities fraud. In the early 1990s, Ziegler began soliciting investors for an offshore newsletter. The special $150 "subscription" fee included the right to sell additional subscriptions for which investors would be paid a commission. New subscribers could then sell subscriptions to newer subscribers, ad infinitum. It was a typical pyramid scheme, but with a macabre twist. Ziegler would deposit all commissions in an offshore account on the Caribbean island of Nevis, where the money would be invested until the subscriber died. At that point, the account would be liquidated and paid to the subscriber's heirs. Some people fell for it. But the Oregon Attorney General's Office didn't and the scheme was taken apart. Ziegler was investigated for various violations, although no formal charges were lodged.

By then, he was unsuccessfully running the Hometown Mortgage Corporation. A brokerage business, it failed and toppled him into bankruptcy. Court records show he'd amassed personal debts of $1.14 million owed to 148 different companies. His assets were $28,440 including $20 in cash, $10 in a savings account, and $10 worth of Hometown shares. At the time he was driving three cars and owed $320,000 in back taxes. His explanation for the debacle puts the blame squarely on someone he names as "Reverend Gregory Peck."

According to him, Reverend Peck told the cops that Ziegler was running a fraudulent investment program because one of Ziegler's mates – whose wife was a Reverend Peck parishioner – had taken up with another woman and she wanted revenge. To help her, Reverend Peck duped the cops because Ziegler refused Reverend Peck a directorship in a bank he wouldn't form for another two years.

If it sounds convoluted – typical Ziegler-speak – that's because he always lays the blame for everything on someone else.

Leaving Oregon under that cloud, and with two failed marriages behind him, Ziegler pitched up in Hawaii, where he bought an existing offshore bank licence and changed the name of the company to Fidelity International Bank. Naming himself executive director, he abbreviated the name FIB, the play on words being totally appropriate as the bank was chartered in Nauru.

A Pacific Islands nation of less than eight square miles and barely ten thousand people, until the mid-1990s Nauru's most important export was phosphate. But they foolishly mismined it and the country tumbled perilously close to bankruptcy. They needed a new export, so the government opted for fraud.

Nauru's offshore banking sector was designed to be con-man friendly. In principle, licences were to be granted only to persons of sound financial standing with good reputations and sufficient expertise. In practice, they were granted to anyone willing to pay an initial fee of around $50,000 and to keep up the annual payments of around $1,000. For an extra $20,000, they would throw in an "investor passport," meaning citizenship for foreign clients. Thousands of passports were sold until international pressure so humiliated the government that the practice was stopped. But banking licences continued. No local directors were required and if you asked nicely they'd throw in an insurance licence at no extra charge. Minimal capitalization was set at a lowly $100,000 with two years after the licence grant to raise the money. Then you didn't have to show it to anybody. All Nauru required was an auditor's statement that it had been paid up. Any word-processing program and cheap ink-jet printer solved that problem.

There were annual reporting requirements but, again, no one in Nauru cared who audited your accounts as long as the letterhead looked real. Applicants also had to provide a reference from an accountant, auditor, or financial associate, who could affirm that the applicant had a net worth exceeding $250,000 in unencumbered assets.

In this case, the person applying for the charter – Ziegler – was bankrupt.

In 1998, the Russian Central Bank reported that $70 billion had been laundered through Nauru by Russian organized-crime groups. At the time, more than four hundred non-resident banks were registered there, all sharing the same mail-drop address. Around half were reputedly managed in the old Soviet bloc. Correspondent relationships with Nauru banks have turned up in criminal investigations throughout the former Soviet Union, especially Belarus, Chechnya, and the Ukraine. Just over one-third of the banks registered in Nauru were said to have been managed in the subcontinent and the Middle East, raising serious questions about Nauru's role in the funding of terrorist groups.

If there ever were any legitimate offshore banks in Nauru – a big *if* – they could be counted on one hand. In 2003, the government ran out of money and the lights on the island were turned off. They've revoked all the banking licences, and recalled all the passports they sold. Yet Nauru's well-deserved reputation as a money-laundering offending nation means that anything and everything chartered there must be considered "extremely suspect."

Ziegler's FIB was no exception. Within a year he claimed that the bank's net worth exceeded $200 million. But records show that Nauru licensed FIB on July 3, 1996, as a Class B bank, which meant that it could not legally function until it had a suitable correspondent relationship with a Class A bank somewhere else in the offshore world. Ziegler shopped around to set up such a bank in Belize, Barbados, and Antigua, but was turned down by all of them. It says a lot about Ziegler that even Antigua refused him, considering that government's lack of shame and the mass of inanities they have licensed.

That's when he noticed a shiny new welcome mat in Grenada. The Caribbean "spice island" nation of ninety thousand people was open for business. And by then, he'd met a man who knew how to make that business work.

Robert Earl Palm also claims to be an ordained preacher. Operating out of Victoria, British Columbia, he tells people he represents a coalition of Christian philanthropists, oversees some European trusts, and has advised both the Thai and Saudi royal families. Two years older than Ziegler, he, too, has been a bank director. But his United National Republic Bank (UNRB), which is supposedly based in Moscow, doesn't seem to be based anywhere. The Russians say they never heard of it, and in an official warning, Canada's Office of the Superintendent of Financial Institutions (OSFI) describes UNRB being of "unknown jurisdiction." As neither a licensed chartered bank in Canada, nor a registered representative office of a foreign bank operating in Canada, the OSFI says, "it may be operating in Canada in contravention of the Banking Act."

Palm and UNRB hit the headlines in 2003 when the Supreme Court of British Columbia finally caught up with them for a twelve-year-old matter. In 1991, using a company called Advance Capital Services Corp. and UNRB as guarantor of the deal, Palm purchased $300 million worth of potatoes and wheat flour from a consortium of Polish farmers. He said it was to send to Russia as humanitarian aid. The Poles shipped $37 million worth, which promptly disappeared. Two years later, still waiting to get paid, a Polish agricultural co-operative sued Palm, his partner

Jason Dallas, and Advance Capital Services. Palm was charged with criminal fraud in Poland but extradition from Canada never happened. Dallas, however, was extradited, convicted for fraud and spent four and a half years in prison.

By the time the Poles had their day in court in Canada, Dallas was in jail, Advance Capital Services had been struck off the companies' register, and, according to the judge, UNRB was not a normal licensed bank and had never operated as one. That left Palm to stand alone. The judge ruled he'd used Advance Capital Services "to effect a fraudulent purpose and to convey fraudulent misrepresentations," and ordered him to pay the Poles their $37 million.

Press reports in Canada allege that Palm has been the object of investigations for more than ten years by the Mounties, Revenue Canada, and police agencies in the States and Europe. Apparently, there is an ongoing racketeering investigation in the Ukraine over a $40-million rubles-for-dollars swap. A similar investigation for a similar currency swap is said to be underway in Finland.

To set up his deal in Poland, Palm and UNRB offered to lend $11 billion in hard currency to the Guangxi Trust & Investment Corp. in southern China. In return, the Chinese handed Palm some two hundred letters of credit, including $80 million written on an obscure Chinese bank on the island of Hainan. The Chinese never got their $11 billion, but Palm used $1 billion worth of this paper to guarantee the potato and wheat flour sale. Scotland Yard has since discovered twenty-two of these letters of credit, worth another $1 billion, in various scams. That leaves $9 billion in Chinese paper still floating around the offshore world.

The same people who have been investigating Ziegler for years allege – but have not proven – that Ziegler paid Palm $2 million for "business advice." If so, his lessons on "how to use phony paper to borrow assets which you put on the bank's books disguised as real assets against which you borrow real money" turned out to be worth the price.

In Grenada, those politicians and businessmen who had just turned the country into an offshore financial centre reckoned it was a great way to cure all that ailed them and ensure economic health. They intended to license a few companies and banks, then sit back and watch the money pour in. To manage it, they established the Offshore Financial

Services Division of the Ministry of Finance and installed Michael Creft to run it.

A crony of Prime Minister Keith Mitchell, Creft had been educated in Canada, worked for Agriculture Canada in Regina, and then spent fifteen years in Winnipeg, working for the Manitoba Department of Highways. His qualification for being named Grenada's first Registrar of Offshore Services was that he'd come home and needed a job.

When he looked closely at Grenada, Ziegler could hardly believe his luck. Here was an island of foolish amateurs perfectly ripe for plucking. Single-handedly, he was about to turn the place into the poster child for what happens to an offshore financial centre when the people running it don't have a clue what they're doing.

He waded ashore, introduced himself as CEO of First International Bank, and gave them a song and dance about creating jobs. He promised to bring wealth to the island by folding FIB into a new entity that he would call First International Bank of Grenada (FIBG), or First Bank for short. And just in case anybody in Grenada thought for a moment that he was legit – which, obviously, they did and which, clearly, he wasn't – he arrived sporting a passport issued by the Dominion of Melchizedek.

Unlike Nauru's designer-fraud "investor passport," this is utterly fake. Melchizedek's first address was the Isla de Malpelo, a rock in the Pacific that just happens to be owned by Colombia. Next, Melchizedek moved to Karitane, an island one thousand miles south of Tahiti, claiming to have purchased sovereignty from the Kingdom of Polynesia. Except the Kingdom doesn't exist and, anyway, Karitane is most of the time thirty feet under water. Other addresses have included Antarctica, Clipperton Island in the north Pacific, Solkope Island off Rotuma in the south Pacific, and Taongi Atoll, an uninhabited rock barrier owned by the Republic of the Marshall Islands.

Over the years, Hong Kong police arrested fraudsters trying to pass cheques drawn on Melchizedek banks; Texas issued cease-and-desist orders against Melchizedek insurance companies; British cops raided a company flogging a Melchizedek investment scheme backed by the German Weimar Republic; Philippines police arrested three people, including a British lawyer, for selling $1 million worth of Melchizedek passports at $3,500 each; two thousand investors in Singapore, Portugal, and the Caribbean lost millions of dollars in a fraud perpetrated by Credit Bank International of Melchizedek; and the SEC filed fraud charges against a lawyer and his investment advisory firm for running a Melchizedek bank Ponzi scheme.

The creation of David and Mark Pedley, a father-son team of multi-convicted felons, Melchizedek first appeared in the late 1980s when Mark, disguised as Consortium Finance Corporation, began selling banks chartered there. He added passports to his product line, then formed International Auditors, bogus chartered accountants, to provide fraudulent financial audits for those banks. He invented an embassy in Washington – the address is a mail drop, the phone number is an answering machine – and forty others around the world, professing accreditation to the United Nations, Canada, the Vatican, eight countries in Europe, five in the Pacific, five in Africa, plus Oklahoma, Kansas, Missouri, California, Chicago, a sovereignty called "Europe," and another called "Central America."

"Everything about Melchizedek is fraudulent," notes John Shockey, the legendary fraud expert from the U.S. Office of the Comptroller of the Currency. "Here you have a phony government consisting of fraudsters creating phony citizenships, ambassadorships, embassy and legation offices, issuing diplomatic passports, registering financial aid, granting business licences, and creating a stock exchange. There is absolutely nothing legitimate about Melchizedek."

Ziegler's Melchizedek passport introduced him as "Ambassador-at-Large to the Caribbean."

To capitalize FIBG, Grenada's banking laws required Ziegler to put up $2.2 million. Needless to say he didn't have it. But knowing that the regulator wouldn't look too closely, he produced documentation that suggested he could substantiate a claim to $500,000 cash and $17.25 million in publicly traded securities. Those turned out to be collateral for a loan that never happened and had simply never been returned. But even Ziegler must have been stupefied when regulator Creft didn't question the bank's biggest supposed asset – a $20-million, 10,000-carat carved ruby called Boy On Water Buffalo. Ziegler listed it on FIBG's books at the "fire sale" value of $15 million.

The only problems were Ziegler didn't own it; Ziegler didn't have any rights to it; and Ziegler never saw it.

What he provided to Creft was a photocopy of an appraisal for the ruby. Not the actual appraisal, which was suspect enough, but a photocopy. No original documentation has ever been produced by Ziegler, or anyone else, to support the valuation of the stone, or the assignment of it to him. In fact, when the FBI located the real owner of the ruby, they established beyond any doubt that the man had owned it for more than two decades, still owned it, had never given up any interest in it, and had never heard of Ziegler.

Besides that, a ruby is not a liquid asset and, under Grenada law, could not be used as initial capital. Yet, on October 9, 1997, Michael Creft licensed FIBG as Class I Offshore Bank #005.

Having reinvented FIB, Ziegler's next step was to reinvent himself. In addition to companies and banks, Grenada was also, in those days, dealing in one of the more shameful aspects of the offshore world, the sale of national sovereignty. Under the guise of "economic citizenship," Ziegler was allowed to buy a Grenadian passport. It cost $50,000 – a $22,000 fee to the treasury, a $17,000 donation to a government-approved project, and an $11,000 fee to an approved agent. Then, instead of having it issued to Gilbert Allen Ziegler – after all, he was already known as that in the States and in Melchizedek – he legally gave himself a new name, Van Arthur Brink.

The same people who have been investigating him for years, the ones who link him to Robert Earl Palm, say that what happened next clearly points to the influence of someone like Palm. And while Ziegler/Brink might think of himself as intelligent, they insist he is not smart enough to come up with the intricate rip-off that is FIBG.

First, he set up the International Deposit (re)Insurance Corporation in Nevis. Known as IDIC, the name is purposely similar to America's Federal Deposit Insurance Corporation (FDIC), inferring a relationship and/or suggesting that this is even better than the FDIC because it is the international version. He next announced that, as a result of "arm's-length negotiations" – his own words, which were plainly untrue – FIBG had entered into an agreement with IDIC to insure FIBG's depositors. In other words, your money is perfectly safe because IDIC says so. He claimed that as FIBG was holding over $200 in deposits for every $1 insured, IDIC had awarded the bank its "AAA Rating." Needless to say, the rating was as worthless as IDIC's insurance because Ziegler/Brink simply made it up.

After that, he set up a series of IBCs throughout the Caribbean, opening accounts for them in other jurisdictions, such as Jersey and Austria, to create the mirage of business activity and to obliterate money trails. To induce people to invest with FIBG, he established the Given In Freedom Trust (GIFT), a recreation of the subscription pyramid he'd worked in Oregon. He would ultimately claim that GIFT benefactors had accumulated $1 billion in the trust. It's not true.

Once that was done, he concocted the World Investors Stock Exchange (WISE). It was, he said, "An opportunity to create a market for venture capital in which the risk factor is reduced to negligible in order to help small businesses achieve seed capital and mezzanine-level financing in a world that is increasingly inhospitable to business formation and development financing."

Whatever that means.

In truth, WISE was yet another hollow promise of more insurance. Shares purchased through WISE were guaranteed by FIBG and IDIC, so that if the price fell below what the investor paid, IDIC would reimburse the loss. Besides the fact that there was never a secondary market for companies listed on WISE – meaning that once you bought shares there was no place to sell them – the companies he was flogging were described as "emerging," which means they probably couldn't get funding anyplace else, which says a lot about what these companies were emerging from and what they would end up emerging into.

At the same time, he began constructing a franchised network for his frauds. He helped his "agents" set up sub-banks of FIBG, many of them chartered in Grenada with the help of a company he formed there to act as a government agent for company licensing. The idea of the sub-banks was to create a conduit for income derived from frauds that would flow into FIBG, where the proceeds could be disguised as legitimate accounts. Most of FIBG's nearly two dozen sub-banks – such as Wellington Bank, Cambridge International Bank & Trust, Crown Meridian Bank, and Sattva Bank – were run by alleged fraudsters, previously convicted fraudsters, or since convicted fraudsters.

Ziegler/Brink now brought potential victims to Grenada, put them up at a good hotel, wined and dined them, dazzled them with white sand beaches and scuba diving, confirmed their worst fears about oppressive government tax regimes, set up accounts for them, and helped himself to their money. He assured them that, in addition to IDIC's insurance of their funds, FIBG maintained cash, cash equivalent instruments, and gold held at various international banks, including gold-bullion Certificates of Deposit (CDs) from Union Bank of Switzerland. The documentation for the UBS gold turned out to be photocopies of photocopies. And in any case, banks do not issue gold-bullion CDs. Nevertheless, he bragged, "I know of no other bank in the world which operates with First Bank's underlying financial strength in support of its obligations to depositors."

Sadly, in that regard, he was wrong. The offshore world is filled with banks whose underlying support of its obligations to depositors are just as fraudulent as his.

Sadder, too, during a twenty-five-month span – from March 1998 to April 2000 – Ziegler/Brink was able to pull off one of the most spectacular financial rapes in the history of the offshore world.

⟿

His game was nothing more than basic "Prime Bank" fraud.

Estimated by the U.S. government to be a $2.5-billion-a-year global scam – thriving and flourishing offshore – it's based on the totally bogus assumption that certain banks and governments will pay other banks and governments annual interest rates in the 100 to 500 per cent range for well-kept-secret reasons.

A typical script goes like this:

The government of Japan, realizing that its largest commercial banks are about to go bankrupt, has put together a pool of fifteen major international banks – so-called "prime banks" – to rescue the economy. Through them, Japan is offering $12 billion worth of financial instruments, at a guaranteed 12.5 per cent interest per month. That's 150 per cent a year. However, while the Japanese stand firmly behind the debt, and the fifteen prime banks are entitled to a tightly regulated 2.5 per cent monthly commission on every $10 million instrument they sell, there are two important restrictions legally placed on any bank's participation. First, no bank can sell any of these instruments to any entity other than a foreign government or another prime bank. And second, no bank or government involved in this can ever admit publicly that these financial instruments exist.

With that in mind, an offshore bank makes it known through its agents onshore that it has miraculously tapped into this lucrative market and obtained a portfolio of these ultra-high interest notes. Understanding how the average investor cannot possibly pay $10 million for one, the offshore bank has subdivided each parcel into $100,000 tranches. After it takes a mere 1 per cent commission per month, investors are invited to reap $9,000 monthly interest on each $100,000 investment.

It goes without saying that anyone with half a brain should instantly question 9 per cent monthly interest on anything. But, by combining a "risk-free" element – each investments is guaranteed by IDIC – and the aura of something clandestine, even a mediocre con man can erase common sense with greed.

You must remember, comes his caveat, that the secrecy clause forbids governments and banks from acknowledging the existence of these unique and exclusive investment opportunities. And even if they were allowed to tell you about them, they wouldn't because they don't want you in on it. Various governments and prime banks have conspired to keep this for themselves. Therefore, if you pick up the phone and ring a prime bank, or if you ask a government agency about this, they will go blue in the face telling you it doesn't exist. They will probably even try to frighten you away by saying it's nothing more than a con game.

As unlikely as it sounds, thousands of people fall for variations on this absurdity every day. They phone a bank, ask about ultra-high-yield interest investments, are assured by someone that they don't exist, and instantly conclude that the guy at the offshore bank who offered this unique and exclusive opportunity was right, governments and prime banks are covering up, so obviously this stuff does exist.

For every site on the Net warning the public about prime bank fraud – the RCMP (http://www.rcmp.ca/scams/primeinvest_e.htm); *Offshore Alert* (http://www.offshorebusiness.com); the U.S. Securities and Exchange Commission (www.sec.gov/divisions/enforce/ primebank.shtml); Quatloos (www.quatloos.com); and the Office of the Comptroller of the Currency (http://www.occ.treas.gov) – there are literally thousands that beckon investors to lose their money.

In the beginning, Ziegler/Brink targeted his marketing to members of evangelical churches in Canada and the States, showing a special affinity for pensioners. He shamelessly played off their financial insecurities and religious beliefs, claiming, as he did in one video, "God means for everyone to have the kind of freedom that comes with wealth." Before long, he turned his attention to other groups, ultimately abandoning all of them to take money from anyone at all foolish enough to give it to him.

He also turned double-talk into an art form. In a lengthy exchange of e-mails with journalist John Greenwood of Canada's *National Post*, Ziegler/Brink displayed considerable skills, explaining how FIBG could offer such ultra-high interest rates on deposits.

It came down to "understanding what you can do and by leveraging." He wrote, "I discovered that there are holders of major assets (in the hundreds of millions of dollars and in the billions of dollars) that are willing to deed those assets to a bank for a price, the price including a joint venture contract on sharing the profits that could be achieved by the effective utilization of those assets."

His formula for success was: "(1) create credit lines against the assets; (2) utilize the credit lines to achieve a profit; (3) do it some more."

To acquire $200 million in deposits, he tried to make Greenwood believe, it might cost $500,000 in special service company formation and operating expenses, $500,000 in bank operating expenses, and $1 million in acquisition costs. "As a result, the bank has achieved an enormous amount of potential leverage for its initial investment. I use the word potential because it is unrealized gain at this point. If you do nothing with the asset, you still haven't realized a cash-in-hand profit (although you have an enormous paper profit)."

With that $200 million, Ziegler/Brink promised, he could easily achieve an 80 per cent loan against assets, producing $160 million. "I know mortgage brokers in Oregon who do nothing but buy and sell first and second mortgages and earn not less than 70 per cent per annum on their working capital."

This from a mortgage broker who went bankrupt.

Earning 20 per cent per annum on the $160 million, he claimed, produces an income of $32 million. Paying $16 million as cost of the credit line, then splitting the rest with a joint-venture partner leaves $8 million. Paying 200 per cent interest to his depositors, claiming this represents the initial $2 million, takes $4 million out of the pot, leaving $4 million as "net-net-net profit."

It is, of course, unadulterated bullshit.

Enter now the Ponzi element.

If the risk-free investment isn't paid out early on, word spreads that the whole thing is bogus. Ziegler/Brink needed to take care of the first people in, paying them the published high interest in order to entice new pigeons into the game. The faster the game gets – the more Peters that sign up, in principle creating more money to pay Paul – the slower the payments are to those who are actually getting something out of it. Excuses about faulty wire transfers and mistakes by distant correspondent banks fend off people looking for their money. By the time most of them open their eyes to the scheme, the bank has folded and the culprits have gone to Uganda.

Which is exactly what happened.

If you believe in fate, then it's easy to assume that David Marchant's path in life was always destined to cross Ziegler/Brink's because while Ziegler/Brink was learning his trade as an offshore con man, Marchant was learning his as an investigative journalist who hunts down offshore con men.

Born in South Wales, Marchant studied journalism in Cardiff and began his reporting career in the Welsh valleys, covering the violent miners' strikes of the 1980s. Ten years later, in search of new stories and better weather, he emigrated to Bermuda, where he spent six years annoying officialdom by exposing their follies. He wrote about local businessmen stripping Bermuda Fire & Marine Insurance of $40 million before the company went belly up. He exposed dubious share listings on the Bermuda Stock Exchange. He wrote about Bermuda's best and brightest and hung out their dirtiest financial laundry, until he'd finally upset so many people that the government lifted his work permit.

In 1996, he pitched up in Miami, started a newsletter called *Offshore Alert* – and a sister publication called *Inside Bermuda*, because he's not the kind of guy to let go that easily – and is still pissing off a lot of people. Being an equal-opportunity offender, he fearlessly takes on crooked banks, phony shell companies, and corrupt governments throughout the offshore world.

Marchant was the first journalist to target Ziegler/Brink. And predictably, when Ziegler/Brink fought back, Ziegler/Brink lost.

"It wasn't exactly the greatest piece of detective work in the world," Marchant admits. "You know, figuring out that Van Brink was running a scam. I mean, come on, he was offering 250 per cent interest rates. What was ingenious about it, however, was how he used FIBG as a marketing ploy, how he obtained banking licences for his mates, and set up those sub-banks. He understood that by franchising his fraud, the brokers who owned the sub-banks would double their efforts to raise money for him because they were also doing it for their own bank."

Within days of Marchant's first exposé of Ziegler/Brink, a major Florida law firm filed a $100-million libel suit against him. On behalf of Ziegler/Brink, they accused Marchant of "deliberate lies, innuendoes, unsubstantiated allegations and misleading statements." They also tried to injunct him from further exposing their client, but the court refused to grant them a hearing on that. Just as Ponzi had tried it on with the *Boston Post* – and Marc Harris had with Marchant, as well – Ziegler/Brink was using the courts as a truncheon to beat up a journalist. The con-man's gamble is that most journalists can't afford to defend a suit and learn to steer clear. But Marchant stood his ground and a court date was set. Ziegler/Brink did not file his action on time and never appeared. Inevitably, his attorneys advised Marchant that the action would not be pursued.

Ziegler/Brink accuses Marchant of being in the pocket of the FBI, and/or the CIA, and/or competing banks, and/or unnamed evil doers who were determined to put him out of business. In his own head, conspiracy theories abound.

Sifting through the massive amount of self-aggrandizement that Ziegler/Brink has posted on the Internet, you find stories laced with secret meetings, mysterious go-betweens who have sought his advice on how to solve all the world's problems, and mistaken identity. Someone called Gil Ziegler who was once involved in a gold scam is not him, someone called Zig Ziegler who was selling a suspect investment scheme is not his brother Zig. He rationalizes his perpetual victim-mode with pure Ziegler-speak. Just because he has a caring heart, he says, and just because he simply wanted to help the common man, the big banks despised him, the press lied about him, the auditors hated him, and governments deliberately set out to get him. When it was discovered that the hard drive of his laptop computer in Grenada was bookmarked with

Internet porn sites, he needed the world to understand that those book-marks were put there by some poor kid he'd kindly hired to teach him how to use the computer.

He says his current troubles began in 1999. "Less than thirty days after writing and widely circulating a paper highly critical of the Organisation for Economic Co-operation and Development (OECD) Council's report on 'Harmful Tax Competition,' I became the target of a well-financed Florida Internet writer determined to smear First Bank and me with (seemingly plausible, but wholly unsubstantiated) allega-tions of being a fraud and operating a Ponzi scheme (can't be the case, since total deposits are less than one per cent of the bank's retained earn-ings/net worth) or money laundering (also can't be the case, since it is impossible for private international banks to absorb cash deposits – all funds must come in by way of wire transfers or cheques drawn on com-mercial banks which 'know' their customers and are satisfied as to the non-criminal origin of funds)." The parentheses are his.

Marchant just laughs. "He's always got someone else to blame. Sure, everyone's out to get him because he attended a conference and sub-mitted a seminal paper on how the countries of the world are ripping everyone off. Come on, he was perpetrating one of the crudest frauds imaginable and ruined a lot of people's lives. But, don't forget, he never could have managed it had the government of Grenada not let it happen. Someone told me you could literally put your right hand on FIBG's front door and put your left hand on the regulator's office door."

❧

It is possible that certain people on the island believed Ziegler/Brink was an original thinker who could work magic in the global economy. It is more likely that certain people on the island had a relationship with him that constituted a conflict of interest.

Prime candidate for villain-in-chief is the former regulator, Michael Creft.

A soft-spoken man who is clearly not comfortable discussing the scandal, he says there's no question that, if he had it to do all over again, Ziegler/Brink would never have been granted a licence. "But, remem-ber, Grenada had just started, just come into this business, we didn't have enough experience."

Oddly, Creft states that when Ziegler/Brink filed for FIBG's licence, he asked the FBI for a background check. In all the paperwork on the matter, there doesn't seem to be any mention of the FBI's involvement in Grenada's fledgling regulatory due diligence. But Creft insists it was done. He also says the report sent back from Washington "wasn't bad, it wasn't damning." As far as he can recall, it made no mention of Ziegler/Brink's bankruptcy. "They did say he had some problem in Oregon, but they didn't say bankrupt."

When you mention David Marchant's name to Creft, he comments, "Marchant was a fellow who was just after us." Then he thinks about that for a moment and backtracks. "Certainly Marchant caused us to do some hard thinking on this whole thing."

But hard thinking didn't happen until late in the game and Marchant was writing about the bank right from the beginning. He exposed IDIC – which was publicly claiming to provide up to $100 million in coverage – pointing out that it was not licensed in Nevis as an insurer. Certainly the regulators on that island did some hard thinking because they started asking questions about the word *insurance* in IDIC's name.

Ziegler/Brink took Marchant seriously also, telling the regulators in Nevis that IDIC was not an insurance company but an administrator of assets for member banks. When asked to name the member banks, he refused, citing secrecy agreements. The truth of the matter is, he couldn't name them because there weren't any, besides FIBG and the sub-banks. No legitimate bank was ever found to be a client of IDIC, which is hardly surprising, considering that IDIC was nothing more than a garden-variety shell company with no offices and no employees. But FIBG's clients didn't know that Ziegler/Brink wasn't going to tell them and Michael Creft didn't seem to want to find out for himself.

To keep the regulator in Nevis happy, Ziegler/Brink changed the name to International Deposit Indemnity Corporation. Even then, IDIC would still be in violation of Nevis law if indemnity meant insurance. Which it clearly did. So on January 26, 1999, the Nevis Ministry of Finance shut it down. Ziegler/Brink arranged to reopen it in Dominica. When Dominica said no, he brought it to Grenada.

On January 29, Marchant's *Offshore Alert* detailed more wrongdoings at FIBG, WISE, IDIC, and other parts of Ziegler/Brink's empire. Four days later, Creft faxed Marchant: "No company registered and/or doing business under the Laws of Grenada has been involved in any alleged wrongdoing." Creft cleared both WISE and IDIC of illicit dealings, despite the fact that IDIC had been put out of business in Nevis for illicit dealings. Creft concluded, "We have no complaints or allegations of wrongdoing made by offshore investors in the State of Grenada."

Two weeks later, on February 12, Creft wrote a letter to Marchant, reconfirming what he'd already said. As far as he was concerned, FIBG was operating wholly within the law. "This office has not received one substantiated complaint concerning its banking operations."

Creft reiterated that he did not see any proof of wrongdoing at IDIC, and was somewhat surprised that Nevis had taken such drastic action. He said, if real evidence of fraud or misconduct were to be forthcoming, he would act accordingly to law. However, he warned, "reckless smear campaigns hurt not only offshore companies but also the Government and the people of Grenada and casts aspersions on the integrity of our jurisdiction."

Tellingly, this letter was not mailed to Marchant on the stated date, but faxed to him at five o'clock in the morning from a fax number – which appears on the top of each page of Creft's letter – registered to FIBG. The suggestion is that Creft never intended it for Marchant's consumption. Instead, it was for FIBG to file with their court documents as part of Ziegler/Brink's lawsuit against Marchant.

Creft was aware, by then, that FIBG was offering unrealistic interest rates because he was quoted as saying, "I don't know how they do it." He now says that FIBG's ultra-high interest rates did, indeed, worry him at the time. "I was very concerned." But he never showed much concern. One suspects that a serious regulator faced with transparent fraud might have made some inquiries. Instead, on February 24, Creft wrote that he had never received any complaints from depositors of First Bank, or any other parties with a financial interest in First Bank. "First Bank has not engaged in any such wrongdoing or suspicious circumstances and therefore has never been investigated."

Yet, Nevis had shut down IDIC, the Comptroller of the Currency in Washington had issued an official warning that First Bank was illegally soliciting deposits in the United States, and the Financial Institutions Commission in British Columbia had issued a cease-and-desist order against FIBG, IDIC, and several sub-banks.

Much later, in e-mail correspondence between Ziegler/Brink and some of FIBG's directors, it would be revealed that "$30,000 was loaned to purchase a new car for Michael Creft's significant other who called in desperate need for many months running."

Creft gets very nervous when that subject is broached. Taking "significant other" to mean wife, he categorically denies it, noting that his wife lives in Canada and never had anything to do with FIBG, Ziegler/Brink, or a car loan. Translating "significant other" to mean girlfriend brings the response, "I heard about the loan, somebody asked me, but I don't know anything about that." Eventually he remembers, "There was a friend of mine I knew who used to work with Van Brink. She's the one . . . nothing to do with me. She worked for Van Brink."

By March 1999, FIBG was late in submitting its accounts to the government. Lauriston Wilson, whose local accounting firm served as the bank's auditors, was having trouble getting information out of Ziegler/Brink. He became so frustrated that he voiced his concerns to the prime minister. Keith Mitchell said he wanted something in writing, so on March 26, Wilson wrote a letter to him questioning Creft's competence and honesty, and urging the prime minister to remove Creft from office.

Mitchell now phoned Wilson at home. Transcripts of Wilson's conversations with the prime minister were lodged in court. According to them, Wilson told Mitchell that FIBG's accounts led him to believe that the bank was capitalized at just $2, and that FIBG lacked proper internal controls and accounting systems. Wilson said he had evidence that Ziegler/Brink was cooking the books by listing depositors' funds as revenue. He says he told the prime minister that the operations of the bank "are bogus and fictitious."

Wilson also accused Ziegler/Brink of refusing to provide details of the bank's assets, and of seriously obstructing the audit. He explained that, after reviewing FIBG's bizarre roster of assets – including Egyptian antiquities, pre–Ming Dynasty vases, $8.7 billion worth of suspect gold certificates, and photocopies of paperwork valuing the $20-million ruby – he asked Ziegler/Brink to show him the actual assets. Instead, Ziegler/Brink handed Wilson photographs and photocopied appraisal certificates.

After insisting that the bank was in complete violation of several provisions of Grenada's Offshore Banking Act – including a purported

$200,000 campaign donation to Mitchell's New National Party – Wilson told the prime minister that everything had taken place with the full knowledge of the Registrar of Offshore Financial Services. He accused Michael Creft of failing to take the necessary corrective action, maintained that Creft's demeanour betrayed total ignorance of his responsibilities, and concluded that Creft is "apparently corrupt."

Mitchell was utterly shocked, although not utterly shocked enough to fire Creft, because his party executive saw Creft as a loyal member.

Instead, Ziegler/Brink fired Wilson. He also demanded that Wilson return the bank's accounts. Wilson later claimed that the prime minister expressly asked him to hold on to the accounts, so that the government could investigate them. The prime minister denies it. Ziegler/Brink sued and the court ruled that Wilson had to return the accounts. By the time the liquidators arrived, important documentation – which Wilson says was returned by him to Ziegler/Brink – was long gone.

As all this was played out publicly, Creft could no longer deny that accusations had been lodged against FIBG by someone in a position to know the truth. He now suggests, "I did speak to some FBI people then about this. Sometime around that time. But after that, we become very suspicious of everything." He persists, "I was asking him [Ziegler/Brink] serious questions and I threatened to revoke the licence because he was not complying with some of the regulations."

Still, the bank stayed open for another sixteen months. "That's true," Creft agrees, "but remember, things here . . . we don't do things quickly here. There were lots of communications asking for information and asking –" He stops, then indicates, "It wasn't just me, there was a board, and I was asking directions of the board about what to do."

With Wilson no longer his auditor, Ziegler/Brink needed someone to sign off on the bank's accounts. He approached several firms, but they all turned him down. He then sought the advice of an acquaintance "who used to be a CPA." According to Ziegler/Brink, after the used-to-be CPA admitted he'd served time in prison for bank fraud, he introduced Ziegler/Brink to a man named Kenneth Nelson Craig, another used-to-be CPA, whose licence had been revoked in California in 1996. The two used-to-be CPAs prepared the report together. It's Craig's name that appears on two similar versions of FIBG's "un-audited" annual report for 1998. Issued on the same day, one comes from Craig personally, still representing himself as a CPA with an address in Nevada, the other comes from Kenneth Craig and Associates, with an address in Guadalajara, Mexico.

The report is unmitigated fiction, misstating and misrepresenting the capitalization and assigned assets, and referring to trading that never took place. One declared asset is shares of an unlisted stock. The cost is put at $850,000. The current value is put at $507 million, a figure pulled out of thin air. Another asset listed is $3.8 billion in cheques drawn on Dai-Ichi Kangyo Bank. Except they weren't cheques, they were photocopies of cheques, and a set of the same photocopies were later found at another insolvent bank in another jurisdiction. The City of London Fraud Squad reports that these Dai-Ichi cheques are forged and have been showing up for years. Best of all, in the report, Ziegler/Brink claims to have increased the bank's capital from $110,000 to $14 billion, and states that net income had reached $26 billion. The assertion is so outlandish that, had it been true, FIBG would have been in the same class as Chicago's Bank One Corp., the fifth-largest bank in the United States. But no one in Grenada challenged this.

On July 23, 1999, with David Marchant tenaciously on the case, after months of relentless allegations about the bank, and despite Wilson's warnings to the prime minister, Mitchell proclaimed FIBG to be sound. He said his government had asked the FBI to look into the operations of FIBG and, based on correspondence he'd received from them, there was nothing irregular about the bank. "We had not received any indication as to any illegality on the part of the bank at this particular time."

Three days later, a press release was issued in the names of FIBG, IDIC, and WISE entitled "First Bank Says Thanks." In it, Ziegler/Brink redefines irony with, "It is nothing short of breath-taking how some people will try to exploit someone's unfortunate situation for their personal gain."

Later, misquoting the prime minister, Ziegler/Brink told at least one journalist, "The FBI had concluded that there was no evidence of money-laundering or other criminal activities on the part of First Bank."

By then, Ziegler/Brink was already planning a hasty exit stage left, creating an infrastructure for himself in Uganda, using FIBG's fund to purchase more than $4 million in properties. Presumably, he was also stashing money somewhere as well. To help smooth his landing in Africa, he called on Creft.

In a July 27 letter, written on the official stationery of the Registrar of Offshore Services, Creft told the chairman of the Parliamentary Committee on the National Economy for the Republic of Uganda, "According to audited financial statements submitted by the bank [FIBG], it is in a healthy financial state." That Creft would have written the letter to begin with is odd. That he misrepresented the facts by saying that FIBG's accounts were "audited" is sinister.

"In retrospect," Creft says, "I wouldn't do that again. They had . . . up to that time, while I had a lot of misgivings, concerns about Van Brink and his operation . . . there were people in Grenada who . . . I didn't have enough . . . I wouldn't do that again. That was a mistake."

Marchant was now screaming that the jig was up. "First International Bank of Grenada makes a mockery of the island as a legitimate financial centre."

In a desperate effort to feign legitimacy, Ziegler/Brink offered to guarantee depositors' funds by posting a $50-million bond with the government. The financial instruments he proposed to put up were drawn on an obscure Chinese bank on the island of Hainan.

Shades of Robert Palm.

Ziegler/Brink resigned as CEO and some of his henchmen stepped in to run the day-to-day operations. And still the island authorities clung like rats to this sinking ship. Creft wrote to Ziegler/Brink – again on official letterhead – that the U.S. government had cleared FIBG of any wrongdoing. "The FBI carried out an investigation into the activities, procedures and associations of First Bank. They also made inquiries and checks with respect to the source of many deposits. I can confirm that the result of this investigation has exonerated First Bank regarding the allegations. The procedures adopted by First Bank with respect to all deposits are more than adequate to ensure that all deposits received into the Bank are clean funds and from legitimate sources."

Three weeks later, the U.S. Justice Department informed the island's authorities that they were still investigating FIBG for fraud, had seen evidence that supported the claim, and offered FBI assistance in raiding FIBG's offices. The raid never took place because the government wouldn't allow it.

On December 14, 1999, the pressure on Creft was so great that he finally asked Ziegler/Brink to respond to the general tone of the allegations that had appeared in the press throughout that year.

Already in exile in Uganda, Ziegler/Brink answered with a twenty-six-page rambling monograph entitled, "Overview of the Quasi-Facts Used to Support the Allegation that Van A. Brink and/or First International Bank of Grenada Limited is Operating a Ponzi Scheme, an Illegal Pyramid Scheme and/or a Money Laundering Facility."

Besides laying the blame for injurious and unfounded allegations squarely on a conspiracy between the FBI, the SEC, and David Marchant, he announced that FIBG "has now accumulated over $60,000,000,000 (not a typo, $60 billion) in profits held in cash equivalent instruments issued by top 100 banks."

His parenthesized "not a typo, $60 billion" claim suggested that FIBG had somehow made an additional $34 billion in just nine months. That, too, went unchallenged by the Grenadians. Ziegler/Brink supported this absurdity with the explanation that the increase in net income came about thanks to a secret side of Grenada's banking system, one that other banks purposely hid on their balance sheets. He wrote, "First Bank has a cash equivalent base equal to over 600 times the total amount of its liabilities to depositors."

He also hit out at Marchant's allegations. "A Ponzi scheme? No. Just a bank that chose to report accurately on its balance sheet those matters other banks long ago decided to keep on an 'off ledger' basis. Naive, perhaps, but not dishonest, unethical, immoral, unlawful or illegal."

Undoubtedly, Ziegler/Brink saw the big cash-crunch finale waiting in the wings and desperately tried to finagle $3.8 billion from Malaysia to pay for humanitarian projects in something he referred to as the G77 countries. The proposed collateral were two financial instruments drawn on an Asian bank. When that didn't happen, he went shopping for $21.6 billion, this time for a free-trade zone and health centre in Uganda, soya products in Brazil, and a buffalo ranch in Canada. This time the collateral would be "top rated cash-equivalent instruments that have been deeded to First Bank."

As his various associates began to flee, others took their place. A man described as "a little-known chartered accountant from Yorkshire" came along to do an audit and a report issued in his name – but without his signature – and branded the bank hunky-dory.

Marchant shot back that the audit "triggers disbelief."

To secure his own financial future, Ziegler/Brink tried to buy a co-operative bank from the Uganda government. But his arrival in the country had been greeted with the local newspaper headline: "CONMAN ON THE RUN," and he was turned down on the grounds that he was not a qualified banker. Ziegler/Brink claimed to have negotiated an $80-million deal with a Congolese rebel leader for control over mineral resources in an area that the rebel group controls. He also claimed to have negotiated a $16-million deal with another rebel leader who agreed to appoint Ziegler/Brink to run the nation's central bank, should the rebel group come to power.

By April 2000, the flow of funds from FIBG had come to a halt.

Throughout that spring and summer, the authorities in Grenada refused to believe they'd been had. When they assigned the former accountant general as interim administrator, he reported that millions of dollars were missing and that several millions had been transferred to Uganda.

At the time, the annual jazz festival was taking place on the island, sponsored in part by FIBG. So the government – finally conceding defeat – politely waited until the jazz festival ended before putting the bank out of business.

Apparently someone thought it would look bad if they did it while the music was still playing.

For years, the Eastern Caribbean has been a sink for dirty banks and suspect shell companies. Grenada dragged the region's reputation to a new low.

At one point, in one of the most dim-witted decisions in the history of offshore finance, the government of Grenada actually agreed to grant a new licence to the people running FIBG, calling the Mark II version First International Bank of Grenada 2000. Somehow, better advice prevailed. They revoked Ziegler/Brink's citizenship and a Grenada court formally accused him of stealing $150 million.

The government then set about making substantial reforms to their offshore industry. Seventeen banks directly affiliated with FIBG were shut down. A few months later, they closed six more. Most of the rest of their offshore banks have been shut one by one. Only a couple of the original twenty-nine remain. The government revoked the law that allowed them to sell economic citizenship, amended their banking and companies acts, accepted Michael Creft's resignation – he announced he was doing it for purely personal reasons, so that he could pursue other interests – and established the Grenada Industrial Development Corporation to put in place a more serious regulatory infrastructure.

Hoping to salvage something out of this mess, the government turned to a man who actually knows what he's doing. They appointed Marcus A. Wide, of PricewaterhouseCoopers in Halifax, Nova Scotia, as liquidator. Enormously experienced in the ways of the Caribbean, Wide recognized immediately, "FIBG was a sham from its inception."

In three well-documented reports, Wide describes the fraudulent chaos in which the bank operated. He says that Ziegler/Brink's only intentions were to mislead depositors and to use their funds to line his own pockets. He says that depositors were subject to fraudulent misrepresentation with respect to investment opportunities, and that funds received by FIBG should now be considered proceeds of crime.

As of mid-2003, Wide has found less than $500,000 in assets, although he calculates that the bank took around $125 million in deposits from about six thousand victims of Ziegler/Brink's criminality.

"Brink was indiscriminate about who he sucked money from. Many of his victims were pensioners who were just scraping by, and put their life savings into this, looking for a better lifestyle. Now they have absolutely nothing. And Brink doesn't give a shit. He's a disgusting man. He's the worst of the lot. He's repellent."

The only reason that Ziegler/Brink is not in jail, Wide says, is because he's in Uganda and there's no extradition. But he promises, "It's just a matter of time. Sooner or later, we will get him."

At the end of 2002, Wide obtained a judgment in Grenada against Ziegler/Brink for theft of $125 million. In February 2003, a court in Uganda recognized that judgment, allowing Wide to go after properties there. "He says he doesn't own them, but we've got the trail that clearly says he does. We've now frozen them, so he can't sell them."

Wide also believes that Ziegler/Brink has stashed money somewhere and can't get to it without tipping his hand. "He did such a good job of raping and pillaging, and a great job of putting blinds in the way, using payment centres through which money flowed, that it's very difficult to trace the money. We figure he probably got away with $20 million."

Expressing some sympathy for the islanders — "They didn't appreciate the extent to which they were opening doors to the crooks and thugs and liars and cheats" — Wide concedes they were done in by a masterful scheme. "Out of the thirty-something banks that I'm involved with down there, as a liquidator and receiver, this is the best scam I have seen, by far." Wide is not convinced, however, that Ziegler/Brink came up with it all by himself. "The guy's not that smart. He was nothing but a petty fraudster from way back. I think he learned a lot of this stuff from someone else."

Whether Ziegler/Brink, or anyone else, ever goes to jail for this is up to law enforcement. With the agreement of the courts in Grenada, Wide has made all of FIBG's records, and all of the records of the subsidiary companies, available to the FBI.

Hiding in Uganda, Ziegler/Brink clearly hopes he's out of reach. Just in case, he married a local woman half his age, which, blissful love aside, means he can't now be extradited. Along with his bride comes the possibility of an Ugandan passport. But then, Ziegler/Brink apparently doesn't see any reason why he might be extradited. He maintains that he wasn't the owner of FIBG, just the guiding spirit.

In yet another protracted e-mail to John Greenwood at the *National Post*, Ziegler/Brink waxes lyrical, "Isaac Newton may have not legally owned the Law of Gravity, but when he spoke of it and wrote as concerning it and made recommendations to others as pertaining to it, people tended to listen. He was looked up to as a father, legal ownership notwithstanding. . . . I was looked up to as a father, legal ownership notwithstanding."

He steadfastly maintains that he's not to blame for anything, that everybody else is out to get him, and that, obviously, they did because he's penniless.

When con men get caught out, many of them run a second scam off the back of the first. As long as there are enough defrauded investors clamouring for their money, it's not usual to see someone pop up with an investors' reclamation group. True to form, Ziegler/Brink is doing just that in various Internet forums, hiding behind the alias Ira M. Samuels.

Introducing himself as a fellow investor who's lost money, Samuels explains that he's organizing a team of private detectives, lawyers, accountants, butchers, bakers, and candlestick makers – he never gives specifics and refuses to name names – in order to help get everyone's money back. Ever altruistic, he's doing this for the common good of the human race, and has recently been assured by his team that they are ready to pounce. Like-minded defrauded investors who want to share the booty are invited to split expenses with him.

Which means, send money.

Writing in the same forums under his own name, Ziegler/Brink berates Wide, constantly proclaims his innocence, sings the praises of Ira M. Samuels, and swears that he is ready, willing, and able to do whatever he can to see that First Bank's creditors get their money back. One e-mail even contains his firm promise that he would happily return to Grenada to sort out the problems if someone would simply cover his expenses.

Marcus Wide heard about that and quickly took Ziegler/Brink up on his offer.

But safety in Uganda remains the better part of valour.

As Ziegler/Brink explained it in his answer to Wide: "I have to devote on an average of ten hours a day to generate a living. I have yet to take a twenty-hour airline commute to a destination, spend a day or two there and return twenty hours and not be sick in bed for the following week (and that is flying business class, not economy class – I think in economy class I would require hospitalization on both ends of the flight). Therefore, financially and for reasons of physical health, I say 'No, thank you.'"

10

CABLETRAP

*"Without bank secrecy, the Cayman Islands
would be a fishing community again."*

– former Caymans banker John Mathewson

Gordon Ryan owned a hot-dog
cart on a street corner in downtown Jersey City, New Jersey.
One dog with sauerkraut and mustard, please . . .
It was called Gordon's Hotdogs.
. . . one Dr. Pepper . . .
And for a while, business really boomed.
. . . oh yeah, and a pirate cable box to go.

The Grenadians were pure amateurs who learned some expensive
lessons at the hands of Ziegler/Brink. Instead, they should have taken a
few classes in the Caymans, where learning to fly below the radar is a
required course.

John Mathewson had served in the U.S. Marine Corps and afterwards
ran his own construction company in Chicago. Closing in on his fifty-
second birthday, around 1980, Mathewson decided he'd made enough
money to retire. After all those Midwest winters, it's understandable
why he chose someplace warm like the Western Caribbean. But there
was more to his choice than just sunshine and scuba diving. He had it in
his head to start a second career. This time he was going to be a banker.
And the Caymans was a very good place to do just that. Little did he

know when he moved there that, one day, a New Jersey hot dog would ruin his life.

The first thing Mathewson did after buying a shell bank called Argosy was look around for a more suitable name. He settled on Guardian Bank and Trust Company because there were at least eleven other banks around the world called Guardian and he knew that by creating a bit of confusion, it would be that much more difficult for someone to trace any transactions back to his Guardian.

"This was a key concern," he said later, "because offshore banks in small jurisdictions, by necessity, conduct most of their transactions through international payment systems and need to find ways to minimize detection and disclosure of client information."

Unlike many companies and banks registered in the Caymans in those days, Guardian did have a physical presence, renting office space on the second floor of a downtown low-rise building. The law obliged that his clients be foreigners, but that wasn't a problem because he'd always intended to go after a European clientele. Yet, owning a bank was one thing, bringing customers in was another and no matter what he did, he couldn't secure enough European business to stay open.

Worried for his own investment, he turned to the North American market, advertising heavily in U.S. and Canadian in-flight magazines. His ads hinted that he could help make income tax "an optional matter." Though he never came right out and said, We'll help you evade taxes, he didn't have to. He couched his sales pitches in the usual lingo of "asset protection." And it worked. By 1990, Mathewson would claim to hold $350 million in deposits. More than 90 per cent of his clients were American, of whom 95 per cent were there specifically to evade taxes.

"Without U.S. clients, there wouldn't be a banking industry in the Cayman Islands," he said later. "It is ridiculous to think that anyone would establish an offshore account without tax evasion as the motive."

⌒

Long before Mathewson invented Guardian or Gordon started selling hot dogs, America was wiring-up for cable television.

Even though it took more than a decade, and even though most of the rest of the world opted for satellite, by the 1980s an abundance of sports, movies, cooking, all-news channels, and all-night porn – but especially CNN, HBO, ESPN, Cinemax, Showtime, pay-per-view events, and porn – assured an abundant flow of customers. However, there was a serious flaw in the business. Like the little Dutch boy who needed to keep his finger in the dyke to prevent the sea from flooding his village, cable service providers were constantly wrestling with the way their scrambled signals were so easily stolen.

The problem lay in the chip.

Unlike, say, a cellphone where the computer that allows you access to the network is at the phone company, the cable box that descrambles the television signal lives in your house, usually right next to your set. Given untethered access to the box, anyone who wants to steal service merely has to open the lid, pull out a twenty-eight-prong chip, put in a modified chip, and screw the lid back on. People who can't work their own VCR are able to manage this trick in less than thirty seconds. Cable service providers blame equipment manufacturers for making signal theft too easy. Manufacturers blame advancing technology that is readily available to anybody who wants it.

As long ago as 1984, Washington recognized that cable piracy was a serious problem, tried to help but only made matters worse. Under that year's Cable Act, Congress ruled that the crime was stealing the signal, not buying, owning, or selling a descrambler. Unlike drugs, where possession counts, the weight of the law fell on the use to which you put the pirate cable box. Technically, you can buy and use one without risk of penalty, as long as you pay the cable operator for what you're watching. Therefore, it's been argued, the only person who can break the law is the end user, not the people who build or sell the decoders.

Based on that ruling, pirate descramblers poured onto the market throughout the 1980s. Cable box pirates emerged from the underworld and into the shadows of the legitimate world, in large part abetted by the industry itself, which charges clients per television. If you're paying for cable on a living-room set and you decide you'd also like to hook up your bedroom set, service providers claim the right to add a fee for that second television. Consumers, feeling hard done, argue that because it's not illegal to own a pirate box, if you're already paying for cable on one set, connecting a box to a second set is not theft of services. If it's anything, it's just an inexpensive way to beat the cable companies at their, arguably, greedy game.

And so cable piracy in the U.S. donned the cloak of a perfect crime.

In Canada, the law takes a very different approach. It is illegal to manufacture, possess, sell, offer for sale, or distribute any device that can be used to obtain telecommunication signals or services without payment.

Not that the law stops 700,000 Canadians who are estimated to be using illegal satellite TV equipment. Nor has a 2002 Supreme Court ruling that prohibits Canadians from watching direct-to-home satellite television from providers other than Bell ExpressVu and Star Choice. Even those people who use a U.S. address to subscribe to services, and pay for them, are in breach of the law.

The problem with the Canadian law is much the same as with the U.S. law – it is almost impossible to enforce.

It means that pirates view the industry on both sides of the border as a high-return, relatively low-risk venture. Which is why they even advertise in prominent magazines and newspapers. In turn, the public assumes this must be legit or the pirates wouldn't be permitted to publicize it.

Accordingly, well into the 1990s, more and more product was fed onto the two nations' markets to meet an ever-increasing demand. With the advent of the Internet, pirates headed en masse to cyberspace, offering ready-made boxes on-line. Today, there are sites with instructions for hobbyists who want to build their own. The parts cost around $13 and are cheerfully available in electronics stores found in most shopping malls.

As a result, cable theft in the States has become so widespread that it's said to occur with one in five subscribers. These days, the American cable business is worth around $24 billion a year. Piracy accounts for roughly $7 billion of that. It's hardly surprising then, with so much money at stake, cable pirates employ professional marketing people, top-class engineers, and spend enormous sums on research and development to stay one ahead of the legitimate chip manufacturers.

Understandably, cable operators are very aggressive when it comes to protecting their market. So when a senior executive at the service provider in Jersey City heard that a hot-dog vendor was moving pirate boxes, he alerted the FBI in nearby Newark. Because taking a hot-dog seller off the streets isn't quite like shooting it out with John Dillinger, the job went to the lowest guy on the totem pole.

Bill Waldie had been with the bureau just three years. A New Jersey kid who'd originally been assigned to the Washington, D.C., field office, he'd recently transferred home. His supervisor handed him the short straw. As far as the bureau was concerned, this was a case of low-priority signal theft. As far as Waldie was concerned, his desk was already piled high with grunt work.

"Gordon was selling Oak Sigma boxes," Waldie begins, "which seemed to be the most interesting thing about the case because prior to this, nobody had been able to descramble an Oak Sigma box. Everybody did General Instrument and Scientific Atlanta boxes, but Oak was the tough one. I figured I was looking at two days' work, tops. I'd eat a few hot dogs, do a couple of controlled buys, and take this guy down."

Waldie went to look at Gordon, where hot dogs turned out to be the easiest part of the deal. Lunch came with no questions asked, but Gordon demanded answers before he'd even discuss cable boxes. He wanted to know how Waldie knew he had boxes for sale. He wanted references. Of course, Waldie told Gordon what he wanted to hear and once Gordon was satisfied that this customer was legit, Gordon asked, "Suburban or Jersey City?"

That sparked Waldie's interest. If Gordon could offer Oak boxes with different chips, Waldie wondered about Gordon's suppliers. It's one thing to stick a chip in a box, it's another to provide for variations in the same market. Legitimate cable boxes are worth around $35. Adding a $5 pirate chip to it puts the price up to $250 to $350. Gordon was asking $450 for the Oak Sigmas.

"Where I made my mistake," Waldie admits, "was thinking that this guy is too low level. He was selling hot dogs for a living. It just didn't figure that he could be dealing a lot of boxes. But it was obvious that Gordon's suppliers were running a sophisticated operation. I didn't know how many more Gordons there were, but I was less interested in them than I was in finding the next guy up the ladder, then following the ladder all the way to the top. That's where I made my mistake. Instead of working this case for a few days, I turned it into four years."

Along the way, Gordon got shut down.

But more than ten years after that first hot dog, a lot of people a long way from Jersey City are still getting indigestion.

As a young man, Philip Deming spent five years with the Bureau of Alcohol Tobacco and Firearms (ATF). Although he left ATF to set up as a security consultant to the telecommunications industry, he never stopped thinking like a street cop. It all came back to him in 1993, on hire to General Instrument (GI), then the world's largest manufacturer of cable boxes. Reporting directly to Stan Durey, GI's head of security, Deming had been scouring the country, investigating the major pirates. He'd identified a Lebanese family in Nebraska named Abboud and had approached the FBI in Washington hoping they'd help him shut these guys down, but the bureau hadn't shown much interest.

That's when Durey received a call from a former employee looking to move a load of boxes into South America. It's a critical market for manufacturers because that's where they sell excess descramblers. With newer, more advanced models tempting American consumers to upgrade every few years, out-of-date models sold south of the border represent a significant revenue stream. The former employee told Durey that he and a business partner had a deal to place $4 million to $5 million worth of older boxes in Brazil and wanted Durey to supply them. He was very persistent and Durey didn't want to risk losing the sale, but something about it made him uncomfortable. Durey asked Deming to find out more.

Deming quickly suspected that the former employee was working some sort of scam. But rather than cancel the deal outright, Deming suggested that he and Durey meet with the former employee and his partner to find out exactly what was going on. The encounter was arranged for the U.S. Airways lounge at New York's LaGuardia Airport.

"At the time," Deming recalls, "that was the only airline lounge at LaGuardia inside the security loop. You had to go through the metal detectors to get there. I wanted to make sure these guys weren't wired, that they couldn't use any information against us at a later date. I also wanted to be sure they weren't armed."

Arriving at the club early to make certain that no one could bug the conference room, he wasn't there long before a character in his early forties appeared, looking as if he'd just walked off the set of *The Sopranos*. Dressed in a black suit with a black shirt, and sporting a signet ring that no one could possibly miss – the initial *F* was made out of eight one-carat diamonds – this guy was also casing the place.

When the former employee showed up, he had a brief conversation with the man in black, then left him alone until Durey arrived. The former employee greeted Durey, who introduced Deming, and those three went into the conference room. Only after they settled in, did the man in black join them.

"His name was Frank Russo," Deming says. "And he clearly wanted everyone to think he was seriously connected. We found out later that he'd beaten up a few people and done some loan sharking, but nothing more than that. He was on the periphery, just someone who liked wiseguys. But we didn't know that then. He spent the whole meeting smoking and drinking Scotch. I kept thinking that he was exactly the kind of guy who would show up wired and armed. He made us very ill at ease."

Frank was introduced as the president of a start-up company looking to move boxes south. Durey went to great pains to explain that General Instrument, like all legitimate cable equipment suppliers, kept tight control of boxes specifically so that pirates couldn't get their hands on them to rechip them. He warned that the company vetted everyone they sold boxes to and before they could make any sort of deal, they'd need to run background checks on Frank and his company.

Frank's answer to that was, "Okay, what's your price?"

Durey was stunned.

But Frank was prepared. "Two million to facilitate the deal."

With only $4 million to $5 million up for grabs, a bribe that size made no sense. But Deming immediately saw this as his way in. "The first thing I did was get Durey out of there. I said to Frank that Durey had to leave the room, that he represents a publicly held company and that there's no way he could be party to anything like this."

Durey followed Deming's lead, stood up, and walked out.

Now Deming turned to Frank. "Okay, tell me more. If I'm interested, we'll cut Durey out of the deal."

Frank said that sounded good to him and outlined his plans.

The following day, Deming briefed General Instrument's lawyers on the deal Frank was proposing. When they agreed that this was a case of commercial bribery, Deming rang his FBI contacts in Washington and explained what had transpired. Suddenly, they seemed interested in what Deming had to say.

What he didn't yet know was that, back in Newark, Bill Waldie was making big plans.

⟋

The deeper Waldie got into "the hot-dog case," the more expansive the web of players became.

The more mobbed up the players became too.

Waldie now sat down with Assistant U.S. Attorney Donna Gallucio – a fireball prosecutor who is one of the last people in Newark that defence lawyers volunteer to tangle with – and the two of them started talking "big picture." The presence of the Mob meant this had the potential of a major, nationwide case. But Mob presence also raised the risk of danger. Any case mounted against them would require a lot of "backstopping" – physical backup, established safety measures, evidence-gathering systems securely in place. If they were going to do it right, Waldie and Gallucio decided, they'd need to commit "assets." And that cost money. So Gallucio and Waldie put together an elaborate game plan, seeking permission and the funds to go Group One.

For the sake of definition, when a cop does a "buy-bust" – goes undercover wearing a funny hat and a wig to purchase something from somebody on a street corner – that's a Group Three undercover. When a cop spends a couple of days being somebody else to get evidence on tape, and there is also a danger element, it slips into the category of Group Two. But when there is a heightened element of danger, when human resources are committed and assets are required – "toys" such as registered corporations, leased offices, penthouse apartments, helicopters, jets, Ferraris, gold chains, silk suits, speed boats – then Group One rules apply. For that, a special board is convened by the Justice Department in Washington to approve or disapprove the plan, then to amend the plan, set parameters, establish timing, supervise the back-stopping, and fund the operation.

What started with a couple of hot dogs soon became six months of dreary paperwork and cheerless administrative battles simply to secure Washington's approval. But the case they made for going Group One was sound, the board said yes, and as soon as that happened, everything else moved at lightning speed. Waldie rented a warehouse with a loading bay in an industrial park in Kenilworth, New Jersey. Bureau technicians wired it for sound and video while Waldie purchased furniture for the office, got stationery printed, got invoices printed, got phones and computers installed, and even got himself a forklift truck. He obtained a supply of cable boxes from one of the manufacturers, had them secretly stamped to identify them as evidence, installed a young agent named Jim Kay at the front counter and, just like that, went into business as Prime Electronics. The only thing he didn't have were any customers.

That's when Philip Deming came along with Frank Russo.

"This was the perfect point to introduce our company into the game," Waldie says. "Everything fit together. Prime had boxes to sell and Deming had Frank Russo to buy them."

They played him like a fish. Deming told Frank there was no way General Instrument would authorize him to be a dealer but said he'd located a company willing to act for him. Deming promised that he could get his friend Jim at Prime Electronics authorized, waited a reasonable amount of time before ringing Frank to say that Prime had GI's blessings, and within days Jim was moving cable boxes to Frank. To keep Deming sweet, and make certain that Prime wasn't a bunch of cops, Frank put Deming on the payroll at $10,000 a month, cash.

"We started with the people selling this stuff," Gallucio says. "From there we moved on to the distributors. When we saw how they were getting boxes, we moved up to the wholesalers. Before we knew it, we were doing business with people all over the country."

Cable piracy had never been a priority for the FBI and nobody could recall a cable case initiated by the bureau. But Operation Cabletrap got so huge so fast that it became a seven-days-a-week, eighteen-hours-a-day venture. Gallucio soon needed help, so another assistant U.S. attorney was brought on board.

His name is Jim Carney. "The hot-dog guy was a mope. What made this case exciting, what Bill and Donna did, was go from one guy on a street corner in Jersey City to multimillion-dollar companies operating throughout the States, Asia, Malta, the U.K., and other parts of the world. Prime moved boxes by the thousands, all the time developing and processing a staggering amount of evidence against an ever-expanding network of people."

To convict them, Gallucio and Carney would have to show "intent." Because Prime was dealing in raw, unchipped boxes, the prosecution would need to demonstrate in court that the people buying those boxes from Prime intended to turn them into pirate cable boxes that would allow their clients to steal signals. So with surveillance cameras running, Jim Kay began telling some of his customers, I'll get you one hundred raw boxes but need you to send ten back to me chipped because I've got some friends. And just like that, chipped boxes started coming back to Prime.

In one instance, Kay didn't have to do anything because the bad guy did it by himself. He swaggered into the warehouse, sat down in front of a hidden camera, and lectured Kay, "The FBI can't catch you unless they know you're stealing, and we know we're stealing, but they don't."

Another genius chipped a bunch of boxes in front of Waldie and Kay, not realizing that he was being taped or to whom he was bragging. "The only way the FBI is going to catch me," he said, "is if they're standing here right now watching me do this."

From the start, Frank Russo was moving so many boxes that he was always going to be Prime's biggest customer. But what made Frank even more interesting was his partner, Joe Russo. The two were not related but shared a Hollywood, Florida, company called Leasing Ventures. They also owned a company called Cable Box Services and had several large warehouses in Port St. Lucie, Florida, through which they moved pirated boxes.

Where Frank was a poser, Joe was the real thing, a major player hooked into the Gambino Mob. The man behind Joe – his silent partner who backed several large purchases of raw boxes – was John (Johnny Black) Trematerra, an aging and respected wiseguy with the Luchesse crime family. It was Joe who elevated Cabletrap into the big leagues.

The Russos bought boxes when they could get them and stole boxes when they couldn't buy them. Hand in hand with Joe's connections came guns and violence. When Joe heard about a thief named Willie Pagan who'd stolen forty thousand boxes from a warehouse in Baltimore, Joe moved in on him. Willie had been so adept in lifting the $5 million worth of boxes that the company didn't even know it had been ripped off until Bill Waldie told them. But Willie made a critical mistake while moving the boxes to a fellow in Florida, who was, in turn, selling them to Frank and Joe. He'd accidentally left the original labels on a few. Joe tracked the labels back to Willie and, accompanied by one of his leg breakers, informed Willie that from now on he was selling to the Russos direct. Joe also decided how much he would pay for the boxes, which was considerably less than the Russos were already paying. Willie became the Russos' new supplier and, every now and then, Frank Russo would sell some of Willie's stolen boxes to Jim Kay at Prime.

"These guys didn't care who they did business with or how," Waldie points out. "They robbed everything they could, and even robbed from themselves. Frank and Joe set up a company called Greenhouse Electronics in order to rip off John Trematerra. They used Greenhouse to buy stuff, which they'd mark up, then sell to Leasing Ventures at the higher price. Leasing Ventures paid for it with Trematerra's money and the markup got split between Joe and Frank."

Joe's legbreaker friend and Willie Pagan were not the only sleazebags to stroll into Cabletrap with the Russos. The legbreaker introduced his mate "George the Animal" into the circuit, and George sold stolen boxes to Prime, which Prime sold on to Frank Russo, who often commented on tape that he knew the boxes were hot.

"These guys are not exactly what you'd call intellects," Waldie continues. "But they're streetwise. Their problem is, greed blinds them. It's about money. How much can we make? How much more can we make? They become pigs. They don't trust each other and rightfully so. They do backdoor deals. There were times when Frank would say to us, Don't tell Joe because he doesn't know about this so you've got to get me cash, send the money to my house."

With tens of millions of dollars pouring in, Frank bought himself a Mercedes convertible. Joe decided he wanted one too but still had a year left on the lease of his Lexus. To get rid of it, he arranged to have the car stolen, then trashed. Unfortunately, he reported it stolen the day after it was recovered. And every bit of this was recorded on tape as the guys bragged to Jim Kay.

Also on tape was the Russos' benevolence to Deming. Once, when Deming went to Florida to collect his monthly ten grand, Frank pulled a stack of fresh $100 bills out of the dishwasher.

Before long, Deming announced that he wanted more. "We were moving boxes by tractor-trailer loads. One of the things that concerned me was that the sums of money changing hands wouldn't mean much if we went to trial in Newark. Think about someone sitting on a jury from a working-class neighbourhood downtown, and you tell him that the defendants are doing millions of dollars' worth of business. He sees a businessman and figures that's what businessmen do. So I suggested to the bureau that we needed to show the jury that these weren't ordinary businessmen, that they paid their bills in extraordinary ways. The FBI agreed and so I asked Frank for a Porsche Carrera."

Keeping Deming happy made sense to Russo, who paid $52,000 for the car in Florida and delivered it to Deming in New Jersey.

"It was beautiful," Deming says with a tinge of anguish in his voice, "but the FBI wouldn't let me keep it. I tried to convince myself that I shouldn't be too disappointed. I rationalized the whole thing away by saying, Anyway, it's an automatic."

Feeling his pain, the bureau let Deming drive it – once – and then, like everything else collected in the case, the Porsche was stored as evidence. Later Russo offered Deming a cigarette boat, but the operation got closed down before he could drive that once too.

⟶

Mathewson always held his clients' hands as he walked them each through the same routine.

He started by selling them a shell company and into the shell went whatever bank and brokerage accounts the client wanted. To access their money, he gave them a gold Visa or MasterCard – always in the name of the shell – and a spending limit that could go as high as $1 million a month, depending on how much the client had on deposit with the bank. He also coached them to sign the back of the card with a signature that was "reproducible but hard to read."

Clients wishing to deposit cheques were instructed by Mathewson to make them payable to a Guardian-owned shell – they had names like Fulcrum and Sentinel and Tower – and warned never to endorse the cheques. Instead, he told them to send the cheques with their Guardian account number written on a separate plain sheet of paper. In turn, Guardian stamped each cheque for deposit in the name of a correspondent bank, without any reference to the Cayman Islands.

Guardian's correspondents included Credit Suisse in Guernsey; Cayman National Bank, Bank of Bermuda, and Bank of Butterfield International in the Caymans; SunBank, Popular, Capital, First Union

National, Eurobank, and Bank of New York in the States; and Royal Bank of Canada, Toronto-Dominion, Credit Suisse, and Canaccord Capital in Canada. Guardian also had correspondent relationships with brokers, including Prudential, Wheat First, Smith Barney Shearson, Charles Schwab, and Richardson Greenshields.

According to Mathewson, none of those correspondents requested any information about Guardian's clients. As far as he could tell, "I don't think any of them ever attempted to monitor the account."

If funds were being wired in, Mathewson told clients to use a non-U.S. correspondent bank, so as to keep documentation held in the States to a minimum. Again, no personal information was to be included. Clients would simply phone Guardian to advise them of the transfer.

The easiest way to get money out of an account was with the credit card. But clients who wanted chequebooks could have them. They were usually issued by one of the correspondent banks, either with the word *Guardian* printed on the top – but without any address or phone number – or, with nothing at all printed on it, except the number of the Guardian account at that correspondent bank. Furthermore, Guardian also maintained its own chequing accounts with correspondent banks, which did not identify Guardian, so that any client wishing to make a large purchase without leaving a trail could have Guardian pay the bill, writing as many cheques as it took to skirt any reporting requirements. That meant cheques were usually written for sums under $10,000.

Doing business with Mathewson was not cheap. Guardian's charges were $5,000 to open an account, and $3,000 annually to maintain it. Clients paid an additional $5,000 for a standard shell company – they only cost Mathewson $500 to buy from the local authorities – and $12,000 to $16,000 if they needed an "aged" shell. That's a company incorporated several years before, which allowed clients to backdate invoices and create fictitious trading records. The required nominee shareholder for each shell was often a Guardian subsidiary, for which there was a fee. Mathewson also supplied company directors – usually another Guardian subsidiary – for another fee. On top of those, he charged $100 per wire transfer, sent or received.

Additional services included invoices in the name of any company to help clients defraud their own companies with transfer-pricing scams, and shell companies incorporated in Holland to work back-to-back loans disguised as mortgages. Mathewson's fees for transfer pricing ranged from $1,000 an hour to a flat sum of $25,000 per year, plus a percentage of the cost of the product invoiced. His fee for the back-to-back loan scam was $30,000.

It all added up to a lot of money, but Mathewson knew that whatever it cost, it was still cheaper for his clients than paying taxes. "Why would any citizen wish to go through the time and expense required to establish an offshore account unless it was for the evasion of taxes or the hiding of funds? Even when an offshore account looks innocent, it very probably has a hidden agenda."

Bill Waldie's investigation of the Russos – which included Frank's wife and son – soon caught the attention of an FBI team in Florida. Together they set up surveillance on a load of new targets.

Around the same time, the FBI finally turned its sights to Deming's Lebanese pirates in Nebraska. The Abboud family was among the most visible of the cable pirates. They advertised, and were active in a pirate cable consumer's association that held regular meetings in Las Vegas. There, pirates openly lectured on how to avoid forfeiture by the FBI, what to do if you got caught with cable boxes, and how to hide pirate goods. Trailing the Abbouds, agents also showed up at conventions, took a lot of notes, and added names to the target list.

One of them was William S. (Trey) Prevost, III. Something of a cult hero in the trade, the twenty-nine-year-old owned and operated several businesses in Sun Valley, California, including two pirate cable firms, Novaplex and Gage Systems Group. Prevost had run up against the police before, in the early 1990s, when he was raided and the cops seized 3,500 cable boxes. The judge put him on probation, ordered him to stay out of the business, and to pay $2.75 million to the southern California cable operator he'd defrauded.

The quarter of a million dollars' worth of boxes that the cops seized from Prevost wound up in a Los Angeles Police Department evidence facility, which happened to be a used jail that they occasionally rented out to television and film production companies. Somehow, Joe and Frank Russo found out where that was and, along with a connected guy in L.A. whom Joe knew, convinced the LAPD that they were an MTV crew. They rented the jail for a music video, arrived in an empty van, located the boxes, cut the bars, filled the van, and drove off.

As if stealing evidence from the LAPD wasn't audacious enough, they came back two more times, until they had all 3,500 boxes.

Needless to say, when Prevost found out who did it he was extremely annoyed. He knew he'd never get the boxes back from Joe and Frank, but reckoned he could get something out of it from the LAPD. So he sued the cops, claiming that the police had a responsibility to safeguard his possessions while they were being held in custody. It was a good try, but didn't work.

The Russos sold some of Prevost's boxes to the Abbouds, and the rest to Prime. Frank Russo even explained to Jim, unknowingly on camera, how he'd cooked up the perfect alibi. He said he had receipts proving that he'd purchased the boxes from a fellow named Ken. Making the alibi watertight, Frank declared, "Ken's fuckin' dead and dead men can't talk." To which he added proudly, "I thought of that all by myself."

In the meantime, Waldie's investigation of Prevost revealed that he was still very much in the business and, therefore, in violation of his probation. He had a fifty-thousand-square-foot warehouse filled with seventeen tractor-trailer loads of pirate cable boxes. He'd also formed a consortium with Joe, Frank, and a group of other guys, called Cable Box Central, which served as an umbrella under which they concealed several companies, their own identities, and a great deal of illegal activity. They brought components into the country from the Orient addressed to aliases and sham corporations, sneaking past Customs with false declarations. They also hijacked tractor-trailers carrying cable boxes. While law enforcement in California and Arizona investigated those thefts, Waldie watched the stolen cable boxes arrive at Prime's front door. He added interstate transportation of stolen property to the growing list of charges he could bring against both Russos.

Targeting Prevost also led Waldie to the computer nerd who masterminded the chip technology. For his services, Prevost was paying him more than $1 million a year.

"It was a huge web," Waldie continues. "All the big players were intertwined. They all dealt with each other. They were each other's competitors, but they all needed raw cable boxes and Prime became the centre of this. It got so hectic that Jim Kay and I were in the warehouse every morning by six, sometimes seven days a week, sometimes staying there eighteen hours a day."

There were days, he says, when a load would come in with a couple thousand boxes. They'd have to unpack them, micro-stamp each one so they could be used as evidence, then repack them, and ship them. In summer it was 110°F inside that warehouse.

"Prime was making money hand over fist and we weren't even the ones who were chipping the boxes. We were selling raw boxes in big numbers. Nobody walked in off the street to buy one or two. In fact, unless you knew us, you couldn't even get in the front door. Frank Russo would show up to buy two thousand boxes. That might be a $135,000 deal for us, he'd flip it for $250,000, somebody would chip them and retail the load for $350,000. Everybody made money."

Including the FBI.

"Once we got this thing off the ground, we were self-supporting. We didn't use any bureau money. Prime paid for the entire investigation, all four years' worth. Our warehouse, our travel, our food, our buy money, everything we did, got paid for out of the profit from Prime. Then, when it was all done, we sent the bureau something like a million dollars that we still had in the bank." Waldie thinks about that for a moment, then jokes, "Of course, when you break it down, Jim and I were working for a buck an hour."

<hr>

With so many cable boxes moving out of Prime and so much money coming into Leasing Ventures, the Russos started to worry about protecting their stash. They wanted to put their money somewhere safe, where no one could find it. Should the day ever come when they got busted, they needed to make sure there'd be no money trail to follow.

It was Joe Russo who knew about Guardian Bank. He told Frank, who mentioned it to Jim Kay, and that's how the bureau first heard about Mathewson. Frank's idea was to move all their banking to the Caymans and run everything through Guardian. He wanted to use false invoices to justify payments, and to pay Deming's monthly ten grand with a credit card on a Guardian account. So a trip to the island was planned. Originally it was to be Frank and Joe – who'd make the introduction to Mathewson – Kay and Waldie, plus a few other people from

Leasing Ventures. But Joe pulled out at the last minute and the rest of them had to walk into Guardian cold.

Not that Mathewson would have turned them away. If someone had money to deposit, he didn't particularly care who they were or where their money came from. He set the Russos up with a shell company called Hanson. Frank put $20,000 into the Hanson account and Mathewson issued credit cards, including one to Deming. From that moment on, the Russos paid Hanson, Mathewson supplied invoices to justify the payments, and the Russos used the invoices to deduct those deposits as business expenses on Leasing Ventures' books. From that moment on, as well, Mathewson and Guardian were placed high on the list of people the FBI intended to indict.

Waldie and Kay now started working Mathewson, bringing cash to him, always making certain that Mathewson understood the money was the proceeds of unlawful activity. Mathewson happily accepted it and even advised Waldie how to get large amounts of cash out of the United States, in direct contravention of U.S. laws, and into the Caymans, in direct contravention to Caymanian law.

"Mathewson knew all the tricks," Waldie says. "He warned us, don't wear a lot of jewellery to attract anyone's attention, and don't put any cash in your bag. Instead, wear cowboy boots. Which is what I did. I filled each boot up with cash, about fifty grand worth, and walked right through the detectors. They did the wand on me, and I stood there thinking to myself, If they find the money, I'm going to get arrested. That would probably blow the case. We definitely didn't want to do that. So I stood there with tens of thousands of dollars stuffed in my boots while they inspected me and, frankly, I was in a little bit of panic."

But no one ever found the money and Mathewson never suspected he was being set up.

In January 1995, seven months after Mathewson incorporated Hanson for the Russos and inadvertently opened the door to the FBI – and just two months before Waldie, Kay, Gallucio, and Carney planned to take down Cabletrap – the Cayman Islands government surprised everyone by shutting Guardian.

The Caymanians claimed the bank was going under and that they needed to step in to protect the depositors. Mathewson's version is very different. He insists that a bank regulator demanded a $250,000 bribe and, when he refused to pay it, the regulator launched an investigation for some vaguely stated malfeasance. No matter which version is true, the government sent in the liquidators. Shortly thereafter, Mathewson left the island with his Caymanian wife and three children, settled in San Antonio, Texas, and started planning his comeback, this time with a bank in the Bahamas.

~

After recording more than three thousand conversations, and going up on nearly as many wiretaps, after spending months listening to all those tapes and all those wiretaps, and after compiling all the evidence gathered by Waldie and Kay, prosecutors Gallucio and Carney obtained sealed indictments against dozens of conspirators in four states. The charges were mail fraud, wire fraud, bribery, receipt and sale of stolen property, money laundering, unauthorized use and unauthorized reception of cable television services, various types of conspiracy, and interstate transportation of stolen goods.

Waldie now needed to co-ordinate a massive, national takedown. "We had sixty to seventy subjects spread out over the country. I can't tell you how many dozens of search-and-seizure warrants we had to put together, but the paperwork was massive. We planned a simultaneous hit on twenty-four locations across the country."

Thinking he might be able to turn Frank Russo against Joe Russo and some of the others, Waldie and Kay plotted to bring Frank to New Jersey on the same day that the arrests were happening. So ten days before the takedown, Jim called Frank to say that there'd been another hijacking and that two thousand of the hottest new boxes were coming onto the market. He asked, "Do you know anything about the hijacking?"

Frank said he didn't but begged Jim to get those boxes, "'Cause I need 'em like blood."

Jim promised to try. Frank started ringing back every few hours, pleading with Jim for the boxes. When Jim announced that he could get them, but that the price was $150,000 for the load, Frank haggled him down to an even $100,000 cash, and agreed to pick them up on the appointed day. But at the last minute, Frank announced that Joe was coming with him and Waldie knew his chance to turn Frank was gone.

The Russos arrived at the warehouse with $100,000 in cash just as three hundred FBI agents were spreading out across the country serving warrants and locking up suspects. The two men were sitting with Jim, talking about the deal, when Prime's front bell rang. Jim opened the door and eight agents wearing FBI vests – including Waldie – burst in with weapons drawn. There was a lot of screaming, "Freeze, freeze, get your hands up, freeze . . ."

Frank and Joe looked at each other, looked back at the agents, looked at each other again, then simply put their hands on top of their head. Waldie separated Frank and Joe, then introduced Frank to FBI Special Agent Jim Kay. Frank couldn't believe it. Waldie explained that not only was Jim an agent, but Deming was working with them too.

Frank kept saying, "No way, no way." Waldie confirmed that it was true. Eventually Frank said, "Let me get this straight. Jim is an FBI agent? And Philip . . . Philip's a prick!" There was a long pause before Frank shrugged, "I guess this means I don't get the new boxes?"

Waldie assured him, "No new boxes."

Still, Frank gave it one last try. "Come on, guys, we can make a lot of money."

And that was the end of Frank Russo.

Being the real thing, Joe played it cool. He lied right from the beginning and kept lying right to the end, insisting that he had nothing to do with any of this, that he was simply Frank's accountant.

Waldie insists, "Joe can't even spell accountant."

Joe also denied knowing anything about the suitcase filled with cash that the two of them had carried into the warehouse. He swore it wasn't his. Of course, Frank said the same thing. But neither had any wiggle room because it was all on video.

The Russos were in handcuffs by the time all the other warrants were served. Some forty premises were raided and around fifty thousand cable boxes were seized. The bureau also got computer and electronic equipment, vehicles, and cash. The sting had been so well put together that five of the targets gave up and pled guilty right away, and some of them, like Frank Russo, also agreed to co-operate.

In June 1996, fourteen people were additionally charged by the FBI with stealing and selling millions of dollars' worth of illegal decoder boxes. Among them were Frank and Joe, sharing seventy-one counts that included conspiracy, wire fraud, interstate transportation of stolen property, theft of cable television signals, and money laundering. Both of them went to jail. Further indictments followed, including a laundry list of charges against the Abbouds. They pled guilty, assets were seized, fines were imposed, and the family business was, to all intents and purposes, dismantled. It would later come to light that the Abbouds had banked at Guardian as well, moving around $27 million through the Caymans. Records would reveal that they'd also transferred funds to Venezuela, which opened an entirely new line of investigation.

Prevost, who was originally charged with ninety-three counts, had been enjoined by a California court to stay out of the cable business. But he'd violated the order by establishing a sham company in Ireland, called Hazeltown Trading, with a mail-drop address in London's Knightsbridge. When his customers wanted pirated chips, they paid Hazeltown and that money was moved by one of the Big-Four British banks to Malta. From Malta, some of it came back to the States, and some of it disappeared into a void. Now, at his Cabletrap hearing, when asked about Hazeltown, Prevost swore under oath that he knew nothing about it.

Comments Waldie, "Frank and Joe Russo were pigs and they were dumb. But Trey was smart. He had a very sophisticated set-up. His problem was that he testified in court that he wasn't Hazeltown, which was really stupid, because we knew he was."

Released on bail, when Prevost heard he was about to be rearrested for lying to the court, he fled the country. He was located living in Costa Rica under an assumed name. The FBI "invited" him to return to the States, and in May 1998 he surrendered to federal agents. Now he was charged with flight to avoid prosecution, new counts of money laundering, false reporting, and criminal conspiracy. He worked out a plea agreement, was fined $500,000, and was sent away for five years.

And still there was unfinished business.

———

The FBI banged on John Mathewson's door early one morning in June 1996. He was pushing seventy, had a heart condition, and now faced the prospect of spending the rest of his years in prison. He was petrified. Right away, he waived his right to counsel, fessed up, and agreed to cooperate fully. He asked, What can I do to keep from going to jail? The agents told him the truth, that there was probably no way he could avoid jail time. He pledged to help them. They said they doubted there was much he could do at this late stage. How about, he wondered, if I had copies of the bank's computer backup tapes and was willing to hand them over? Before that day was out, Mathewson and the FBI had found room for discussion.

The following day he turned over the tapes, containing fourteen months of transactional activities for around one thousand Guardian clients in sixteen hundred accounts. All but seventy-three of the clients were American. In addition, Mathewson gave the FBI his electronic Rolodex, which linked the shell company listed for each account with the name of the beneficial owner. The only problem was, the tapes were encrypted.

The bureau wanted the Caymanians to help decipher them. The island authorities flew into a rage, vehemently refused, announced that the tapes had been stolen, insisted that they rightfully belonged to the Cayman Islands Monetary Authority, and demanded that they be returned. When the FBI reminded them there was no chance of that happening, the bank's liquidators – obviously with the encouragement of the local government – filed a suit in U.S. federal court demanding their return. The liquidators also asked the court to prohibit the United States government from publishing, communicating, or otherwise acting upon the information contained on the tapes. They insisted that the information needed to be protected to preserve client confidentiality, to safeguard the integrity of the Cayman banking system, and to stop the Americans from embarking on "a fishing expedition" for tax evaders.

Gallucio and Carney responded that the Caymans' position had no basis in U.S. law, was disingenuous and otherwise pretty silly.

Up to this point, the Cayman authorities regularly asserted that their reputation as a money-laundering sink was based largely on "a media stereotype" rather than "objective reality." The bank's tapes proved them dead wrong, and plenty of islanders understood that. If the tapes were decrypted, officials wrote, it would have "a significant negative impact on the integrity, confidentiality, and stability of the financial services industry of the Cayman Islands."

In other words, this had nothing to do with protecting clients, this had to do with protecting themselves. In one court brief it is clearly stated, "The Cayman Islands and, indeed, the economy of the territory, could suffer irreparable injury."

Those concerns are echoed in confidential correspondence between the liquidators' attorneys, the liquidators themselves, other lawyers, and the Royal Caymanian Police, making it very clear what the government was really worried about.

Attorney John Rodger, acting for the Caymans, wrote in one letter, "In the likely event that the Federal authorities share the information they obtain from the disks with the Internal Revenue Service, we would antic-ipate widespread investigation and possible prosecution of Bank clients."

The Guardian bank liquidator, Christopher Johnson, further warned the police, "I believe these events will be potentially very damaging to the wider public profile of the jurisdiction and the reputation of its banking industry."

These days in the Caymans, they contend that Mathewson was always suspect. The official line from the government is, "We got rid of him because we didn't like what he was doing." The Bankers Association maintains that the liquidators were justified in trying to block American access to Guardian's records and steadfastly affirms that tax evasion is not why people deposit money there. They say they were shocked to have found themselves on the FATF blacklist and, in response to that, tightened their statutes on criminal money laundering. They say they've taken steps to become as transparent as commercially possible, which obviously pleased the FATF sufficiently to remove the Caymans from the blacklist.

Looking back, John Carney finds it difficult to believe how two-faced the Caymanians have been through the Guardian saga. "While they were saying publicly, we have no idea what the bank and its clients were doing, their correspondence shows that they knew damn well why these banks existed and why people banked in the Caymans."

Mathewson was charged with money laundering, aiding and abetting the evasion of income tax, and conspiracy to commit wire fraud. He pled guilty and asked the court for leniency. "I have no excuse for what I did in aiding U.S. citizens to evade taxes, and the fact that every other bank in the Caymans was doing it is no excuse."

Gallucio, Carney, and Waldie went to bat for him, telling the judge that the nature and extent of his co-operation had been tremendous. To his detriment, Mathewson had never much cared with whom he did business. In addition to abetting fraud, theft, and tax evasion, drug money and organized crime money also moved through Guardian. Still, U.S. District Court Judge Alfred Lechner, Jr., agreed that Mathewson's assistance to federal authorities was "unparalleled," and that saved him from prison. Noting that he'd received an extraordinary number of requests for leniency, the judge sentenced Mathewson to six months of house arrest, five years' probation, a $30,000 fine, and five hundred hours of community service.

He showed less sympathy to the Caymans. The judge decided that possession of the tapes by the U.S. government was lawful and that the liquidators had no right to seek their return. "The interest of the Cayman Islands in maintaining confidentiality of records protected by the Cayman Confidential Relationship Law, while vital, does not overcome the interests of the United States Government in investigating violations of its criminal laws."

Unwilling to abide by spirit of the Judge Lechner's ruling, the liquidators did whatever they could to keep the tapes from being decrypted. They threatened the foreign software company that had written the program, and threatened Mathewson as well. Suitably intimidated, the software company told the FBI they wouldn't co-operate. But Mathewson did and, with his help, the bureau broke the code. The FBI then handed the Guardian client list to the IRS.

"There are so many people," confessed one IRS agent working his way through the Guardian cases, "I don't know if we've got the manpower to handle them all."

The IRS rounded up a con man who'd transferred $25.3 million through the bank as part of a gigantic credit card fraud, and a doctor who'd filed false returns, saving around $22,000 in tax. They fined a lumber broker $30,000 for illegally diverting corporate funds to his account and sent a man to jail for forty-six months for defrauding the government out of $14.6 million. They charged a video producer with evading $40,000 in taxes, and charged the owner of a computer retail chain with evading $2 million.

Hundreds of cases have been prosecuted and hundreds more are awaiting court dates.

The IRS estimates they will still be working on Guardian's files well past 2005 and expects to have collected nearly $300 million in back taxes and penalties.

Not a bad return for the price of admission.

One dog with sauerkraut and mustard, please . . . one Dr. Pepper . . . oh yeah, and a pirate cable box to go.

PUMP 'N' DUMPS
AND OTHER GAMES

"If you're a guy who runs pump 'n' dumps, and you're not channelling your money offshore, you're committing malpractice."

– Wayne Carlin, attorney, U.S. Securities and Exchange Commission

As a kid growing up in Cranston, Rhode Island, back in the 1960s, Stephen Saccoccia bought gold coins from his school friends – after encouraging them to steal the coins from their parents – and sold them to dealers, making so much easy money from petty theft that he decided, when he grew up, he wanted to be a substantial thief.

Finishing high school in 1973, he opened a gold and coin shop and, within a few years, had built up such a huge cash business that he was able to swindle gigantic sums from the tax collector. Although it took the IRS until 1985 to bust him, when they did they sent him away for three years. As soon as he got out, he went straight back into gold and coins, turning Trend Precious Metals and Saccoccia Coins into one of the world's most substantial laundromats. His clients were the Medellín cartel of Pablo Escobar and the Cali cartel of the Orejuela brothers. It is a testament to his abilities that Stephen Saccoccia is the only laundry-man ever to do business with both groups at the same time.

Saccoccia's method was fairly straightforward, even rudimentary by modern standards. Drug cash was collected at jewellery shops in New

York and Los Angeles, bundled as gold shipments, and crated to him in Rhode Island. He converted the cash to cashier's cheques, backed by false invoices and sales receipts to explain the sudden increase in turnover, and deposited them into his own company accounts. From there, the funds were wired offshore and, eventually, made their way to Colombia. For the service, he charged his clients a flat 10 per cent commission.

In 1991, the Feds finally said enough was enough, but before they could handcuff him, Saccoccia bolted. Months later, he was arrested in Switzerland. He fought extradition, lost that battle, was shipped back to the States, and lost the next battle too. Convicted on fifty-four counts of money laundering and conspiracy, he was fined $15.8 million, subjected to a confiscation order for $136.3 million – the documented amount of his drug-money laundering – and sentenced to 660 years in prison.

When he heard the sentence, he demanded of the judge, "How am I supposed to serve that long?"

The judge responded, "Just do the best you can."

While dissecting Saccoccia's Colombian connections, the government stumbled across his relationship with the Patriarca crime family. From there they discovered he'd been handling contract laundering for New York's Genovese clan. Those money trails led to Britain, Austria, Switzerland, and back into the Caribbean. With each new money trail came new players. But, investigators soon realized, many of those new players did not have drug connections. And that confused them. It hadn't yet dawned on many cops that dirty money is dirty money, and it doesn't matter how it got dirty. It hadn't yet hit home that money laundering is a business and that the laundrymen who work in that industry don't particularly care where their product comes from.

It was Stephen Saccoccia's money that would rewrite the textbooks.

—

Way back in time, in those Dark Ages when people only had landline telephones and there was no such thing as the Internet, boiler-room fraud was one of the biggest games around and Canada was the world capital.

Canadians have been exporting telemarketing scams for decades. The business flourishes because it's easy to set up – all you need is a basement with a lot of telephones, a lot of phone books, a high-pressure selling script, and a lot of people willing to work under terrible conditions for a small percentage of a whole lot of money – the phone system is good and the market to the south is lucrative.

What's more, the police are singularly inefficient in shutting it down. It's akin to digging up crabgrass.

Dozens upon dozens of folk sitting in airless rooms for ten to twelve hours at a stretch cold call one name after another – typically targeting the elderly and inexperienced investors – flogging financial instruments, low-interest credit cards, land investments, subscriptions of all kinds, and shares in obscure companies listed on the woollier stock exchanges, like Vancouver and Alberta.

In the beginning, the scripts were monologues and the cold callers were ordered to stick to the pitch word for word. But as the scams got more sophisticated, so did the scenario. Instead of one call, now there are a series of calls. The initial contact man hands off to the expert, who quantifies the potential for profit, who hands off to an executive, who has special powers to authorize a special deal just for you.

And time is always of the essence.

I've only got fifteen minutes left to sell these because this market closes early and if I don't sell them now I've got to toss them back into the pool, which means the instant profit will be lost, so you've got to let me know yes or no right now, and if it's yes you make the 7 per cent I told you about when I explained how the spread on these things works, and you'll double your money in three months, but if it's no it's lost forever and I won't be able to get you in on it.

If you're operating from Canada, common sense dictates, never scam a Canadian. If you do, you risk getting a knock on the door from the Mounties. By going after folks in Florida or Arizona, you lengthen the odds against ever having to face justice. The victims have to find you in Canada, there would have to be enough victims for the Mounties to take action, and then the victims would have to show up to testify against you. As long as your victims are outside Canada, you're likely to get away with it. The proof of that is, so many do.

Also, always keep your money offshore. If it's in the same country as your victims, they can get at it. If it's in Canada, the cops can get at it. If it's sitting in the Caribbean, or in Gibraltar, or in Hong Kong, in the name of a shell that nobody ever heard of, then only you can get it.

One still-ongoing case out of Toronto is based around low-interest loans. Telemarketers inform American seniors that they've been pre-approved for special cards. Rather than the more usual rates of 18 per cent, this new card carries 8 to 9 per cent annual interest. However, there's a fee involved. But before the seniors even agree to the fee, the telemarketers say they need to run a security check, just to make sure these seniors are the ones who are, indeed, qualified. That requires the senior to give up his or her current credit card number and the expiry date. Two weeks later, a statement arrives showing that some company in Scotland has debited anywhere from $249 to $399 — in pounds sterling — for the new credit card subscription fee. That's followed by a package of literature about the card. But the low-interest credit card never arrives. Six months later most of the victims are still calling a 1-800 number that doesn't get answered.

The perpetrator of this particular scam spent $32,000 buying specialized phone lists of U.S. seniors. He lives in a small town in Ontario. His victims are all in the States, the credit card processor is in Scotland, and his banks are in Mexico. The operation is run out of four boiler rooms, with at least twenty telemarketers per room. And in just ten months, the man running this scam is estimated to have made $24 million. At least, that's what his own records show. The cops reckon he's fudged those books so that his partners can't figure out how much he's been skimming.

His boiler rooms represent just four out of an estimated 200 to 300 that the Mounties believe are at work in Canada every day. Why the country remains a hotbed for this kind of fraud is down to several factors, but most of them add up to one simple conclusion: the business pays better in Canada.

In some jurisdictions, for instance the State of Georgia, if you commit telemarketing fraud against the elderly, it's considered a violent crime and you're looking at twenty years hard time. In Canada, telemarketers pay their costs in Canadian dollars, earn their income in U.S. dollars, and if they do get caught, it's a non-violent crime so the penalties aren't too severe. If they do get caught and the case goes to trial, the costs involved in bringing victims to testify can be excruciatingly high. On top of that, many victims have shown a reluctance to travel to Canada either out of fear, or because they believe they won't get their money back and just want to forget that they've been scammed.

Interestingly enough, police report that Canadian telemarketers generally have a godfather in New York to provide connections to Puerto Rico. Because Puerto Rico enjoys all the privileges of a territory and none of the downside of a state, there are no customs checks on travellers flying from New York to San Juan, making it easier to bulk cash down there. Once in Puerto Rico, it's an easy hop to the Eastern Caribbean.

These days, a lot of telemarketing scams also spread through the Internet. The global explosion of e-mail has made it much easier for criminals to hide in the anonymity of cyberspace. But the Net is a long way from replacing phones, and satellite communications has seen phone-based boiler rooms thrive in faraway places like Thailand.

Still, Canadians lead the major leagues of telemarketing fraud. But back in the 1970s, Canadians and telemarketing fraud were synonymous and Canada owned the game outright. It wasn't until European phone systems disengaged themselves from state-owned post-office monopolies and modernized that new markets opened. By far, the most attractive was Holland. So Canadian con men colonized the Netherlands. The Amsterdam stock exchange was a free-for-all, the country came equipped with built-in island laundromats – Aruba, Sint Maarten, and Curaçao – and the Dutch speak English. Best of all, lax Dutch laws meant that even if they got caught, there wasn't much anybody could do.

An added bonus was the confusion created by Holland's drug trade. Banks there were used to taking cash, while the cops were generally too busy worrying about heroin, coke, and even marijuana to care about a telemarketing scam. The drug wars distorted law enforcement on all levels, rearranging prerogatives and monopolizing international police relationships. Every time a foreign cop travelled to Holland to ask for help in busting a drug trafficker, white-collar crime was demoted another notch on the priority table.

It remained that way until the 1990s when stock markets boomed. With fraud squads everywhere fighting for their budgets, two things occurred to change the landscape. The cops in New York orchestrated the demise of the Mafia's $50-million control of the Fulton Fish Market, clearing out rackets that had been going on for more than a hundred years. Around the same time, they smashed large chunks off the Mob's $500-million rubbish-hauling cartels, a racket they'd been working since Prohibition. A severely wounded Mob needed to find a new act. They looked around, spotted opportunities in the booming markets, and limped over to Wall Street.

The Russians were already there. Particularly clever at staying below the radar, they've tended to work off-market scams – private placements and unregistered offerings. Sometimes, the company they're selling is a start-up but has no functioning business or any real prospects. At other times, it's a completely non-existent company. Cold callers in boiler rooms tell you how well the company is doing and how you can get in on the ground floor now because there's going to be an initial public offering. They invite you to buy shares for $6 a unit, a golden opportunity and really cheap because in three months the company is going public for $20 a share. When you finally realize you've been had, your money is in Cyprus, Vladimir has changed his name to Grigori, and the boiler room has moved down the block.

Of course, the five New York La Cosa Nostra (LCN) families had worked Wall Street before. But in the 1990s there was so much money flying around, and the excitement of a racing bull market was contagious. What's more, they felt the pickings would be easy because law enforcement was forever struggling with drugs.

At the Securities and Exchange Commission, they're fast to tell you that white-collar crime and boiler-room fraud have never been low-ticket items for them. They've been on the case since 1934 when Congress passed the Securities Exchange Act and President Franklin Roosevelt appointed Joseph Kennedy – JFK's father – as the SEC's first chairman. Prior to that, regulation of the markets was a non-starter. There wasn't a government in the world that cared. But the stock-market crash of 1929 changed that. Roosevelt needed to restore investor confidence.

That idea didn't dawn on Canada for a lot of years. Until recently, the smaller markets were an arena for down-and-dirty scams that worked off the back of telemarketing fraud, while the bigger markets were an arena for sophisticated scams that also worked off the back of telemarketing fraud. Provincial securities commissions were put in place to clean them up but still haven't managed it.

Nor did the idea dawn on the British for quite a while. Until recently, the City of London had conned parliament into allowing self-regulation, which left the city wide open to decades of astonishing abuse.

The best of Canadian and British intentions notwithstanding, by contrast, the SEC has always been a humourless, no-nonsense sheriff. It goes into any area of the financial industry to investigate insider trading, manipulation of the market, theft of investors funds, and the illegal sale of securities. Though its remit is strictly civil, many of the 400 to 500 actions that the SEC brings each year are in tandem with federal, state, or local law enforcement. They also keep an eye on cross-border securities fraud and have, in recent years, alongside Canadian regulators, gone after some Canadian companies.

"If I had thirty more people I could keep them fully employed," explains Wayne Carlin, a regional director of the SEC's New York office. "But I was saying the same thing three years ago, and saying it six years ago too. There's always more that comes to our attention than we can adequately pursue. Does that mean that if something significant comes to our attention we won't pursue it? No, it never means that. When we need to go after someone, we do."

Once the SEC sinks its teeth into a company, or the people behind the company, it doesn't tend to let go. One of the keys to the commission's success lies in hiring young lawyers who are especially ambitious and particularly aggressive. SEC recruiters troll law schools for the best, the brightest, and the most combative, offering young lawyers a unique opportunity. Their pitch goes something like this:

Many of you are dreaming of walking into a Wall Street firm and earning a cool three-mil a year. But no one's going to pay you that kind of money unless you've got a three-million-dollar reputation. So, come to work for us and we'll help you get that reputation. We'll pay you less than you could earn as a first-year attorney on Wall Street, but we'll give you the powers of a federal officer, we'll introduce you to some FBI agents with guns and handcuffs, and we'll let you round up all the crooks you can find. Then, once you make a name for yourself as an exceptionally vicious good guy, if you really want to, you can cross over to the dark side and defend bad guys and earn yourself three mil, because by then the people you've been terrorizing will pay you whatever it takes to have you on their team.

It clearly works, because each year the SEC brings in a new crop of sharp young lawyers and turns them loose on Wall Street. They never earn anywhere as much as they could in that other world, yet many of them stay because rounding up bad guys is, as one of them explained, "Almost as good as sex and you never have to buy them a drink."

In this respect, the SEC stands apart from other regulators, like the Canadian Securities Administration, the OSFI, and the various provincial regulators who collectively take a much more gentlemanly approach to regulation. The SEC puts the fear of God into people while Canadian regulators, doing the best they can with limited resources and weak laws, are effectively little more than an annoyance.

"We don't do raids and shout, Hands up, stand where you are," Carlin explains. "But our examiners show up unannounced and when we want to see something, we want to see it then and there. We'll be polite if someone says, Have a seat while we get our lawyers. But we'd better start seeing things in the course of that morning or we go into federal court for an order. No, we don't barge in and yank open file drawers. But when our examiners show up, it's too late to turn on the shredders and cart out boxes of documents."

Although the SEC does not have the power of arrest, it does have the statutory authority to walk into any brokerage or any investment house or any mutual fund and demand to see whatever they want to see without a search warrant. It's a different game, Carlin notes, when the people they're looking at are mobbed up. That's when they show up with their FBI friends bearing guns and handcuffs.

"Be careful not to overstate the presence of the Mob on Wall Street. Our view is yes, there is an organized-crime presence. But it's confined to a very small segment of the securities marketplace. Their activities, in general, are pretty much limited to the bulletin-board market. That's not to say that when you find it, it's not tremendously egregious. It's awful conduct. But it's a very small slice of the market."

Still, it's the SEC's close partnership with the police and criminal prosecutors that makes it a force to reckon with. In the end, battling the SEC on its own is much less worrisome than battling the SEC and the FBI and the U.S. Attorney's Office at the same time.

Carlin agrees. "We can get an injunction from a federal judge that says don't do it again. We can get a judgment that says pay back your profits. We can get a judgment that says you have to pay a civil penalty in a large amount. But when it comes to some people, if you're not able to put them in jail, they're not going to be real worried about you. For certain people, the only thing that's really going to get their attention is the threat of incarceration."

Just as white-collar crime was once considered low priority by the police, criminal prosecutors historically showed very little interest in securities fraud. Besides the fact that securities fraud is usually complicated and document intensive, cases are often filled with unexciting accounting issues. The last thing a criminal prosecutor wants to do is put a jury to sleep. Which is one reason why criminal prosecutors weren't interested in the SEC's 1996 case against Salvatore Mazzeo.

Five years previously, the forty-three-year-old Mazzeo and his partners opened Westfield Financial Corp. in the Seagram Building on Park Avenue in midtown Manhattan. The address was impressive. Their intentions were less so. Mazzeo had set up Westfield to look like a dealer-brokerage, but underneath it was a brokerage-laundry. He was using the markets to wash funds through sixteen offshore shell companies that a British lawyer had registered for him in Moscow, Gibraltar, and Liberia. He was also bulking cash to Europe in suitcases. In the four years that Westfield operated, Mazzeo and his partners made around $17 million for themselves.

The SEC only happened along after Westfield was out of business. They never knew about the cash and, anyway, they weren't looking at Westfield for money laundering. They wanted Mazzeo and his partners for four specific violations of Regulation S of the Securities Acts of 1933.

Known simply as Reg S, it's a set of rules designed to make it easier and less expensive for small companies to raise capital through special sales of shares to foreign investors. Because they take place outside the regulated securities markets, companies don't have to file all the usual statements, or make all the various disclosures, they would otherwise be obliged to in a registered offering. The thinking goes, as long as these shares are sold into another jurisdiction, it should be up to that jurisdiction to regulate the matter and protect its own citizens. The major restriction placed on Reg-S sales is a holding period – originally forty days, it's since been changed to one year – during which time the offshore buyers cannot resell the shares onshore in the U.S. markets. That's mainly so that companies can't use Reg S to get around U.S. reporting requirements.

However, because Reg-S shares are sold at a deep discount offshore and because the buyers can resell them in the U.S. markets after the waiting period – meaning that there's a potential for immediate profit – Reg-S sales can involve foreigner buyers acting clandestinely for U.S. sellers. That's patently illegal. And that's what bothered the SEC about four of Mazzeo's Reg-S deals.

In March 1993, Mazzeo and Westfield sold fifty thousand unregistered shares of a woman's footwear company called Candies at a discount to a foreign entity in return for a short-term, unsecured promissory note. Mazzeo negotiated the sale directly with the foreign purchaser's attorney in London. The attorney provided a $150,000 unsecured IOU for the shares. Forty days later those same shares were sold by Mazzeo on behalf of the foreign buyer and the money from that sale paid off the IOU. Two months later Mazzeo sold 727,272 shares at a discount for $2 million to four foreign entities. One of them was a Liberian shell whose address was listed as "P.O. Box 26, Moscow 117049." No other information was provided. The same London attorney handled the deal for the buyers and, again, IOUs were used. When the forty-day period was up, the sale of the shares in U.S. markets grossed $2.8 million and the IOUs were paid.

Two more Reg-S discounted sales followed, using the same formula. There were 25,000 shares of Candies' stock discounted for $75,000 and 600,000 shares of a company called Response USA – manufacturers of personal emergency-response systems – discounted for $1.5 million. The same lawyer in London acted for the foreign buyer in both instances, bought the shares with IOUs and paid off the IOUs when the shares were sold, forty days later, in the U.S. market.

The SEC ruled these were an illegal ruse to avoid properly regulated sales, and therefore a Reg-S violation. Mazzeo was ordered to cease and desist and was suspended from being a broker, dealer, investment adviser, investment company, or municipal securities dealer for a period of five months. The SEC moved on to fry bigger fish and Mazzeo let out a huge sigh of relief.

As a direct result of the demise of the Fulton Fish Market and the Mafia's rubbish-hauling rackets, offices all over Wall Street, and in the backwater financial neighbourhoods too, got turned into boiler rooms. And boiler rooms were being made to look like offices. The new game became microcaps – minutely capitalized, thinly traded companies that you find swimming along the bottom of the smaller, less regulated, slightly murky exchanges. Because microcap companies are not required to submit audited reporting to the SEC – some do but most don't – it's often impossible to find out what the company does or what it's really worth. Combine that with totally fraudulent sales methods and it's easy to understand how prices can be manipulated, how investors can be duped, and why the Mafia loves this.

The crooks behind these deals feed the shares into boiler rooms, where the telemarketers, disguised as brokers, pump up the price by moving shares to the unsuspecting – and bribe and intimidate other dealers to do the same thing – until the share price is high enough, at which time the crooks dump whatever they're holding onto the unwitting market. Investors lose everything while the crooks conceal their profits offshore and move on to the next microcap swindle.

Mazzeo had managed it, for example, with a microcap called Guardian Technologies International. A bulletproof vest manufacturer founded by Oliver North, whose own money-laundering exploits were highlighted by the Iran-Contra scandal back in the 1980s. Thanks to Mazzeo, his sixteen shell companies, and his ability to manipulate share prices, Guardian Technologies jumped $12 on the first day. He then dumped shares on unsuspecting investors and the price sank like a stone to a few cents.

He got away with it because his was common, everyday Reg-S stuff at a time when criminal prosecutors were looking for big-deal, mobbed-up swindlers. Which is why the SEC, the FBI, and the Manhattan District Attorney's Office came to bust Meyers Pollock Robbins. Operating out of New York, Las Vegas, and south Florida, Meyers Pollock Robbins ran a standard pump 'n' dump on more than two dozen microcaps, swindling sixteen thousand clients out of $176 million. Sitting at the heart of the scams were the Genovese and Bonanno crime families, who not only backed certain deals but handled the "incentive" side of the business – the bribes and intimidation.

The Manhattan District Attorney's Office followed the money trails and located $1.5 million on the Channel Island of Guernsey. Some of the sham companies Meyers Pollock Robbins used had also been registered there.

No sooner had the SEC and their criminal prosecutor pals put Meyers Pollock Robbins out of business when they joined up again to bust another mobbed-up microcap dealer-brokerage, A.S. Goldmen.

The 1988 brainchild of brothers Anthony and Salvatore Marchiano, those two decided that if their business worked, they'd be worth their weight in gold. The *A* and *S* of the firm's name were their first names, the Goldmen part was what they hoped to become. The brothers opened offices in Naples, Florida, New York, and New Jersey and by the mid-1990s had more than three hundred brokers and fifty thousand customer accounts. In just one of their fraudulent offerings, the Marchianos moved three million shares of a microcap called Millennium Sports Management. They walked away with $7.5 million. They spent a lot of it on their own lifestyles, but also dumped plenty into offshore accounts. It would later turn out that the Millennium offering was financed by some Genovese mobsters.

In total, A.S. Goldmen moved ten microcap companies into the world, bilking investors of $100 million. Some of that money went through the Bahamas. Some of it turned up in the same places that Meyers Pollock Robbins money did. But then, there was a lot of cross-over between the two firms, with many brokers moving back and forth. Like Meyers Pollock Robbins, A.S. Goldmen was shut down and people went to jail. Anthony got ten to thirty years, Salvatore got five to fifteen.

Before long, the SEC and the FBI came down on DMN Capital Investments. That firm was backed by the Bonanno and Gambino families with some participation of all five LCN families. DMN had fraudulently traded in the shares of nineteen companies and in the private placement of sixteen others. There was also racketeering and physical violence. A ten-month investigation resulted in a roundup that saw six hundred FBI agents and police officers grab 120 people in thirteen states. Investors had suffered losses of up to $50 million. Some of it has been found in the Caribbean. Some of it is still hidden offshore.

"There's always an offshore connection somewhere," Carlin maintains. "If you're not offshore, you didn't go to the right school, you didn't have the right mentor, you just don't get it. Offshore makes the task of tracking you down that much more difficult. It doesn't mean you can't be tracked down, but when you're offshore it takes longer and it is much more difficult."

He notes that all the usual suspects show up all the time – Switzerland, the Bahamas, the Caymans, Liechtenstein, Antigua – but adds that he also sees many jurisdictions that he describes as "not on the all-time hits list," such as Gibraltar, Cyprus, and phony operations in the Pacific like Nauru and Niue.

"We see them all. And we try to go after it all. But don't assume for a moment that when we come knocking on their door they're necessarily very helpful. There was a judicial decision not long ago in Switzerland that was decidedly unhelpful. The Supreme Court there narrowed our ability to obtain financial evidence. I think it's fair to say that the most popular places for dirty money continue to be popular, and the places that are the least helpful when it comes to letting us in to look for dirty money continue to be the least helpful."

Policing the investment world, the SEC's Carlin adds, is a juggling act. "We watch activity in the market. We have informants. We listen to complaints. We conduct field audits. Our guys are very good at realizing what they've walked into. Many times, it's not by accident that they're going into a certain office. When a share suddenly blips 300 per cent in just two hours, we want to know why. There's all kinds of surveillance that goes on. We have all sorts of ways of spotting activities that shouldn't be going on."

There's no doubt that, while they come up with the goods very often, they didn't in 1996 with Sal Mazzeo.

What they didn't know was what happened when Mazzeo learned that the SEC was sniffing around Westfield's crooked Reg-S deals. He panicked. He couldn't afford to have the SEC looking too closely at the offshore companies that had purchased the Reg-S shares because, if they did, they'd also see the money laundering. So he decided to make the ownership of those offshore shells disappear. He wanted to find someone who would stand up and lie, "We own those companies."

The one man he knew he could count on was the lawyer in London who'd set up those sixteen shells for him. He was the same lawyer in London who'd worked the foreign end of those Reg-S deals. Mazzeo rang him for help and the lawyer assured Mazzeo it would be no problem to supply a beneficial owner for the shell companies. Even better, the lawyer claimed, the person he had in mind was a minor Liberian diplo-mat and, minor or not, his diplomatic status would provide a certain immunity to the whole business. As a diplomat, he couldn't be called on to testify in court.

Mazzeo thought it was perfect.

If it wasn't for Stephan Saccoccia, it might have been.

⟶

The Americans knew that some of Saccoccia's money had gone to Europe but didn't know how much he'd stashed away there or where he'd hidden it. However, they had a pair of names in the U.K. who might know something about it. So they asked Britain's Southeast Regional Crime Squad (SERCS) for help.

Details of the U.K. side of this investigation are revealed in an official confidential report begun in 1991 and continually updated throughout the decade. It explains that one of the two men was Robert Dick, a stocky fifty-three-year-old who claimed to be in the film business, at times telling people he was a producer, at times telling people he wrote screenplays. The other was John Joseph O'Carroll, a thirty-five-year-old workaholic who'd made a fortune in commodities during the boom days of the 1980s.

SERCS officers interviewed the pair separately. Both categorically denied laundering Saccoccia's drug money and neither of them was ever charged in the matter. However, both men admitted to having met Saccoccia. Dick acknowledged that he'd been holding $75,000 for Saccoccia and handed it over to the police. O'Carroll, who said that Saccoccia was a minor acquaintance, divulged that he'd helped Saccoccia obtain a safety deposit box at Selfridges Department Store on Oxford Street, in which the police found $530,000.

According to the report of those interviews, both men denied knowing anything about Saccoccia's funds outside the U.K. But the FBI had intercepted telephone conversations between Saccoccia and O'Carroll, suggesting that the two were more than simply minor acquaintances. Anyway, accounts had already been discovered in Austria, opened on Saccoccia's behalf in 1988. One of Saccoccia's American attorneys had shown up in Vienna to withdraw funds from an account the Austrians had already frozen. The attorney was arrested and found to be carrying papers relating to another code-named account in Vienna, this one, the report says, registered to O'Carroll.

The attorney was prosecuted in Vienna for his involvement in laundering Saccoccia's money but, against the odds, was acquitted by the bench. The trial judge later received a reprimand from the Vienna High Court, the acquittal was overturned, and a retrial was ordered. By then, the American attorney was back in the States and not planning on ever visiting Austria again.

That's where the British inquiry ground to a halt. No charges were lodged against Dick or O'Carroll. The officers who'd been working the case moved on, and the matter lay dormant for nearly nine months. Then, in November 1994, Gordon Hutchins was assigned to SERCS.

A rugged Metropolitan Police detective, he'd been working mostly murders and organized crime until the team he was on decided to see if they could follow a money trail left by drug traffickers working around London's King's Cross Station. That was his introduction to financial crime. When Hutchins came to SERCS, he went straight to the money-laundering team and the first case he picked up was Saccoccia.

Several inquiries abroad hadn't been answered, so he started following them up. Over the course of the next thirteen months, he discovered a bunch of offshore companies that opened new lines of inquiry. One of them, registered in Ireland but administered in the Channel Island of Jersey, was called FRM. Hutchins tied that company to O'Carroll. Records showed that $8 million had passed through FRM's account at the Bank of Ireland-Jersey. The money was a consolidation of wires from stockbrokers in the States addressed to other shell companies. Most of $8 million was then wired back to the States, addressed to six different recently registered shells – two in the British Virgin Islands (BVI), one in the Isle of Man, one in Liberia, one in Panama, and one registration was unknown. Four of the six were managed out of Guernsey.

An FRM payment that did not go to the States was the $89,000 transfer to a Bank of Ireland account in Jersey in Dick's name. Looking at that account, Hutchins saw two deposits in a two-month period – one for $54,096 and another for $130,000 – which Dick wired on to Barbados.

Hutchins was also able to establish that of the six recently registered shells, the two BVI companies and the Liberian company had been receiving monies from FRM in Jersey. Those three had, in turn, made some substantial payments to a third BVI company, this one administered Guernsey with accounts held there by the Royal Bank of Scotland.

From the account of this third BVI company, a payment was made for $1,631,000. Around the same time, a payment for $1,950,000 was made from FRM in Jersey. A third payment, this one for $200,000, came from the Liberian company. The recipient of all three – totalling $2,151,631 – was a company in California called Scorpion Technologies.

﹀

While Hutchins was nosing around the accounts in the Channel Islands, the SEC – without knowing about the British investigation – was nosing around Scorpion Technologies.

A Colorado-registered company with offices near San Jose, California, Scorpion's business was computer software conversion systems and imaging processing technology. But business wasn't good. Scorpion's shares were flat in the basement at forty-eight cents. The company's president and CEO, Terry Marsh, knew they were about to go bust. Drastic measures were needed, so Marsh and others plotted to save the company and, at the same time, to save themselves.

Marsh hired a man named Barry Witz. It's not clear whether Marsh approached the three-hundred-and-fifty-pound Witz looking for help, or if Witz came along on his own offering to solve Marsh's problems. But Witz was clearly a man who knew how markets functioned in the real world. A lawyer by trade, he'd worked at both the SEC and the New York Stock Exchange and, for a while, was employed by corporate take-over specialist Carl Icahn. In any case, it was Witz who took Scorpion to Reg S.

The day after Witz joined the company, Marsh announced that newly developed imaging software would generate $12 million in revenues. The Reg-S issue followed that. Almost overnight, the company's shares shot up, going as high as $7.59. A lot of people made a lot of money very quickly and Scorpion duly reported revenue of $12.5 million. Except $10 million of that was a sham.

Within eighteen months, the FBI had raided the company, NASDAQ had halted trading on it, and the share price had sunk to nineteen cents. The bureau's investigation revealed how Marsh and others in the company used bank accounts and shell companies in twenty countries to generate fraudulent sales and trading figures. After pumping the price, Marsh and others dumped twenty-two million shares onto the market.

Foreign buyers in the Reg-S offering illegally split their profits with Scorpion, which now moved money back into the company, creating a cash flow that made it look as if Scorpion was actually selling software.

Federal prosecutors would eventually lodge fraud and money-laundering charges against Marsh and eight others. And Marsh would go to prison for that. According to depositions filed in the case, it was alleged that Witz had bribed brokers to pump Scorpion's share. Witz denied it and was never charged. However, a pair of class-action civil suits brought by Scorpion's shareholders followed the criminal case and in one of those Witz is named as a defendant.

When the SEC unravelled Scorpion's Reg-S scam, they found that two shell companies were listed as buyers. One was registered in the BVI, the other in Panama. Both were owned by O'Carroll. The Panamanian company, Mayfair Financial, had purchased four million shares offshore and had unloaded them quickly through a small New York brokerage. The BVI company had purchased four million and unloaded them through the same broker – Westfield Financial Corp.

It meant that O'Carroll and Witz both knew Mazzeo.

⟶

And Witz knew O'Carroll.

Hutchins's investigation in the U.K. revealed payments from O'Carroll's FRM to several shells that Witz was involved with in the States.

The U.K. investigation had simply grown too big and too complex for one man, so two more detectives joined Hutchins in the search. Neil Jeans had been a uniformed constable working out of a central London police station. But he'd also once been a stockbroker, and when Hutchins heard that, he requested that Jeans be assigned to SERCS. With him came a young general CID detective, Martin Woods.

"Neil and Martin came along," Hutchins explains, "because the investigation had broadened out so much and I needed help. I'd got stacks of details from Jersey that showed all sorts of stock trading, but I didn't understand what it was all about. Neil, having once been a stockbroker, understood it immediately. That's when we identified some $2.2 billion going through one of the companies. These were stock trades by Mazzeo at Westfield Financial. One company, for instance, issued one million shares and wound up trading ninety-three million shares. In other words, here was a company that sold itself ninety-three times."

Only now did the Brits, looking at Saccoccia's money, and the SEC lawyers, looking at Scorpion, became aware of each other. The SEC had filed a request for mutual assistance with the U.K. Department of Trade and Industry (DTI). They wanted to find out more about O'Carroll, about Mazzeo's lawyer in London, and about whatever dealings Mazzeo and Westfield Financial had with either of them. The request included a long list of companies, among them FRM, Mazzeo's shells, and at least one in which Witz was involved. After scrutinizing the SEC's request, the DTI discussed the matter with senior managers at SERCS. Companies and names on the SEC list matched companies and names that Hutchins, Jeans, and Woods were looking at.

Of particular interest was O'Carroll's Panamanian company, Mayfair Financial. Hutchins, Jeans, and Woods learned that he'd first tried to register it in BVI, but the name wasn't available. Wondering why he needed that specific name, the Brits found that six weeks before the company was registered in Panama, Scorpion Technologies had already noted in its Reg-S subscription a sale of one million shares to Mayfair Financial. In other words, the shares had been assigned before the company was formed. The Scorpion paperwork, which declared both O'Carroll and Mayfair Financial non-U.S. citizens and therefore made them eligible for the Reg-S offering, was signed by Barry Witz.

Those same folks showed up again with a BVI company called Saturn Enterprises. O'Carroll appeared to be the beneficial owner of it, and the only reason for the company's existence appeared to be the purchase of Reg-S shares in a firm called Osicom Technologies.

That company was the creation of a man called Parvinder Chadha. A publicly held company, Osicom made personal computers but had been struggling for years. In 1992, it looked as if it was going under. Until Barry Witz came along. He said he knew an overseas investor willing to buy a piece of Osicom's floundering business. Saturn Enterprises acquired Osicom's U.K. subsidiary for $1.25 million worth of shares and $2.5 million of debt. The next thing that happened was that Scorpion Technologies acquired Saturn. When the SEC looked closely at that sale, they suspected it was part of Scorpion's Reg-S fraud. They believed the deal was done in an effort to make Osicom look profitable and augment Scorpion's balance sheet.

The SEC was also concerned about the paperwork they saw supporting the deal. In one document, Saturn's president – a Bolivian national – signs his name, Mario V. Andrade. In the other, identical to the first, the president's name and signature is said to be O'Carroll's. Sworn depositions by at least one of the defendants in the Scorpion Technologies case names Witz as the power behind FRM and Mayfair Financial. Witz answered that it wasn't true and that his only dealings with O'Carroll were to represent him as his lawyer. O'Carroll has steadfastly maintained his innocence and has never been charged in any of these inquiries. Nor has Witz.

Worryingly, some of the money from Scorpion's Reg-S sale was wired into Bolivian bank accounts associated with a company in La Paz apparently run by a man also named Andrade. When the FBI looked at that, they couldn't find any reference anywhere to the company, but did recognize the name. They informed the British officers that there were open drug inquiries on several Bolivians named Andrade. The three British investigators never found out whether the Andrades involved with Saturn were the same ones being looked at by the Americans for drug trafficking. But according to the Americans, two Bolivians named Andrade had been caught in a sting in Los Angeles, instructing undercover agents to deposit large amounts of drug cash into bank accounts in London and Switzerland.

That sting was part of the Saccoccia investigation.

So now Hutchins, Jeans, and Woods looked again at the relationship between Witz and O'Carroll, and Mazzeo kept showing up. That brought Hutchins, Jeans, and Woods straight back to Mazzeo's lawyer in London.

At least one of the companies that the lawyer in London had incorporated in Liberia for Mazzeo was managed in Jersey for the benefit of Westfield Financial. Some of the deals that were moved through that account were Reg-S sales that tied back to Witz. From there, Hutchins found one of Mazzeo's BVI companies, set up by his lawyer in London and also managed out of Jersey. Then he found another Liberian company. Then he found a Dutch company. And then he found several bank accounts where large sums moved in and out very quickly.

The more the three British officers thought they were looking for Saccoccia's drug money, the more they kept seeing what appeared to be the proceeds of securities fraud.

Dozens of companies popped up all over the offshore world – but especially in the Channel Islands, BVI, Antigua, and Ireland – many of them linking back to one another. As the ties between those companies grew more complicated, the officers started seeing commercial paper, including a $10-million note signed by Mazzeo that related directly to the drug laundromat BCCI. Then they started seeing Russians, with money moving through companies that used false addresses and would eventually link back to the Bank of New York.

Senior managers at SERCS soon decided that the Americans would have to handle that side of the inquiry because they wanted to focus on Mazzeo's London lawyer.

Andrew Warren was born in 1946, had practised law at a solicitor's firm called Rutherfords, and was now with one called Talbot-Creggy. His partner there was Stuart Creggy, born in 1939. But Creggy was not only a practising solicitor, he was also a sitting magistrate at the North Westminster Petty Sessions court.

If Warren was bent, the police worried, his partner might be as well.

If Magistrate Creggy was bent – putting criminals away for the same crimes he was committing – the ramifications for the British judicial system could be enormous.

I2

WHEN PARALLEL LINES MEET

*"You'll only ever have two friends in life,
your mother and your bank balance."*

– advice to her son from Stuart Creggy's mother

W hile the British were starting to investigate Andrew Warren and Stuart Creggy, John Moscow had worries of his own.

In the mid-1990s, with markets going wild and organized crime taking full advantage of confusion bred in greed, Manhattan District Attorney Robert Morgenthau put Wall Street on notice that microcap fraud would not be tolerated, and put the Mob on notice that they were not welcome on Wall Street. His point man was Moscow and there was plenty to keep him busy.

Broker-dealer Stratton Oakmont made $28 million in illicit profits on five microcap offerings. Broker-dealer D.H. Blair excessively marked-up on sixteen microcaps. Broker-dealer GKN Securities excessively marked-up on eight microcaps. Broker-dealer Sterling Foster made illicit profits exceeding $50 million on three microcap underwritings.

There was market manipulation at La Jolla Capital and at Hibbard Brown and at Chatfield Dean and at H.J. Meyers. A four-year probe of Mob activities on Wall Street brought indictments to nineteen people, including six La Cosa Nostra guys and some Russians, for running multimillion-dollar scams. At Globus Group, eighteen Russians were indicted on twenty-two counts of securities fraud and conspiracy to commit murder.

Along the way Moscow busted A.R. Baron.

A small-time bucket shop pretending to be a legitimate broker-dealer, A.R. Baron was run by an aggressive young con man named Andrew Bressman. Over the five years that Baron was in business – July 1991 to July 1996 – Bressman and his cohorts managed to steal more than $75 million from eight thousand investors. The National Association of Securities Dealers (NASD) caught up with them in July 1995, fining Baron $1.5 million for excessively marking up on clients. Restitution was ordered, and some executives, Bressman included, were given a slap on the wrist with minor suspensions. It was, nevertheless, the NASD's largest enforcement action that year. A year later, Baron was in such terrible financial difficulties that liquidation became inevitable.

The company was later described by Robert Morgenthau as a place "where every conceivable form of dishonesty was used. It was created and it existed for no other reason than to line the pockets of its executives and employees at the expense of unsuspecting members of the public."

In July 1997, Moscow convened a grand jury, which handed down a 228-page, 174-count indictment against A.R. Baron and thirteen employees. Moscow charged them with enterprise corruption, grand larceny, a scheme to defraud, and other crimes. Bressman was charged with the theft of $8.5 million.

The SEC now ordered Bressman to return $6,038,412 to his clients. In response, he filed for bankruptcy. Some people believe that his money remains hidden offshore. Bressman owned some Liberian shell companies in Jersey and had hidden illegal profits in an entity called Mid-Ocean Trust, which was registered in the Pacific backwater of Rarotonga, Cook Islands.

Confronted with the overwhelming evidence that Moscow had gathered against him, Bressman pled guilty to enterprise corruption and grand larceny. Facing twenty-five years in jail, he agreed to co-operate with the authorities while sentencing was pending.

In London, Gordon Hutchins, Neil Jeans, and Martin Woods were trying to build a case against lawyers Andrew Warren and Stuart Creggy.

The three officers had identified funds going back and forth between the U.S. and the U.K., and knew that some of those funds were the proceeds of crime, specifically securities fraud. But under U.K. law, as it was then in force, to pin money laundering on Warren and Creggy, they needed a predicate offence in the U.K. And in those days, parliament was still foolishly insisting that money laundering was a crime only when the predicate offence was drug, terror, or major fraud related.

In search of that predicate offence, the detectives spent three entire months putting names into various databases, desperately hoping to find one little shred of evidence that would allow them to nab the two lawyers.

"It was very frustrating," Hutchins recalls. "The more we looked, the more difficult it seemed to become."

Exasperated one lunchtime, Jeans left the office and headed down the block to buy a sandwich. As he approached the local news kiosk, he noticed a story in that day's *Evening Standard*: fifty investors, including Sir Anthony Pilkington, chairman of the family glass company, and the late Duke of Atholl, had been victims of a fraudulent securities dealer in New York named A.R. Baron.

Jeans recognized those names and bought the paper. Then he spotted Andrew Bressman's name. He knew that Bressman was a Creggy client and that Creggy had set up some Liberian companies for Bressman in Jersey. He rushed back to the office and, within an hour, Hutchins was on the phone with Clark Abrams, a bright, go-getter lawyer he knew at the SEC.

Hutchins told Abrams about the Creggy-Bressman connection and asked if he knew John Moscow. Abrams said he didn't, but promised to call Moscow to see if he was interested in knowing more about this British connection. Within an hour of speaking to Abrams, Hutchins was on the line with Moscow. And when Moscow heard what Hutchins had to say, he responded, "Come to New York."

A few days later, Hutchins and Jeans flew to New York to lay out their case for Moscow. "We were selling, not buying," Hutchins says.

It was apparent that the cases on each side of the Atlantic were parallel. But being parallel, they were also separate. Moscow now included Creggy and Warren on his list of people to look at, while questioning Hutchins and Jeans about the lawyers' links to Russians who were showing up in the Bank of New York money-laundering investigation.

One of the companies that Hutchins, Jeans, and Woods had spotted in Jersey was tied into a second offshore company, controlled by Russians living in the U.K. Those Russians were connected to the Russians that Moscow was investigating in the Bank of New York case. One money trail led directly to Benex and Becs International. Another pointed to Semion Mogilevitch, the Russian accused of being at the very heart of the YBM Magnex scandal that fed into the BoNY case.

Over the course of three days in New York, the parallel lines moved closer together. By coincidence, at one point during those three days, Moscow mentioned that he was hiring staff. Hutchins put in a bid for his pal Abrams. Not long afterwards, Moscow hired him away from the SEC.

Hutchins and Jeans returned to Britain, but the phone and fax lines to Moscow's office stayed open and active. Moscow expanded his BoNY investigation to Europe, particularly to the Channel Islands. Hutchins, Jeans, and Woods continued to focus on Creggy and Warren. A few months later, when they felt they had sufficient evidence to take a crack at Creggy and Warren, the British officers obtained search warrants for their offices.

The law firm of Talbot-Creggy was at 38 Queen Anne Street, a block north of Wigmore Street in London's West End. Creggy's office was on the first floor of the building, Warren's on the second floor.

The search warrants were written specifically to permit access to all materials concerning twenty named offshore companies, like the ones in Jersey, and to several named people including Bressman, O'Carroll, Witz, and Mazzeo. Hutchins handed a copy of it to Creggy, who looked down the list and said that none of the names meant anything to him. Hutchins then went upstairs and presented a copy to Warren, who looked down the list and admitted to knowing Mazzeo. Warren also said he had some documents in the office relating to some of the named companies and provided the officers with twenty-one files.

Many of the documents the officers obtained that day duplicated documents they'd already acquired in the Channel Islands. Of the ones they hadn't already seen, some added substantially to what they knew about Sal Mazzeo and Westfield Financial. But one file in particular would stand out. It contained copies of correspondence and faxes to and from a lawyer in Montreal, Canada, named Harry J.F. Bloomfield.

One of those faxes, dated April 6, 1994, and addressed to Bloomfield on Talbot-Creggy letterhead, had obviously been returned by Bloomfield, because it had a handwritten note at the bottom of it.

The original message from Creggy to Bloomfield read: "Dear Harry, we have the need of the services of Charles again. Could you be kind enough to fax through a phone number where we can make contact with him (if necessary), although I do not think it likely. So that we can have it just in case. Or would you like his phone number to be yours? Could you please reply to my partner Andrew Warren in my absence."

The handwritten note back from Bloomfield read: "Dear elder colleague, Wilson 613-830-6901. I have advised him of a possible call. Send dollars, dollars."

The "Charles" and "Wilson" in question turned out to be a minor Liberian diplomat with that name, then stationed in Ottawa. He was the same minor Liberian diplomat who'd signed off as the beneficial owner on Sal Mazzeo's sixteen shell companies. The same sixteen shell companies that Mazzeo had asked Andrew Warren for help with when Westfield Financial was being investigated by the SEC for Reg-S fraud.

⌁

Harry Bloomfield moved in rarefied circles.

Born in 1944, he was a Queen's Counsel and senior partner in a Montreal law firm that bore his name, Bloomfield Bellemare. His father, Bernard, was a high-profile businessman and philanthropist in Montreal. His uncle Louis Mortimer Bloomfield was a lawyer with ties to the Bronfman family. Louis had served during the Second World War as an officer in the British Special Operations Executive – a euphemism for the spooks – and afterwards was chairman of a decidedly shady operation called Permindex. Conspiracy buffs link Permindex to nefarious goings-on and criminal intrigue in Cold War Europe, all of it managed on behalf of some spy service somewhere. From there, they tie Permindex and Louis to the same organized crime guys in New Orleans, who eventually form part of the conspiracy buffs' endlessly mutating DNA of the Kennedy assassination.

Various reporting suggests that Louis, through Permindex, was associated in money laundering – again, supposedly at the behest of a spy service – with Tibor Rosenbaum's Banque International de Credit (BIC). At least one of Permindex's main accounts was held in Rosenbaum's bank in Geneva. There have also been reports that a company once owned by Mafia boss Joe Bonanno owned shares in Permindex. That company was taken over by fraudster Robert Vesco. And while it could be unsound to draw inferences about a businessman by the company he keeps, there are enough odd circumstances surrounding Permindex and Louis Bloomfield, at least, to make one wonder.

An unconfirmed report has it that, as a young man, Harry Bloomfield worked for a time at BIC.

In later years Harry Bloomfield was president of a private charity, the Eldee Foundation, and a director on several company boards. He'd also been an unsuccessful parliamentary candidate in Canada's 1980 election, running as a Conservative for a riding in the Town of Mont Royal, next door to Montreal. Seven years after failing to win a seat, his pal Brian Mulroney appointed Bloomfield to the board of the Business Development Bank of Canada (BDBC), where he served as chairman of the audit committee for four years. He left the BDBC board in 1996.

Described by one Canadian newspaper as "a man who collects titles like lesser mortals collect postage stamps," Bloomfield comes by it naturally. His father was honorary consul general for South Korea and Uncle Louis had some sort of unofficial status as an adviser to the opposition party in British Honduras, now Belize. Harry also had a diplomatic relationship with the Government of Belize and appeared to have an honorary title from Djibouti.

But the title that really mattered, the one that Uncle Louis also had, was honorary consul general for Liberia.

—

Sal Mazzeo moved in less rarefied, decidedly more dangerous circles.

In 1994, two young men who'd briefly worked at Westfield Financial stepped into Sal's midtown office and one of them shoved a pistol into the side of Sal's head. The man with the gun was Albert Alain Chalem, a French-born broker who'd made a name for himself pumping microcaps. The other was Maier Lehmann, a similarly dodgy broker and Chalem's sidekick. Chalem nervously reminded Mazzeo that he and his pal were still owed money, and because Mazzeo had been warned before, and because Mazzeo didn't take those warnings seriously enough to pay up, they intended to settle the debt their way.

Mazzeo somehow managed to calm them down, then slowly talked Chalem and Lehmann out of doing something stupid then and there.

Eventually, he persuaded them to leave. The instant they were gone, Mazzeo phoned someone who could guarantee his safety. He had a lot of those connections. But whomever it was that he begged to intervene with Chalem, that man needed credibility because Chalem was personally close to Phil Abramo, a DeCavalcante crime family *capo*. The two had been buddies in Florida at A.S. Goldmen, where, among other fraudulent deals, they manipulated Osicom Technologies shares during that Reg-S offering.

Whether Mazzeo had markers he could call in, used family connections that he definitely had, or simply paid in cash, it worked. The Chalem problem went away. But another serious problem would soon manifest itself – the identification of Charles Wilson and his fraudulent claim to being the owner of Mazzeo's sixteen shell companies.

John Moscow wasn't going to let anyone make this one disappear. He moved on Mazzeo and his two partners, George Carhart and James Cohen, even though Westfield Financial was already out of business. Moscow charged Mazzeo – who was by then running a small gourmet food shop on Long Island – with attempted enterprise corruption. At the end of October 1997, Mazzeo pled guilty to illegally obtaining over $17 million from investors. Based on his evidence, his partners Carhart and Cohen were also arrested and charged. But before anyone could discover that Mazzeo had turned, Moscow sealed Mazzeo's plea. He kept it secret for nearly nine months, specifically to allow the officers in Britain time to work their end of the investigation.

In March 1998, Hutchins and Jeans returned to New York to interview Liberian diplomat Charles Wilson, who was now attached to his country's delegation there. As a result of conversations with Wilson, the parallel lines were about to meet.

On June 23, Moscow unsealed Mazzeo's plea. The following morning, in London, Stuart Creggy and Andrew Warren were arrested.

Mazzeo's sentencing was delayed another ten months. Under normal circumstances, it happens relatively quickly. When it's put off for any real length of time, it's usually because the prosecutors want access to that person. The reason why is, generally, because that person has something to say. Mazzeo was free, awaiting sentencing for nineteen months, until July 1999, when he was found dead.

Officially he died of natural causes in his sleep at home. But not everybody believes it, because forty-one-year-olds don't usually die in their sleep of natural causes. Anyway, this was a man who moved in circles where death is one way of doing business. There are even a few people who believe Mazzeo is not dead at all, that he was able to fake it. His death certificate was signed by a relative. Limited toxicology was done by the coroner's office. The photo of his body on the medical examiner's table is inconclusive and may or may not be him. Cremation took place before the D.A.'s office was informed that Mazzeo was dead.

Far-fetched, perhaps. But certainly not the first time that such things have occurred to people who move in the same circles as Sal Mazzeo.

On the night of October 25, 1999, Albert Alain Chalem and Maier Lehmann were found dead in Chalem's home in New Jersey. In this case there's no doubt that they're dead. Or that someone wanted them dead. The cause of death was multiple gunshot wounds to their heads.

In June 1998, new search warrants had been issued for Andrew Warren's office, for Stuart Creggy's office, and also for an office in Brighton where the police believed other documents might be. On the morning of June 24, only hours after Moscow unsealed Mazzeo's plea, Hutchins, Jeans, Woods, and other officers from the National Crime Squad raided Talbot-Creggy. They were joined by a couple of people from Moscow's office in New York, including his chief investigator, Andrew Finan. Also accompanying the raiding party was a technical team from Scotland Yard for the computers, and representatives from the Law Society because searching and seizing documents from lawyers' offices is a delicate matter. The client-attorney privilege of people not involved with the case needs to be protected.

Another group of officers raided the Brighton premises.

But when Hutchins and his team arrived at 38 Queen Street, they were in for a surprise. The brass plate that bore the name Talbot-Creggy had been removed from the front of the building, and there were signs that the place was not fully occupied. Asking inside, Hutchins was told that Talbot-Creggy was no longer practising at that address. A hasty discussion took place on the sidewalk as the officers tried to figure out what to do next.

As luck would have it, that's when Andrew Warren happened along. So what Hutchins did next was arrest him.

The officers brought Warren inside, read him his rights, and started bundling documents. While this was going on, Warren gave Hutchins a phone number for Creggy. Hutchins dialled it, Creggy answered, and Hutchins explained that the police were in the midst of executing a search at Queen Anne Street. Hutchins invited Creggy to join them there. Creggy said he knew about the raid because he'd already got a call from his staff in Brighton, but, unfortunately, he could not attend because he was on his way to the airport to fly out to the States.

Hutchins asked for his new office address, which Creggy gave him. And as soon as they hung up, Hutchins and Jeans jumped in their car, got to Creggy before he left for the airport, and arrested him. More officers now showed up at Creggy's new office and documents were seized there too.

"With the first search warrant," Hutchins explains, "we believed we were investigating money laundering. As a result of the additional information we managed to obtain, it now became obvious to us that we were also looking at conspiracy to defraud."

During the move to his new office, Creggy had shipped a large portion of his files to a garage lock-up in another part of the country. The officers found out about that, obtained access to the garage, and seized those files too. In all, the police acquired seven full pallets of paperwork from Creggy and Warren, an estimated half-million documents. It would take them a year just to begin to realize the full extent of incrimination these documents held, how relationships had come together, and where the money trails would lead.

Among the documents was a wealth of correspondence between Bloomfield and Creggy. Much of it refers to Wilson's services as their for-hire diplomat. One letter, dated December 1994, mentions a Liberian honorary consulship on sale in Germany for $25,000. Another, dated September 1995, has Bloomfield explaining how he's been selected as an "Approved Immigration Consultant" by the government of Belize and is now in a position to help people buy citizenship in that country. The price he quotes is $75,000 plus fees, for which a new passport can be issued immediately. He asks Creggy if he has any potential clients.

Some of the documents opened entirely new lines of inquiry. In one file, Martin Woods stumbled across a *Times Law Report* that discussed aspects of offshore company ownership as raised in a 1993 case called *El Ajou v Dollar Land Holdings*. Creggy sent the report to one of his clients in Canada, who was a defendant in that suit. Woods contacted the lawyers who'd represented El Ajou and learned how their client lost $12 million in the deal. The lawyers told Woods that several Canadians had perpetrated this fraud, including one who could be tied directly back to Meyer Lansky. The lawyers also described the money trail in the case – starting in Geneva, going to Gibraltar, then on to Panama, back through Geneva, and finally to London. The more Woods found out about the Dollar Land Holdings case, the more he saw unmistakable similarities with the Creggy and Warren case. Several new areas now needed to be looked at.

In another file, a Canadian suspected of fraud was linked to Creggy. When Creggy was first asked about this man, he said they'd met in 1993. But this file proved they'd met as early as 1989. That caused the officers to look again at other relationships Creggy had denied. And other inconsistencies began appearing.

In an offshoot from information discovered in these files, a gentleman in Canada was stopped with an attaché case containing CAD$200,000. The police wanted to know what this money was. The man explained that he'd just withdrawn it from his account at a Swiss bank in Montreal to pay for a new kitchen. The Mounties seized the money, pending their own inquiries. But when officers interviewed employees at the Swiss bank, they were told that no such withdrawal had taken place. It subsequently turned out that the money had been brought into Canada from the Bahamas. When the police confronted the man with that fact, he denied it. So the Mounties decided to hold on to the money until the man was able to satisfy them that this was not somehow tied to the proceeds of crime. Rather than expose himself to the inquiry, the man simply walked away from the $200,000.

Also among the papers found in Creggy's files were copies of false export documents that he'd supplied, either to Bloomfield for a Canadian company or directly to the Canadian company, so that the company could fraudulently reclaim taxes and duties on goods it hadn't exported. Further documents led to a Canadian boiler-room operator set up in England seemingly with Creggy's help. The money from that scam was shipped off to Malta, a matter still being investigated.

In a bizarre twist to the story, documents were discovered indicating that a company called Panavest U.K., which was registered in Gibraltar, owned several shell companies registered in Guernsey and Luxembourg, which owned an historic church in Toronto. But in 1995, St. Paul's Trinity United burned to the ground. The matter is still officially listed with police as a $5-million unsolved arson. Panavest U.K. bought the church in 1992 to redevelop the property. During the ensuing investigation, a fire marshal looking into the possibility of arson received threats to his family, which the police say they took seriously. Creggy told the police that Panavest U.K. was owned by two Israelis and two South Africans, whom he would not name. Creggy himself was once managing director of Panavest U.K. Insurance investigators in Canada say the company was secretly owned by a Canadian and that the Israelis and South Africans were fronts set up by Creggy, the same way he used Wilson. That investigation also continues.

However, it was in New York that the Creggy and Warren files really had an effect. Through them, Moscow was able to tie up several loose ends involving Mazzeo, to open several new lines of inquiry in the Bank of New York matter, and to begin putting together a case against Creggy, Bloomfield, and Warren.

In June 1999, a New York grand jury indicted Andrew Warren on seventy-eight charges, including enterprise corruption in connection with the offshore companies and false documentation to conceal Westfield Financial's criminal activities in the United States. Warren refused to come to New York to answer the charges and extradition proceedings were opened against him. Warren chose to tough it out. His defence was that he was mentally too depressed to stand trial. In March 2003, a British court ruled that it was up to the American courts to decide whether Warren could stand trial, and ordered him sent to the States. In mid-2003, Warren pleaded guilty to attempted racketeering in connection with an international fraud conspiracy. The case against him continues in the U.K., with inquiries into front companies that link him with Benex, Becs International, certain Russians, and the Bank of New York.

While Warren was fighting extradition, a grand jury in New York also indicted Bloomfield and Creggy on twenty-two counts of criminal conspiracy. Bloomfield presented himself to the New York authorities.

Creggy was invited to New York but refused. Instead, he planned to hole up in his condo in south Florida. His lawyer implored him, "For God's sake, don't go to America." But Creggy was a guy who believed he was fireproof.

John Moscow's guys proved he wasn't, and arrested him there.

Eighteen months later, the Manhattan D.A.'s Office faced off in court with Bloomfield and Creggy. Because Bloomfield and Creggy knew they'd lose in front of a jury, they requested and were granted a bench trial. It would be left to one judge to hear the evidence and decide their fate.

From the beginning, certain people involved with the case found an unsettling arrogance about Bloomfield and Creggy. Spotting Bloomfield coming into the courtroom one morning, one of the detectives who'd investigated him told the Canadian, "I like your tie."

Bloomfield stopped, looked at the detective, and promised, "When, not if, but when I win this case, I'm coming back to New York to give you this tie."

Having seen the evidence stacked against Bloomfield, the detective shook his head. "When you lose, I'm going to ask you for your shoelaces and belt too."

Moscow handled some of the courtroom work, but most of his time was taken up with work on the unfolding Tyco case, and the $600-million looting of that corporation by its senior executives. So responsibility for the day-to-day lead fell to Clark Abrams. Together with Kenneth Chalifoux and Rebecca Roiphe, the three assistant D.A.s went at Bloomfield and Creggy with everything they had, turning the job into eighteen-hour days and seven-day weeks.

Abrams, Chalifoux, and Roiphe, with Moscow to backstop them when he was needed, laid it all out for the judge. Their case was that, from around January 1980 until mid-March 2001, Bloomfield and Creggy had conspired to falsify business and banking records, and to forge securities to assist their clients in violating the law. Specifically, Bloomfield and Creggy had agreed to establish and operate offshore companies and offshore bank accounts for which they'd misrepresented the identities of the owners and directors of those companies and bank accounts. By going offshore, the conspirators were deliberately trying to prevent anyone from discovering the true owners of the companies and bank accounts.

By using a diplomat as a front, they were counting on his diplomatic immunity to block subpoenas and other legal inquiries into the actual owners of the companies and bank accounts. Their assertions of attorney-client privilege would be yet another layer of protection.

In one instance, Bloomfield had a friend in Canada who'd built up a chain of nine pharmacies. Over the years, the man had squirrelled away $400,000 in an offshore bank account. Because Revenue Canada didn't know anything about it, he couldn't just repatriate the money and spend it. On his behalf, Bloomfield and Creggy invented a scheme that involved a Declaration of Trust in the name of two Creggy clients from Cyprus. This was 1995. Creggy agreed that the paperwork should be dated to coincide with the formation of an offshore trust in 1979. Creggy even cooked up the story that his Cypriot clients had met Bloomfield's friend in 1979, decided that Canada was a wonderful place to invest their money, and that their investment was still sitting in that offshore trust all these years later.

Bloomfield told Creggy it would be helpful to have the Declaration of Trust "drawn up in October or November of 1979, just prior to the opening of the account in early December of 1979." He also wanted a letter written by the Cypriots confirming the arrangements plus, "One or two letters over the years that you might have sent him [Bloomfield's friend] to his office asking whether or not investment opportunities were foreseeable."

A few days later, copies of passports and bank references for the Cypriots arrived. So did a draft copy of the Declaration of Trust dated December 1, 1979. It turns out that neither of the people whose names Creggy was using were aware of the transaction. But then neither Bloomfield nor Creggy ever imagined the two would find out about it.

There was, however, a problem that seriously worried Bloomfield about the paperwork Creggy supplied. "Your draft appears to have been produced on a word processor."

Creggy realized that if this stuff had been written in 1979, a word processor would not have been used. He faxed Bloomfield, "We do have a typewriter. It (the draft) was sent to you in great hurry, as and when it will be typed on the old fashioned typewriter."

Needing to make sure that Creggy had his dates and places correct,

Bloomfield reminded him that one of the Cypriots "traveled to Zurich in May of 1976 and stayed at the Hilton Hotel. He also visited Interlaken, Geneva and Montreux. Of course he was also in Nassau in December of 1979 and I am sure he could have met you in Canada or Florida at different times over the years."

Bloomfield wanted Creggy to make sure that it would be obvious to any authorities reading the phony paperwork that his friend had maintained contact with the Cypriots throughout the intervening years. "I therefore again suggest that you look at my October 10 letter for guidance on correspondence that would be in your file, e.g., a letter by which the Cypriots suggested to [Bloomfield's friend] that they stay in touch through you; and one or two letters over the years where you state that you are aware that the funds are accumulating, but no suitable investment has been found, the funds are still not large enough, etc."

The address Bloomfield supplied to Creggy for his friend was where he'd lived in 1979.

Over the course of the prosecution's case, it was shown how Bloomfield and Creggy were doing this sort of thing for loads of people. When a New York plastic surgeon saw one of his patients die on the operating table, he decided to put his assets offshore to render himself judgment-proof. It was Creggy who supplied everything the man needed. Creggy did the same for a heavyweight New York criminal, setting up an offshore network for "Spanish" Raymond Marquez, the man who ran Spanish Harlem's biggest numbers racket.

In yet another example of fraudulent deception, Bloomfield knew a man named Matthew Snyder in New York who was concealing from his employers at Chemical Bank, the bank's regulators, and presumably the IRS, money he was receiving from a client at the bank. Snyder needed Bloomfield to help him hide it, so Bloomfield went to Creggy, who decided to set up a Liberian corporation called Bloomfield and Bloomfield Investment Management Limited (BBIM). But when Creggy tried to open a bank account for BBIM at Bank of Butterfield Bermuda, he was informed that, under the money-laundering laws in force in Bermuda, the bank would require details on the beneficial owner of BBIM. Bloomfield didn't want to put his own name to the account, nor did Creggy. Knowing that it would defeat the purpose to use Snyder's name, Bloomfield asked Charles Wilson for the use of his name. Wilson agreed and supplied photocopies of his diplomatic passport. Bloomfield sent Wilson $3,000.

Two months later Creggy forwarded paperwork to Bank of Butterfield falsely claiming that Wilson was the owner of BBIM, reminding them that "the gentleman is a diplomat." Still, to comply with Bermuda laws, Bank Butterfield insisted that a reference come from a bank and a lawyer in order to open the account. Instead, Creggy opened an account for BBIM at Barclays Bank in Jersey. To be sure that the paper trail was covered, records for the Liberian-registered BBIM, with a bank account in Jersey, were held in Gibraltar. Snyder's money was deposited in Jersey, then regularly wired in amounts of $5,994 to his personal account in New York with the reference "Consulting fees re: BBIM."

Shortly after that, in April 1994, Creggy told Bloomfield he needed Wilson again. This is when Wilson was asked to sign the documents falsely declaring that he was the beneficial owner of the sixteen shell companies set up by Warren for Mazzeo and Westfield Financial.

Seven months later, Creggy called on Bloomfield to supply Wilson's signature on the share certificates of the fund Concord Capital Growth. Wilson was already listed as president of the corporation.

By now, Wilson was growing concerned that he was being asked to do something illegal. He needed reassurances. He reminded Bloomfield that he did not want to be "tangled into any unlawful and illegal business."

In November 1994, when Bloomfield and Creggy asked him to sign more papers, Wilson repeated his anxieties. "About two years ago when you requested I sign some papers for you to open an account for yourself, I raised the concerns that I did not want to be tangled into any unlawful and illegal business. You immediately assured me that this was not the case and in our relationship you will never mislead me nor talk me into anything illegal. As you are aware, I appreciate all the assistance you have granted me but I am concerned if these documents will not eventually be used for that purpose. You are equally aware that I have a family that depend on me for support that would not like to see me fall into problems. I need your reassurances if possible, written, before I can proceed further. Please understand I am trying to protect myself from problems."

Bloomfield answered Wilson, "Creggy assures me that these are regular business accounts. I know him and trust him. Be assured that we will always try and protect your position."

When originally asked about all this correspondence, lawyers working for Creggy and Bloomfield attacked the letters as fakes. Later, when shown the correspondence in which Bloomfield admits to asking Wilson to claim, deceitfully, that he is the beneficial owner of the sixteen shells, Bloomfield's lawyer acknowledged his client might have asked Wilson to do that but insisted, "Bloomfield had zero to do with the fraudsters."

In court, Bloomfield's attorneys painted a picture of an innocent man unwittingly seduced into a scheme that he knew nothing about. Wilson had been representing his country in Canada when civil war broke out in Liberia. The government in Monrovia could no longer afford to pay its overseas diplomats and Wilson had a family to support. He needed an income. Bloomfield was simply helping Wilson get through those hard times.

Not true, Abrams, Chalifoux, and Roiphe countered. The defendant was "borrowing, then renting, and then essentially stealing Charles Wilson's identity."

No longer a diplomat at the time of the trial, and therefore no longer shielded by diplomatic immunity, Wilson's testimony painted a different version of events from Bloomfield's and Creggy's. Wilson claimed that when Bloomfield first contacted him in 1993 about using his name and signature on certain documents, it wasn't for shell companies but for a Swiss bank account that Bloomfield wanted to open to put money away for his children. "He said that because I was an accredited diplomat, I didn't have to pay taxes in Canada."

As a result of the civil war, Wilson said, Liberia stopped paying foreign service workers and he was left penniless in Ottawa. He had five children to feed and was also coping with health problems. The money from Bloomfield was a great help. But Bloomfield, he swore, had assured him it was not illegal. "I trusted his judgment. . . . He said I was not breaking the law."

Wilson was not charged in the matter.

When the judge added everything together, he found Bloomfield and Creggy guilty on sixteen of the twenty-two charges. Moscow, Abrams,

Chalifoux, and Roiphe were all hoping the judge would now do the right thing and send Bloomfield and Creggy away for a couple of years. Hutchins, Jeans, and Woods were hoping for that too. They'd all put in a lot of work, and the condemnation of guilt, branding Bloomfield and Creggy convicted felons, was the cake. Sending them to prison would be the icing.

But lawyers for Bloomfield and Creggy had one last card to play – Creggy's health.

At the sentencing hearing, in February 2003, they made a passionate plea to the judge that their client was in remission from leukemia. They begged the judge to understand that jail would be detrimental to his health. Moscow vigorously reminded the judge that medical facilities in prison were just as good as they were outside prison, and that the State would appropriately look after Creggy's condition.

In the end, staggeringly, the judge fell for the emotional appeal.

He sentenced Creggy to treble-fives – five years' probation, a trifling $5,000 fine, and five hundred hours of community service. He then turned to Bloomfield, who maintained his freedom only by clinging desperately to Creggy's coattails. The judge said he felt it would be unfair to send Bloomfield to jail when Creggy was equally or more culpable in the offshore shell scheme. So Bloomfield got the same treble-fives.

After twenty-one years of aiding, abetting, and laundering money for fraudsters, Creggy went back to Florida, to fight deportation to Britain where an arrest warrant is waiting for him.

And Bloomfield went home to Montreal, along with his tie, considerably freer than he might otherwise have been.

13

YOU GOTTA HAVE A GIMMICK

"You gotta have a gimmick if you want to get ahead."

– career advice given to legendary stripper Gypsy Rose Lee

Cole Bartiromo, who sometimes called himself Tom Manning, spent most of spring 2001 hunched over his bedroom computer manipulating the share price of fifteen publicly traded companies. With an initial borrowed stake of $60,000, he purchased several million shares – in some cases as much as 50 per cent of the day's volume on his target company – posted as many as six thousand false messages on Internet bulletin boards touting the company's prospects, waited for the price to rise, then unloaded the shares at a profit. He salted away a lot of money in offshore accounts before, apparently, quitting for the summer.

That autumn, he was back on-line, this time with a Web site called Invest Better 2001. Bartiromo, as Manning, promised investors huge returns on "safe bets" that he was making – or at least that he said he was making – with on-line sports bookie. He claimed he'd cracked the secrets that Las Vegas gamblers employed "to make billions" and was now employing those "guaranteed" and "risk-free" methods for everyone else's benefit. If investors wanted to join him, he pledged to repay them anywhere from 125 to 2,500 per cent of their stake over a period of three days to a month. The minimum in was $50. There were no maximums.

Yet again, P.T. Barnum was right – "There's a sucker born every minute." The money poured in, thousands of dollars at a time, with the unwitting help of the Internet's most popular digital money exchanges – PayPal, Evocash, and E-Gold. All Bartiromo had to do was move it electronically to banks in Curaçao, Dominica, Bermuda, and Panama, and from them into his account at an on-line gambling site in Costa Rica. By Christmas, he'd bilked three thousand investors out of more than $1 million.

What he didn't know was that the Securities and Exchange Commission monitors the Internet all the time, that they'd stumbled across his Christmas Miracle Investment, that they'd refused to buy into the metaphysical aspect of it or, for that matter, his use of the word *investment*, and that they were coming to get him.

Dogged persistence and skilful detective work led the SEC to Costa Rica. There, with the co-operation of the offshore gambling site that Bartiromo was using, they followed the money trail back to Mission Viejo, California. The SEC not only put him out of business but reclaimed a large portion of the money he'd stolen.

Yet Bartiromo's ability to move money over the Internet and through the offshore world demonstrated how cyberspace and the offshore world are made for each other, how the Net provides a highly effective, easy-to-use tool for fraud, and how the offshore world is a purpose-built firewall. The ease with which Bartiromo manipulated the Internet made the offshore world look like a place where even a kid was welcome.

Which is exactly the way it was because, at the time, Bartiromo was just seventeen.

———

Liberian shell companies should have been a giveaway to anyone looking into the affairs of Messrs. Bloomfield, Creggy, and Warren. For three men who doubtless considered themselves intelligent, their raw stupidity could not have been more apparent because the offshore world is filled with much better gimmicks than Liberia. That they staked so much on such a patently dumb ploy reinforces the notion that common sense and greed are mutually exclusive.

In the end, they turned out to be a bunch of dull-witted crooks who failed to comprehend what the offshore world does best: it creates confusion so that real secrecy is mistaken for acceptable privacy.

The Merriam-Webster Dictionary defines privacy as "the quality or state of being apart from company or observation; freedom from unauthorized intrusion." The same dictionary defines secrecy as "the condition of being hidden or concealed."

While the two sound as if they are the same, in practice they are anything but. Privacy is what you expect in your bedroom with your spouse; secrecy is what you count on at a motel with your lover. Put another way, your income is secret to your neighbours, but merely private as far as the government is concerned. The inference being that your neighbours can't get to your secrets, but the government is permitted to breach your privacy.

Peddling secrecy in the guise of privacy is what makes the offshore world effective, and profitable.

The Ansbacher Bank scandal is a perfect example. The biggest money laundering and tax debacle in Irish history, it featured evasion on a huge scale and was littered with prominent business and political figures, not least of whom was former prime minister Charles Haughey. It didn't do much for the reputation of the Caymans either.

The story starts with Desmond Traynor, who, as an old man in the 1990s, was described as taciturn, respected, trustworthy, fiercely loyal, and one of the leading figures in the Irish business community. More than forty years previously, he'd been articled to Haughey at the chartered accounting firm of Haughey Boland, where a lifelong friendship began.

While Haughey climbed his way up the political ladder of the Fianna Fáil party, Traynor stayed at the accounting firm until 1969, when he was named a director of the bank Guinness & Mahon (Ireland) Limited (G&M). A few years later he was named deputy chairman and, in effect, chief executive of G&M. An accountant who clearly understood the need for secrecy in a banking environment that merely permitted privacy, one of the first things Traynor did when he took control of the bank was to open a tiny investment company in the Caymans and turn that into a bank called Guinness Mahon Cayman Trust Limited (GMCT).

His man in the Caymans was John Furze, an ex-pat banker who'd been there since the mid-1960s working for Canada's Bank of Nova Scotia. Furze knew every offshore trick then in the book, having cut his teeth helping the Bank of Nova Scotia earn the money-laundering reputation that would dog it for much of the 1970s and 1980s. Traynor, recognizing talent when he saw it, named Furze managing director of

GMCT in 1973. Furze then set about designing the various discretionary trusts that Traynor used to help wealthy people in Ireland hide their money. For all intents and purposes, G&M in Dublin and GMCT in the Caymans functioned as a single unit. Traynor became a one-man money-laundering sink, personally accepting deposits and getting them into the system, while Furze controlled everything in the Caribbean.

The system went through a series of name changes, but for two decades it remained essentially the same. In 1984, GMCT was sold to Guinness Mahon & Co. in London, parent of Traynor's Dublin bank. The following year it was sold again, this time to a private group headed by Traynor and Furze. They unloaded 75 per cent of it to the London bank Henry Ansbacher, who changed the name from GMCT to Ansbacher Limited, then changed it again to Ansbacher (Cayman) Limited. It was later sold to the First National Bank of Southern Africa.

Traynor and Furze offered clients three essential services.

First was a discretionary trust. That's an offshore account so con-structed as to appear that the beneficial owner is independent of his money and, therefore, not liable for taxes on the income. The specific gimmick Furze used was the same that made Liechtenstein famous as an offshore centre – "Red Cross Trusts." Money is held for a named charity. No taxes are therefore due. But that's followed with a "letter-of-wishes," in which the beneficial owner secretly informs the trustees that the charity will only receive a peppercorn and then lists the real benefi-ciaries. It's the ploy that tycoon Robert Maxwell was using when he announced to the world that his family members were not the bene-ficiaries of his wealth, held in trust in Liechtenstein.

Second was a facility through which people could deposit and with-draw offshore monies in Dublin, as if their account was onshore. Traynor, presumably at Furze's suggestion, established two shells – Amiens Investments Ltd. and Amiens Securities Ltd. – both of which held non-resident accounts at G&M. Deposits and withdrawals in Dublin would be credited and debited against funds in the Caymans, skirting the usual Irish resident-account requirements of tax and exchange controls.

Third was back-to-back loans. A favourite gimmick of drug traffickers, Traynor's clients could use their own money on deposit in the Caymans as security for a loan from a bank onshore. This allowed them to make large purchases without the tax man realizing they were actually repatriating their own funds.

It is now believed that perhaps as many as two hundred tax-liable Irish residents moved as much as $60 million through four hundred shells to hide their money in the Caymans. And it is just possible that none of this ever would have come to light had it not been for a Dunne family feud.

In 1992, Ben Dunne, then the chief executive of Dunnes Stores and one of the wealthiest men in Ireland, got into a fight with some of his relatives about lifestyle matters and during it, they discovered that he'd been writing cheques to Haughey. The press got wind of it – these didn't appear to be political donations – and the stories that followed forced a board of inquiry. The investigation established that, around 1987, Haughey had run into personal money problems. His friends decided they would ask half a dozen folks to offer $230,000 each to ease the prime minister's financial pain. Dunne was approached. He is said to have retorted, "Christ picked twelve apostles and one of them crucified him," and volunteered to pay the full amount himself. Over the course of the next couple of years, he reportedly gave Haughey $2 million.

The most interesting thing about the payments was the way Traynor and Furze handled them. The official report on the matter reveals that the first cheque from Dunne to Haughey, for $310,000, was given to Traynor, who sent it for collection to Guinness Mahon & Co. in London. Four days later in Dublin, before the funds cleared in the U.K. and were credited back to the Irish bank, the equivalent amount in Irish punts was wired out of an anonymous GMCT account for the benefit of Amiens Investment Ltd. Two days after that, the money deposited in London was wired to Dublin to fill the hole left in the GMCT account.

Flashback two weeks prior to the cheque from Dunne. Records show that the same sum, in Irish punts, was withdrawn from that Amiens Investments account and deposited into a special loan account at the Agricultural Credit Corporation, to be applied against monies allegedly owed to them by Haughey. A decidedly convoluted process, it obliterated the trail and separated Haughey from any association with Dunne's money.

Further payments were moved through Haughey Boland clients' accounts, a Swiss trust company, Credit Suisse, a bank on the Isle of

Man, Barclays, Royal Bank of Scotland in London, and the Irish Inter-continental Bank in Dublin.

The discovery of the Dunne/Haughey money sparked an investiga-tion into the way Traynor, Furze, and their banks were assisting in tax evasion. Irish authorities petitioned records from the Cayman Islands, which, of course, prompted a lot of excuses from the island as to why they couldn't possibly be helpful. Dublin put pressure on Ansbacher hoping to force disclosure, but account holders objected. After all, they were paying for secrecy and expected Ansbacher and the Caymans to live up to their end of the bargain. The case wound up in court.

Cayman Chief Justice Anthony Smellie heard arguments for six days in camera before coming down with a ruling that showed the island to be co-operative without really co-operating. He ordered the bank to divulge account records to the Irish inspectors, but only after the names, addresses, and any other descriptions of clients were removed.

As if to contend that privacy and secrecy were the same, Smellie justified his decision by writing: "This court must stand ready to reject any request for disclosure which may proceed upon a presumption that the mere fact of doing business with a Cayman Islands financial institu-tion points to some reproachable objective such as tax evasion."

Inquiries followed in Ireland, and little by little the story came out, much to the embarrassment of many of the protagonists. It would have happened sooner and more completely had the Caymans played ball, but that's not what the offshore world does. In the Caymans they actu-ally declared Smellie's decision "a win-win." This, while much of the rest of the world decided the islanders had simply run true to form.

Plainly, for the Caymanians, the cost of making clear distinctions between privacy and secrecy would be high. But a situation now arose in the States that would send tremors through the entire offshore world.

Three people in Florida were targeted by the IRS in a criminal tax-evasion case. They were clients of Ansbacher using a "pass-through account" (PTA), a variation on the two Traynor-owned Amiens accounts at G&M. Ansbacher was a client of Marine Midland in New York, allowing Ansbacher's clients access to Ansbacher's PTA account there. They could make deposits and withdrawals, exactly as if this was Ansbacher, but without anyone at Marine Midland knowing offshore funds were involved.

When the IRS discovered that the three Floridians were using a PTA, they demanded that Marine Midland produce transaction records. Marine Midland objected and, not surprisingly, so did Ansbacher, arguing that the summons was much too broad because it would include records of people unrelated to the targets. The IRS argued that, because of the way the accounting was done, they were entitled to see everything in order to establish what their targets were up to. The court agreed with the IRS and ordered Marine Midland to turn over the records.

Suddenly, a U.S. bank was required by U.S. law to give up offshore banking information that was otherwise protected elsewhere. The only way the offshore world could get around this was by eliminating any business that left traces in a U.S. bank. So now, most offshore banks with PTA accounts in the States keep those records well outside U.S. jurisdiction.

———

Keeping records outside U.S. jurisdiction was at the heart of the Enron scandal.

The Texas energy corporation pinned a lot of private hope and aspirations on offshore secrecy. And Enron knew a lot about that because they'd been offshore since the mid-1980s. From 1985 to 1987, several Enron executives diverted $142 million in company funds to offshore shells and Panamanian banks. At the time, CEO Ken Lay claimed total ignorance of such fraudulent activities.

He can't say as much these days.

The company created 881 foreign subsidiaries, including 692 shells registered in the Caymans that were designed for no other reason than to fool shareholders and regulators into thinking they were legitimate companies. There were also 119 shells in Turks and Caicos, 43 in Mauritius, and 8 in Bermuda. Lay and his mates used their offshore empire to shelter profits, enrich themselves, and avoid taxes to the extent that Enron paid no corporate income tax to the U.S. government for four out of the five years between 1996 and 2000. As a matter of fact, thanks to sham accounting, during one of those years the company actually worked out a $382-million refund.

Much of what Lay was doing to avoid taxes was transfer pricing, moving onshore profits to an offshore shell where taxes don't count. But Enron took it to new depths of sleaze. For example, Enron had several negotiated deals to sell oil and natural gas to a company called Mahonia, registered in Jersey. Mahonia's bankers, Chase Manhattan – which later became J.P. Morgan Chase – financed the deals from mid-1998 to the end of 2000. On paper, when payments were due, Chase would pay Mahonia, which would pay Enron. But the way it actually worked was very different. In a typical deal – this one dated December 28, 2000 – Enron sold a gas contract to Mahonia for delivery from April 2001 to November 2005 at an agreed price of $394 million. Off that came a discount for full payment up front, making the total $330 million.

Chase paid Mahonia, which paid Enron. However, that same day, Enron agreed to purchase from another Jersey company, Stoneville Aegean, the same amount of gas for delivery during the same period of time. The price was $394 million but did not include the upfront full payment discount because Enron chose to pay monthly, which is standard industry procedure. So Enron now had $330 million to put on their books as revenue, with a debt of $394 million due in the future. That worked out to a fifty-five-month loan of $330 million at 7 per cent interest.

The Mahonia and Stoneville Aegean contracts were signed by the same man, who happened to be a director of both companies. But that's hardly a coincidence. Mahonia and Stoneville Aegean had the same address in St. Helier, Jersey, which they shared with a local law firm, and the man who signed those contracts was a partner in that law firm. Company filings in Jersey show that Mahonia's shareholders were two shell companies: Juris Limited and Lively Limited. Those shells owned shares in each other. The local law firm also owned shares in Juris and Lively. Company filings in Jersey show that Stoneville Aegean's corporate structure was exactly the same. This is not to suggest there's anything untoward with the offshore governance of either company, simply that it refutes claims that the deals with Enron were unrelated.

The deals were structured in such a way as to keep up appearances, while allowing Enron to use the bank's money and still have the same amount of commodity on hand to sell a second time. Call it "commodity laundering" – a loan disguised as a trade. Over the years, Enron materially benefited by being able to disguise borrowings of $3.9 billion. Instead of listing that as debt, they added it to revenue. For some people at Enron, putting Mahonia and Stoneville Aegean offshore and keeping the records offshore too was a good idea. These days, to much of the rest of the world, what Enron did looks exactly like fraud.

It was another Enron partnership where loans were disguised – a shell called Chewco – that came to light during a U.S. Congressional hearing and lit the spark that became the Enron bankruptcy. Dissecting the corpse, it's blatant that none of this could have happened without three very important ingredients:

First, the company needed to be run by crooks. They designed a dishonest structure for their own benefit. Second, it required the collaboration of hundreds of financial professionals. Enron's crooked management could not possibly have pulled this off without bankers, lawyers, and accountants playing along. At best, they were myopic. At worst, they were criminals. Third, it had to be offshore. Without a place to hide, Enron could not possibly have perpetrated such a gigantic lie.

Unfortunately, Enron is hardly unique. There's Worldcom, Tyco, and multinationals like the French oil company Elf Aquitaine that have used the offshore world to throw bribes at every tin-pot dictator in Africa with an oil well. All typical examples, notes attorney Jack Blum, of what happens when people are allowed to say, I'm going somewhere else so that I can break all the rules.

"You want to understand the offshore world? Just look at what's gone on in the last five years. Corporations have reached a point where they cannot continue to compound earnings at 20 per cent. So what's the next step? They cook the books. Why? Because the board has stock options and the only way they can get the price up and steal more is if they cook the books."

The place to do that, he insists, is away from home. "Because it's much more fun to play where there are no rules. That is, forgetting at the end of the day, that we could be rocketing towards a global catastrophe with absolutely no capacity to fix anything. The whole enterprise is based on, How do we get out from under the rules? The truth of the matter is that the rules are there for a reason. If you want to see where we are running without rules, look at Enron and WorldCom."

Equally illuminating, look at the way certain tobacco companies allegedly used the offshore world to deal with organized criminals and break UN sanctions.

In 2002, the European Commission filed suit in the United States against R.J. Reynolds (RJR), claiming that, for much of the 1990s, RJR knowingly sold cigarettes to Italian, Russian, and Colombian organized criminal groups. The claim states that to keep payments from those criminals secret, RJR directed, managed, and controlled money-laundering operations in several offshore jurisdictions. Furthermore, the EU says, the company violated UN trade sanctions by doing business with Iraq.

The suit outlines a criminal conspiracy, beginning with a company in Puerto Rico called Japan Tobacco (JT). Acting under licence of RJR, JT shipped 5,340 master cases of Winston cigarettes from the U.S. factory to Valencia, Spain. There are 10,000 cigarettes in a master case, making for 53.4 million cigarettes in this shipment. That's enough to fill five forty-foot containers. The accompanying bills of lading showed the shipment bound for Cyprus.

When the containers got to Spain, they were offloaded from one vessel and onto another that sailed to Cyprus. There, the containers were unpacked, and the master cases were then repacked into new containers, with new bills of lading that showed the shipment bound for Russia. By changing the containers and the bills of lading, these cigarettes could no longer be identified as the same ones that had gone from the States to Spain. Leaving Cyprus, the vessel sailed first to Lebanon, then to Turkey. The cigarettes were unloaded there and trucked overland to Iraq. The EU maintains that RJR and Japan Tobacco knew the people they'd sold the cigarettes to and knew what those people intended to do with them. RJR and JT steadfastly deny this, insisting that any allegations of deals with the Mafia or terrorists or sanction breaking are absurd.

But that hasn't stopped similar accusations coming from other sources and, allegedly, RJR is not alone. A major investigation conducted by Washington watchdog The Center for Public Integrity accused senior executives at British American Tobacco (BAT) and Philip Morris of having sold cigarettes to individuals directly connected to organized crime in the States, Canada, Colombia, Italy, and Hong Kong. BAT and Philip Morris both deny the allegations.

Trade in black-market cigarettes – product produced for one geographical area and smuggled into another to sell at a lower price – is gigantic. It's said that one out of every three exported cigarettes winds up on a black market somewhere. The cigarette companies disavow complicity, insisting that they do everything they can to stop it.

For every black-market cigarette sold, a cash register rings in the offshore world. Italian criminals launder cigarette money in Montenegro, an emerging sink on the Adriatic. Russian criminals launder cigarette money through Cyprus. It's believed that some of it is then reinvested in Russian-Cypriot joint-venture factories that manufacture counterfeit cigarettes for the Eastern European black markets. In the Caribbean, the two major cigarette-smuggling centres are Aruba and Panama, both of which come complete with built-in money-laundering facilities.

The EU suit claims the criminals couldn't function without product from the big manufacturers. Notes Kevin Malone, a lawyer representing the EU in its suit against the big companies, "What you have is one big smuggling conspiracy. The cigarette manufacturers, their distributors, the money launderers, it's the same people doing the exact same thing."

Again, the companies deny it.

A major test of Malone's theory came in 1999, when Canada started an action in U.S. Federal Court against RJR-Macdonald, R.J. Reynolds, and related companies. The claim was that the manufacturers conspired to export and illegally reimport cigarettes into Canada, thus depriving Revenue Canada of taxes. It was happening, they said, along the border that Ontario and Quebec share with New York State, on land designated official territory of the St. Regis Mohawk Indians. Known as Akwesasne, organized gangs of native Americans living on the reservation have, for years, moved cigarettes north or south depending on the tax situation.

The manufacturers argued the "Revenue Rule." That's eighteenth-century common law that says a court can refuse to hear a case if its judgment would serve only to enforce another country's tax laws. Appeals went all the way up to the U.S. Supreme Court, where, in November 2002, a decision came down for the manufacturers. By then, Canada had run out of appeals.

Next, a suit was filed in the U.S. by the European Commission against Philip Morris and RJR. Their claim was that the tobacco companies had been running a global smuggling operation to deprive EU member states of tax revenue and had become a money-laundering outlet for criminal organizations. This time, lawyers for the cigarette companies convinced the judge to throw the case out on the technicality that the European Commission could not act exclusively on behalf of the member states.

So the European Union refiled, now joining ten member states with the European Commission. In February 2002, that case was dismissed based on precedents set in the original Canadian trial. The EU appealed and began reshaping its case, yet again, this time to play off the terrorist and money-laundering aspects of the U.S.A. Patriots Act, which Congress had passed in response to 9/11.

At the same time, the EU filed a money-laundering version of its suit against RJR. The company has promised to take this one all the way too. And the EU doesn't seem ready to let the matter drop either.

In the meantime, the offshore world is gearing up to make it easier for big companies to function. It's part of the new image the big jurisdictions are polishing. For them, shell companies and private banks that cater to small-time crooks and tax evaders are too much trouble. The big jurisdictions – notably Hong Kong, the Bahamas, and the Caymans – seem intent on getting out of what might be called retail money laundering, because the wholesale side of the business is safer and more profitable. They see their future in tax structuring, in multinational financial chicanery. It's no longer about the Cali cartel, it's about tomorrow's Enron. It's about catering to companies like Halliburton and Bechtel and the Carlyle Group, huge multinationals with massive global investments that need to be protected from the whims and fancies of any single government.

An added incentive for the big jurisdictions is reputational risk. If due diligence fails and drug money or al-Qaeda money turns up, it's the jurisdiction that takes the heat. If due diligence fails and another Enron happens, it's the company's problem.

At least in the big jurisdictions, the days of small-time crooks are numbered. Sure, there will always be someplace else for them to go, but for multinational giants with money to hide, Hong Kong, the Bahamas, and the Caymans are laying out the welcome mat.

Of course, the big jurisdictions all talk the due diligence game. But the way the cards are getting shuffled, chances are nil that their due diligence will ever get in the way of: a cigarette company looking to move into an untouched black market; a pharmaceutical company looking to transfer price its drugs so that it never pays any taxes anywhere; an insurance company looking to run reinsurance around the offshore world to the point where it never has to pay on a huge disaster; or an imitation Ansbacher helping people evade taxes because it satisfies all the requirements of being a legitimate bank.

⟶

That said, because the offshore world is a competitive business, while the big guys move to wholesale, smaller players will upgrade their retail side. For them, due diligence creates room in the game for small to medium-sized players with street cred. Except you can't always tell whose cred is cred. Just ask Mark Edward Valentine.

Once the darling of Bay Street, Valentine was born in 1970 in Brazil, where his father was a career diplomat. Douglas Valentine would go on to serve as Canada's ambassador to Saudi Arabia and to Colombia. Mark attended Concordia University in Montreal before getting a job as an investment adviser. A loner at heart, his workaholic energy and money-making talents quickly turned him into one of Canada's hotshot dot-com brokers, a feat that did not go unnoticed by the otherwise venerable fifty-year-old financial services firm Thomson Kernaghan (TK).

Where TK had prospered through strong and reliable research in some of the less exciting areas of investment – mining, power generation, and machine makers – the firm was now old, tired, and falling behind its younger, more vigorous competitors. The Kernaghan brothers, who were running their late father's firm, wanted to breathe life into it and Valentine seemed like an exciting choice. He was less than half the firm's age when they hired him in 1994.

Within a year, Valentine's partners were so appreciative of the business he brought to the company, and the way he'd begun taking them into sexy high-tech, that they gave him a thank-you Ferrari with the special licence plate, GIDDYUP. Within three years, Valentine was making so much money for TK that the partners agreed to sell him 25 per cent of it, and let him turn the company into a technology specialist house. He moved the firm out of its dismal Bay Street offices and into shiny new ones around the block, then opened branches in Calgary and Vancouver. Before long, one hundred employees became two hundred.

By 2001, Mark Valentine was chairman and Thomson Kernaghan was on the verge of bankruptcy. The company was overextended in high-tech at a time when high-tech was heading south. Also, the Ontario Securities Commission (OSC) was investigating Valentine for the way he'd been financing certain deals. Their concern was a game called "death spiralling."

Simply put, a death spiral is a scheme devised to run a company's share price into the ground, while all the time selling shares to hapless investors who don't know the cards are stacked against them.

A variation on the pump 'n' dump, it begins with what appears to be a big investment into a thinly traded microcap. Because the company doesn't have access to large investors, when someone comes along with money to spend, its willing to give up "floorless warrants." Those are guarantees that the investor can convert into shares at a later date. But unlike agreements that put a price on the shares to be issued to the investor, these put a value on the investment, which means the number of shares fluctuate.

For example, with "floorless warrants," if $1 million is the agreed investment and the shares are $1 each, the investor has the right to one million shares. But if the share price drops to eighty cents, the investor gets 1.25 million shares. In other words, as the value of the shares changes, the number of shares issued changes to match the investment.

Knowing that he has a guaranteed supply of shares, the investor starts pumping the shares to other investors, while all the time selling short, which means he's unloading shares that he doesn't yet own. He's betting that the price will drop, which, as more shares come onto the market, it invariably does. By selling at eighty cents, when the price drops to sixty cents, the investor makes the difference. Of course, if the share price goes up to $1.20, then he has to buy them back at that price and winds up losing the difference.

Many brokers consider short-selling a mug's game because it's not an investment, it's a bet. But if you've got inside knowledge or can control the share price, then it's not really a bet, it's a sure thing. You're guaranteed a supply of shares all the way down, creating the financial equivalent of perpetual motion. The more you sell, the more the price drops; the more the price drops, the more shares you get from the floorless warrants, and, consequently, the more you can sell.

Investors out of the know wind up holding worthless shares. The company that falls victim to this almost always goes bust. Players on the inside walk away with fortunes.

All the various securities commissions are supposed to be on the lookout for this scam. They may know it when they see it, but it isn't easy to prove. A source in Canada suggests that TK under Valentine made $2 billion in six years playing the death-spiral game.

No one noticed because the action was funnelled offshore.

Valentine was connected in Bermuda to a fellow Canadian named Paul Lemmon, who owned the Voyager Group of financial services companies. The two guys intertwined their offshore entities. Valentine had a Bermuda company called Ashland Resources. Lemmon was listed as the trading authority for Ashland Resources and for a fund called Hammock Account. Valentine was the controlling shareholder of Hammock and the agent for Hammock Group, which was actually registered in BVI. However, the address listed for Hammock was the same one in Hamilton, Bermuda, that Lemmon listed for Voyager Group. Valentine also owned a company called VMH Management, in which he put a hedge fund called Canadian Advantage Limited Partnership, which had a sister incorporated in Bermuda, Advantage (Bermuda) Fund. He mirrored that with VC Advantage Limited, a company that managed a hedge fund called VC Advantage Fund Limited Partnership, and its sister, VC Advantage (Bermuda) Fund.

Enter Valentine's pal and partner in the VC Fund, Cameron Brett Chell. In a previous incarnation, Chell had been a salesman for a securities firm in Calgary but ran afoul of the Alberta Stock Exchange and, in 1998, admitted to violations. He was banned by the exchange from acting in any capacity for five years, placed under supervision for two years after reregistration, and fined $25,000. Now he ran the Chell Group, which owned an Internet company called Jawz Inc. The OSC and TK investigations found that, in late spring 2000, Valentine and Chell worked a death spiral with Jawz. Valentine is accused of using TK to issue a buy recommendation on Jawz, while motivating other TK clients to sell. Valentine and Chell short-sold as well.

It now appears that Valentine might have been working both sides of a trade with another Chell company, C-Me-Run. One of his hedge funds was buying C-Me-Run shares at the same time when several offshore entities controlled by Lemmon were selling. Funds held at Thomson Kernaghan lost $4.5 million. The offshore funds made $6.4 million.

Valentine always maintained that he did nothing wrong. But the movement of large blocks of Chell Group shares in and out of these funds – creating profits for Valentine at the expense of TK's investors – worried the OSC. Thomson Kernaghan's Management Committee mounted an inquiry that ended by ordering Valentine escorted from the building. The OSC then issued an order banning him from working or trading in the markets.

Ever intent on making money, Valentine turned his attention to Germany's poorly regulated penny-share market. What he didn't know when he flew to Frankfurt in August 2002 was that, instead of coming directly home to Canada, he'd be detouring for a very long time through Miami.

A year and a half before, he and Lemmon concocted a deal with an investment office in Boca Raton, Florida, to move overpriced shares through a U.K.-based unit trust run by a crooked manager, in return for a multimillion-dollar kickback. It was a pretty good gimmick and they weren't the only ones working it. The owners of one company agreed to sell shares to the unit trust for $8 million – which was more than seven times the actual market value – for a $3.2-million kickback. Another company CEO offered to sell two million shares at $4 each – when the share price was sixty-five cents – for a $4-million kickback.

Because none of these could be straightforward and on-the-books transactions, U.S. regulators were bound to realize that something was wrong. So both money and shares were moved through Canada and the Caribbean. There were shells in the Bahamas, a bank in Barbados, a bank in the Caymans, and, of course, Valentine's and Lemmon's companies in Bermuda.

There was only problem with the scam – it was a scam.

The U.K. unit trust didn't exist, the British fund manager didn't exist, and the office in Boca was run by an undercover FBI agent. Called Operation Bermuda Short, it was a full-frontal attack on fraudulent penny-share promoters. Along with the FBI came the RCMP, the SEC, the U.S. Postal Inspection Service, and the National Association of Securities Dealers.

By the time Valentine was ready to board his flight from Germany to Canada, the U.S. Justice Department had unsealed indictments and issued arrest warrants for fifty-eight people, including him. The Germans grabbed him and held him for nearly five weeks until U.S. Marshals arrived to escort him to Florida. Valentine and Lemmon were charged with conspiracy to commit wire, mail, and securities fraud. Valentine pled not guilty, maintaining his innocence and, as of mid-2003, is still fighting his corner. Lemmon took a plea to one count of conspiracy to commit wire and securities fraud, and agreed to testify against Valentine. Lemmon was sent away for twenty-one months.

14

ENTANGLED ALLIANCES

"If we lose sight of the threat that organized crime poses,
even for a short while, it will take us years to regain
all that we've accomplished during these past five years."

– RCMP Chief Superintendent Ben Soave

Thanks to films like *The Godfather* and *Goodfellows*, over the past thirty years there's been a real interest in and increased understanding of organized crime. That's reflected in today's never-ending diet of Discovery Channel, History Channel, and Biography Channel insights into the Mob, Colombian drug cartels, the Russian Maffiya, and the mysterious gangs of the Orient. But as public fascination grew, a small movement took hold among a close-knit group of academics, which, in the simplest of terms, denied the existence of organized crime.

Admitting that serious crime was happening, that some of it was very well organized, that most of it was economically motivated, and that all of it posed a threat to our communities, these scholars accused law enforcement and politicians of deliberately misleading the public. They refused to recognize a united conspiracy driven by a hierarchy seeking riches, and blamed law enforcement and politicians for camouflaging reality and misdirecting enforcement efforts.

The overwhelming response from law enforcement and politicians is that this bunch has a lot in common with the Flat Earth Society.

As the revisionist theories of this group hardened, it's not clear that they've taken on many new recruits or, for that matter, influenced public perception in any meaningful way. The popularity of *The Sopranos* suggests that, when given the choice between a professor guaranteeing that organized crime doesn't exist and the dysfunctional antics of a New Jersey crew, Tony and the boys win, hands down.

This is not to say that the academics don't make some valid points. The problem is that being academics, they're too used to talking to each other, and for non-academics theirs can be a foreign language.

For example, this from two of the group's chief cheerleaders: Dr. Margaret Beare, director of the highly respected Nathanson Centre for the Study of Organized Crime and Corruption at the Osgoode Hall Law School of York University in Toronto; and Professor R.T. Naylor, a recognized authority on enterprise crime, financial fraud, black markets, and criminal justice enforcement issues who works out of McGill University in Montreal.

In their 1999 treatise, "Major Issues Relating to Organized Crime – Within the Context of Economic Relationships" – prepared for the Law Commission of Canada – they state: "The danger is of course a self-fulfilling process whereby the police, believing in a national criminal conspiracy (in part because of the advantages in this interpretation), focused their attention on these groups and individuals. In police work, one tends to be able to verify the criminal involvement of those groups who are targeted. Over time, if the police focus on Italians, the police files would indicate a dominance of Italian organized criminals, thus confirming the initial belief in the existence of the LCN (La Cosa Nostra) model."

If what they're saying is, just because you set out to look for trees and find some, you can't claim to have discovered a forest, they're absolutely right. But if you set out to look for trees, and you find a whole bunch of them clumped together in the same ecosystem, and after a while there are so many trees that you can't see where you started and you can't see what's on the other side either, well, most people would forgive you for calling it a forest.

Still, the academics remain vociferous. Law enforcement has an agenda, they insist, which is to manipulate statistics and create a fear of criminal power in order to increase budgets and, consequently, their own power. To recognize the validity of the point, the argument goes, you merely have to observe how law enforcement and politicians play on easy-to-understand images of "an assortment of bogeymen such as the Russian Mob, the Colombia drug cartel, and biker gangs."

Accepting the theory that increased threats – perceived or real – lead to increased budgets, it's still a stretch to deny the existence of organized crime.

Perhaps common ground lies in the recognition of "networked crime."

This is the concept that disparate individuals and groups are linked through their common interest in criminal enterprise. Without ignoring the vertical or ladder image of crime groups, syndicates, families, whatever you call them – from foot soldier on the street corner to godfather in a fortress – the "networked crime" picture is laid out flat. You need to look down on it, the way you would a map of a ring road around a city.

You start at any point and follow it around until you get back to the beginning, and every so often there is a street or highway feeding off it to take you in another direction. These intersections represent those disparate individuals and groups as they go about the business of crime. But while they may appear at first glance to be totally independent of all the others along the ring road, they are in fact joined by it. The connection from the first to the second may be a banker, the connection from the second to the third may be a drug trafficker, the connection from the third to the fourth may be a money-laundering jurisdiction.

Granted, when money laundering becomes part of this – as it inevitably does – the ring road will be multi-jurisdictional. That creates the problem of multi-jurisdictional co-operation. But the point is, when you join up all these individuals and all these groups with that ring road – when you find the common bits that network them – you have another target to attack. By identifying the network, then breaking into it at a few strategic points, by blocking off some of the streets that feed off the ring road, you can cause such an enormous traffic jam that, effectively, you've brought the entire network to a halt.

Unlike the old rhyme about "the man who shook hands with the man who shook hands," you don't need six degrees of separation to spot the connections. Start with Ken Taves, a man in his early forties who, one day, decided to go into the Internet porn industry.

The Web is so filled with sexually related material that, as a single category, it is believed to be the most visited and most profitable. But designing a site and uploading a lot of hard-core porn does not automatically a porn king make. The California-based Taves found that a few thousand subscriptions at $19.95 a month was not enough to retire on. So he invented nine hundred thousand more.

His bank, Charter Pacific, maintained a massive database of all its credit card transactions and, under the guise of fraud control, was willing to make that database available to certain merchants. In 1997, Taves paid Charter Pacific $5,000 for access to 3.7 million account numbers. He got through nearly a quarter of them, submitting the account numbers to the merchant's service he used with instructions to charge each account $19.95 a month. In the credit card fraud business, that's known as "cramming," and by the time the Federal Trade Commission (FTC) clamped down on him, he'd crammed himself $37.5 million.

Understanding that he would, eventually, get caught – after all, he had to expect that a lot of the nine hundred thousand people he was defrauding monthly would question this recurring bill on their credit card statements – Taves turned for help to the Cayman Islands.

He opened an account there with Eurobank, one of the less reputable financial institutions still in business at the time. On his behalf, Eurobank incorporated a company called Benford Ltd. in Vanuatu. That's the island chain in the South Pacific about a thousand miles northeast of Brisbane, Australia, that used to be called New Hebrides. Its status these days as an offshore centre is highly suspect.

Within hours of incorporating Benford for Taves, Eurobank opened an account in the company's name at European Bank in Vanuatu with a wired $100,000. In all, European Bank would eventually move $7.5 million from the Caymans to Vanuatu.

Although it took the FTC two years to investigate the thousands of complaints that were filed against Taves, his wife, their friends, and all of their companies, when the agency finally lowered the boom, it was to put them out of business. The FTC filed a civil suit in Federal Court against Taves and the others for deceptive trade practices, and successfully proved that this bunch had used at least five different merchant accounts and four totally fictitious businesses to steal people's credit card numbers and bill them for services they had not subscribed to.

As a consequence, the court appointed a receiver to go after Taves assets and repay his victims. They ordered Taves to disclose all his financial interests and to repatriate any offshore assets. They then barred him for ten years from having anything to do with any business that handled credit or debit card accounts.

Taves, who sometimes used the name Kenneth Till, had been in trouble before, involved with counterfeit cheques, fraud, and even attempted murder. In 1980, he was arrested for hiring someone to kill a con man who'd swindled him out of $100,000. But the case dried up when the hired gunman, who'd agreed to testify against Taves, was killed in a car accident.

Here, too, Taves was sidestepping criminal prosecution. His victims were spread out across twenty-two countries – including the U.K., Ireland, and Canada – and many of them would never be able to testify against him. What's more, in places like Japan, thousands of victims were so embarrassed about being bilked by a porn site that they refused to complain.

However, Taves got stupid and did his victims an enormous favour when he lied about his financial interests. He didn't tell the court about the $23.5 million sitting in Eurobank. Or about Vanuatu. Or about any of the shell companies he owned, such as Satmax Family Limited Partnership and Coastal Holding Limited, which owned a $3-million mansion along the Pacific Coast Highway in Malibu. Not only was this his home – a fact he also neglected to mention in court – but when the judgment came down against him, he rushed to move the property out of those companies and into a Canadian shell called Trans Global Development Corporation. He also started moving his offshore money around to make it safe.

It was about this time that the authorities in the Caymans decided they'd had enough of Eurobank and, using Taves as the excuse, shut it down.

By now, too, the receiver was all over Taves's offshore holdings. But Taves was fighting back. Lawyers in Vanuatu and more lawyers in the Caymans put up hurdles to keep anyone from getting inside the various accounts, especially those at European Bank in Vanuatu. According to papers in the Cayman Islands, European Bank in Vanuatu had known for some time that Eurobank was "open to business when other doors are closed to it, very much lower end of the local banking business, dubious, three months ago there were rumours that they might fail, not well respected, advise caution when dealing with them." The papers continue, that reputable banks such as Barclays would not accept a reference from Eurobank and "would certainly not do business with them."

One reason why Taves's bankers in Vanuatu might have chosen to ignore the warnings was that the Benford account was too big to lose, representing about 15 per cent of European Bank's total deposit base.

As soon as Eurobank was forced into liquidation, and it became obvious that the Benford monies were proceeds of fraud, European Bank transferred the Benford money into a non-interest-bearing account and froze it, so that neither the U.S. receiver nor the Eurobank liquidators could get their hands on it. Without advising their correspondent bank in New York that the funds were dirty, European Bank left them on deposit in a high-interest-bearing account, for the benefit of European Bank.

Authorities in the Caymans took the big step in February 2000, charging three Eurobank officials with money laundering in the Taves's case. It was the first time the Caymans brought a money-laundering prosecution against a bank or bank officers based there. Similar charges were also lodged against Taves and five other people involved with him.

Realizing that Taves had lied about his assets, the U.S. receiver went back to Federal Court in August 2000 to have Taves ruled in criminal contempt. Taves further aggravated his situation by refusing to reveal his assets and the judge tossed him into jail until he did.

In the Caymans, where Eurobank had been a local embarrassment for quite a while, secret banking laws prevented foreigners in civil actions from getting to the bank's records and laying claim to any funds. Yet, once the liquidators stepped into Eurobank and the Taves case became a criminal matter, everything changed. The U.S. receiver put in his claim for Taves's money and the liquidators agreed to it. But the attorney general of the Cayman Islands didn't. He placed a restraining order on the funds because the bank was a defendant in a criminal matter. The U.S. government applied to exclude the Taves's money from the order and the attorney general opposed the motion. But the Caymanian court noted that because this was a criminal matter the funds could be repatriated, and ruled in favour of the Americans.

From that point, it became much easier to establish a money trail. From mid-1997 until late-1998, Taves moved $25.3 million through four different companies to Eurobank, where it wound up in two Taves-controlled accounts, and moved from there into other Eurobank accounts, including one in Taves's parents' names. Records in the Caymans reveal that Taves owned property there in the name of a shell company, and had accounts at Barclays Bank, the Bank of Nova Scotia, and the Cayman National Bank. In addition, he maintained investment accounts at Morgan Stanley Dean Witter and the Royal Bank of Canada, and through Eurobank there was also an investment account in Germany. He moved money from the Caymans to Vanuatu to Citibank, Australia, and then to Citibank, New York; to a lawyer's client account in the Bahamas and from there back to the States; from the Caymans to Jamaica; from the Caymans to the account of a Taves's company called Global International Media at Landesbank in Liechtenstein; and from the Caymans to the Toronto-Dominion Bank in Victoria, B.C. Furthermore, Eurobank had issued Taves a MasterCard that worked off one of the accounts, so he could spend money in the States without the IRS finding out. In just under two years, Taves ran up nearly $300,000 on that credit card.

Taves has since pled guilty to the biggest credit card fraud in history, and is spending a considerable part of the rest of his life in a federal prison.

While the U.S. receiver was chasing Taves's money, and the Feds were building a case to put him behind bars, Brian Gibbs in the Cayman Islands was working for too many masters.

A sturdily built man in his early fifties, Gibbs had joined the Metropolitan Police in London in 1964 and had spent the next twenty-two years working on any number of squads, investigating all sorts of criminality, including organized crime. In 1986, he was asked to form the Met's first Drugs Profit Confiscation Unit, which is how he got interested in money laundering. Three years later, an opportunity came up to live in the Caribbean, seconded to the Royal Cayman Islands Police (RCIP), and he took it. There, he set up the island's first drug-money-laundering unit and although he retired from the Met in 1994, he remained on the Caymans' force, rising to the rank of detective chief inspector. He continued running the money-laundering squad until the end of 2000, when the Caymans, to comply with FATF requirements, established a Financial Reporting Unit. Gibbs and his money-laundering team were slid sideways out of the RCIP, renamed, and placed under the auspices of the Attorney General.

From that point on, money-laundering cases on the island were dealt with by the FRU. The unit established its own intelligence sources, analysts, and investigators, and had direct access to prosecutors.

"The reason it was taken away from police," Gibbs explains, "is because it consists of civilians and police officers and attorneys and the whole idea was to make it independent of everybody. It wasn't a political situation and the politicians don't like it."

A confidential unit that, he points out, was "charged with maintaining confidential information in confidence," the FRU was designed to operate as a closed unit right from the beginning. That meant, among other things, it had to be totally detached computerwise from any other arm of government, so that whatever came in – reports, intelligence, evidence from confidential sources – would not be available to any other authority on the island or in any way compromised. But because the attorney general has overall control of the FRU, it appears as if the executive council now has its own police force.

It's a situation that hasn't sat well with at least one well-known critic of the system, who claims, "It is dangerous to have more than one commissioner of police."

The jury is still out on how independent the politicians permit the FRU to be. Proof of the pudding will come when a relationship between a politician and a local bank gets closer than arm's-length. The wisdom of taking the FRU away from the police might then be called into question.

Still, the Caymanians shut down Eurobank. The stated reason for it was money laundering and the Taves fraud. But behind the scenes there were other, more sinister concerns. The bank was started in 1981 and maintained a physical presence on the island. This wasn't just another brass-plate operation, there was an office and there was staff on the island. The reason was that certain people needed it to be a real bank. Several men with banking backgrounds were behind it. One of them was a Canadian accountant with residence in the Caymans and Monaco named Donald Fraser. He had a connection to Saudi arms dealer Adnan Khashoggi, who'd spent most of the 1970s encouraging rumours that he was the richest man in the world.

He never was that, but by the time Eurobank was up and running, Khashoggi was definitely one of the more amusing ultra-rich Middle Eastern eccentrics running around the world making money, flaunting money, and marrying rather gorgeous women.

Along the way, Khashoggi established a business relationship with Canadian wheeler-dealer Peter Munk. While it's clear that the two did a number of deals together, less clear is the extent to which Khashoggi helped Munk get his company, Barrick Gold, off the ground and then keep it off the ground. Depending on whom you believe – Barrick's official version of events denies this – Khashoggi rescued Munk on at least one occasion and, at least for a while, owned a controlling share in Barrick. Again, it depends on whom you believe and there are several versions of the story around, many of them contradictory, each of them suspiciously serving the person telling it. But what is certain is that Khashoggi was holding Barrick shares in 1985 when he got involved in the Iran-Contra scandal.

This was a concoction of the then CIA director, William Casey, who envisioned selling arms to Iran and using that money to support the paramilitary Contras in their revolution in Nicaragua. His guys were a bunch of CIA refugees from the Nugan Hand Bank in Australia, which itself had been an offshoot of Paul Helliwell's Castle Bank in the Bahamas and Caymans. Star player was Marine Lieutenant Colonel Oliver North, then on assignment to the National Security Council. He was the man most directly involved in the day-to-day arms dealing and money laundering. But it was Casey, in his role as puppet master, who pulled most of the strings. It was Casey who invited in Khashoggi, having access to him through their mutual friend, Kamal Adham, the Saudi intelligence chief.

Never one to play the shrinking violet, Khashoggi promised Casey he could deliver the goods, which in this case was missiles. But when it came time to do that, Khashoggi discovered that he needed to come up with $15 million. He found $5 million from one source, then called on his mate Donald Fraser to help with the rest. Eurobank loaned Khashoggi the money. Khashoggi's collateral was his shares in Barrick.

By 1986, as Khashoggi and Fraser were sighted together all over the Caymans, some people came to believe that Khashoggi was one of Eurobank's original investors. Instead, his reason for hanging out there was that his wife, Saroya, was in the midst of dumping him and he needed someplace safe to stash his money so that her lawyers couldn't find it. Until this point, Khashoggi had regularly banked in Liechtenstein. Now he reregistered his Triad Holding Corp. in the Caymans and packed his real estate wealth into a Cayman's Trust. He incorporated a company there called AK Holdings for his toys – his plane, his yacht, his cars – the kind of stuff his ex-wife's lawyers would have loved to get their hands on.

Although BCCI was deeply involved with Iran-Contra, and maintained a significant presence in the Caymans, a lot of money still moved through Eurobank to the Contras. U.S. Senate investigators also discovered in 1991 that there were dozens of transactions between Eurobank and BCCI. But other people were moving money through there as well, including at least one American fugitive from justice, prompting the local inspector of banks to complain quietly to the management that too many bad people were associated with the bank.

There's no doubt that drug barons were among the people washing money through Eurobank. Nor is there any doubt that, in the wake of 9/11 – given its pedigree – certain intelligence agencies around the world had an interest in who walked through Eurobank's doors. One of those intelligence services was Britain's MI-6.

Their guy on the ground was Brian Gibbs.

Surveillance of Eurobank and its clients was code-named Operation Victory. To manage it, Gibbs had a source inside the bank – Edward Warwick, code-named Warlock. The two had met some years before, when Warwick was at Finsbury Bank. Gibbs and his unit at the RCIP investigated Finsbury for drug-money laundering, and the government shut it. Gibbs maintained contact with Warwick, who came to be considered a high-value source by MI-6. According to documents in the Caymans, there were several people Warwick spoke with Gibbs about over the years.

One was Donald Stewart. Before coming to Eurobank, Stewart had been country manager at the Royal Bank of Canada. While there, Gibbs had served Stewart with a production order to hand over certain bank documents in connection with a drug case. According to Gibbs, Stewart did not fully comply and withheld information.

Another was Brian Cunha, a Eurobank officer who'd previously been manager at First Cayman Bank. Gibbs had served him with a production order in a case involving David Namer, a now-convicted fraudster out of Tennessee. Namer had been laundering the proceeds of his crimes through the Caymans, and working Reg-S fraud with Meyers Pollock Robbins, the mobbed-up brokerage that the SEC and John Moscow had busted.

Warwick was also a source of information about David Bockius, a man running insurance fraud out of Pennsylvania. Bockius was laundering funds through an investment account at PaineWebber in New York, and was also using the casinos in Atlantic City to wash some cash. The rest he merely carried with him to the Caymans. On his initial trip down, using the alias Louis Middleton, he stashed half a million dollars into secret compartments of his suitcases. He formed a shell called Little Mermaid Holdings and through that, with some of his cash, bought himself a house. He intended to put the rest of the cash into Canadian banks, making multiple deposits of under $10,000 to escape reporting requirements. But either some of the banks flatly refused him, or he found out that the others would probably report him anyway. At Eurobank, they welcomed him and his cash.

A certain Russian whose name popped up frequently during the 1990s involved with offshore scams was also brought to Gibbs's attention this way, although intelligence on that person was coming from several sources at the same time. Gibbs wrote in a report about this Russian, "The matters on record concerning (name omitted) were ongoing not just from Mr. Warwick, but from the National Criminal Intelligence Service U.K., press reports, City of London Police, FBI and other sources."

As outlined in a confidential report written by a New York private eye, this particular Russian was an intermediary in the purchase of certain financial instruments by a small Moscow bank. The money was being run through three shells in the Caymans, all of which had accounts at Eurobank. The first two deals, totalling $9.7 million, worked fine. But the third, for $4.75 million, went missing. The Moscow Bank asked Eurobank for the return of the money, but Eurobank refused. On further investigation, it was determined that monies had been moved out of Eurobank in various directions. A large sum was sent to an account at Citibank, New York, for credit to Bank von Ernst et Cie in Zurich. Another large sum was sent directly to an account at Bank von

Ernst in Zurich. The supposition was that the Russian intermediary had ordered the transfers and controlled the two accounts.

But the Russian claimed that the two transfers were forgeries. Investigators in New York, the Caymans, Switzerland, and London never accepted his excuse at face value and are continuing to look into the Russian's business affairs. One area of interest are his associations with certain people involved in the Bank of New York laundering scandal.

Two other names that were brought to Gibbs's attention by Warwick were Jay Bartz and Patrick Smythe. Both of them were stock-piling money at Eurobank, and both of them would be the next stop along the ring road of networked crime.

But Brian Gibbs wouldn't be around to do anything about that.

The Caymans brought charges against Eurobank and some of its officers – including Stewart and Cunha – and took the case to trial. Back in London, MI-6 grew increasingly nervous about the possibility that its position might be exposed. Paranoid about publicity anyway, the last thing it wanted was for evidence to be presented in court that would require it to "neither confirm nor deny" an active presence in the Caymans, expose Gibbs as its agent, compromise any of its ongoing inquiries, or expose Warlock.

Early on in the trial, when the defence attorneys and the judge began to realize that certain documents had not been made available to them by the prosecution, attention focused on the FRU and Gibbs. The prosecution pressed Gibbs about the documents too. There were then discussions with London about possibly sanitizing the missing information, loading it onto Gibbs's computer, and making some excuse about having misplaced it until now.

That's when word came to Gibbs that the RCIP was about to raid him. If that happened, MI-6's work in the Caymans would be destroyed. So the decision was made to shred certain documents. When the judge discovered this – and was led to believe that MI-6 might even have been bugging his phones – he castigated Gibbs and tossed the Eurobank case out of court. He declared all of the defendants not guilty.

Gibbs resigned from his post at the FRU and quickly left the island.

‒

In 1990, the financial position of the National Heritage Life Insurance Company, a subsidiary of LifeCo Investment Group, became tenuous as a result of a series of bad deals, and the company's future was at risk. The Delaware Insurance Department, which had oversight authority, threatened the company that unless they raised additional capital, the department would take regulatory action. But instead of bolstering the company's bank accounts, several directors of LifeCo decided to sacrifice National Heritage in favour of their own bank accounts.

Over the course of the next seven years, Patrick Smythe, then president and chief operations officer of LifeCo, together with a group of corporate insiders and at least one professional fraudster, ran through a series of scams to embezzle $440 million from the company.

Among the scams was one revolving around non-performing mortgages. Smythe announced that he was in the midst of negotiating a $200-million reinsurance deal and that National Heritage would have to come up with the money to fund it.

One of his partners-in-crime, Lyle Pfeffer – who served on LifeCo's board – moved the National Heritage money to other associates who, in turn, sheltered it away in various shells. That money was then used to buy a portfolio of non-performing mortgages, which were eventually grouped into another shell company. Bonds, with grossly exaggerated values, were issued by the shell company holding the essentially worthless non-performing mortgages, for which National Heritage paid $118.3 million.

Smythe's second partner-in-crime was Jay Bartz, whose name had come up at Eurobank. He was an attorney in Arizona who also sat on LifeCo's board and served as Smythe's laundryman. Bartz's primary task was to make money safe, which he did for Smythe by moving $2.2 million first to the Channel Islands and from there to the Caymans. In the end, Bartz was put in prison for three years and disbarred.

Two other men now come into play.

The first is Michael Blutrich, a New York attorney and convicted pedophile who, through his friendship with Pfeffer, was brought into the LifeCo swindle. Blutrich helped Smythe and Pfeffer divert $47 million from National Heritage by creating a ruse that made it look as if the money was being spent on capital investments.

With their share of the money, Blutrich and Pfeffer bought themselves a strip joint and turned it into Manhattan's first lap-dancing club, Scores. Not only was this a place where they could hang out, but they'd worked out a way to help their friends at LifeCo launder money through the business. What neither of them understood, however, was that in New York, the five LCN families had long ago divvied-up the strip-club market. It's one of many traditional businesses where one of the families is always a silent partner. In this case, the Gambino family, then run by John Gotti, moved in with Blutrich and Pfeffer at Scores.

At the same time, the Gambinos were laundering drug money through an upmarket strip joint in Atlanta called the Gold Club. The man running it for them, Steve Kaplan, had turned it into a hot spot for celebrity athletes, which he easily did by pimping some of the dancers. At his trial, stories of sex at the Gold Club came from NBA stars Patrick Ewing and Dennis Rodman and Atlanta Braves baseball player Andruw Jones.

Kaplan, who was looking to move up in the world, tried to convince his masters in the family that he could work the same routine at Scores. So pressure mounted from at least one faction of the family to install Kaplan. Blutrich never liked the idea that the Gambinos were setting the terms of his own business. They were skimming wherever they could, overcharging him for booze, rubbish collection, doormen, bouncers, and the girls. Now they wanted to run him out. Blutrich realized he needed some help and turned to the Feds. He let them wire the club in their effort to target Gotti.

Push came to shove when Blutrich fired the Gotti-installed manager. Kaplan wanted a showdown and the only way Blutrich could save his business was to ask for arbitration. John Gotti, Jr., agreed to hear both sides, and ruled in Blutrich's favour. He then sent Blutrich a bill for $200,000 for settling the matter.

When the LifeCo case came down, Blutrich pled guilty to eighteen felony counts of racketeering, conspiracy, wire fraud, and money laundering. Along with Smythe and Pfeffer, the judge handed him twenty-five years. Rather than do all that time, Blutrich and Pfeffer offered to turn state's evidence against Junior Gotti, the Mob, Kaplan, and the others at the Gold Club. They helped to expose what they knew about seven Mob-controlled corporations and the money-laundering apparatus attached to them.

It pretty much worked, because Gotti and Kaplan and most of the rest went down. For their trouble, Blutrich and Pfeffer were made life members of a witness protection program, were allowed to spend the next sixteen and a half years in the relative safety of solitary confinement and, eventually, if they live long enough to get out, will be given new identities.

The other man who got involved in the LifeCo scam and went on to bigger and better things was Blutrich's friend, Shalom Weiss. A professional fraudster, he was the genius behind the non-performing mortgage rip-off. It was his shell company that acquired the mortgages and another of his shell companies that sold them.

When the cops came looking for him, however, Weiss decided it would be a good idea to abandon his wife and children in New York, and spend time with his girlfriend in Brazil. He went on the lam for more than a year, until he was found in Vienna and brought back to the States to stand trial. Ordered to pay a fine of $123 million, plus restitution of $125 million to National Heritage's policy holders, Weiss was sent away for 845 years.

Previously convicted of mail fraud, Weiss had been working Reg-S scams for several years and had close ties to various Russian mobsters also working securities fraud in the States. There are connections through those Russians to the Gambinos.

Weiss is linked to Phil Abramo, of the DeCavalcante crime family. The same Phil Abramo who'd once worked at A.S. Goldmen in Florida with Albert Alain Chalem – the man who'd threatened Sal Mazzeo – and had helped manipulate the Reg-S offering of Osicom Technologies.

The two showed up again in an investigation in Vancouver. The British Columbia Securities Commission (BCSC) spent two years investigating a local brokerage house, Pacific International Securities, which had been named in three U.S. money-laundering indictments. As a result, several brokers were arrested for dealing with mobbed-up clients. In a press release, the BCSC even announced some of the names of the mobbed-up clients. High on the list were Weiss and Abramo.

Sal Mazzeo was also on that list.

Slightly lower down the list was a convicted stock manipulator from Las Vegas named Barclay Davis. He'd been involved in a series of fraudulent microcap offerings that were moved through several brokerages in Vancouver. Among the promotions complained of were Systems of Excellence, Combined Companies International Corp., and Bio-Tech Industries Inc., which was originally called Twenty-First Century Health.

A Davis comrade in at least one of the fraudulent offerings out of Vancouver is Thomas Clines. And he brings the ring road back to the beginning.

In 1990, Clines was convicted for income-tax evasion for failing to declare $260,000 that he made in arms' shipments to the Nicaraguan Contras as one of the CIA refugees working the Iran-Contra scandal for William Casey and laundering money through Eurobank.

15

A BETTER MOUSETRAP

"Build a better mousetrap and the world will beat a path to your door."

– Ralph Waldo Emerson

There was a time when drug-money laundering was a fairly straightforward business. You gathered up all the cash from street-corner sales, walked it around to lots of banks, dumped a little bit here and a little bit there, then consolidated the accounts and wired the whole stash out of the country and into some secret jurisdiction.

That's the way Stephen Saccoccia did it.

That's also the way Gary Henden did it, although this legendary Canadian laundrymen had a variation on the theme. Instead of having the money delivered to him, he used a delivery boy to take it to the banks – a fifteen-year-old on a bicycle.

It was basically the same method for the drug trafficker who bragged when he was arrested that he employed an army of Smurfs – named for the cartoon characters – who could make up to two thousand deposits a day at 513 different banks.

Law enforcement figured out that approach pretty quickly and although it took politicians a while to catch up, eventually they passed laws making it more and more difficult to get cash into banks. So much so that Pablo Escobar, the late Colombian cocaine cartel boss, once had to write off $40 million because he couldn't get it into banks fast enough. The cash was found rotting in a California basement.

Without any doubt, when you get right down to it, cash is the most difficult problem that drug traffickers face. Holding on to it is dangerous and trying to get rid of it is clumsy. Because street sales are made in small denominations, cocaine and heroin can generate six to ten times their weight in banknotes. Smuggle fifty kilos of coke into the country and your street sales will net approximately three hundred kilos worth of cash. Import ten kilos of heroin, and you've got to worry about one hundred kilos in small bills.

As laundering became more difficult, traffickers looked to bulk money out of the country and get it into laundry-friendly jurisdictions. In many cases they used the same methods to get money out as they did to bring the drugs in.

Customs officers at Kennedy Airport in New York stopped a woman from boarding a flight to Europe and asked her how much money she was carrying. She answered, $9,000. When they searched her luggage, they found $24,000 stuffed into shampoo bottles. When they examined her, they found she'd hidden six wads of $100 bills vaginally and had swallowed a dozen condoms with another $20,000 rolled in them. Their cohorts at nearby Newark Airport stopped another woman wearing a lot of clothes about to board a flight to Colombia. Underneath her dress, girdle, and stocking she wore a surfer's wetsuit stuffed with $75,000.

Inspectors all over the world report money hidden in toys, sealed inside wax candles, stuffed inside resealed boxes of popcorn, pancake mix, and sacks of rice. Some $695,000 was found by inspectors in biscuit tins and packages of baby wipes inside the luggage of a man boarding a flight to Egypt. Another $625,000 was located in plastic bags that had been professionally sewn into the lining of a comforter. Bulk cash has been found rolled into carpets, shoved inside laptop computers, packed into fridges, and, in one case, hidden inside a stuffed animal just back from the taxidermist. Cash has been found in vats of battery acid and toxic waste, and some years ago $6.5 million worth was found at the bottom of drums filled with bull semen on its way to South America.

At Heathrow Airport, it is becoming more and more common to see HM Customs officers with specially trained "cash sniffer" dogs doing spot checks of people flying out of the country. Not long ago, a team with dogs was checking people leaving on a flight to Miami. When the team leader was informed by a nosy passenger that he was wasting his time, the officer wondered why. He was told that he'd do better to check flights going to Canada – where laundering cash was more viable – because no one in Miami wanted cash. Instead, every laundryman in Florida was paying over the odds to get rid of cash.

Either the HM Customs officer refused to believe it or he didn't understand, which, in either case, says a lot about Britain's war on dirty money.

Although sniffing dogs checking the wrong flight do create a presence – which might, if HM Customs gets lucky – have a knock-on effect in deterring some amateur money launderer from carrying cash through the airport, more effective methods can be deduced from understanding how creative money launderers need to be.

Brokers at the Wall Street firm MLU Investments were well aware that the Colombians had found a better mousetrap, because they were part of it, helping the Colombians move $8 million through the markets.

The president and chief laundrymen of MLU Investments was Ron Rose. Now in his mid-forties, athletically lean, with bright eyes and a laid-back friendly smile, he grew up on Long Island, graduated from John Jay College in Manhattan in 1978, and got himself a job working in the inspector general's office at the New York City Department of Finance. He wasn't there long before he realized what he really wanted to do was to be a cop. So he signed on with the NYPD, did all the usual uniformed street patrol stuff, and got himself interviewed for a detective's position. Transferred into plain clothes, he was assigned to the Organized Crime Control Bureau.

"It's really just the luck of the draw," he recalls. "I spent time working in Public Morals, the vice squad, doing gambling and loan sharking. I also worked traditional organized crime, racketeering cases on the Bonanno crime family, and did a lot of cases going after the Colombo family. Then somebody asked me if I wanted to move into something new. They were setting up a money-laundering unit. I didn't seek it out, didn't even know much about it. But one day I was working the Colombos, next day I was working the Colombians."

In 1992, as Lieutenant Rose, he and his NYPD money-laundering unit moved into offices leased by U.S. Customs at the World Trade Center to become an integral part of a joint task force known as El Dorado.

Literally billions of dollars had been going through New York banks each month in a well-organized, professional manner. The bad guys were frantic to get their cash out of the country, while the good guys were trampling over each other's feet to try to stop them. The idea behind the two-hundred-strong El Dorado team was to unite the thirty-five federal, state, and local agencies that were working money laundering throughout the New York metropolitan area. The feeling was that the good guys were outgunned, outfinanced, and outlawyered, so that by combining forces – by putting law enforcement together with prosecutors, intelligence, and analysts – they might stand a chance at interrupting the cash flow and reinvestment that the traffickers needed to keep their business flowing.

One of El Dorado's senior managers, U.S. Customs agent John Forbes, believed that if El Dorado could target money remitters in some of New York's high-density drug-trafficking neighbourhoods, they could interrupt the cash flows and, in turn, affect trafficking. Forbes wanted to target a Colombian neighbourhood in Jackson Heights. About a mile south of LaGuardia Airport, it's a lower middle-class section of Queens where, in those days, the average family earned about $20,000 before taxes. But so much money was going to Colombia that it averaged out at $30,000 to $40,000 per family.

Forbes sold the idea to the then-undersecretary of the treasury for enforcement, Ray Kelly – later commissioner of customs and then police commissioner for the City of New York – who signed a geographical targeting order (GTO). Among other things, this restricted the amount of money a person in Jackson Heights could wire to Colombia without filing certain forms.

The money-laundering laws limited the amount to $3,000. The GTO reduced it to $750. And almost immediately, Forbes's idea proved right. Big sum wire to Colombia from Jackson Heights virtually ceased. At the same time, the cost of sending wires dropped from 7 to 3 per cent. Forbes, Rose, and other managers at El Dorado knew that reflected increased competition. So they went after the remitters.

These were, ostensibly, mom-and-pop businesses – beauty parlours, candy stores, travel agencies – which offered a remitter service in the shop. Some of them also sold cellphones and phone cards, so that anonymous calls could be made. All of them advertised ENVIO, which meant they wired money. Along Roosevelt Boulevard, running through the heart of Jackson Heights for about a mile and a half, there were more than 175 ENVIOS and these places were moving $1.1 billion to $1.3 billion a year.

Of course it was dope money, and El Dorado started shutting the remitters down. But typically, whenever they closed one, two more would open up. After a while the traffickers understood that they were being targeted and the money being wired out moved across Manhattan, to Washington Heights on the upper West Side, where Dominicans controlled the drug trade. Forbes went back to Kelly and got another GTO to target the Dominicans. Before long, some of the action left town, heading south to Florida, which meant that El Dorado was having an effect.

Around 1998, some disquieting news came out of their surveillance of the wire remitters. Instead of seeing money moving to Colombia, they were seeing Colombian drug money wired out to Pakistan. Forbes grew very concerned, and went to his superiors to say, We need to look at this. No one up the ladder felt the same sense of urgency about it. Forbes simply couldn't get anyone to commit to it. That Colombian drug money was heading to the subcontinent – with all the ramifications of money moving through there to the Middle East – didn't seem important.

Three years later, when El Dorado's offices were destroyed by the 9/11 attacks, Colombian drug money going to Pakistan took on a whole new meaning.

El Dorado was focused on Jackson Heights when Rose got a call from his boss at police headquarters saying that the commissioner had met a couple of retired FBI guys with an informant who knew a couple of guys looking to invest some dirty money. Rose was told to look into it.

The retired FBI agents explained to Rose that their informant had connections with Mexico's ruthless Gulf cartel and that this would be a way to land some heavyweight money launderers. Rose thought about it and decided he might be able to set up some sort of an investment firm to handle their money. If he worked it right, the money trail should lead to the cartel's investment brokers. But the more he talked to these guys, the less enthusiastic he was about dealing with them. They wanted to run the whole thing by remote control from another part of the country and Rose saw too many problems with that.

Undercover operations are inherently risky, and Rose knew from experience that the stakes in this one could run very high. He decided he didn't want any part of it and explained to the commissioner why he felt the NYPD should stay away. He returned to El Dorado, thinking that's the end of that. But a couple of days later, one of the retired FBI guys decided that he and his mate would be willing to do it any way the NYPD wanted to, so Rose's boss asked him to write up a game plan and cost it. He did, putting the price tag for the operation at around $100,000, and sent it up the chain of command.

Normally, proposals like this one get sent from office to office and a year later someone remembers to say yes or no. So Rose wasn't counting on anything happening for a long while. But two days later someone called to say, Go ahead.

He was shocked. "Most of the time I couldn't get ten dollars out of them to buy batteries for a tape recorder, now in two days they're telling me to spend a hundred grand."

The commissioner wanted the operation run in conjunction with the New York District Attorney's Office, which teamed Rose with Assistant District Attorney Gilda Mariani.

Describing her depends on the circumstances of how you met. If you've been introduced by mutual friends, she is a charming, bright, sophisticated woman with a deep love of animals, whose mind and door are always open to new initiatives and new ideas. As chief of the New York D.A.'s money-laundering and tax crimes unit, Mariani is a genuine authority on money laundering and one of the driving forces in getting an effective money-laundering law implemented in New York State. If, on the other hand, you've been introduced to her by cops who have locked you in handcuffs, she is a tenacious and resolute workaholic who categorically will not quit until she gets the result she wants, which usually means putting you behind bars.

So Rose and Mariani now spent a year setting up everything they needed to go into business as investment brokers. It began with a lot of backstopping that had to be put in place – undercover identities, driver's licences, credit cards, personal histories, credit histories, and work histories. Because Rose and his guys were going into the markets, they needed memos of understanding with the SEC and the NASD. They also needed, and got, some professional training.

Next, Rose and Mariani had to form a company. They incorporated themselves and set up bank accounts as the MLU Investment Group Corporation. It was their little inside joke. MLU stands for Money Laundering Unit.

"We had to assume," Rose says, "that we might come under a lot of scrutiny. If these people were actually going to trust us with their money, they would want to know who we are. We were going to do cash management and investment for companies that were cash intensive, so we wrote a business plan that showed us dealing with video arcades, amusement parks, video rentals, supermarkets. We then created accounts in the names of Lake Wholesale Foods, American Video, Funtime Arcade. Our story was that we could place their money in the bank. From there, we would send it wherever they needed it, and hold on to whatever they wanted us to invest for them. We set it up so that when some bad guy looked at us, he'd think to himself, these guys can wash our money for us and nobody will ever know."

With backstopping in place, MLU Investments needed an office. It had to be in the right part of town and it had to have the right look. At the same time, it had to be secure enough that they could run the undercover safely. They settled on a twenty-second-floor suite at One World Trade Center, a building where security had been seriously increased following the 1993 attack. Unless you had an ID card, you couldn't walk into the elevator banks and go upstairs. Anyway, the last thing Rose wanted was someone just stopping by. To get upstairs, you needed to ask at the desk in the lobby and someone from MLU would have to come down to escort you up.

The MLU office was behind a secure door, with cameras guarding the entrance. Naturally, the place was wired for sound and video. It wasn't plush, but it was typical and adequate. Rose filled it with $25,000 worth of furniture – cherrywood desks, high-backed leather chairs – and computers and market wires to make it look like a boutique investment firm.

Rose, case officer Joe Thompson, and four undercover detectives would work the office. The rest of the crew – about ten people – would handle surveillance and backup. They also needed to put in place some administrative support, which meant bookkeeping and accounting and someone to type transcripts when they were running wiretaps.

Once they had it all equipped, when Rose and Mariani and everyone else were all ready to go, Rose told the guys running El Dorado what was about to come down. Around that office, he was always pushing for equal footing, always reminding the Customs and IRS guys running it that the locals had to have an equal share. So he told them about his undercover, and invited El Dorado to play a support role.

"They didn't know if they wanted in or out. They hemmed and hawed about it. I asked them not to tell anybody about it, because it was under-cover and we weren't looking to advertise, and gave them time to think about it. I went to Puerto Rico on a job and while I was there I get a call from my boss at NYPD, who said, Your new case is in the newspaper. Except we hadn't done anything yet, we were still in the process of setting it up. We hadn't even started and it's already in the newspapers."

Rose later learned that one of the higher-ups at El Dorado had men-tioned the undercover to a friend at the U.S. Attorney's Office. The Feds like to think of Wall Street as their turf, and don't necessarily like it when the New York D.A.'s Office plays there too. On at least one occasion, District Attorney Morgenthau is known to have reminded a certain U.S. attorney, "Last time I looked out my window, Wall Street was in Manhattan." So when someone at the U.S. Attorney's Office heard about Rose's undercover, and realized that he was working with the D.A.'s Office, whoever that person was decided to remind the New Yorkers that the Feds were not to be ignored. The D.A.'s Office had locked up a woman for insider trading. Over one weekend, an assistant U.S. attorney visited her in jail and got to her to take a plea on federal charges. Essentially, the U.S. Attorney's Office stole the case. That person then leaked a story to the *New York Times* about how the Feds had scored some points, mentioning in the last couple of paragraphs that there was a dispute going on with the D.A.'s Office over an undercover investiga-tion that the NYPD was running despite objections from the U.S. Attorney's Office.

That didn't please Rose and Mariani. It didn't sit well with the El Dorado hierarchy either. They decided they didn't want to upset the U.S. attorney and opted out of Rose's undercover. They also ruled out any participation by anyone assigned to El Dorado. That placed Rose and his team in the middle of a power struggle between El Dorado's masters and the NYPD. So now, with everything ready to go, the NYPD simply pulled their guys out of El Dorado and went ahead with MLU.

They called it Operation Bluechip. Right from the beginning, Rose put out the word that they weren't going to do street pickups. He wanted his customers to know that cash had to be delivered to his office. And not just to the lobby. Cash had to be brought upstairs to the office, and only after the person making the delivery was behind the locked office doors would MLU take possession of the money.

"We did that for several reasons," Rose goes on. "Number one, it helped support our story that we were brokers and investment advisers, not just some slugs on the street. It showed them that we knew we had a lot to lose by doing it any other way. It showed them we didn't intend on getting robbed by some mutts. We don't do pickups, that's not us, we're not going out there. Number two, it protected my guys from getting ripped off. No one could set us up where one guy gives you the bag here and the next guy comes around the corner with a gun and takes it from you. Number three, we needed to protect ourselves from other law enforcement people out there. We didn't want to get arrested in a sting that someone else might be running. So our guys never touched anything until the money was handed to us upstairs, behind our locked door with our cameras running."

Because attention to detail is always so vital in any undercover, Rose set up a system where the guys working in the office were not the same people who took the money out of the office to the bank. Nor did anyone taking money out use the same bag that brought the money in.

Yet with all their planning, and all the tension that had been caused by the *New York Times* article, and all the political problems with El Dorado, Rose and Mariani suddenly found themselves dressed to the nines but with no place to go. They'd sent their confidential informant (CI) out into the world, seeded him with $10,000 to spread around, and only got promises in return.

They both understood how an undercover like this could produce major results. And they were determined to make it work. So Rose and Mariani tried to find someone who would authorize them to branch out. But the powers that be were nervous about that – branching out wasn't written into the game plan, which meant the bosses wouldn't have their butts covered if something went wrong – and they kept coming back to Rose and Mariani with remarks like, Give the CI a chance to deliver, hang in there, something will happen.

Except it didn't.

Months passed and the only thing they had to show for MLU was one guy who offered to sell them some phony Paraguayan bonds.

Refusing to give up, Rose and Mariani got permission to use their own contacts, reached out to certain people, and let it be known that MLU Investments was able to do stuff that no one else on Wall Street could do.

That's when a call came in from someone who knew someone who might be interested in doing business.

With Rose and Mariani in the background, Detective Jimmy Ricaurte, a Spanish-speaking undercover, negotiated with the intermediary, who had a friend in Colombia who had some money stashed at a wholesale clothing place in midtown Manhattan. The intermediary explained that if MLU wanted to do business with his friend the Colombian, MLU would have to pick up the cash.

Right away, Ricaurte explained that they didn't do collections. He told the intermediary, "We're brokers, not guys who pick up bags of money."

But the intermediary insisted and Rose knew that tapping into the Colombian could lead to bigger things. To facilitate the deal, Rose nodded to Ricaurte, who told the intermediary that he'd contract out the pickup, but just this once. What Rose and Mariani didn't find out until much later was that this particular wholesale clothing business was being watched by an NYPD narcotics team. Luckily, when one of Rose's guys made the pickup, the narcotics team didn't get in the way.

Once the money was moved, the Colombian himself – call him Jorge – phoned Ricaurte to say, I want to work with you but I don't know you, you don't know me so we have to get together before we can do anything else. Jorge suggested they get together in Colombia. That was out of the question for the good guys. Rose wanted Ricaurte to meet Jorge in the States. That was out of the question for the bad guy, who now suggested Panama. On Rose's advice, Ricaurte compromised by setting up the meet in Curaçao. The Dutch island off the coast of Colombia would be safe because Rose had law enforcement connections there. Curaçao is also an offshore banking centre, which gave Ricaurte the built-in excuse of being able to say that he needed to be there on business anyway.

Jorge agreed and the meeting took place on schedule. He told Ricaurte that he was a money broker who got in the middle of other guys' deals. Rose and Mariani couldn't yet tell how important Jorge was because these guys always play themselves up to be a lot more important than they really are. But even a small broker was capable of moving tens of millions of dollars. And anyway, the MLU undercover didn't have anyone else to play with.

During the meeting in Curaçao, Ricaurte reminded Jorge that money moving wasn't their business, that they did investments but that he might be willing to do a certain amount of money moving for serious investors. Jorge became MLU's first client.

"Getting into Jorge was a big step," Rose points out. "These guys have associates who are always looking for outlets to move money. When they find one, they never tell their friends about it because then their friends can deal directly. Instead, they broker deals for their friends. We moved his money, he trusted us and his friends trusted him. Before long we were moving money with our guy for a lot of other people, wiring it all over the States and all over the world. Hong Kong. Shanghai, Italy, London. This guy put us in the middle of a huge black-market peso exchange."

The Black Market Peso Exchange (BMPE) was, indeed, the better mousetrap.

Based on the same ancient system of barter that Middle Easterners and Asians call *hawallah*, it was perfected in the Western Hemisphere by smugglers who needed to do double-sided trades to thrive in the underground economy.

It's a system where goods move and money stays put. Traffickers, faced with the increasing difficulties of shifting money, latched on to the idea in the mid-1980s. By 1990, they'd perfected the system to the point that Colombia's Black Market Peso Exchange was a $5-billion bazaar. Today, it's anyone's guess what this market is worth, but estimates of two to three times as much as it was in 1990 could be in the ballpark. An official Colombian estimate suggests that 45 per cent of the country's imported consumer goods are paid for through the BMPE.

The reason for its indisputable success is that money laundering doesn't have to be about money. In fact, these days, it seldom is. Money laundering in the globalized twenty-first century is about honey and diamonds, charities, and paperless networks like *hawallah* banking that you find throughout the Middle East and subcontinent. Recently, money laundering was also about sporting memorabilia – a Mafia loan-sharking operation washed money through collectible baseball cards, Michael Jordan–autographed basketballs, signed hockey pucks, and a pair of Muhammad Ali's boxing gloves.

In its most basic form, a broker sitting in Colombia arranges to buy a trafficker's drug cash in Britain at a discount. At the same time, he takes pesos from a legitimate businessman in Colombia looking to import a product, say a large shipment of Scotch. The broker uses the pesos in Colombia to buy the drug trafficker's cash in Britain, then uses the drug cash in Britain to buy the Scotch for the businessman in Colombia.

Traffickers and legitimate businessmen both have to trust the broker with their money. But as he's in Colombia, if anything goes wrong, retribution is simple. So it's the broker who takes a risk by trusting associates outside Colombia to facilitate transfers, deposit cash, and sometimes make payments. But then, these brokers frequently work like bookies, laying off parts of contracts to spread the risk.

The system flourishes because it is efficient. Whether the product is Scotch or household appliances, consumer electronics, cigarettes, used auto parts, precious metals, footwear, cars, boats, whatever, everyone gets what he wants. The trafficker winds up with pesos, which means his drug money has been laundered. The businessman get his goods and, because the purchase is outside normal channels, he usually beats the taxman. The broker has made money on the spread between buying and selling dollars and pesos, plus a commission on the deal. And the company selling the goods has probably made a sale it might not have otherwise made. Except that the company selling the goods has also laundered drug money – albeit unknowingly. Still, very few serious companies want to get caught doing that.

Just ask the folks who make Bell Helicopters.

In 1998, a man with links to drug traffickers and paramilitary groups in Colombia wanted to buy a Bell 407 helicopter. The company didn't know anything about his background or his business dealings. Nor was there any requirement for them to do so. This was simply a guy looking to buy a helicopter and selling helicopters is the business Bell is in. He agreed to pay them $1.5 million for the machine and nobody at Bell thought twice about it.

Yet alarm bells should have gone off when Bell saw how he was paying for it. They received twenty-nine third-party wire transfers from sixteen different sources, in addition to a third-party cheque signed over to Bell from yet another source. None of those third parties had any sort of relationship with Bell. As it turned out, none of them had any sort of relationship with the man buying the helicopter either. The third parties were following instructions from a BMPE broker who was moving drug money into negotiable paper, payable to Bell. The actual buyer had already put down $1.5 million in pesos in Colombia.

Bell's response was understandable. *How could we know this was drug money? If we'd known this was drug money, we'd never have done the deal.*

U.S. Customs response was then – and is now – *You should have known.*

Bell was hardly alone in getting duped. The investigation that uncovered this sale led to investigations into half a dozen other companies that had fallen victim to the same ruse. In every case, the company denied intentionally taking drug money. In some instances, the denials are believable. But it's not always easy to understand why a legitimate business doesn't question payment methods that are so out of the ordinary. That said, BMPE brokers count on the fact that most companies would rather have a strange sale than no sale at all.

And many of those sales are decidedly strange.

Take, for example, the order that arrived at the sales office of a world-famous sporting goods company for $10,000 worth of soccer gear. It was to be shipped to Colombia. Payment was a pile of money orders, but the envelope that it came in didn't even have a return address.

One U.S. company, General Electric, instituted a very strict money-laundering compliance program in 1995 after getting burned by a BMPE broker buying a load of refrigerators. The program was in place and effectively stopped another BMPE broker when he tried to pay for $40,000 worth of air conditioners with thirty-five money orders.

In October 1997, an anonymous BMPE broker went before a congressional committee and named several international companies with whom she'd placed deals. Among them: Sony, Procter & Gamble, John Deere, Whirlpool, Ford, Kenworth, Johnny Walker, Swatch, Merrill Lynch, and

Reebok. As she explained, "These companies were paid with U.S. currency generated by narcotics trafficking. They may not have been aware of the source of this money, but they accepted payments from me without questioning who I was or the source of the money."

By the mid- to late 1990s, the volume of money moving through the Black Market Peso Exchange was so large, it's hardly surprising that Ron Rose and Gilda Mariani were not the people setting up a sting to get inside one.

In Operation Juno, the DEA and the IRS rented office space in suburban Atlanta to set up a stockbrokerage called Airmark. Although they never did any actual stock trading, they found some peso brokers who believed they were for real and contracted Airmark's undercover agents to make drug pickups. Juno was followed by a U.S. Customs sting called Operation Skymaster. It was the same kind of sting, where undercover agents arranged pickups for black-market peso brokers. The two operations resulted in more than 250 arrests, drug seizures totalling more than eight tons, and money seizures in excess of $36 million. The two operations also exposed thirty-four U.S. banks and fifty-two foreign banks to warrants, seizures, and further scrutiny.

One of the banks that showed up in those operations was the British Bank of Latin America (BBLA), a tiny offshore affiliate of Lloyd's TSB. Licensed in the Bahamas, it only had a couple of hundred clients, but they were all Colombian and all of them used this offshore facility to maintain dollar accounts. In turn, BBLA had correspondent relationships with Bank of America, Bankers Trust, Barclays Bank, Chemical Bank, and Citibank, plus Lloyd's in the U.S. and in Panama. Towards the end of its life, BBLA had a strong working relationship with the Bank of New York.

Hardly surprising, BBLA maintained no anti-money-laundering procedures and was subjected to no real oversight. The British, the Colombians, and the Bahamians were all depending on one of the others to watch the bank. BBLA finally folded in 2000. By then, it had been operating as a sink for Colombian brokers for a good part of its nineteen years.

Enter Luz Mariana Gómez Alzate, a five-foot-tall Colombian woman in her late thirties with bleached blonde hair.

Known to her friends as Patricia, she had a small business in one of Bogota's many illegal markets – they're called *sanandrecitos*, named for the Colombian smugglers' island, San Andres – which is how she got to know Jorge. When he needed somebody to do pickups in the States, she moved her five kids to Florida – her first son Hernan was twenty, her second son Andres was sixteen, and the other three were little – and decided to teach her boys the business.

She showed up with Hernan the first time he made a delivery for Jorge. The surveillance team in the lobby spotted this woman and this young man immediately, but didn't know who she was. Hernan went to the desk to ask for MLU and Patricia stayed off to the side, waiting alone while Hernan went upstairs. She returned with him on his next delivery, and the delivery after that. It was Hernan who then happened to mention that his mother liked the way they did business. He asked if MLU was interested in dealing directly with her.

Rose answered right away, "Who are we to say no?"

So Patricia became an MLU client. Jorge didn't know that she'd gone into competition with him. Nor was she the only one. Word quickly got out that MLU Investments could move money. Several people working for Jorge double-crossed him by going behind his back and doing deals directly with MLU. But none of the others was ever like Patricia. She became the exception to everything they did at MLU.

It wasn't enough that she was moving money through them, before long she announced that she wanted sixteen-year-old Andres to stay in New York to work deliveries, and asked Ricaurte to help find an apartment for him. This was not part of their original plan, but Rose decided it was a good idea to keep Patricia close, so his guys located a flat for Andres in a good neighbourhood in Forest Hills, Queens. They also got him a cellphone and a pager, and of course put wires on everything so they could listen to his calls.

Through Andres's conversations with his mother, the team was able to learn about other deals being set up. They also listened as people working with Patricia in Colombia started ringing Andres too. It gave Rose and the team access to both sides of these deals – the money side and the drug side. Which was important because they needed to tie the two sides together.

Mariani, who would take these cases to court, had to prove to a jury that the money they were laundering was drug money, and that the brokers they were working for knew that this was drug money. In a few instances, it was easy. A bag of cash arrived at the office one day with so much coke on it that the counting machine jammed. But getting brokers and delivery guys to admit on camera or on a wire that they were dealing in drug money was another matter.

When money came in, there was hardly ever any paperwork attached to it. Most of the time hundreds of thousands of dollars were simply handed over, just like that, by people who didn't know the guys at MLU and never expected to see them again. When there was a slip of paper with a total, the count was usually wrong. So Rose decided that they had to keep their clients informed. On the premise that MLU didn't want any trouble, the team rang every broker with a ballpark figure of how much money had been delivered. It was during those conversations that one of the MLU guys would say something like, We counted the money and my table was covered in white powder. Or, the guy you sent up here looked like he just sold crack on the corner. The brokers started talking about drugs and Mariani started to collect the evidence she'd need.

A couple of months into the sting, Jorge phoned Ricaurte to ask if he'd heard about a BMPE case that the IRS had taken down in Miami. Drug money was going through computer and electronics stores. Ricaurte said he didn't know anything about it, but after the call he and Rose researched it and decided they could use it to throw back at Jorge. During their next conversation, Ricaurte warned Jorge, "If you're involved in that case in Miami, we don't want any of this coming to us."

Jorge admitted to knowing those people but assured Ricaurte he didn't have anything to do with them. When Ricaurte faxed Jorge some newspaper articles about the case, Jorge got so worried that he started pleading with Ricaurte not to throw him out. And all the time, he kept acknowledging that he was doing the same thing as the guys in Florida, which added to the evidence that Mariani was compiling against him.

Demand for MLU's services quickly grew to the point that Rose could do to other brokers what he'd just done to Jorge. "Usually you have to prove yourself to the bad guys. They're always questioning you. They want to know, who are you, who do you know, how do I know you're not the cops? But when word got out about us, we started saying to them, who are you, who do you know, how do we know you're not the cops? We'd make them prove themselves to us."

Before long, he adds, they had a UN of crime going on. "An arrangement was made through a Colombian broker for a guy to deliver money to us. He's a white Canadian guy of Italian descent, supposedly half tied into the wiseguys up there. He's wearing a blue windbreaker with Wayne Gretzky's number on it, is carrying $100,000 in a bag, and is wearing a fanny pack around his waist. Right away we figure he's an undercover DEA agent and that he's got a gun in the fanny pack. We take the money from him, then set up on him. We follow him to a meeting, where he hands 40,000 ecstasy pills to a Russian who takes the pills to Brooklyn. Meantime, the Canadian guy goes to Queens to hang with a Korean kid who turns out to be doing home invasions as part of a local gang. So here we are getting instructions from Colombians, taking money from a Canadian of Italian decent who's dealing ecstasy with a Russian and hanging with an Asian gang guy."

⟶

As it turned out, laundering drug money, setting up brokers, and gathering evidence was only half the job. The rest of the time, Rose and the team were babysitting Patricia and Andres.

When Patricia lost $300,000 of the cartel's money, she wound up getting kidnapped – not once, but twice. The second time, some people in Patricia's office begged MLU to help.

Ricaurte had to remind them, "Hey, we're brokers."

Patricia's friends wanted MLU to forward some of her money to the kidnappers to pay her ransom. In the end, the Colombian police rescued her. She still owed a lot of money to people in Colombia and, feeling the heat, ran to Spain. Rose figures she was dipping into the till, which is pretty common with lower-end brokers. It's also pretty stupid because the deal with the drug cartels is, you're responsible. If the money goes missing for whatever reason – if it gets seized or stolen – that's your problem, you've got to make it up. Patricia got too deep in the hole and needed to put a little space between herself and some of the people she owed money to.

Then Andres lost $200,000. The story he made up was that some Dominican guys came to the apartment, pushed the door in, and robbed him.

But Rose knows that's not true. "When we got him the apartment we told him, nobody comes here. His mother told him the same thing. Meanwhile, he's sixteen years old with a nice apartment in Forest Hills that he's not paying for. So what does he do? He has everybody in the world partying there. He had that money in the apartment and I'm sure he got drunk one night and passed out and somebody found it."

Adding to Rose's worries, Andres got himself kicked out of the apartment so they had to find him a second one.

The MLU guys didn't like it when Patricia suddenly showed up with her two youngest kids to live with Andres. They liked it even less when they overheard her telling Andres to forget about school and do a pickup. And they couldn't believe how stupid she was when she told Andres to show the younger kids how to count money.

Rose just shakes his head. "Dealing with that family was a nightmare."

Then came the night that someone offered Andres an unexpected gift.

He got a call to meet some people in Times Square. A surveillance team followed him. When Andres arrived at Times Square he received another call telling him to go from there to Second Avenue and 22nd Street and then call a certain number. So Andres walked over there, phoned the number, and was told, "Halfway down the block is a pizza place. There's a blue car parked in front of it. The keys are in the car. The money's in the trunk. Keep the car."

Andres didn't understand. "What?"

The guy said, "Keep the car. It's a gift from me to you," and hung up.

Andres walked down the block, found an older model used car in decent shape, got in, found the keys, and just sat there for twenty minutes because he didn't know what to do. Rose wasn't even sure if Andres had a driver's licence. Eventually, Andres phoned the number again and said, "I'm going to take the car, drive around the corner, park there, take the money, and leave the car."

The guy told him, "Keep the car. It's yours. It's a gift. Goodbye."

Getting out of the car, Andres popped open the trunk – there was half a million dollars in a duffel bag – got back in the car and still couldn't figure out what to do. Rose's guys were watching this and so, too, Rose assumes, were the people who owned the money. But they never showed their faces, nor did Rose's guys. The car was obviously bought for just this deal. The registration was in a phony name.

After a very long time, Andres started the engine. He drove a couple of blocks, turned onto a side street, then suddenly pulled over. He got out of the car, took the duffel bag out of the trunk – it was so heavy that one of the straps broke – and lugged it for several blocks, looking for the subway. He rode that home, abandoning the car. Later, he told one of the MLU guys, "The whole thing was just like the movies."

Throughout the operation, MLU Investments wired money offshore, mainly to the Caymans, Panama, and Barbados. They also wired money to Sun Life Assurance of Canada, Eagle Star International Life Services, Kia Motors in Korea, Lineas Aereas Suramericanas, Tissot Watches, Avianca, Daimler Chrysler in Germany, the Dole Company in Chile, Dynamic Cassette International in Britain, and to brokerage accounts at Merrill Lynch and Charles Schwab. Money was used to purchase textiles in Shanghai, car parts and electronics in the Orient, goods from import-export companies scattered around the world, and gold from jewellery businesses throughout Latin America.

MLU also wired money into personal accounts, including some held by diplomats. They also facilitated capital flight for wealthy Colombians who were looking to hide money by selling pesos in the markets there and having the dollars in the States moved into investment accounts in New York or insurance trusts offshore.

Among the one hundred banks to whom they wired money were Royal Bank of Canada, HSBC, Lloyd's TSB, Standard Chartered, SunTrust, Citibank, Bank of America, Chase Manhattan, Mellon Bank, Bank of Miami, Bank One, Republic National, Bank of New York, First Union, Wells Fargo, Banco Santander in Spain, Banca Popolare di Bergamo in Italy, Union Banque Suisse, Bank of Tokyo, Industrial Bank of Korea, Korea First, Thai Farmers Bank, and Banco do Brasil.

The nature of the BMPE being what it is, the various companies and banks to whom money was wired almost certainly had no direct knowledge that it was drug money, and their mention here should in no way be construed to mean that they knowingly engaged in any criminal activity.

"We sent money to some of the largest manufacturers in the world," Rose says, "and to small companies, and to individual accounts. We sent money everywhere. Europe. Latin America. Japan. Hong Kong. We even saw people using Latvian banks."

As part of this operation, Rose says, MLU was asked to make pickups in Egypt. He declined. They were also asked, several times, to make pickups in Australia. He declined those as well. Rose thought about accepting some work in Spain, until he heard how difficult it was to deal with the Spanish in an undercover operation. At one point there was talk about putting undercovers in place elsewhere in Europe. Rose refuses to go into too much detail, but says it didn't happen because they didn't need to. However, there were meetings with officers from other countries and arrangements were made.

"Just getting that far couldn't have happened five years ago. That it happens now demonstrates how levels of co-operation between law enforcement in various nations have greatly improved." Still, he adds, "it's too bad we had to turn down so many opportunities, but a lot of countries in Europe aren't set up for undercover work. They can't do it legally or operationally. Yet tons of money is going through Europe."

One place Jorge asked them to go was London. He begged Ricaurte to do a $200,000 pickup there. Rose said no. Although, he did set up a company and some bank accounts in Amsterdam, just in case he needed to bounce money from New York to Holland. He felt that, for the sake of appearances, it would look good if they had accounts all over the place. After all, they were moving a lot of money to a lot of different countries, especially Italy, Britain, Guernsey, and the Isle of Man.

Canada came back into the picture when MLU agreed to arrange pickups in Toronto. Mounties were recruited for that part of the under-cover. As Rose recalls, "Someone wanted us to work Montreal, but that's also where the approaches were coming from. We said we'd take the money, but they had to get it to Toronto. And they did. They shipped it to Toronto and then the Mounties got it down to us."

Startlingly, Rose says, while moving money MLU stumbled across other law enforcement undercovers doing the same thing. "We uncov-ered all sorts of other government operations laundering money. And let me tell you, it's sad. Customs. DEA. Guys in Florida. Guys up north. Guys out west. You name it, they were doing it everywhere. What's really sad about it is that everyone is sending the money to the same places. They're all dealing with the same people, the same brokers, and nothing is co-ordinated, nothing is shared. So much information just goes down the toilet."

Rose isn't sure how much of the money he saw had terrorism written on it, but he has his suspicions. "There's a big Lebanese and Middle Eastern community in Colombia. A lot of those people are in the jewellery business and some of them are clearly facilitating. A certain amount of them are brokers. But whether any of them are taking some of their money and funnelling it back to terror groups, there's no way to know for sure."

By summer 2001, MLU was starting to wind down.

Dozens of indictments came down and arrests followed in the States and in Colombia. Several brokers were taken down and $6 million was seized. Another $1.2 million has since been seized as a result of leads developed during the case. MLU more than paid for itself by collecting around $1 million in fees from the bad guys. Patricia was sentenced to four to twelve years, while Hernan and Andres both got a couple of years. Other warrants are still outstanding.

When Patricia's arrest made the papers in Colombia, Rose pretty much figured that the operation was finished. He didn't know for sure if anyone had sussed that MLU was involved, but that hardly mattered now. He and Mariani had got inside a BMPE network – taken apart this better mousetrap – and no one had ever managed that before. There probably wasn't much else they needed to do. But Rose kept the MLU office open, anyway, just in case the phone rang.

On the morning of 9/11, the fellow who was supposed to stop in to check the answering machine was late getting to work.

16

TOO MANY BAGPIPES

"I used to love bagpipes.
But then there were all those police funerals.
And all those firemen's funerals.
And . . . and there were just too many bagpipes."

– Joe Webber, 9/11 hero

Joe Webber was in a staff meeting that morning, on the seventh floor at Six World Trade Center, when the first plane hit.

Many of the agents who worked with him at the New York field office of U.S. Customs had been there during the 1993 bombing, and the instant the explosion rocked the building, they knew what was happening. People began to evacuate very quickly. But Webber, as special-agent-in-charge of U.S. Customs for New York, at first refused to go downstairs. Instead, the tall, solidly built Texan ordered everybody to reassemble at Seven World Trade – at the emergency command post that the City of New York maintained there – then ran through the various floors of Six World Trade to make sure everyone was getting out.

By the time he arrived at Seven World Trade, debris and bodies and mass confusion were raining down all over the block. The doors to the command post were locked. They couldn't get in. That's when the second plane hit. Webber and the others were right there, on the street below, with the fireball and debris coming down.

Webber and the others rushed farther down the block to a day-care centre where they commandeered phones and called headquarters in

Washington to tell them what was happening. Some of the other senior agents announced that they were heading for the FBI headquarters. Webber watched them leave, then went back to Six World Trade. He got into the building and raced upstairs to make absolutely certain that everyone was out and that his offices were secure. Electricity in the building was coming on, then going off, then coming on again. Alarm systems were going on and off too, adding to the noise from all over the block. Many of the electronic locks were shut, keeping him out of certain rooms.

Going back like that nearly cost him his life.

Webber was just thirty feet from the North Tower when it crumbled. Fire ripped through the building. He was trapped. He tried to make it down the stairs, but there was too much smoke. The rooms around him were caving in. From inside, Webber could see that firefighters were trying to get in. Two men from Ladder Company 11 had managed to get up to a balcony on one side of Six World Trade. From there, they rigged another ladder up to the fourth floor. But he was on the fifth floor. There was nothing he could do but brave the flames and the smoke and make one desperate dash down the stairs.

Somehow, he made it. The firemen grabbed him and dragged him down the ladders to safety.

Two weeks later, Webber and two of his agents went back inside.

It was around 2 a.m. Fires were still burning below ground and the air smelled of destruction and death. Crews were working nonstop, still hoping beyond hope to find survivors, finding instead limbs and body parts and horrible reminders that 2,800 people had been murdered here.

Webber identified himself to one of the senior fire officers and explained why he needed to get back inside. It took some convincing, but for the men and women who were working there, Webber's request was one more remarkable gesture in a place where days and nights were replete with remarkable gestures.

The fire department launched a crane in front of what was left of the building. Joe and two other Customs agents – Alysa Erichs and Tina Zimmerman – bravely climbed into a cherry picker along with some emergency workers, and the NYFD lifted them up to the fifth floor. It was pitch dark inside. The fire department brought up some flood lights and with long shadows cast against the eerie, burnt-out walls, the agents and the emergency workers made their way through each floor of what had once been U.S. Customs–New York.

In the main seizure vault there were 3,200 pounds of cocaine, 983 pounds of heroin, and some ecstasy. They got it out.

In another part of the offices, there were firearms, including a cache of fully automatic weapons and 1.4 million rounds of ammunition. They got them out.

In one safe there was cash and in others there were thousands of classified documents, confidential informant source files, and case files. They got them out.

"We recovered about 96 per cent of all the controlled substances we'd had in the office," Webber says. "There's no evidence that any of the rest of it ever hit the street. We worried about that because it was all packaged and tied together with U.S. Customs tape around it, and finding any of that back on the streets would have been terrible."

His voice gets very quiet. "You can't imagine what it was like. This had to be the crime scene of all crime scenes. In just one morning, 2,800 people were murdered. And the frustration of not being able to help, the sense of helplessness . . ."

Shaking his head, he stops for a few seconds, then continues. "They started taking down the building, so we established a detail, working like everyone was, twenty-four/seven, so that as the building came down, our agents were right there going through the rubble. We recovered guns, some of them still fully operational, some of them melted. We worked that detail for six months."

Within three months of the disaster, El Dorado and U.S. Customs were back in business in new offices uptown. Webber's big corner room is on the wrong side of the building to see downtown. He doesn't say if that's on purpose.

Then his voice gets quiet again. "I used to love bagpipes."

———

While Ron Rose and his team at MLU Investments were working Patricia, his old mates at El Dorado had stumbled across a group of Colombians – brothers Hermes and Luis Torres and Norberto Romero Garavito – whom they identified as Black Market Peso Exchange (BMPE) brokers for Colombia's North Coast drug cartel.

Through relationships built up over time, the El Dorado agents were able to call on the assistance of Colombia's Departamento Administrativo de Seguridad (DAS) to set up an operation that would, for the very first time, take in both sides of a BMPE network.

Known as Operation Wire Cutter, it began in September 1999. With introductions arranged by informants in New York and Colombia, the El Dorado guys started doing cash pickups in New York. When the BMPE brokers saw that these guys could be trusted, the pickups extended to Chicago, Miami, Los Angeles, and San Juan, Puerto Rico.

Once the cash was collected, the brokers would tell the undercovers what they wanted them to do with it. Some cash got bulked out by private air charter to Colombia. Some was deposited in banks – including Lloyd's, HSBC, and Deutsche Bank – some was handed off to other brokers, some was wired to shell companies. Money went to Singapore, Canada, and the U.K. Some of the money was laundered through shares on the NYSE and NASDAQ. Some of the money went into purchasing merchandise. The shopping list included helicopters, fridges, and electronics. The purchases were made through manufacturers, wholesalers, and distributors who were happy to accept cash or third-party payments.

While this was going on, undercovers in Colombia – from U.S. Customs, the DEA, and the DAS – were working with the brokers. The Americans spent a year with the Colombians, identifying the brokers in Bogota and trying to get inside the system they would eventually dismantle.

"We had successfully done a number of BMPE cases," Webber says, "and we'd done loads of pickup cases in the city. What we had never done, however, was to take one case full cycle, to watch the monies picked up in Manhattan and watch that money come out the other end in Colombia."

Over a period of thirty months, the undercover agents gathered evidence on eight BMPE brokers in Colombia and twenty-nine brokers and money launderers in the States who were driving this BMPE.

The World Trade Center disaster got in the way, and the possibility of losing the evidence stored in the offices at Six World Trade jeopardized the case. All of the Wire Cutter evidence was there, including original tapes of wiretaps, agent reports, and transcripts.

Webber, Erichs, and Zimmerman got them out.

Within a few days of 9/11, Webber says, they got a call from a citizen in Brooklyn who'd found documents in her backyard. To this day, he still finds that scary.

"It was a synopsis of wiretaps we'd been running on the Mafia hit man Sammy 'The Bull' Gravano. We got them back, but it made us think about what else might have blown away. This stuff turned up ten to twelve miles from the World Trade Center. It frightened us because we didn't know what else we might have lost. We were worried about losing prosecutions and about compromising our undercovers. But I think we got lucky and that turned out to be an isolated incident. What we did lose in the building were some surveillance photos. You know, 'fenoo-lenoos.'"

That's *f-n-u-l-n-u*, as in "first name unknown, last name unknown."

When they brought down Wire Cutter, the thirty-seven targets were arrested and more than $8 million was seized. So were 400 kilos of coke, 100 kilos of marijuana, 6.5 kilos of heroin, and several weapons.

"All these folk wanted to do was move money quickly," Webber continues. "I found it remarkable how, unlike legitimate business, which is always about the bottom line, these people weren't interested in profit margins. Not at all. There's so much profit built into the drugs that they don't have to worry too much about cost. They'll pay whatever the price is because this isn't about profit, it's about how quickly they can place the money."

Another surprise came in the methods they used. "All of them. Whatever worked. They showed us that there's no single traditional way. And that was one of the problems we'd had in the past. We'd sit on one type of money-laundering scheme and while we were drilling on down to the bottom of that we'd miss other stuff. These guys were all over the map."

As often happens during one investigation, the good guys stumble across bad guys they don't know about and other good guys chasing bad guys they don't know about either. Just a year into Wire Cutter, U.S. Customs in Miami was working a major Colombian drug-money-laundering case of their own, looking at a BMPE network.

At the same time, Britain's National Criminal Intelligence Service (NCIS) had picked up word on the street that large amounts of cash were being laundered through some *bureaux de change* around London. A surveillance operation was set up and officers were able to watch cash coming into these storefronts and, from there, leaving the country. The money was either bulked out to South America – the ring had an Avianca air hostess carrying cash for them – or wired out to various places, including the U.S. This was the first time that the British had seen money laundering in this purest of forms, where the suspects were strictly laundrymen and not traffickers involved with drugs.

Several suspects were tagged for observation, but two names emerged at the top of the target list – Juan Miguel Salgado, who ran the Latin Linkup *bureau de change* in north London, and Luis Edwardo Hurtado, who ran the World Express *bureau de change* in south London. Both were Colombian-born, naturalized Britons. Code-named Uproar, the operation sent thirteen people, including Salgado and Hurtado, to prison for laundering more than $70 million, the proceeds from the sale of two and a half tons of cocaine.

In the old days, it's likely that none of the dots would have connected. But in recent years, one of the major advances in law enforcement has been a recognition of the global scope of organized crime and terror, and an understanding of the need for law enforcement to think global too. The Brits gave the Americans a heads-up about how some of the *bureau de change* money was coming their way. Miami Customs took a real interest in it and discovered a connection between this money and some of the people Webber and El Dorado were dealing with in New York. They also spotted a connection with Ron Rose's MLU Investments.

The common link was the Isle of Man.

The seventy-seven thousand people who live on this self-governing British territory have had their own parliament for more than one thousand years. This dogged independence has allowed them to create a financial services environment that, at times, has been wild and woolly enough to earn the island its offshore laundromat reputation. But eventually, some people on the island said enough was enough and they started to clean up their act. Law enforcement now actively co-operates with international investigations. By the beginning of 2003, there were around thirty-six thousand IBCs on the island, but that figure is down 15 per cent from what it had been just four years previously. The Isle of Man requires strict due diligence and no longer licenses bearer-share companies. There are 59 banks on the island, 16 life assurance companies, and about 160 collective investment schemes. Nearly $8 billion are managed through funds, and bank deposits total more than $44 billion.

There was a time, however, when money came onto the Isle of Man and no one there gave a damn where it was coming from, who owned it, or what anyone intended to do with it. Change came slowly, but it came, and for the Americans – many of whom had been severely critical of Man – the first real sign of change came in 1999.

Cops in the States had been after a major fraudster named Robert Brennan for more than twenty-five years. His First Jersey Securities had bilked tens of millions of dollars from investors. The SEC filed civil proceedings against him, and in 1995 a $75-million judgment was lodged against him. Brennan elected to avoid paying up by declaring bankruptcy. And for a while, it looked as if he was still sidestepping the authorities.

Four years later, the New York District Attorney's Office was actively seeking better co-operation from the Channel Islands. A real effort was being made to improve relations. After several trips back and forth by prosecutors, as working friendships grew between New York and Man, results started coming in. The Americans were trying to gather evidence in several securities fraud cases. The authorities in Man helped them get it. Then Brennan's name came up. The authorities in Man helped the Americans file the necessary paperwork – as required by Manx law – then helped them find where Brennan had hidden several million dollars, money that had not been disclosed during his bankruptcy hearing. Brennan maintained a nominee account at the Bank of Scotland in Man, from which he used a Bear Stearns brokerage account in New York. At one point he had $22 million in three trusts there, but during the bankruptcy hearing, records show, he moved one of the trusts to Mauritius and, from there, to St. Kitts and Nevis.

With the evidence they'd collected in Man, the Feds and the State of New Jersey – where Brennan lived – hustled him back into court and charged him with ten counts of bankruptcy fraud, money laundering, and manufacturing evidence to cover up his crimes. The jury found him guilty and the judge sent him away for nine years and two months, without the possibility of parole.

Now the Americans started singing praises for the way the authorities in Man had co-operated. And the authorities in Man – especially those who'd been so reluctant to co-operate – decided that being a responsible member of the global financial world wasn't quite as painful as they'd imagined it could be.

The Brennan case turned out to be a prelude of what was to come.

Back in Miami, U.S. Customs were putting a case together against several drug traffickers and their BMPE networks, one of whom was Rodrigo Jose Murillo. A trafficker on everyone's radarscope, he'd been indicted in San Diego for trying to smuggle thirteen tons of cocaine into the U.S. Having shipped the drugs from Colombia to Mexico, he then was moving them north in small boats and over land. The guys in Miami were able, through their various undercover operations, to target one of Murillo's money launderers – a small investment company that was using banks in Mexico, Hong Kong, and one in Latvia to put money into a Murillo account at the Bank of America in Fort Lauderdale.

The Latvian connection was interesting because it's not one of the more glamorous money-laundering centres. That said, more and more dirty money gets moved through Latvia, and the authorities there seem less than interested in doing much to stop it. In Murillo's case, $697,000 was transferred through a Latvian bank, where it was not considered suspicious enough to report because no one there knew anything about it. The bank manager would later explain that, because the bank had no information that would have linked this money to drug trafficking or money laundering, and had never heard of Rodrigo Murillo. He didn't bother flagging it.

Which, of course, is why the money was sent through Latvia in the first place. Then again, this was not the first time that the same bank had been used in a laundering scheme. In 1997, $1.2 billion was wired in from a bank in the Ukraine with instructions to wire the money out again right away, this time to a bank in Nauru. The Latvian bank did what was asked of it, because it had no reason to suspect that $1.2 billion they knew nothing about, especially going from the Ukraine to Nauru, was suspicious.

In this case the Customs guys in Miami knew better. What worried them was why some of Murillo's money was also coming back from the Isle of Man as insurance policies.

Miami contacted Man and based on information they received from the Americans, Manx Customs and Excise officers started looking into their side of this money trail. What they saw worried them. Over the next two years, investigations were launched in Man (Operation Basking), the States (Operation Capstone), and Colombia (Operation Fan). The three countries shared information, and what they uncovered was a highly sophisticated plot by Colombian BMPE brokers to launder drug money through the offshore insurance industry. Before long, money washing through the Hurtado-Salgado network showed up as part of this, as did money being washed through Ron Rose's MLU Investments.

It worked off the back of investment-grade life insurance. These policies function like a mutual fund. You buy one, then overfund it. In principle, you're supposed to wait until the end of the term before recouping your investment, but you have the right to cash in early, although there are penalties to discourage you from doing that. Writing that off as the cost of doing business, cashing in a policy bought with drug cash nets you seemingly clean money wired into your bank account.

Some of the money that wound up in Man originated from the Hurtado-Salgado network in London. Some of it came from Mexico. Some of it also came from MLU Investments in New York. Ron Rose's undercover brokerage wired $500,000 for three different cells to more than a dozen different accounts at Eagle Star International Life Services. Although that company was not charged in this matter, MLU Investments documents show that it wrote policies and accepted wire transfers from several third parties.

That these policies were coming in from, and being topped up by, third parties should have been a tipoff that something was strange. The traffickers were putting these policies – worth as much as $1.9 million each – in the names of all their relatives and, in most cases, the relatives didn't know anything about it. That the third parties were then cashing in these policies, and paying 25 per cent penalties for the privilege, really should have sounded alarm bells.

From Man, money was sent back to the States – to banks in Florida, New Jersey, New York, Texas, and Puerto Rico – but also to Spain, Portugal, and Panama. Over the course of two years, it's estimated that traffickers laundered nearly $80 million through 250 insurance policies. Although on the Isle of Man someone hints, "Actually, it's considerably more."

By early 2003, with parts of Capstone/Basking/Fan still running, U.S. Customs in Miami had seized $9.5 million and indicted five Colombians, including Murillo's launderers and his son. The amount of money seized in Man has been announced at $8.75 million. The DAS in Colombia arrested ten people and seized $20 million worth of insurance policies, bonds, and cash. In Panama, $1.2 million was frozen.

Using the BMPE to wash money through offshore insurance caused a lot of people in post-9/11 law enforcement some sleepless nights because if the system worked for drug traffickers, it could work for terrorists. At one point, a rumour started circulating around law enforcement and the insurance world that Osama bin Laden had moved some of al-Qaeda's money through the offshore insurance world.

Authorities in the Channel Islands, well aware of those rumours – and worried about them too – checked them out as best they could but found nothing to substantiate them.

At least, not yet.

⟶

Once upon a time, the Colombians controlled the product and their one product was cocaine. They might have turned it over to the Mexicans for smuggling, but before it hit the streets, the Colombians were in charge again.

No more. Now they do what McDonalds does – they franchise. They've sold street-sale rights to Mexicans and Dominicans and even Vietnamese gangs, who work the retail side. In the meantime, the Colombians have diversified and increased the number of products they deal in.

For the three hundred mini-cartels that picked up where the Cali and Medellín cartels left off, it's no longer just coke on the menu, it's marijuana, heroin, and there are some indications that they're also dealing ecstasy.

"They're fully diversified," Joe Webber says. "They're selling the product outright to the Mexicans, which means the Colombians aren't running the risks. With the brokers in Colombia, they're getting their money outright, so they're not even running those risks. They've positioned themselves as businessmen. Maybe they're not realizing the profit margins they once did because they're sharing the profits with the Mexicans and the peso brokers, but the risk is way down and the diversity of the product they're shipping means they're doing fine."

The Mexicans are also making out better. Which means more bulk cash going to Mexico. While Customs and the DEA and local law enforcement keep trying to attack bulk cash on the southwest border, Webber feels there are better ways of going about it.

"You attack it in New York City and in Chicago, in Los Angeles, in Boston. You attack the cash where it's generated. The opportunity to attack it along the southwest border relies on a cold hit, a lucky inspection, or some inside information."

Anyway, the Mexicans who move money are well prepared for whatever law enforcement has in store. They keep coming up with all sorts of new ways to hide cash – containers within containers within containers – and then they have learned to become very compartmentalized.

Webber continues, "A number of years ago we got six tons of cocaine in a warehouse in Los Angeles. If you dissect that case and dissect that organization, you see how they work. They'd moved cocaine across the border for years, one load at a time. Like an army of ants. There was one group who would pack the car and leave it somewhere. There was another group who drove it across the border and left it. A third bunch would pick up the car and take it to a warehouse. A fourth would move it to another warehouse. Even if you picked up one of those violators, he couldn't give you the whole picture because he wouldn't know it. You might get one load, but you weren't going to get the warehouse."

It's the same with money, which is why he says that the best place to attack money is where it's generated.

"The banking community has a wealth of experience in moving money. If something attracts their attention, it's probably right on. I think too many banks are too concerned with their image being tarnished. Some banks are better than others. Some banks will close the account down instead of calling us because they're concerned with the bank's reputation. There's one individual whom we're looking at pretty hard, and four banks closed him out before we stumbled across him. Rather than call us, they sent him away. The banks were in compliance, but they just didn't want the controversy."

Occasionally, though, banks can be extremely helpful. Valley National in mid-Manhattan was just that, only a few months after a U.S. Customs' border team intercepted five hundred kilos of cocaine concealed in a rolled-up carpet.

It was one of those fortunate inspections that happens now and then. With luck still on their side, Customs was able to get some background information on the shipment. They passed it along to the DEA. In turn, that agency had contacts in Colombia, who pointed to a fellow named Antonio Pires de Almeida. Watching him led the DEA to a bank account in Connecticut, where they were able to seize $6.87 million, some of it associated with the drugs in the carpet. Exactly two weeks after de Almeida lost his money in Connecticut, he switched banks. The DEA told Webber's team about it, and El Dorado couldn't wait to take a closer look at the way de Almeida was conducting his affairs at Merchant's Bank

His money was being handled by Maria Carolina Nolasco, a Portuguese-born naturalized American in her early forties. She was an assistant vice-president for international and private banking, and the more they looked at her, the more interested they became, because she was a major player.

They watched her for quite a while, and kept an eye on de Almeida's accounts too, until the bank was taken over by Valley National. When it was, Nolasco stayed on in her same role at the Madison Avenue branch, in midtown Manhattan. But the new management gave Webber and his crew a chance to get closer. Webber approached certain people at Valley National, explained what they wanted to do, and the bank gave them permission to put someone inside the branch.

A female U.S. Customs undercover officer who spoke fluent Portuguese was put in place as Nolasco's assistant, and the extent of Nolasco's business soon became clear. She managed 250 accounts. Her records, including identification documents and wire transfer instructions, were locked in her private office safe. Not only did no one else at the bank know who her customers were, everything she did for the bank was in Portuguese. In effect, she was running a bank within a bank.

The undercover was able to determine that 44 of Nolasco's 250 clients were shell companies with "hold mail" notices, meaning that none of them received statements. She soon suspected that all of those shells were involved in BMPE payments. Three of them – Sorabe SA, Harber Corp., and Gatex Corp. – carried the signature authority of Antonio Pires de Almeida, who was listed on the accounts as the representative of two South American companies. One of those companies appeared to be a *bureau de change*.

Nolasco accounted for a very large percentage of the branch's daily wires, but the wires only showed money in and money out, leaving a lot of unanswered questions. However, based on what the undercover was able to glean, the El Dorado team felt they had probable cause for a wiretap. A judge agreed and they were able to go up on Nolasco's office.

They now saw that deposits into the three de Almeida accounts were either wire transfers from outside the bank or transfers from other accounts controlled by Nolasco. All of the withdrawals were also either transfers to other accounts or wires to Brazil. Reviewing hundreds of the outgoing wire transfers, the team learned that they were payments made on behalf of companies other than de Almeida's shell companies.

This was drug money going through Nolasco's end of a BMPE.

For the period May 4, 2001, through December 31, 2001, Sorabe's deposits and withdrawals were negligible. Harber Corp. saw $39.5 million come in and $39.7 million go out. But Gatex Corp. had deposits of a whopping $136.5 million and withdrawals of an equally astonishing $137.3 million.

When they finally got to look at Nolasco's bank inside the bank, her twenty-six most active business accounts, including Gatex and Harber, showed that for the same period, deposits exceeded $538.5 million and withdrawals exceeded $534.6 million. Over an eighteen-month period, Nolasco had moved more than $2 billion through those accounts to Brazil.

As luck would have it, one of the other operations they were involved with crossed this one, and through a money launderer in Florida, El Dorado was able to get an undercover in to meet with Nolasco about laundering some money. On one occasion she was handed $30,000 in cash by this undercover. She suggested that deposits be made in amounts under $10,000 to avoid reporting requirements. She agreed to deposit $9,000 immediately and hold the rest in her safe to be deposited over the next few days. She then asked the undercover how he brought money into the country, and he told her he carried it on his body and in bags. She warned him that was dangerous and said she could put him in touch with money remitters in Brazil who could do it for him safely.

Eleven days later, the undercover brought her $50,000 in cash. Now she told him that she was worried this might be drug money and that if he was caught she might wind up involved in the case. She told him from now on he had to have it wired, and that she wouldn't take cash from him again.

The original intention was to continue surveillance on Nolasco for as long as possible, hoping to get inside the entire BMPE network and dismantle it, not only in the States but in Colombia and especially in Brazil. The problem was they weren't sure about the Brazilian side of it, didn't know how secure it would be, and began to worry that if they stayed up too long, the undercover might get compromised. That's when Nolasco announced she was going to take a trip to Brazil. And that's when the decision was made at El Dorado to take the case down.

They arrested her and seized thirty-nine bank accounts with about $20 million.

If the same case came along today, El Dorado would certainly consider it, and the likelihood is that they would probably take it. But it's not a given.

Since 9/11, the only given is terror money.

Joe Webber has since left New York and is now stationed in Texas. But El Dorado is still in New York, and even in Texas, Webber's priorities remain the same. "It's terror. We haven't shifted resources away from drug cases, because we're still working those. But our priorities on September 10 are not what they became on September 11. Life as we know it changed forever that day."

Pre-9/11, he says, if someone came in the office with a money-laundering scheme that moved a total of $300,000, it wouldn't raise anybody's eyebrows. "By the standards of this group, that's a Class III case and we really didn't have the time to be bothered with that nuisance. We were dealing in big numbers. If you came in with $3 million, then you'd have gotten my attention. Now, post-9/11, tell me there's $300,000 associated with a potential terrorist incident and that just became a Class I case with a number-one priority."

The heart of El Dorado is the huge, open-plan office filled with desks and agents and bulletproof vests dangling over the backs of chairs. Off to the side are huge tables. That's where they count the money.

"There's something special about seeing millions of dollars of stacked cash sitting on the counting table. It's a difficult feeling to explain. The guys have arrested people for their whole careers. Big dope cases, big fraud cases, they've arrested loads of people and sent them away. But there's something special about millions of dollars stacked on the table. I think the most I've seen there is six million. That's a lot of money."

In the end, he says, it's all about money. "If you follow the money, you're going to back into every criminal scheme known to man, eventually. The money is the key to everything. The cartel members in Colombia may never touch the cocaine, never touch the heroin, but they will touch those pesos. That's the motive. So if you can attack the money, you get so much further. They can replace a mule, they can replace the product. The most disruption you can cause them is taking the money away. I would rather see a couple of million stacked on the counting table than the powder itself. Of course, I'd love to get the powder too. But the impact is greater when we take the dollars off the street."

In that respect, drug dealers and terrorists are similar.

"The real key to dismantling some of these organizations," Webber explains, "is infiltrating the command and communications structure. We learned that doing pure dope cases. If we can identify their means of communication, if we can identify the command structure, infiltrate it through informants or Title 3s" – wiretaps – "that's when we have the most impact. The goal is to dismantle the organization. The old school of picking money up on the street corner is attacking the organization, and we continue to do that. But now we do that with an eye towards moving up. All too often in money-laundering operations, people see attacking the money as an end, in and of itself. From our standpoint, especially looking at terror groups, that's just the beginning."

The problem with many terrorist organizations is that, like modern drug-trafficking groups, they're highly compartmentalized. Except more so. They are also more resilient and have an ability to change faster than drug groups.

"There have been instances where we've watched them collect money and forward it to support other groups in Pakistan, Indonesia, the Philippines. There's a steep learning curve here for us because they've demonstrated the ability to shift course very quickly. So we watched them, studied how they concealed bulk cash in a multitude of ways, and then did a full-court press to hit some bulk cash outbound. We hit FedEx and express courier packages and suddenly they switched to cheques. For a brief period of time we were seizing cheques. Within a matter of less than thirty days, they moved to bearer instruments. There were choke points we tried to focus on. But as soon as we had a few successes, they would dry up quickly."

These terror groups also launder money through gold and honey and diamonds, and that makes it all the more difficult because they mask their laundering as a legitimate enterprise. They also use all the offshore tricks. "We see shell companies everywhere. And charities. They do whatever they can to look like a legitimate business with money moving through them."

And of course, there are drugs.

The Taliban were the largest heroin business in Europe and, until February 2001, they had a liaison office in New York, not far from the United Nations. The Americans finally got fed up and demanded that they leave. There were indications that heroin proceeds were being handled by certain people associated with that office.

Webber won't talk about that, but he will say that heroin money and terror groups tie together. "But we're not seeing the heroin, just the money generated from the sales. I find that troubling. Seizures in New York amount to about half of all the heroin seized by U.S. Customs. So it's troubling when we see the proceeds of Afghan heroin sales and can't find the heroin."

Equally troubling is a new drug that's come onto the North American scene in recent years, khat.

A stimulant derived from the *catha edulis* shrub, it is strongest when the fresh leaves are chewed. Being perishable, it loses its potency in a few days, but even then it can be made into a tea or chewed as a paste. The plant comes primarily from East Africa and the Arabian peninsula and is traditional in that part of the world.

The United Nations estimates that the international trade in khat is worth $50 million and notes that Kenya is the largest supplier to the international market. The UN also believes that khat sales have funded terrorist activities in the Horn of Africa. They are especially concerned with khat exports from Nigeria to Somalia, where some tribal leaders are known to sponsor terrorism. In recent years, Somalia has become a transit point for terrorist groups.

Sold openly in ethnic shops throughout Britain at around $6 a bunch, khat is illegal in Canada and the U.S. The RCMP says that khat enters Canada as air cargo, arriving in Toronto aboard flights from the U.K., Netherlands, Germany, and Kenya. In 2001, Canada Customs seized eleven tons of khat. The groups moving it are generally Ethiopian, Yemeni, and Somalian.

Historically there have been very few prosecutions. However, khat generates an income for some groups, selling for around $350 a kilo in North America. "This is not a drug used on college campuses or in the bar scene. The average street cop wouldn't recognize it. Khat has a unique audience and is clearly associated with a network of people we're interested in. We've had two cases where khat is mentioned, where money has gone through the system back to the Middle East. It's below the radar. We're concerned."

His concern gets right back to money.

"In money-laundering events that relate to terrorism," Webber says, "you don't find huge amounts of cash. And that can be a problem for us. So relying on those types of indicators are not always productive." He pauses for just a second, then nods, "If you look at some estimates that say the 9/11 event was funded with as little as $300,000, imagine what $6 million can represent to a terrorist. If we can take that money away from him, if we can get his six million . . ."

Webber nods slowly . . . "That's twenty September 11ths."

17

BLOOD MONEY

"How much does a terrorist attack cost in Britain?
Of course, the answer is 2p."

– a conclusion reached by the National Terrorist
Financial Investigation Unit (NTFIU)

As the ferry arrived at Black Ball
Terminal in Port Angeles, Washington, that December night in 1999, a
weary group of U.S. Customs agents made ready to look at what they
expected to be the usual assortment of Canadians heading south from
Victoria, British Columbia, and the usual assortment of Americans
coming home.

Christmas was still eleven days away, so traffic was light.

Some cars were waved through. Others were randomly stopped.
Agents asked drivers a few standard questions – they weren't looking for
anything in particular, just people who answer standard questions
uncomfortably – and when the agents were satisfied with comfortable
answers, they let those drivers go on their way. But a female agent
noticed a thirty-three-year-old Arab man in a brand-new rented
Chrysler with Canadian plates and something about him bothered her.
She motioned to him to pull over. He tried to run for it.

Agents chased him and grabbed him, and others opened the Chrysler's
trunk. There was a timing device, a substance used to make military-
grade C-4 explosive, and a nitroglycerine equivalent in two glass jars.

The suspect was carrying cash, false IDs, and the business card of
someone called Dr. Haydar Abu Doha in London. The suspect refused

to give up his real name, so the agents fingerprinted him and within a few hours they'd linked this man – Ahmed Ressam – to a terrorist "sleeper" cell in Montreal.

His mission was to blow up Los Angeles International Airport in three weeks' time. The millennium was about to happen and that's how al-Qaeda wanted to celebrate it.

Within hours of his capture, cops in Canada were trying to find Ressam's pals in Vancouver and Montreal, cops in New York were grabbing some of Ressam's friends there, and cops in London were checking out Dr. Doha.

Ressam came to Canada in 1994 with a false French passport. The first thing he did was apply for asylum. When that was refused and a deportation order was issued against him in 1996, he obtained a bogus Canadian passport and continued living in the country. It's known that he travelled on his Canadian passport, because shortly after he got it, he went to France. Authorities there have since tied him into some bombings. Back in Montreal, he was arrested no fewer than four times for theft. At no point was Canada Immigration ever notified. In all, Ressam only served two weeks for just one theft.

He shared a flat in Montreal on Lacordaire Boulevard with Said Atmani, an active member of the Groupement Islamic Arme (Armed Islamic Group), otherwise known as the GIA. A small, violent bunch formed in 1992 specifically to destroy the secular government of Algeria, many of the original GIA recruits had fought against the Soviets in Afghanistan and trained with Osama bin Laden when he and the Taliban moved in. The GIA claimed responsibility for assassinating President Boudiaf in 1992 and for hijacking an Air France plane in 1994. Although their agents failed in an attempt to destroy the Eiffel Tower, the GIA was successful in launching two series of nail-bomb attacks in the Paris Metro, which killed eleven people and injured more than one hundred.

Atmani was one of GIA's document forgers. He'd been arrested in Canada in 1998 for credit card fraud and extortion and deported to Bosnia, despite the fact that there was an active arrest warrant for him in France. Three years later peacekeeping forces in Bosnia arrested him, and this time he was deported to France to stand trial for terrorist activities there.

Ressam's contact in Vancouver was Abdelmajid Dahoumane, another former roommate in Montreal. The two had met at al-Qaeda's Khalden Camp training camp in Afghanistan. Dahoumane came to Canada a year after Ressam, and he, too, sought asylum. Like Ressam, his request was turned down. By then, Dahoumane had managed to enrol himself for welfare benefits and was receiving regular cheques at the same time that Canada Immigration was looking for him to deport him. Dahoumane was the subject of an Interpol "red notice" – arrest immediately – for his ties to the training camp and the GIA.

In Vancouver, Ressam and Dahoumane spent several days together at a motel, making the explosives that were found in Ressam's car.

As soon as he heard of Ressam's arrest, Dahoumane fled. Fresh warrants were issued for him in Canada and the U.S., but Washington wanted him more and put a $5-million price on his head. The reward was substantially higher than most because the Americans had reason to believe that Dahoumane was close to a Muslim radical living in Calgary, who in turn was close to, and supposedly in daily contact with, Abu Zubaida, bin Laden's so-called right-hand man. In March 2001, Dahoumane was arrested by Algerian Security Forces.

But the most interesting man to come out of Ressam's arrest was Abu Doha. Not only did Ressam have Doha's business card, but when the police searched the Montreal apartment they found a diary from a Swiss bank that contained names and phone numbers of several people, including Abu Doha.

When terrorist squad officers from Special Branch searched Doha's home, they discovered that his real name is Amar Makhlulif. They found passports and fake IDs in several names, and documents that linked him directly to the timing device found in Ressam's car. Furthermore, the timing device in the car was identical to timing devices used by bin Laden–trained terrorists in previous attacks.

The thirty-seven-year-old Algerian-born Doha/Makhlulif had been a senior officer at the Khalden Camp, where he'd recruited Ressam and Dahoumane for their assignment in Canada. He moved to the U.K. in 1999. From that base he planned attacks on Strasbourg Cathedral and a market in that city. Neither happened. Since then, it is known he met with bin Laden in Afghanistan to negotiate a plan that saw GIA's international operations come under a loose umbrella arrangement with al-Qaeda. He also maintained regular communication with a terrorist cell in Milan.

Suspecting Doha/Makhlulif of being both an operational chief and a financier, British police sat on him for more than a year, trying to establish who his contacts were and where and how he was moving money. When it became clear in February 2001 that he was about to flee, they arrested him at Heathrow Airport. He was checking in for a flight to Saudi Arabia with a Spanish passport.

Based on an indictment against him for conspiracy to commit terrorist acts and for providing money, safe houses, and other material support to terrorists, the Americans requested his extradition. A British court ruled in favour of the U.S., but Doha/Makhlulif appealed. A year after the court decision against him, he was still in Bellmarsh top-security prison, desperate to avoid the trip across the Atlantic.

That Ahmed Ressam was trying to enter the States on the ferry from Victoria made sense, because the border stop there is notoriously easy. But the fact that he was coming into the States from Canada raised eyebrows in Washington, because the U.S. intelligence services had been saying for years that Canada's immigration policy was dangerously lax and that the border was no longer safe. Canada could no longer claim that Canadian asylum laws were strictly a Canadian problem. The fact that anybody who could get into Canada could slip into the States – and try to blow up an airport – made it Washington's problem too.

Eventually, the Canadian Security Intelligence Service (CSIS) conceded, with some embarrassment, that they'd identified fifty terrorist groups in the country comprising 350 people, and that the U.S. intelligence services were right – Canada had become a haven for terrorists.

Because Ressam and the others in Canada needed to earn a living while plotting to blow up Los Angeles Airport, they turned to some of the trades in which they'd been trained: credit card fraud, identity theft, counterfeiting cheques, forging documents, and breaking into cars to steal portable computers and cellphones. They lived quietly, and what money they accumulated in excess of their living expenses was sent through an established network to finance other cells in France, Belgium, Italy, Turkey, Australia, and Bosnia.

The big-money trade they didn't get involved with was drugs. The reason why is simple – drugs get you noticed much faster than credit cards, forged cheques, and stolen cellphones. And for these guys, not getting noticed was also something they were trained to do.

So here were pre-9/11 terrorists, already installed in North America, doing what terrorists usually do when terrorist cells are "sleeping" – working as criminals.

The difference between terrorist-criminals and non-terrorist-criminals is that one thieves for politics, the other thieves for profit. In Britain, the GIA thieves for politics, and makes so much money doing it that the group intentionally avoids violence. No one wants to kill the cash cow.

———

For years, nine British cops banished to a lonely room at the end of the corridor of the Metropolitan Police Special Branch Intelligence office – known locally as SO-12 – were just nine cops at the end of the corridor.

When you asked the others about them, when you spoke with someone at SO-12 who was busy spying on Irish terrorists or tracking down Turkish drug traffickers, he'd scratch his head and say, I'm not really sure, but I think those nine blokes at the end of the corridor might have something to do with the Internet, or maybe it's not the Internet, maybe it's banks, but, like I said, I'm not really sure.

The office where the nine worked was officially called FISAC – the Financial Investigation and Special Access Unit – and it did have something to do with banks. That was the financial part. It also had something to do with the Internet. That was the special access part. But most of the people who referred to them as the nine guys at the end of the corridor couldn't have cared less.

The unit was made up of one detective inspector, two detective sergeants, and six detective constables who, no matter how hard they tried, were never really an integral part of most investigations. Even when SO-12 started realizing that IRA cells operating inside England were supporting themselves with financial fraud, no one did very much about it.

The FISAC guys would try to remind the others, We should find out how the IRA pays their rent, and where they buy their bombs, and how they pay their phone bills. But everyone else worried more about those bombs going off. How a terrorist paid his rent didn't seem terribly important if people were about to get murdered.

Then came 9/11. Someone in the States decided that bin Laden managed the whole thing for under $300,000. Around SO-12, senior management started wondering, How much does a terrorist attack cost in Britain? The FISAC guys told them, of course, the answer is 2p. That's what it cost someone to phone in a bomb threat and stop the Grand National at Aintree and cause millions of pounds' worth of damage.

That made sense to senior management, so now they listened as the FISAC guys explained how an act of terrorism is cheap, but to live as a terrorist is expensive. After all, terrorists need to pay rent and buy food and reconnaissance targets. They need to sustain themselves and that costs money. So the FISAC guys asked the senior managers, Isn't it about time we interrupted their lifestyle, which might stop them from buying a bomb?

For all sorts of reasons, but mainly traditional-bureaucrat thinking, it took some senior managers a long time to grasp the simple concept that money was at the heart of terrorism. But once they understood, they changed FISAC to NTFIU – the National Terrorist Financial Investigation Unit – and made certain that the NTFIU guys were in on every meeting. And now everyone knows exactly what the guys at the end of the corridor do – they follow the money.

To get to their end of the corridor isn't easy. You have to go through security when you come into the building, and then you have to be escorted upstairs to a secure floor where five hundred SO-12 officers make up Special Branch Intelligence. It takes a security check to get on the floor, and then anybody at all who even gets near the front door of the NTFIU needs to be vetted at a very high level. Few people get into their office, and nothing leaves their office, like paperwork, or laptops, or anything case-related. That's how seriously they now take this unit.

The office is a dump. It's a long room that was barely big enough for nine, and now there are twenty. The windows are sealed shut, so it's baking hot in the summer and, they say, the heating doesn't work good in the winter, so they freeze. There aren't enough desks, there aren't enough cubbyholes, and there aren't enough computers. Go to the loo and you lose your workspace. But there is enough work to keep twice as many people busy.

The unit is run by a superintendent with a chief inspector as deputy. There are two detective inspectors, four sergeants, ten detective constables, and a couple of analysts. Of course, Special Branch is elite and its units are customarily staffed only with Special Branch officers. But the NTFIU is a little different because the management was brave enough to defy tradition and bring in two non-branch guys – both highly experienced financial investigators with twenty-five-plus years' experience. These are old fraud squad guys who know about money laundering and how to work a financial case and aren't shy about banging on doors to confront people for answers, which is not necessarily the way most investigations are handled at SO-12. So in a way, it's a new ethos. But then, since 9/11, nothing's the same.

The likelihood of terrorist violence happening in the U.K. sharpened everyone's focus, the NTFIU became pro-active, and SO-12 began to look at several groups known to be operating on British soil. They include the Tamils from Sri Lanka – there appear to be some drug connections with them – Afghanis, Iraqis, and the Algerian GIA.

Attention also turned to the man who'd led those attacks in France. He'd been granted political asylum in Britain several years before, which set the stage for the U.K. being used as a financial base for small groups of GIA members. The arrival of Abu Doha in Britain merely upped the importance of the U.K. as a money source.

Officers at the NTFIU believe there are around fifty to one hundred hardcore GIA members in the U.K. at the centre of some very fluid groups with young soldiers on the periphery. GIA hasn't formed cells in the IRA sense, but work in ad hoc bands of four, five, or six. A financier or manager from the hard-core group supervisors the others, who are foot soldiers. They come together to work cheque fraud and credit card fraud to finance the GIA's activities abroad. Many of the hard-core group are Afghan veterans, men who have had military training and who fought for the Taliban. These are not your normal burglars or just streetwise kids. These are men who have killed. And Special Branch operates on the assumption that they will kill again.

When a group goes out to work, their average take seems to be in the region of $22,500 to $32,000. Then multiply that by fifty to one hundred. When you understand that these groups are going out on a very regular basis, you start to see the kind of money involved. Not long ago when Special Branch raided a house of a suspected GIA terrorist, they found several hundred chequebooks and cheque guarantee cards that controlled fifty-two bank accounts. In addition to what they steal through cheque and credit card fraud, many of the members are in the U.K. under the asylum laws, so there is also large-scale benefit fraud.

For these guys, opening a bank account in the U.K. is easy, because British banks accept IDs from anywhere in the EC. And the EC is rife with stolen passports, counterfeit national ID cards, and counterfeit driver's licences – all documents that the U.K. accepts under the Know Your Customer regulations.

On the rare chance that one of these men arrives in Britain without a phony ID, there are plenty of places where they can be bought. The police across the country have located cafés and bars where young foreign students hang out and where, just before they leave the U.K. to go home, they can sell their empty bank accounts and cash cards and passports too. They're mostly French and Italian, but any passport will do. And there are plenty of places where new photographs can be put expertly into a passport or a driver's licence or a national ID card.

That, combined with a chequebook and cheque card, gives anyone in Britain access to the financial system.

You go to the bank and say you've moved house and need to change your address, and while you're at it, you say that you need a new chequebook. So the bank sends you one to your new address. And after a while, you tell the bank you never got that one and ask for another one. And over the course of a year, you stockpile chequebooks. During that time, you kite your accounts. You go to the bank and put money into your account, then go to an ATM and take the money out. You put money back in and take money out and put money back in again, so that when someone looks at your account, it's not only being used properly, it's responsibly kept in credit.

After a while, you visit your bank manager and ask for a small loan. The bank manager looks at the monthly figures, decides you're credit worthy, and agrees to the loan. You pay it all back within a few months, move more money in and out, and eventually return to ask for a bigger loan. The bank manager looks again at your account, likes what he sees, and grants you the bigger loan.

When you've worked your way up to borrowing $20,000 or $30,000, you empty your account. And that's the last time the bank manager ever sees you. In the meantime, you've stockpiled all those chequebooks, and along with a bunch of your mates, you start hitting the chain stores.

That's how the police first discovered Pierre.

An Algerian man in his late twenties had driven four younger foot soldiers – including Pierre – down to the south coast to work the major retail chains. The four went into the same store, each with one cheque and a cheque guarantee card, to buy something for under $150. The Algerian man circled the block, waiting for a call on his cellphone to say that purchases had been made. When he got the call, he picked up the team and drove them to the next retail chain store.

The group hit towns from Brighton all the way to Southampton, but that afternoon, they ran into a minor problem. Pierre tried to shoplift something from a store, got spotted on closed-circuit TV, the cops were called, and he got busted. The others did what they were told to do in such a situation, they melted away.

At the police station, Pierre showed the young arresting officer a French passport. He didn't seem to speak English so they got a translator. But Pierre didn't seem to speak French either. The young arresting officer thought that was odd. Pierre got binned up overnight, was taken to magistrates' court the next morning. He pled guilty, was fined on the spot, and released.

And that might have been the end of the story as far as Pierre was concerned, except that the young cop was still bothered about a French guy who didn't speak French. He kept thinking about it, then remembered seeing something that had come in a couple of weeks before from a unit in London called the NTFIU.

It was a "heads-up" they'd sent across the country, to say they were interested in knowing about any cases which fit exactly this type of MO with exactly these types of people. The young officer didn't know if anyone in London would really care about Pierre, but he wrote it up anyway and sent it off.

The NTFIU was very interested. They checked Pierre's address and examined the photocopies of Pierre's passport, the single cheque he'd been carrying and his cash card. With that in hand, an NTFIU officer went to see Pierre's bank manager.

British money-laundering laws require financial institutions to keep copies of whatever ID documents are used to open an account for six years after the account is closed. In the real world, however, the copies get lost, or they're filed offsite and take forever to retrieve, or the photocopies are useless. But one of the many assets that those two old-time financial investigators brought to the unit is a network of helpful contacts in the financial industry. Of course, all necessary paperwork must be filed by the police. The NTFIU does everything by the book so that whatever evidence is collected can be used in court. But some bankers are more co-operative than others, and the old-timers know how to start with the helpful ones.

So the officer asked Pierre's bank manager about any other accounts Pierre might have, and the bank manager came back with several. The officer threw Pierre's name and address into his computer system and discovered that the address matched for ten other people. At this point, the NTFIU brought in some experts to sit on the house, and everybody in it, which is something that Special Branch really knows how to do.

"The expertise built up over one hundred years of doing that kind of work," says one Metropolitan police officer who has regularly seen them in action, "is where Special Branch is the best in the U.K. You could be the number-one bugger in the U.K., and you would never know you've got Special Branch up your bottom. They can get that close."

Which is almost as close as they got to Pierre and his friends. They watched him for weeks, got to know the people he knew, and got to study their cheque fraud routine. Police officers tailed them as they went out on a daily basis, working one town after another, always operating the exact same way. They would buy enough goods to fill up the car. After a few days of doing that, they would head up north and start returning things to different branches of the same store, handing sales staff the untouched item, producing the receipt, pointing out that this had been bought with a cheque, and getting a cash refund.

Pierre appeared to be one of the more senior guys in this crew. He was the one who appeared to control the lockup where the goods were kept.

As more people showed up in the surveillance, more names got added to the NTFIU list. Cellphone numbers were added too. But as each phone was getting passed to someone else every few days, and the SIM cards were getting moved too, tracking calls became next to impossible.

It became clear, nevertheless, that Pierre and his friends were working within a structure and that someone somewhere was pulling the strings. Identifying this group was one thing, linking it to terrorism was the big leap.

Realizing that some of these men had fought in Chechnya, Afghanistan, and Bosnia – they often reminded others that they were *jihad* veterans – the Special Branch guys sent pictures and names and addresses to Immigration to see what they knew. They also sent fingerprints of Pierre and all his friends to various law enforcement and intelligence agencies in Europe to see if any matches come back.

Sometimes you get lucky, and this time they did. A file appeared from Immigration and a print match came back for that file, which identified Pierre – now they had his real name – and tied him directly to the Paris Metro attacks.

Knowing where Pierre's lockup was, they waited for the right moment to document what was in there. This is another area where Special Branch is among the best on the planet. A specialist team got inside the lockup, photographed it, videotaped it, inventoried it, and got out without leaving any sign at all that they'd been there. Not a single item was out of place. It's very specialized work and the only thing anyone at Special Branch will say about that team is, "The people who do this for a living really know how to do this very well."

What the people who do that for a living found were bags filled with merchandise waiting to be returned. There was so much stuff that in order to keep track, Pierre had stapled the receipts to each bag. That would come in handy when it came to proving which cheque had bought which item.

With his lockup inventoried and his banking records in hand, the cops had built up a sufficient evidence package to make an arrest. They got the necessary warrants and raided Pierre's home. Although he turned out to be a non-violent family man, the T in NTFIU stands for terrorist, so the officers came suitably equipped and Pierre was immediately handcuffed.

Naturally, the first thing Pierre did was swear that he didn't know what this was all about. They explained it to him, and he still said he didn't know they were talking about. They kept explaining it and he kept denying it. While a few of the officers were interviewing him, one of the others found a key ring. Pierre claimed it was old and that he didn't know what any of the keys were for. He was obviously lying, and one of the officers had a hunch. He left with the key ring and went to Pierre's lockup, opened it with one of the keys, then had another officer photograph the key in the lockup door. He came back to Pierre's house and showed the photo to him. The moment Pierre saw it, he broke down and cried.

The search of his house produced $22,500 in cash, chequebooks, ATM cards, diaries, address books, phone books, and computer files. With all the money that passed through Pierre's hands, the officers were surprised to see that he was living in squalor. Where all the money has gone is a question they're still trying to answer. They know that some money was transferred out to Algeria. And there is a sign that some went to Tanzania. But at the other end, they don't know who picked it up or what it's being used for.

Pierre went to trial and got sent away, but only for two years. The judge was told about the Paris Metro connection, but didn't take it into consideration and, for security reasons, whatever information the unit had connecting Pierre to Paris was not brought up in enough detail to charge him for that.

While Pierre was getting used to his new accommodations, the NTFIU was working through the many leads they'd picked up during the investigation. Some information they'd acquired matched information they were already holding. Patterns evolved and associations evolved. Half a dozen good cases came out of Pierre and those six have since led to others. Although no one at the NTFIU will make the connection, some high-profile cases have taken place since Pierre's arrest.

There was the raid on the Finsbury Park Mosque. There was the case of two Algerian men who entered Britain in 1997 and almost immediately began collecting council tax benefits and housing allowances, sustaining themselves by defrauding banks and credit card fraud, until they were arrested carrying false passports and were found to have direct links to the GIA. There was the operation launched by Special Branch officers to round up seventy-five suspects, a vast majority of them Algerians, who'd entered the U.K. under the asylum laws. And in February 2003, there was the Algerian man arrested at Waterloo Station getting off the Eurostar from Paris who was widely believed to have had a connection to a plot to develop the deadly ricin toxin in North London.

"It is fair to say," explains one of the NTFIU team, "that a lot of these investigations do not end in simple fraud cases. That's absolutely true. The power of financial investigations has, at long last, been grasped by our senior management and the people who lead intelligence in the United Kingdom, and the NTFIU is being used the way it should have been used decades ago."

And that's all anyone at the NTFIU will say about that.

———

Other terrorist groups have been just as successful in other parts of the world. In certain ways, they've also been more clever.

As long ago as 1986, an Abu Nidal cell in the States demonstrated a real knack for earning money. It looked for negotiable instruments that it could hijack to fund its war against Israel. The answer it came up with was right there staring back at them from the breakfast cereal box – fifty cents off your next purchase of cornflakes!

Discount coupons on cereal boxes and soap powder and the booklets filled with them that come with the Sunday papers have been a popular marketing tool for hundreds of different products for a long time. The idea is to induce consumers to buy a product by offering a discount on the purchase. But the whole thing is based on trust. There's no way for the manufacturer to know for sure if the person cashing in the coupon actually bought the product. Retailers accepting coupons are supposed to be honest about it and only reward the customer when a purchase is made. But, at the end of the day, the coupons are batched up by the retailers and sent to the manufacturers with this understanding: we sold your product so you owe us the money for the total face value of the coupons plus a handling charge.

Because there are no controls on this, there's widespread fraud. And no one ever demonstrated the breathtaking magnitude of this fraud better than Rick Bowdren, today a very senior supervisory agent with the U.S. Postal Inspection Service. In 1977, as a young agent assigned to New York, Bowdren was working on a number of different investigations, looking at a lot of different criminal enterprises, when he discovered that some organized crime groups were making a lot of money working discount coupon fraud.

He contacted people in the coupon business to find out more and they concurred that this was a huge money spinner for organized crime. In normal fraud cases, jurisdiction goes to the local police. Coupon fraud wasn't an obvious area of concern for a postal inspector. But to cash in the coupons the retailer had to mail them, and the moment he put a fraudulent coupon in a letter and stuck a stamp on the envelope and dropped it in a mailbox, that was mail fraud.

"The mail fraud statute," Bowdren explains, "was created in about 1865 because there were frauds occurring between states and no law enforcement agency had jurisdiction. We were the only people set up to do anything about it. Today, that's changed. But the statute hasn't. Today, if you commit a crime and use the mails, you've got mail fraud. It's a catch-all-type statute."

Armed with that, Bowdren set up a catch-all-type sting. The way to prove that a retailer didn't sell the product, he decided, was with coupons offering a discount on a product that didn't exist. And so he invented Breen – "The detergent that cleans away dirt and grime."

The coupon he designed for it offered twenty-five cents off the next purchase, and contained all the standard warnings: purchase required; non-transferable; any other use constitutes fraud. The address on the back, for retailers looking to reclaim the coupon, was a company he invented, CFCP Coupon Redemption, with a P.O. box in Clinton, Iowa.

Bowdren secured the co-operation of three greater New York newspapers – the *Daily News* in New York City, *Newsday* on Long Island, and the *Newark Star Ledger* across the Hudson in New Jersey – whose combined circulation was 3.38 million. A totally legit-looking Breen coupon was inserted in the three papers on one day only, December 11, 1977.

He then waited to see what would happen. "Within four months we got back over 77,000 coupons from over 2,100 stores in 42 different states. It was unbelievable. This was a product that did not exist."

The coupons he got back weren't copied or counterfeited, they were real. In some cases they had never found their way into the newspapers. In other cases they were stolen by the newspaper delivery drivers. In some instances the stores themselves got hold of them before they reached any consumers. In other instances the coupons were stolen by criminals and sold to the retailers.

"We arrested three hundred merchants in the New York–New Jersey area," Bowdren explains, "and charged them with grand theft for fraudulently submitting bogus coupons. It wasn't a lot of arrests, considering how many coupons we got back. But we couldn't take everybody down. We wanted to show how prolific the crime was and that's what we did.

Unfortunately, the industry never learned its lesson because coupon fraud is still today as prolific as it was then."

The industry might not have learned that lesson, but terror groups did. Palestinian terrorists realized that there were thousands of neighbourhood grocery stores – bodegas and corner shops – across the United States owned by people from the Middle East who would be sympathetic to their cause. The Florida-based Adnand Bahour controlled a network of eight hundred grocery stores across the country, solely to defraud the grocery manufacturers with coupons against sales that never happened. His significance became apparent when undercover agents caught him on videotape claiming to be the nephew of Palestinian Liberation Front leader George Habash. Ten postal inspectors went undercover for five months to expose Bahour and his group, who, over a two-year period, fraudulently submitted $186 million worth of coupons.

In 1987, the manager of a Brooklyn video store was arrested in connection with a ring that turned over millions of dollars in fraudulent coupons. The man was Mahmud Abouhalima, now serving a 240-year prison sentence for masterminding the 1993 attack on the World Trade Center. There is some evidence that Omar Abdul Rachman, the blind sheikh who is also serving a life sentence for the 1993 attack, was involved in coupon fraud as well. The suggestion is that the two funded that first attack on the World Trade Center using the proceeds from those frauds.

In 2002, Canadians were offered 2.32 billion coupons through direct mailings, in newspapers and magazines, and through in-store promotions. Some 110 million were redeemed, accounting for around CAD$125 million worth of goods. But coupon fraud in Canada is rampant, with some criminals known to be hiring school kids to hunt for them in garbage bags and recycling centres. In the United States, it is estimated that one in every ten coupons is redeemed fraudulently. If the figures translate north of the border, that accounts for a CAD$12.5-million Canada-based scam. How much of that winds up in the hands of terrorist groups is not known. But again, based on what happens in the States, a portion of that money gets recycled into terror.

While some groups move discount coupons, others move diamonds. Al-Qaeda has been smuggling embargoed "conflict" diamonds from Sierra Leone into Europe, where they're resold in cities like Antwerp.

Canada has taken the lead in trying to curb the flow of conflict diamonds, but without the total co-operation of all other nations, the battle
can't be won. The money is laundered through legitimate banks in the
Middle East. At the same time, the illicit trade in diamonds continues to
fuel civil strife not just in Sierra Leone but in Liberia and Angola as well.

When diamonds aren't on the menu, other stones are. Within days of
the Taliban's downfall in 2001, ten tons of lapis lazuli vanished from
government vaults, valued at just over $1 million. Not an astronomical
amount by conflict diamond standards, but certainly enough to finance
an illegal weapons purchase. A few months later, al-Qaeda managed to
smuggle $10 million in cash and gold out of Afghanistan.

All over North America, there is a huge trade in knock-off designer
goods – Chanel T-shirts and Nike running shoes, Mont Blanc pens and
Rolex watches. One statistic indicates that 5 to 7 per cent of world trade
is counterfeit goods and another suggests that as much as half of that is
controlled by terrorist organizations.

It's much the same for cigarettes and whisky, although the movement
of those goods across borders and state lines by terrorist groups is driven
almost entirely by taxes, as is evident by the two-way traffic in contraband going on through the St. Regis Mohawk territory, Akwesasne.

In Northern Ireland over the past thirty-plus years, the IRA has actively
funded mainland activities with cigarette tax fraud. One recently traced
IRA money trail leads through Malta. There, an alleged IRA business associate – himself purportedly involved with Gerardo Cuomo, a Mafia
chieftain named in the EU lawsuit against the major cigarette companies
– has used Liberian shells to launder money. Which is hardly a coincidence given the fact that the man in Malta has tenuous ties to Andrew
Warren and Stewart Creggy. There may also be an IRA arms link through
Malta, as part of the cigarette smuggling.

In 1999, drug cops working at the airport in St. Louis spotted a young
Lebanese man acting suspiciously. They were certain he was carrying
something. But instead of drugs, they found $700,000 worth of counter-
feit cigarette tax stamps. That rang alarm bells because similar counterfeit
cigarette tax stamps were found in the apartment of one of the Islamic
jihad cell members who bombed the World Trade Center in 1993.

That $700,000 worth of counterfeit tax stamps turned out to be pocket
change compared with what was going on in Charlotte, North Carolina.

A law in the United States says that you cannot transport more than three hundred cartons of cigarettes per person across a state line unless state tax has been paid on them. So several young Lebanese men would head for JR Tobacco – a wholesaler in the tiny town of Statesville, about forty miles from Charlotte, who calls himself the world's largest cigarette outlet – and each buy 299 cartons of untaxed cigarettes. They'd load them into their van, then drive thirteen hours to Detroit, Michigan, nearly seven hundred miles away, because neither North Carolina nor Michigan puts tax stamps on cigarettes. North Carolina's taxes are five cents a pack and Michigan's are seventy-five cents. With twenty packs to the carton, multiplied by the seventy-cent difference – in business it's called arbitrage – and then multiplied by 299, it works out to $4,186 per person, per trip, before expenses.

Sometimes there would be as many as four guys on a trip, with 299 cartons each. And some weeks they would make five trips.

Needless to say, the trip was not without its perils. They'd get stopped for speeding. Or cops would spot a van load of Arab men and pull them over to find out what they're doing. It's not politically correct to do "profiling" any more, but that's what they called it pre-9/11 and that's what it still is. The cops would see the cigarettes and start asking questions. Because the answers were never very satisfactory, the cops would confiscate the cigarettes. On one return trip when the cops pulled them over, they found nearly $46,000 in small bills that none of the Lebanese men could account for, so the cops confiscated that.

After a while the cigarette smugglers reckoned they could fool the cops by pretending they were on vacation, and strapped mountain bikes to the outside of the van. When that didn't work, one of them married a non-Arab woman and got her to drive the van. But by then, it was probably too late because the security guard at JR Tobacco – who'd seen these guys every few days buying 299 cartons each with shopping bags full of cash – had tipped off the Bureau of Alcohol, Tobacco and Firearms (ATF).

The ATF didn't know it but the Canadian Security Intelligence Service (CSIS) had already taken an interest. One of these men, Said Harb, was delivering money in Vancouver to his old childhood friend, Mohamad Dbouk. CSIS had identified Dbouk as Hezbollah's purchasing agent in Canada. He'd received intelligence training from the

Iranians and reported directly to Hezbollah's military procurement chief. He was spending the money on night-vision goggles, mine-detection equipment, laser range finders, software that was otherwise restricted from export, munitions, global positioning systems, and even ultrasonic dog repellents.

In the beginning, Harb would either bulk cash to Dbouk or, when he could, he'd wire it. As the amounts of money from the cigarette tax scam mounted, Harb established no fewer than eight hundred bank accounts and juggled hundreds of credit cards. Almost as if it was *de rigueur*, when Harb was ready to discard a bank account or a credit card, he worked a scam to defraud the bank of whatever he could get away with.

Most of the electronic surveillance that CSIS was getting on these guys was collected by Canada's Communications Security Establishment (CSE). Along with the U.S. National Security Agency and Britain's GCHQ, they form ECHELON, a global electronic surveillance network that shares information. So as CSE narrowed in on Dbouk and Harb. It told the NSC and, in turn, the NSC told the FBI.

The Lebanese cigarette smugglers didn't have a clue how closely they were now being monitored. But they'd been trained to expect some surveillance and so to make their trail more difficult to follow, each one used several variant spellings of his name on dozens of bogus IDs. They had phony passports, licences, social security numbers, credit cards, credit card histories, and Immigration and Naturalization Service (INS) papers. For good measure, they befriended Arab students at local universities and when those students left for home, these guys bought their passports and IDs to use them too.

In five years, the first-ever Hezbollah terrorist cell in Charlotte, North Carolina, generated more than $2 million for its cause.

The cell leader was Mohamad Youssef Hammoud. He'd come to New York in 1992, at the age of twenty-seven, travelling from Venezuela on a fake visa in his Lebanese passport. When his request for asylum was turned down, he started marrying American women to stay in the country. Apparently, each time the INS ruled his marriage bogus, he got married again.

By the time the Feds were ready to pounce on this crew of seventeen men, they knew they had the cell cold on cigarette tax fraud, conspiracy, and money laundering. What they didn't have was enough of the Hezbollah connection. But they had the Canadians. After a lot of negotiation, CSIS agreed to give up some wiretap transcripts. The judge accepted three paragraphs as grounds for a search warrant on eighteen locations. They found weapons, including an AK-47 automatic rifle, and enough evidence to grab Harb. Once he agreed to talk, the rest of the cell crumbled. Most of them plea bargained. Hammoud was too stubborn and took it to trial.

He was charged with providing material support to a designated terrorist organization. The judge allowed nearly one hundred pages of Canadian wiretap transcripts to be heard, a senior CSIS officer testified, the jury said guilty, and the judge sent Hammoud away for 155 years.

⏤

When terrorist groups pay for black-market products by cheque or wire, if they know how to do it, the money trail can disappear in a nanosecond. Where the product is paid for with cash, other problems arise, like how to get that money back to the people who need it.

One of the first financial victims of 9/11 was a company called Al Barakaat. Within a few weeks of the attack, the White House issued a list of twenty-seven companies whose funds the government was freezing for their suspected links to al-Qaeda. High on the list was Al Barakaat, perhaps the largest financial institution in Somalia. With a bank in Mogadishu and storefront wire remitters scattered around North America, Al Barakaat served Somalis wanting to send money home to their families, much the same way that American Express has served North American tourists in Europe.

The freeze blocked almost $1 million. Arrest warrants saw Al Barakaat managers handcuffed and taken away. What worried the Americans was that some of the cash coming from North America heading eastward was earmarked for terrorist activities in Afghanistan, and that cash coming out of the Middle East destined for North America was being collected by terrorists to fund their activities.

It's a case that, more than three years later, remains to be proven. But the targeting of Al Barakaat was an understandable reaction – even if nothing ever gets proven – because Al Barakaat was nothing more than a *hawallah* banking network with a sign out front. And the first place anyone who understands money laundering and the Middle East would look for bin Laden's money is at a *hawallah*.

The most direct, most traditional, and most invisible way for terrorists to move money, the *hawallah* is an ancient system of IOUs. Invented by the Chinese, who named it *fei ch'ien* – literally, "flying money" – it's known in other parts of the world as *chop*, *hundi*, or *hawallah*. A system born out of political turmoil and a hearty distrust of banks, it is almost always based on family or tribal connections and traditionally reinforced with retributive violence.

Basically, chits or tokens are substituted for cash. Money deposited at a gold shop in Karachi is exchanged for a small, innocuous piece of paper that's been secretly coded, or a $10 bill stamped with a special seal. When the object is presented to a money changer in Dubai, the bearer is given cash. That particular example is one that matters in the terrorist world because the mammoth *hawallah* triangle formed between Pakistan, Dubai, and India is estimated to be worth $4 billion to $5 billion annually. That's four to five times greater than the sums making the same trip through normal banking channels.

While cash machines were used by some of the nineteen hijackers of the 9/11 atrocity, *hawallah* banking can never be ruled out as a main funding source for al-Qaeda's cells in North America. That's made abundantly clear by one of the bin Laden group's many relationships in the Balkans.

By 1991, the war in Yugoslavia had seriously interrupted the traditional heroin route from Turkey and Afghanistan – where heroin was the major export – into Europe. Two alternative routes developed, one through Bulgaria, Romania, and Hungary; the other from Bulgaria through Kosovo and Albania. That became the route of choice.

Albanian gangs moved drugs across the Adriatic into Italy, which created a new alliance between the Italian Mafia and the Kosovo Liberation Army (KLA). Together they smuggled people from the Balkans into Italy, moved counterfeit prescription medicines from Italy to the Balkans, and traded drugs for arms. They also dealt with the Russians, who paid for heroin with rocket launchers and automatic weapons. Drugs alone were bringing the KLA more than $2 billion a year during those years, turning Albania into the Colombia of Europe.

As the war intensified, Albanian refugees spread out across the world. Like the Russian émigrés of the 1970s, these Albanians extended the KLA's influence into Europe and North America, where young Albanian gang members do burglaries, armed robberies, and car theft. Some Albanian émigrés also raise money for Albanian and Kosovo charities. All of which gives them a lot of cash. Bank accounts related to the KLA and certain Kosovo disaster-relief charities have been located in Canada, Germany, Sweden, Italy, Belgium, and the United States.

Any money the bin Laden group might need in one of those countries can easily be provided. It is known that the Taliban traded heroin with the Chechens for arms. Moving the arms to Kosovo means that cash is available to be picked up at disaster-relief charities in the rest of the world.

That's one of the reasons why, when the world went looking for bin Laden's money, they didn't find any.

To begin with, he didn't need to spend his own. Anyway, by 9/11, he might not have had any of his own left to spend. When the world's attention was focused on him that September, bin Laden's personal fortune was estimated at slightly more than $300 million. It's anybody's guess if that's accurate, but it sounded good and so that was the figure that got repeated. But at the time bin Laden was living in a cave and that's a terrible place to keep your life savings. These days there is reason to suspect that by 9/11 he was either broke or about to be.

There's no doubt that bin Laden once owned several businesses in Sudan and Yemen. There was an import-export firm, a concrete factory, a honey business, an Arabic gum business – which manufactures an important ingredient for the production of fruit juices – an investment house that supposedly maintained properties in the West and, perhaps most significantly, a share of Al Shamal Islamic Bank. There is also said to be a Sudanese front company with accounts in Cyprus.

That's particularly important because both sides of the island have Arab banks that are believed to be moving al-Qaeda money into the Balkans through shell companies designed to look like humanitarian aid agencies. That Said Atmani was deported from Canada and arrested in Bosnia and that Mohamad Youssef Hammoud spent time in Cyprus buying U.S. visas is no coincidence. There is serious terrorist interest in these places, and the money has to be the reason.

The bulk of bin Laden's assets were in a part of the world where if you leave your goat untethered someone helps it walk away. He's been away from there for quite a while, with very little prospect of showing up at the next board meeting. So who knows how much, if any, of those assets are under his control or, for that matter, still intact. The Sudanese threw him out, which suggests that his assets there have been looted. In his absence from Yemen many of his assets there, if not all, could have suffered a similar fate.

With that in mind, and based on the way al-Qaeda is known to operate, bin Laden was probably never more than the chairman of a holding company that franchised terrorist activities to autonomous and semi-autonomous subsidiaries. Al-Qaeda maintains cells and alliances throughout the world, most interestingly in Lebanon (secret banking), Malaysia (organized Asian criminal gangs), Uruguay (money laundering), the United Kingdom (offshore banking), and Canada (easy border access to the U.S.). He didn't fund any of them because he couldn't, because he didn't have to, or both. His backers were wealthy businessmen throughout the Islamic world. Some of them may have included disaffected members of the Saudi royal family. Others might have been encouraged to support him through extortion and blackmail. Anyway, whatever cells are out there, "sleeping," they almost certainly fund themselves, much the way that the Montreal cell funded itself.

That possibility of finding offshore shells and bank accounts with bin Laden's name on it is not beyond the realm of possibility, just highly improbable. There was an alleged charity connection in the Channel Island of Jersey that drew a lot of attention in the aftermath of 9/11. But whatever money goes through charities to support terrorist activities, anywhere in the world, is disguised as just that – charity.

Sure, money that funds terrorism may move through any and all sorts of normal-looking accounts. The problem is, none of it gets clearly labelled blood money.

Finding Saddam Hussein's stash is a much more straightforward task, because there are offshore shell companies, somewhere. And Swiss connections too.

In May 2003, reports out of Baghdad revealed that more than $900 million in cash had been withdrawn from Iraq's Central Bank by Saddam's son Qusay only a matter of days before the allied bombing of the city began. Apparently, Qusay and some associates walked into the bank with some sort of official document signed by his father and ordered that the money – made up of U.S. dollars and around $90 million Euros – be loaded onto three tractor-trailers. The press then reported that all three trucks had been spotted heading for the Syrian border.

Undeniably the biggest bank robbery in history – a desperate act of a dictator on the run – it was also a really dumb stunt because it was, simply, too much money.

To begin with, $900 million in its smallest, most portable form – crisp new $100 bills – would have weighed just about ten tons and stacked 3,300 feet high. That's about two and a half Empire State Buildings. Other denominations would have increased the weight and height. So right from the beginning, he had a very serious bulk problem.

As it turned out, bulk proved fatal. He couldn't move it efficiently enough and much of it was quickly found. Around $600 million turned up hidden in one of Saddam's palaces, and another $100 million, plus the 90 million Euros, were found packed into Iraqi armoured vehicles. Later, U.S. soldiers would stop two vans heading for Syria with more than half a billion dollars' worth of gold bullion.

But even if they hadn't found a nickel of it, and even if Saddam had worked out how to bulk it out of the country, he never stood a chance of his seeing any of it. The drug traffickers learned this lesson a long time ago. To get money out of a country, you have to trust people whom you can control. And Saddam lost control long before he lost the money.

Even if he had somehow managed to get it into Syria, he would have had to trust someone over whom he had no control – a banker, a member of the ruling party – somebody who would be sleazebag enough to help Saddam and, by definition, be sleazebag enough to steal the money. What could Saddam possibly have done had he got the money out, and then somehow got himself out, should the person looking after it in Syria then announced, regretfully, "But I never saw a penny of it."

Besides, as soon as news of the theft hit the wires, a lot of people started looking for the money, including the FBI, U.S. Customs, and, perhaps most importantly of all, the U.S. Federal Reserve Bank.

One of the jobs of the Feds is to monitor the flow of dollars around the world. It is estimated that as much as 70 per cent of America's currency is in circulation outside the U.S. Some 60 per cent of that is believed to be inside Russia or otherwise controlled offshore by Russians. While a billion isn't much by Fed standards, were it suddenly to show up in Syria, it would still cause a small blip on the Feds' radar screens.

Saddam's attempt to launder a billion in cash is up there with the war against Iran and the Gulf War on the list of "his mother-of-all stupid mistakes." And it's not even as if he needed an extra billion. His wealth was probably, at the time, already in the $30-billion to $40-billion range. Much of that having been laundered well. Some of that having been washed through Britain.

It is known that in 1990 when he raped Kuwait, Saddam ordered his soldiers to commandeer whatever automobiles they could drive away. A few of the more expensive cars – Rolls, Mercedes, Lamborghinis, Porches, BMWs, and Ferraris – were given to Ba'ath Party officials as a gift. However, fifty of the choicest cars, including an armour-plated Mercedes and an armour-plated BMW, were driven from Baghdad to Amman, then flown to Geneva by Royal Jordanian Airline cargo planes, under the protection accorded diplomatic shipments. Once in Switzerland, they were put on the market and turned into cash.

Not that he needed that either. In the great tradition of despots everywhere, the Central Bank was his personal chequing account. Anyway, long before he moved in on that money, he'd taken some lessons straight out of the Calouste Sarkis Gulbenkian textbook on how to run an oil company.

A Turk of Armenian descent, Gulbenkian founded what was then the Iraqi Petroleum Company. For his efforts, he laid claim to a royalty on every drop of oil produced, giving birth to his nickname, Mr. Five Per Cent. When he died in Lisbon in 1955, the oil royalty was passed on to his son Nubar. Some seventeen years later, Saddam confiscated Nubar's 5 per cent in the name of the Ba'ath Party, and personally assumed joint custody of the funds, sharing signature authority with Defence Minister Adnan Khairallah and Petroleum Minister Adnan Hamdani. In 1979, Saddam ordered the execution of his old friend and co-signatory Hamdani. Ten years later, his pal Khairallah died in a mysterious helicopter crash.

According to a document claiming to be a true accounting of those funds, $51 million was deposited in a major Swiss bank in Geneva in

1972. Within a year, his balance had climbed to $92 million. As the price of oil quadrupled during the Yom Kippur War, the account is said to have been worth $327 million. By the time the Iran-Iraq War broke out sixteen years later, with Saddam firmly in control of the country, his account is believed to have held in excess of $1.69 billion.

One report has it that in 1995 Saddam was reliably believed to control funds worth far in excess of $32 billion. At the end of his reign in 2003, that figure wasn't likely to be less, and could have climbed to twice that.

As witnessed by his palaces, Saddam wasn't shy when it came to spending money, although his monthly outgoings on reverence, loyalty, and, especially, personal security must have been astonishing. He also frequently spent money on whims and fancies. When the Empress Faradiba, wife of the late Shah of Iran, sold a few of her jewels, Saddam pulled $352 million out of Switzerland to buy them for his wife. Faradiba denies it, for obvious reasons. But two sources, both reliable and each independent of the other, confirm the story.

Some sources say, and there is good reason to believe they're right, that Saddam spread gigantic amounts of money throughout the offshore world as a giant safety net for himself, his family, and his closest Ba'ath Party associates. Clearly, he moved money through Geneva and a network of companies. One of them, Montana Management, is registered in Panama and controlled by Midco Financial, a Geneva shell. In 1981, Midco, through Montana, began buying into the French broadcasting and publishing conglomerate, Hachette SA. At one point, Saddam is said to have owned as much as 8.4 per cent of Hachette's shares.

Another Saddam company is Al-Arabi Trading, headquartered in Baghdad, which purchased a large stake in the British-based Technology and Development Group (TDG). In 1987, TDG bought a precision engineering firm called Matrix-Churchill. A few years later HM Customs and Excise became aware of the connection, took a closer look at Matrix-Churchill, moved in on the firm, and confiscated parts of an alleged supergun that was destined for Iraq.

The Americans have been searching for Saddam's money since he came to power and, in April 1991, the U.S. Treasury's Office of Foreign Asset Control identified fifty-two businesses and thirty-seven individuals with direct financial links to him and/or his Ba'ath Party. Of those fifty-two companies, twenty-four were in the U.K., a number of them using the same address – 3 Mandeville Place, London W1. Of the thirty-seven named individuals, a dozen also had addresses in Britain.

For the most part, "Saddam International Inc." was run by his half-brother Barzan al-Takriti, who was living in Switzerland as Iraq's special ambassador-at-large. Barzan was captured right after the fall of Baghdad in April 2003. He knows the intimate details about currency, gold, and jewels that arrived by diplomatic pouch from his half-brother, because he was the one who dumped them into Swiss banks. He also knows about an estimated five hundred shell companies that are believed to have been formed, how they fit into each other, and which direction money flowed through them. After all, Barzan was there for nearly twenty years, bedding down money for safekeeping.

However, here, too, Saddam has a serious problem.

In setting up the network of shells, Barzan built up a cadre of Iraqis outside the country, plus some Jordanians and Palestinians to help him. Saddam's money is said to be in their names – so that there could never be any links back to Saddam or his family – thoroughly washed through double-back loans, investments and trusts, then fed into legitimate businesses that are said to be in Spain, France, Brazil, Indonesia, Hong Kong, Britain, and the U.S.

As long as Saddam was in power, as long as he could shove a gun in someone's mother's ear, his frontmen wouldn't dare steal a penny. The price for bad accounting would be death.

But that threat no longer exists.

The downside of dealing this way in the offshore world is that you have to do business with untrustworthy sons of bitches.

Just as that statue of Saddam in central Baghdad was yanked down, his money was getting washed yet again, through more shells and secret bank accounts and tropical island trusts, this time by those untrustworthy sons of bitches who knew they could get away with stealing it.

18

FUTURE CRIME

"I have seen the enemy and he is us."

– Walt Kelly's Pogo

A few years ago, at a major money-laundering conference in Montreal sponsored by the RCMP, one of the keynote speakers had just finished when a young man raised his hand to ask a question.

"Please tell me, what we are supposed to do?" He explained, "I come from the Eastern Caribbean. Europe and the United States have taken away our bananas. We have no manufacturing. After September 11, there are no more tourists. Now you are saying that we should not be licensing offshore banks and we should not be selling shell companies. But we are already starving today. How will we feed ourselves tomorrow?" He stared, then asked again, "Please tell me, what we are supposed to do?"

The speaker looked at the young man for a long time, then told him the truth. "I don't know," he said. "I can only tell you what we, what all of us, should not be doing."

That speaker still wishes he'd had a better answer.

❧

After the government of Antigua granted an offshore licence to Hanover Bank, and after a bunch of Russians moved $4.2 billion through the Channel Islands and the Bank of New York, and after the Al Shamal Islamic Bank in Khartoum turned out to have a connection with Osama

358

bin Laden, the preachers who were leading the congregation in the anti-money-laundering Sunday mass wanted the world to believe that KYC – Know Your Customer – was the Messiah who would lead us all out of evil.

And the choir sang, *If every financial institution in every country practised KYC, then dirty money couldn't get into the system and that would be the end of that.*

But in the real world, KYC is money laundering's answer to snake oil. Where it is voluntary, it is too often ignored. Where it is legislated, it is too often fudged. So along came "gatekeepers."

This was the group to target because they could disrupt the movement of dirty money simply by withholding their co-operation. They are bankers, lawyers, accountants, investment brokers, middlemen, fund managers, real-estate brokers, auctioneers, and so forth. People who, by virtue of their professional experience, know money laundering when they see it. Or, at least, should know the right questions to ask to properly identify it. And who, by virtue of their professional status, are in a position either to facilitate or to stop it.

To guide the gatekeepers, the key term became *beneficial owner.* Everyone needed to establish who beneficially owned the money that they were being asked to handle. And they were reminded that, should they not be able to establish the beneficial owner, they should not be doing the business.

Gatekeepers fired back, "impractical" and "a violation of our established right to privacy with our customers," and "a Big Brother–like violation of human rights."

While certain aspects of the U.S.A. Patriots Act might have brought Big Brother a few steps closer, at least where money laundering is concerned, there's no doubt that it changed the lexicon. KYC and gatekeepers were still in, but now the two acts – U.S.A. Pats I and the amendments that followed, called U.S.A. Pats II – combined to put a real burden on financial institutions operating in the United States. By proxy, that included foreign financial institutions with subsidiaries and offices in the U.S. as well. With the images of 9/11 still fresh in everyone's mind, Congress was getting serious about money laundering and the financing of terrorist organizations.

The acts prohibit financial institutions from establishing, maintaining, or managing correspondent accounts on behalf of foreign banks that do not have a physical presence in the country of registration. In other words, if an offshore shell doesn't have a roof, you can't do business with it. Every financial institution operating in the U.S. is also subject to stiff penalties for not determining the sources of large overseas private banking accounts. Sanctions under the acts can be imposed on nations as well, if they refuse to provide information about depositors to U.S. law enforcement.

Because U.S.A. Pats I and II apply to everyone who deals with money – including *hawallahs*, which must now be licensed, and on-line payment systems, which must satisfy stricter KYC requirements – renewed emphasis has been placed on gatekeepers and beneficial owners. It goes back to the basic concept that the people who allow money to come into the system are the ones who can best keep it out. Which, like the concepts of KYC and gatekeepers, is fine on paper. But unless you start throwing gatekeepers in jail because they didn't adequately KYC, even the tough-talking U.S.A. Pats acts won't work. If you don't deter those people who could stop it – those same people who otherwise stand to gain by making it happen – why would they bother?

"Implementation is the word," notes Ted Greenberg, former special counsel for international money laundering at the U.S. Department of Justice and now head of money-laundering investigations at the World Bank. Greenberg is also the man generally acknowledged as the father of the gatekeeper concept. "You can have all the legislation in the world, but if you don't implement it, what good is it?"

His point is driven home soundly in a quirky little survey. To determine how seriously the nations of the world were about their own money-laundering regulations, codes, treaties, and laws, the survey looked at 103 countries with stock exchanges to see how well they were regulated. Insider trading laws existed in 87 of those countries, which at first glance is not bad. But prosecutions for insider trading had occurred in only 38.

This is not to say that change hasn't happened. The Proceeds of Crime Act in the U.K. is forcing people to file more suspicious transaction reports. There was a period during the 1990s when the National Criminal Intelligence Service received twenty thousand of them a year, but didn't have the money or the personnel to handle them all. In 2001 they received thirty-one thousand. In 2002, anticipating the Proceeds of

Crime Act, the number nearly doubled. But staff and budget have not.

In Canada, reporting of cash transactions greater than $10,000 is now mandatory. But FinTRAC – the Canadian money-laundering reporting unit – can't work in tandem with its U.S. counterpart, FinCEN, because Parliament legislated ultra-strict privacy safeguards that severely limit the sharing of information. Even Canadian law enforcement has trouble getting intelligence out of FinTRAC.

In Liechtenstein, where banking and related services account for 40 per cent of the tiny nation's economy, legislators made it a crime for bankers and financial institutions to fail to report suspicious financial activity. Bankers fought it for years, stalling as long as they could, insisting that it wasn't necessary because all was fine in Lilliput. That is, until those bankers got caught hiding a slush fund for former German chancellor Helmut Kohl; got caught hiding the profits of an illegal arms deal by Jean-Christophe Mitterand, son of the late French president; got caught hiding money stolen by a whole slew of African despots; and got caught hiding drug money for Latin American traffickers.

The burghers of Vaduz had to come up with something, so rather than knock down the house, they opted for wallpaper. There is legislation. But bankers and financial institutions aren't getting prosecuted for failure to report. Nor are they necessarily reporting everything that is suspicious. But at last Liechtenstein can say that it's complying.

In Nauru, parliament passed legislation abolishing the country's controversial offshore banks. But that only happened when the United States declared economic war on the island, which was nearly bankrupt anyway. Which is why Nauru continued selling citizenship and passports, until the U.S. agreed to pay them to stop.

In Niue, the government announced that they wouldn't sell any more banks. But they refused to stop selling phony shell companies. After all, they argued, why should we?

In Delaware and Nevada and Montana, life goes on as normal. If they were islands somewhere, the FATF would jump on their case. But they happen to be in the United States, and Washington carries a bigger stick than any of the islands. That's why, when certain offshore jurisdictions found themselves getting slapped across the wrists for doing the same things that were happening in Delaware and Nevada and Montana, they objected. The FATF raised its eyebrows in the direction of Washington, and Washington told the FATF to take a hike. There's no way that U.S. trust law was going to get changed just because the FATF didn't like it. In the United States, trusts are the business of attorneys, and Washington is one place where attorneys wield real power.

In mid-2000, when the FATF bared its teeth and published its "report on Non-Co-operative Countries and Territories," placing fifteen juris-dictions on its blacklist – Russia, Liechtenstein, Israel, Lebanon, the Bahamas, the Cayman Islands, Cook Islands, Dominica, the Marshall Islands, Nauru, Niue, Panama, the Philippines, St. Kitts and Nevis, and St. Vincent and the Grenadines – all fifteen feigned shock and horror. Especially Panama, where the head of the country's financial analysis unit told the press, "Panama cannot afford to have a bad reputation."

For bad, substitute worse.

But then, considering how easy it is to fool the FATF most of the time, the fact that Panama was included on the list must be down to that nation's naked venality. When the FATF said Panama was "unco-operative," the Panamanians did what they had to do to pretend to be co-operative. Sure enough, the FATF fell for it. So did some U.S. officials, who should have known better, and praised Panama for becom-ing co-operative.

Except Panama still has secret banking and still has phony shell com-panies and still has the Colon Free Trade Zone, which is regulated by people who don't believe in regulation because it would cost them too much money. Panama simply passed a few new codes that no one ever intended to enforce, and publicly proclaimed that terrorist money would not be welcome there.

Declaring war on terrorist money is like being in favour of apple pie and motherhood. So Panama got removed from the FATF blacklist and it's business as usual, as long as bin Laden's money never turns up.

"When the 11th happened," announced a senior representative of Panama's Banking Association, "we immediately got in touch with all the banks and said terrorist activities are now on the front page. We always said we were committed to helping in this fight."

But the war on drugs has been on the front page for thirty-five years, and so has the growing menace of transnational organized crime, and so has fraud and so has tax evasion, and for that matter, so has the Free

Zone, where all these financial viruses breed the same way mosquitoes did in the swamps where they built their canal.

The Caymans got off the blacklist too. So did the Bahamas. That Nigeria didn't even make that blacklist, nor did the Ukraine, tells you a lot about the FATF and its blacklist.

The problem is that when the FATF bares its teeth, its dentures fall out.

It would be different if, instead of embarrassing jurisdictions, there was a way to ostracize them. This is not just about reputational risk, it's about "terminal" reputational risk. It's about drawing a line in the sand and saying, You're either on-side or off-side, and if you're off-side it's going to cost you dearly, and if you're on-side, you're going to have to work hard to stay there. Albeit well meaning, the FATF needs a cattle prod. It's too gullible. It's also too political. And, in the end, it bottles out when the big kids show up.

If you're going to be a bully, you have to be able to take out the biggest kid on the block. If reputational risk is really going to matter, then entry to the good guys' club must be so strict that membership means something. If Cyprus is going to register a shell to some Russian looking to sell fissile materials on the black market, that should jeopardize all of the other 47,000 shells in Cyprus. If a place like Dominica is going to charter a bank that doesn't have a roof or tellers or real clients, that should put at risk every other company and every other bank chartered on the island. If the Caymans is going to have a Eurobank; or if the Bahamas is going to sell shells to anyone who wants one over the phone; or if Belize is going to sell a passport to anyone with enough money to pay for it; then the economic future of those jurisdictions should be put in jeopardy. If you're willing to sell your soul to anyone with $100 and a mail-drop address, you need to be put on notice that there is no halfway point between on-side and off-side.

Is it Bermuda's problem that some reinsurance company registered there has fooled around with reserves in so many other jurisdictions that, when disaster strikes in Europe or Africa or the Far East, there is no money to make things right? Is it the Bahama's problem that a bank there has issued a credit card to someone in Canada that allows that person to spend money at home without paying the tax on it? Right now, Bermuda and the Bahamas say no, it's not their problem. But the day that the rest of the world makes it their problem, that's the day that the offshore world will take a very different attitude towards responsible citizenship.

Any system that operates outside of legitimate regulatory control – and it doesn't necessarily matter where that regulatory control is, as long as it's legitimate – must be seen to jeopardize every other system that feeds into and off of that one. Think of the offshore world like a series of tributaries flowing into the river that is the global financial system. If one of those tributaries is dangerously polluted, what happens to the river? Does someone downstream have the right to say, Hey you up there, stop dumping mercury into the water and killing my fish?

It may take time, it may be clumsy, it may cost a lot of money, but it can be done. Why should the world tolerate abuse of its financial system by a bunch of crooked politicians who have hoodwinked their own people into believing that this has something to do with sovereignty?

This is not about sovereignty, any more than it's an assault on free-wheeling free-market capitalism. It's about gross abuse, corruption, tax evasion, crime, terror, and dirty money. It's about providing safe harbour to people who will pay whatever it costs to avoid responsibility somewhere else.

—

What's right with the present system, that each jurisdiction knows whether or not it is complying, is also what's wrong with the present system, that each jurisdiction must decide whether or not to let the rest of the world in on the secret.

The concept of "consolidated supervision" means that each jurisdiction employs a local regulator who is responsible for oversight of the financial sector. When the watchdog comes to visit, it's the local regulator who becomes the tour guide.

Over here, ladies and gentlemen, you will see all the wonderful anti-money-laundering regulations we have put in place, and if you look now to your left, you will see the beautifully bound volumes of anti-money laundering codes that every bank must have on its shelves.

The problem with that is magnified a hundred-fold by the smoke-and-mirrors nature of the offshore world, where financial institutions in some places aren't necessarily there, and financial institutions in other places are there, but you can't see them.

The first question is, Who polices this? The answer is, It's supposed to be the legitimate financial institution in the legitimate financial centre.

The next question is, How well can they do it? The answer is, Only as well as some minor employee in some forgotten outpost is willing to let them.

Recognizing that even the most sincere and best-regulated offshore centres are incapable of controlling anything financial beyond the three-mile limit, certain banks have taken it upon themselves to fill the void. Arguably, the most interesting initiative has been the Wolfsberg Principles.

In October 2000, eleven of the world's major private banking groups got together in Wolfsberg, Switzerland, to draw up a set of anti-money-laundering procedures that they hoped would create a level playing field for international private banking. The original eleven were ABN AMRO, Barclays, Banco Santander Central Hispano, Chase Manhattan, Citibank, Credit Suisse, Deutsche Bank, HSBC, J.P. Morgan, Société Générale, and UBS. Since then, Chase and Morgan became J.P. Morgan Chase, and Goldman Sachs joined.

Noticeable by their absence are Canadian banks.

Collectively, the eleven banks moved beyond standard KYC practices, putting in place a much stricter, more precise level of client disclosure. They agreed: to collect as much information as possible about the people whose money they were handling, and about the source of that money; to put curbs on accepting business from politically exposed persons; to define and monitor high-risk category clients, such as senior corporate executives; and to heighten vigilance with respect to money coming from certain jurisdictions where laundering controls were inadequate. Although, if inadequate really means inadequate, they should be eliminating their businesses in Africa, South and Central America, Eastern Europe, a good chunk of Asia, and more than a few of countries in Europe.

Still, they went as far as they did, which is much further than anyone had gone before.

Hand in hand with the watchdog group Transparency International, the Wolfsberg Principles set out to prevent the use for criminal purposes of any subscribing bank's worldwide operations. It's strictly voluntary, so there is no oversight and there are no obligations besides a commitment to try to do better than they have in the past. But the concept is sound. And the next step might be to make the Wolfsberg Principles "seal of approval" the most exclusive club in banking. The day that other banks are banging down the doors to get in, the day when any bank not in the club is automatically suspect, the day when the eleven toss out one of their own for not trying hard enough – that's the day Wolfsberg will really mean something.

Jon Winer, now in private law practice, has spoken about this very road since leaving his post at the State Department. He's observed that too many international financial institutions have weathered scandals that would otherwise have brought down a government. In some cases, where corruption and money-laundering scandals have brought down a head of state – witness Marcos, Mobutu, and even Richard Nixon – the banks at the heart of them go merrily along. The reason is, because the world runs on profit. If a financial institution is profitable enough, shareholders will remain tame enough to save the neck of the man at the top. How else can anyone explain, for example, shareholders not screaming for blood when someone at the Bank of New York gets a bonus while the ink is still wet on the worst money-laundering scandal in the bank's history?

In Winer's view of the world, a compliance officer is a bottom-line debit – the cost of doing business – and a trader is a bottom-line credit because that's where the profits are generated. "Under the circumstances, it is easy to understand why, at any given bank on any given day, those creating a profit-making scheme involving an offshore trust in Belize, that in turn owns a Turks and Caicos company, tend to win battles with those asking questions about the venture."

To change that might be to change a lot. His suggestion is the creation of not another blacklist but a white list. And there is plenty of anecdotal evidence to suggest that a totally transparent, totally open, totally dirty-money-free-zone that bears a real seal of approval can be more profitable than the alternative.

Consider the concept of reputation by association and the case of Guernsey. The government there made a deliberate decision to help foreign law enforcement find dirty money on the island. Almost immediately, much of the dirty money that was there went elsewhere. Guernsey now believes that people doing business on the island can boast, We're clean otherwise we wouldn't be here. Any hiccup could, and should, prove to be a very expensive stumble. So a white list, which would promote reputation by association, has enormous merit.

The framework for it might lie in a permanent Wolfsberg secretariat with the power to decide who's on-side. The stricter the admission policy, the more valuable the membership. Staying on-side should be a ticket to make money. That way, getting thrown out becomes a solar-plexus blow to the bottom line. If the Wolfsberg group can bottle real incentives to do the right thing, if reputational risk can be tied directly to profits, then the eleven banks that came up with Wolfsberg will have done the world a greater service than they ever envisioned.

Winer even suggests a way to jump-start a white list. He says that a select group of organizations – including the United Nations, the World Bank, the International Monetary Fund, and a few hundred big-time NGOs – could pledge to keep their money only in white-list financial institutions. If those white-list financial institutions then had to pass an independently administered "Wolfsberg" test every year – at the risk of losing their status and therefore losing the business of these organizations – at that point, he says, things would change very quickly.

"Financial transparency," Winer continues, "is not a criterion for the selection of one financial institution over another. An international bank involved in money-laundering scandals or terrorist finance has about the same chance of obtaining a lucrative source of government resources as does an international bank that has imposed the highest standards of transparency and anti–money-laundering policies. No wonder the compliance officer is seen as a profit drain."

Change that, and it doesn't matter what kind of window dressing some offshore jurisdiction puts up because now you've changed the shape of the world. If the threat of losing white-list status comes down to a business in some two-bit laundromat, those folks on the white list will be on the first flight out of town.

The legendary Willie Sutton robbed banks because, as he often said, "that's where the money is." It's the same reason why the Colombian cartels deal drugs, Nigerian criminal enterprises run 419s, Triad societies loanshark, the LCN does gas tax scams, and the Russian Maffiya extorts. Product doesn't matter. Cocaine, fissile materials, tobacco, people smuggling – bad guys go where the money is.

So, too, must the good guys.

One estimate has it that 1.5 million ecstasy tablets are dropped in Britain every weekend. Adults can reason with teenagers until they're blue in the face, and the ecstasy death of a teenager every six to eight weeks – a horrifyingly regular event – is still not enough to make kids understand that club drugs are a gamble with a lethal downside. At the same time, the country can patrol its borders and turn itself into a fortress, but drugs will get in.

When you factor money into the problem, the picture changes. Even at a cut-rate $15 a pill, that's $22.5 million a weekend, $90 million a month, $1.08 billion a year. It's a mountain of cash and it has to go somewhere. At some point, while being funnelled into the banking system, spun around the world, moved through shells and secret bank accounts, and brought out the other end, it's under the control of a lawyer, a banker, an accountant, a company-formation agent, a broker, someone. If you can locate that someone, then interrupt the cash flow and reinvestment that this money represents, the business will go bust.

The same principle applies to the methamphetamine business in North America. One group making fortunes selling pseudoephedrine tablets – an ingredient in over-the-counter cold medicines – are Canadian-based Arab gangs. They smuggle the tablets south and sell them to U.S.-based Mexican gangs who use them as a precursor chemical in the manufacture of methamphetamine. A DEA investigation in 2000, dubbed Operation Mountain Express, uncovered this connection and, shockingly, revealed a $10-million money trail that tied those Canadian-based Arab gangs directly to Hezbollah.

Interrupt the cash flow and reinvestment of the methamphetamine traffickers and you bankrupt the pseudoephedrine smugglers. Bankrupt the smugglers and there's no money for Hezbollah.

It really isn't any more complicated than that.

The illicit drug business is a business. Global terrorism is a business. The product may be different, but they both depend on cash flow and reinvestment. Like all multinational enterprises, transnational organized crime and global terrorism need parts of the legitimate financial world. In this respect, criminals operate exactly like multinational corporations.

They use the same global financial infrastructure to handle their corporate affairs.

At the height of its power, the Cali cartel had annual profits of close to $7 billion – more than three times those of General Motors – and was organized exactly along the same lines. As a business, it could not possibly have survived without the direct help of lawyers, bankers, accountants, company-formation agents, brokers, foreign governments, and others who, for a fee, echoed the philosophy of the Hong Kong banker when he proclaimed, "It's not our business to inquire into our clients' morals."

Because criminals shifting drugs hire professionals to handle money, and because professionals handling money never have to touch drugs, those professionals – the laundrymen – live comfortably in a world of "plausible deniability." Lawyers, bankers, accountants, company-formation agents, and brokers may or may not know the origins of the money they're handling, but most of them know they don't want to know. The excuse goes, "My client is an attorney and I don't need to risk losing my fee by probing too deeply about his client."

That is precisely what must change.

If politicians are serious about going after the bad guys, then lawmakers need to look no further than the laundrymen. Criminals may deliberately put themselves beyond jurisdiction, but their money is local and the laundrymen are local too. Without cash flow and reinvestment, no business can survive. So the aim must be to cut into the cash flow and reinvestment to bankrupt these criminal businesses.

Again, no business, no product.

It is a fact of life that there will always be someone willing to do the wash. It's like sticking your finger into a balloon: the air doesn't come out of it, you simply displace it. As America cracked down on money laundering, the criminals turned to softer jurisdictions, and the European Union is one of the softest.

A collection of fifteen borderless countries – with more countries to come – not one of them has a truly effective money-laundering law. All of them depend on suspicious cash reporting, at a time when cash is not the problem, leaving the laundrymen themselves to decide what suspicious means. The new Proceeds of Crime Act in the U.K. doesn't prevent money laundering, it's a tool designed to prosecute money laundering. And none of the other countries in Europe have anything even half as good. Instead, Europe combines inefficient laws with a lack of commitment in many of the countries to enforce the law. Factor in the double-edged sword of intra-European free trade. If it's great for business, it's great for illicit business too.

And now add into the mix a single currency that comes in very large denominations.

Before the EU invented the euro, it was impossible to stash $1 million in an attaché case. Today, with five-hundred-euro notes, it is possible. Equally unfortunate, the euro furnishes a free service that drug traffickers used to pay for. It automatically separates the money from the crime, which is one of the most necessary stages in any money-laundering cycle.

Pre-euro, if you smuggled coke into Spain and sold it on the streets of Madrid, you wound up with a pile of pesetas. You needed to reduce the bulk – high-volume sales with small-value pesetas created too much paper – and to get out of pesetas because Spanish cash was a sure indication that you'd sold drugs in Spain. So you pre-washed, turning pesetas into deutschmarks, and then washed, turning deutschmarks into dollars. At each step you had to pay a commission. But at least you wound up with dollars going into your offshore accounts.

Along came the euro and while dollars are still easy, euros are almost as easy. Now you sell your coke in Madrid and your stash of euros gives no indication of where you committed your crime. That means there's no reason to pre-wash. In fact, you might not even need to wash at all. If your laundering strategy includes businesses or real estate within the euro-zone, you're home free. Euros are also welcome in every jurisdiction doing business in Europe, many of which are happy to take cash. Try Eastern Europe. Try the Baltic states. Try the Middle East and the Gulf states.

If Walt Disney had designed "Moneylaundryland," it would look exactly like Europe.

But tell that to Europe's politicians, and they'll tell you how wonderful the money-laundering legislation is throughout Europe.

What they fail to understand is that legislation that pretends to make specific kinds of financial transactions more transparent doesn't work. If tomorrow, magic wand in hand, total and absolute transparency was imposed in, say, Switzerland and Liechtenstein, the only tangible result would be unemployment in Switzerland and Liechtenstein, because the money would instantly relocate to a more user-friendly jurisdiction.

Somewhere, there will always be an aspiring Antigua.

Despite constant protestations from countries who sell secret banking and bearer-share shell companies and their own sovereignty – despite the gripes about sovereign rights to protect one's own interests and to determine one's own future – there is this indisputable fact: the world offshore is a smoke-and-mirrors fiction, purposely constructed so that money can be in one place, the management of it can be halfway around the world, and the beneficial owner of it can remain well hidden, somewhere else again.

Until the wars on crime and terror are fought on the beaches of the offshore world, organized criminals and global terrorists will remain what they have worked so hard to become – the most powerful special interest group on the planet.

EPILOGUE

The worst is yet to come. Cuba is one heart attack away from throwing the offshore world into total pandemonium.

While the forty-plus years of the American embargo have prevented American businesses from developing interests in Cuba, both the Brits and the Canadians have been busy establishing a foothold there. Before Fidel's body is even slightly cold, British and Canadian open-market-capitalists will flood the island with holiday resorts and casinos.

America's whorehouse will rise gleamingly from the ashes.

At the same time, Cuba's long-time trading partners – the Russians – are poised to claim their right to do business there. Russian organized crime has had a presence in Cuba since the demise of the Soviet Union. Their interests include gambling, drugs, and prostitution. With vast amounts of dirty money to invest, the Russians are preparing to solidify their base, from which they can safely operate throughout the Caribbean.

Once that happens, Cuban exiles and Russian organized criminals living in Miami – who are firmly tied into Florida's Colombian and traditional Italian organized criminal groups – will build a crime-bridge linking Havana with south Florida.

Eager to respond to demand, casinos, offshore banking, shell companies, and money laundering will flourish, marking Cuba's successful return to its crime-capital roots. But this replay – in digital colour and Dolby Surround sound – of the "wild west" that Meyer Lansky and Lucky Luciano built before Castro will be at the expense of the other islands.

Cuban prosperity will sound a death knoll to casinos, banking, shell companies, and money laundering throughout much of the rest of the Caribbean. That is, unless those other islands are willing to compete.

With survival at stake, they will compete.

They will offer better facilities to criminals looking to launder money; create new markets with designer drugs; put out the welcome mat for tomorrow's Enrons and Halliburtons and Carlyle Groups; establish better, more efficient transshipment routes for cocaine and heroin; become the world's major transshipment point for the global trade in illegal aliens; offer safe haven to anyone's money, while all the while "plausibly denying" that it has come from, or is destined for, a terrorist cell.

Ironically, those foreign banks and financial institutions that are lining up impatiently to march into Cuba, and the U.S. banks and financial institutions that will bridge the gap from Miami to Havana, will flourish off the back of all this criminality.

But then, the United States and Canada and Great Britain have – either deliberately, short-sightedly, or simply through greed – spent years putting all the pieces in place for exactly this to happen.

ACKNOWLEDGEMENTS

There are many people to whom I owe a sincere debt of gratitude for their time, insights, inspiration, help, and encouragement.

In the United States, I wish to thank: Judy Fitzgerald and Dave De Young at the National Insurance Crime Bureau; plus Betty Cordial and James Gordon of Maryland First; Jim Vaules and Don Wadsworth of the National Fraud Center; Les Joseph, Ted Greenberg, and Stephen Flamer at the Department of Justice in Washington, D.C.; special agents Bill Waldie, Tom Fuentes, Ross Gaffney, and Drick Crawford at the Federal Bureau of Investigation; special agents Joe Webber, John College, and Mickey Pledger at U.S. Customs; Wayne Carlin, Stephen Cutler, and Alex Vasilescu at the Securities and Exchange Commission; attorney Jonathan Winer; from various U.S. Attorney Offices, Donna Gallucio, John Carney, Marvin Smilon, Herbert Hadad, Steve Cole, Thom Mrozek, and Marjorie Selige; Rick Bowdren of the United States Postal Inspection Service; special agent Joe Kilmer of the Drug Enforcement Administration; former law officers Philip Deming, Joe Occhipinti, and Lenny Lemer; professors Holger Henke, Howard M. Wachtel, and Mike McIntyre; Dan Glazer at the U.S. Department of the Treasury; Steve Kroll at the U.S. Senate; Jody Myers at the National Security Council; Elise Bean and Robert Roach at the United States Senate Committee on Governmental Affairs, Permanent Subcommittee on Investigations; David Marchant at *Offshore Alert*; Joan Wright in Chicago; Howard Arvey in California; Warren Tyron and Gerry Cashin in the office of Representative Spencer Bachus, United States House of Representatives; the Chicago Crime Commission; historical societies and museum resources in Miami, Chicago, Las Vegas, and Cuba; plus various friends and acquaintances.

In Europe, may I thank: Metropolitan Police detectives James Perry and Steve Ratcliffe; former Met detectives Gordon Hutchins, Martin Wood, and Neil Jeans; Henk van Zwam of the Dutch police; Stan Morris at Interpol; Denis Maxwell on the Isle of Man; Doug Reeman at the City of London Police; Dave Monk at the Bank of New York; Mark Steels at the National Criminal Intelligence Service; Geoffrey Rowland, Steve Butterworth, and Peter Neville in Guernsey; Dave Minty and David Hall in Jersey; Gerhard Muller of the German National Police; plus various friends and acquaintances.

In Canada, a very sincerely thank you to the following law enforcement officers, current and retired: John Unger, Brad Demarais, and Tom Hansen of British Columbia; Doug Coates, Brian Guinard, Bill Henderson, Don Panchuk, Kevin Burk, Dave Truax, Mark Sheffer, Dave Taylor, Tony Warr, Garry Clement, and Garry Nichols in Ontario; John Mair and Pierre Camire in Quebec; plus various friends and acquaintances.

And in the Caribbean, my many thanks to: David Thursfield, commissioner of the Royal Cayman Islands Police; Brian Gibbs; Marshall Langer; Marcus A. Wide; Sir Ronald Sanders; Michael Alberga; Lauriston Wilson; Michael Creft; plus various friends and acquaintances.

Several people contributed information, helped make contacts, and provided leads but did not wish their names to be known or the extent of their participation to be mentioned. I trust they know that I am grateful.

May I also say a very special thank you, for all sorts of reasons, to a bunch of people I am very proud to call my pals: John Moscow and Gilda Mariani at the New York District Attorney's Office; the best press officer on the planet, Dean Boyd at U.S. Customs; Ron Rose; John Forbes; Bob Levinson; Joe Petro; Jack Blum; Tim Baldwin; Terry Burke; Rod Carscallen; and the inimitable Ben Soave.

My enormous gratitude goes to Jonathan Webb at McClelland & Stewart, whose sensitivity, wisdom, guidance, and friendship has made all the difference; to my Canadian agent, Linda McKnight; to Carol O'Brien and Dan Hind at Constable Robinson; to my worldwide agents, Eddie and June Bell, Pat Lomax, Ed Breslin, and Paul Moreton; and, *comme d'habitude*, La Benayoun.

SELECTED BIBLIOGRAPHY

BOOKS

Adams, J.: *The Financing of Terror*; New English Library, London, 1986

Adams, James Ring and Frantz, Douglas: *A Full Service Bank: How BCCI Stole Billions Around the World*; Pocket Books, New York, 1992

Alexander, Shana: *The Pizza Connection*; Weidenfeld, New York, 1988

Allsop, Kenneth: *The Bootleggers*; Hutchinson, London, 1961

Anderson, Annelise Graebner: *The Business of Organized Crime*; Hoover Institution Press, Stanford, 1979

Abadinsky, Howard: *Organized Crime*; Nelson Hall, Chicago, 1990

Abadinsky, Howard: *The Mafia in America: An Oral History*; Praeger, New York, 1987

Albanese, Jay: *Organized Crime in America*; Anderson Publishing, Cincinnati, 1996

Anastasia, George: *The Goodfella Tapes*; Avon Books, New York, 1998

Appleton, Peter and Clark, Doug: *Billion $$$ High: The Drug Invasion of Canada*; McGraw-Hill Ryerson, Montreal, 1990

Balboni, Alan: *Beyond the Mafia: Italian Americans and the Development of Las Vegas*; University of Nevada Press, Reno, 1996

Balsamo, William and Carpozi, George: *Crime Incorporated, or Under the Clock: The Inside Story of the Mafia's First Hundred Years*; New Horizon Press, New Jersey, 1991

Baum, Dan: *Smoke and Mirrors: The War on Drugs and the Politics of Failure*; Little, Brown, Boston, 1996

Beare, Margaret E.: *Criminal Conspiracies: Organized Crime in Canada*; Nelson, Scarborough, 1996

Beschloss, Michael: *Kennedy Versus Khrushchev: The Crisis Years 1960-1963*; HarperCollins, New York, 1991

Block, Alan: *Masters of Paradise*; Transaction Publishers, New Jersey, 1991

Blum, Howard: *Gangland: How the FBI Broke the Mob*; Simon and Schuster, New York, 1993

Blumenthal, Ralph: *Last Days of the Sicilians: At War with the Mafia, the FBI Assault on the Pizza Connection*; Times Books, New York, 1988

Bonanno, Joseph and Lalli, Sergio: *A Man of Honor*; Simon and Schuster, New York, 1983

Bonavolonta, Jules and Duffy, Brian: *The Good Guys*; Pocket Books, New York, 1996

Brashler, William: *The Don: The Life and Death of Sam Giancana*; Harper and Row, New York, 1977

Campbell, Duncan: *That Was Business, This Is Personal*; Secker and Warburg, London, 1990

Carrigan, D. Owen: *Crime and Punishment in Canada: A History*; McClelland & Stewart, Toronto, 1991

Charbonneau, Jean-Pierre: *The Canadian Connection*; Optimum, Ottawa, 1976

Clark, T. and Tigue, J.J.: *Dirty Money*; Millington Books, London, 1975

Clifford, Clark: *Counsel to the President*; Random House, New York, 1991

Clutterbuck, R.: *Terrorism, Drugs and Crime in Europe after 1992*; Routledge and Kegan Paul, London, 1990

Colodny, Len and Gettlin, Robert: *Silent Coup: The Removal of Richard Nixon*; Gollancz, London, 1991

Cummings, John and Volkman, Ernest: *Goombata*; Little Brown, Boston, 1990

Davis, John H.: *Mafia Dynasty: The Rise and Fall of the Gambino Crime Family*; Harper Collins, New York, 1993

Dean, John: *Blind Ambition*; Simon and Schuster, New York, 1976

De Grazia, Jessica: *DEA: The War Against Drugs*; BBC Books, London, 1991

Denton, Sally and Morris, Roger: *The Money and the Power: The Making of Las Vegas and Its Hold on America*; Vintage Books, New York, 2002

Dinges, John: *Our Man in Panama*; Random House, New York, 1990

Eddy, Paul: *The Cocaine Wars*; Century Hutchinson, London, 1988

Eisenberg, Dennis, Uri, Dan and Landau, Eli: *Meyer Lansky: Mogul of the Mob*; Paddington Press, New York, 1979

Ferer, Tom, ed.: *Transnational Crime in the Americas*; Routledge, New York, 1999

Fiorentini, G. and Peltzman, S.: *The Economics of Organized Crime*; Cambridge University Press, Cambridge, 1995

Fogel, Jean-François: *Le Testament De Pablo Escobar*; Grasset, Paris 1994

Fox, Stephen R.: *Blood and Power: Organized Crime in 20th Century America*; Morrow, New York, 1989

Friman, Richard H.: *Narco Diplomacy: Exporting the U.S. War on Drugs*; Cornell University Press, Ithaca, 1996

Faith, Nicholas: *Safety in Numbers: The Mysterious World of Swiss Banking*; Hamish Hamilton, London, 1984

Frances, Diane: *Contrepreneurs*; Macmillan, Toronto, 1988

Franklin, R.: *Profits of Deceit*; Heinemann, London, 1990

Freemantle, Brian: *The Fix*; Michael Joseph, London, 1985

Gage, Nicholas: *Mafia, U.S.A.*; Playboy Press, Chicago, 1972

Gambetta, Diego: *The Sicilian Mafia: The Business of Private Protection*; Harvard University Press, Cambridge, 1993

Gardner, Paul: *The Drug Smugglers*; Robert Hale, London, 1989

Garrison, Jim: *A Heritage of Stone*; Putnam's Sons, New York, 1970

——: *On the Trail of the Assassins*; Penguin, London, 1992

Gately, William and Fernandez, Yvette: *Dead Ringer: An Insider's Account of the Mob's Colombian Connection*; DI Fine, New York, 1994

Gentry, Curt: *J. Edgar Hoover: The Man and the Secrets*; New American Library, New York, 1992

Giancana, Sam and Giancana, Chuck: *Double Cross*; Warner Books, New York, 1992

Goldfarb, Ronald L.: *Perfect Villains, Imperfect Heroes: Robert F. Kennedy's War Against Organized Crime*; Random House, New York, 1995

Goode, James: *Wiretap: Listening in on America's Mafia*; Simon and Schuster, New York, 1988

Gosch, M.A.: *Last Testament of Lucky Luciano*; Little Brown, Boston, 1975

Gugliotta, Guy and Leen, Jeff: *Kings of Cocaine*; Simon and Schuster, New York, 1989

Gunst, Laurie: *Born Fi' Dead: A Journey Through the Jamaican Posse Underworld*; H. Holt, New York 1995

Hess, Henner: *Mafia and Mafiosi*; Saxon Hall, New York, 1973

Hogg, Andrew, McDougal, Jim and Morgan, Robin: *Bullion*; Penguin Books, London, 1988

Ianni, Francis and Reuss-Ianni, Elizabeth: *The Crime Society*; New American Library, New York, 1976

Jennings, Andrew, Lashmar, Paul and Simson, Vyv: *Scotland Yard's Cocaine Connection*; Cape, London, 1990

Jacobs, James B.: *Busting the Mob*; New York University Press, New York, 1994

Johnson, Vassel: *As I See It*; The Book Guild, Sussex, England, 2001

Karchmer, Cliff: *Illegal Money Laundering: A Strategy and Resource Guide for Law Enforcement Agencies*; Police Executive Resources, Washington, D.C., 1988

Katcher, Leo: *The Big Bankroll*; Harper and Row, New York, 1959

Kefauver, Estes and United States Senate: *Crime in America: Special Committee to Investigate Organized Crime in Interstate Commerce*; Doubleday and Co, Garden City, 1951

Kelly, Robert J.: *Handbook of Organized Crime in the United States*; Greenwood Press, Westport, 1994

Kempe, Frederick: *Divorcing the Dictator: America's Bungled Affair with Noriega*; Putnam, New York, 1990

Kenney, Dennis Jay and Finckenauer, James: *Organized Crime in America*; Wadsworth Publishing, California, 1995

Kerry, John: *A New Kind of War: National Security and the Globalization of Crime*; Simon and Schuster, New York, 1997

Kessler, Ronald: *The FBI*; Pocket Books, New York, 1993

Kessler, Ronald: *The Richest Man in the World: The Story of Adnan Khashoggi*; Warner Books, New York, 1986

Kleinknecht, William: *The New Ethnic Mobs: The Changing Face of Organized Crime in America*; Free Press, New York, 1996

Kobler, John: *Capone*; Michael Joseph, London, 1972

Kochan, Nick with Whittington, Bob and Potts, Mark: *Dirty Money: The Inside Story of the World's Sleaziest Bank*; National Press Books, Washington, D.C., 1992

Koster, R.M. and Borbon, G.S.: *In the Time of the Tyrants*; Secker and Warburg, London, 1990

Kwitney, Jonathan: *The Crimes of Patriots*; Touchstone, New York, 1987

———: *The Fountain Pen Conspiracy*; Knopf, New York, 1973

Lacey, Robert: *Little Man: Meyer Lansky and the Gangster Life*; Little Brown, Boston, 1991

Lallemand, Alain: *L'Organizatsiya: La Mafia Russe à L'Assaut Du Monde*; Calmann-Lévy, Paris, 1996

Lamothe, Lee and Nicaso, Antonio: *Global Mafia: The New World Order of Organized Crime*; MacMillan, Toronto, 1994

Lance, Burt: *The Truth of the Matter*; Summit, New York, 1991

Lane, Mark: *Plausible Denial*; Plexus, London, 1992

Lavigne, Yves: *Good Guy, Bad Guy: Drugs and the Changing Face of Organized Crime*; Random House, Toronto, 1991

Lernoux, Penny: *In Banks We Trust*; Anchor Press, New York, 1984

Loftus, John and McIntyre, Emily: *Valhallas Wake*; Atlantic Monthly Press, New York, 1989

Lyman, Michael D. and Potter, Gary W.: *Organized Crime*; Prentice Hall, New Jersey, 1997

Lyman, Michael: *Gangland: Drug Trafficking by Organized Criminals*; Charles Thomas, Illinois, 1989

Maas, Peter: *The Valachi Papers*; Putnam, New York, 1968

MacDonald, Scott: *Dancing on a Volcano: The Latin American Drug Trade*; Praeger, New York, 1988

McAlary, Mark: *Crack War*; Robinson Publishing, London, 1990

McCarl, Henry N.: *Economic Impact of the Underground Economy: A Bibliography on Money Laundering and Other Aspects of Off-the-Record Economic Transactions*; Vance Bibliographies, Monticello, Illinois, 1989

Marchetti, Victor and Marks, John D.: *The CIA and the Cult of Intelligence*; Dell, New York, 1980

Martin, John M. and Romano, Anne T.: *Multinational Crime: Terrorism, Espionage, Drug and Arms Trafficking*; Sage, California, 1992

Milgate, Brian: *The Cochin Connection*; Chatto and Windus, London, 1987

Mills, James: *The Underground Empire*; Doubleday, Garden City, New York, 1986

Mokhiber, Russell and Weissman, Robert: *Corporate Predators*; Common Courage Press, Maine, 1999

Mustain, Gene and Capeci, Jerry: *Mob Star: The Story of John Gotti, the Most Powerful Man in America*; Penguin, New York, 1989

Nadelmann, Ethan: *Cops Across Borders: The Internationalization of U.S. Criminal Law Enforcement*; Pennsylvania State University Press, University Park, 1993

Nash, Jay Robert: *World Encyclopedia of Organized Crime*; De Capo Press, New York, 1993

——: *Hustlers and Con Men*; Evans, New York, 1976

Naylor, R.T.: *Bankers, Bagmen and Bandits*; Black Rose, New York, 1990

Naylor, Tom: *Hot Money and the Politics of Debt*; Unwin, London, 1987

Nicaso, Antonio and Lamothe, Lee: *Global Mafia: The New World Order of Organized Crime*; Macmillan Canada, Toronto, 1995

O'Brien, Joseph and Kurins, Andris: *Boss of Bosses*; Simon and Schuster, New York, 1991

O'Kane, James M.: *The Crooked Ladder: Gangsters, Ethnicity, and the American Dream*; Transaction Books, New Jersey, 1992

O'Neill, Gerard and Lehr, Dick: *The Underboss: The Rise and Fall of a Mafia Family*; St. Martin's Press, New York, 1989

Padilla, Felix M.: *The Gang as an American Enterprise*; Rutgers University Press, New Jersey, 1992

Peterson, Virgil W.: *The Mob*; Green Hill Publishers, Illinois, 1983

Petrakis, Gregory J.: *The New Face of Organized Crime*; Kendall/Hunt Publishing, Iowa, 1992

Pileggi, Nicholas: *Wiseguy: Life in a Mafia Family*; Pocket Books, New York, 1985

Possamai, Mario: *Money on the Run*; Viking, Toronto, 1992

Perisco, Joseph: *Casey*; Penguin, New York, 1990

Powers, Thomas: *The Man Who Kept the Secrets: Richard Helms and the* CIA; Pocket Books, New York, 1981

Raufer, Xavier: *Les Superpuissances Du Crime*; Plon, Paris, 1993

Robinson, Jeffrey: *Minus Millionaires*; Grafton, London, 1988

——: *The Laundrymen*; Simon and Schuster, London, 1998

——: *The Merger: How Organized Crime Is Taking Over the World*; Simon and Schuster, London, 1999

Roemer, William F., Jr.: *Accardo: The Genuine Godfather*; Ballantine Books, New York, 1994

——: *The Enforcer*; Ballantine Books, New York, 1994

——: *War of the Godfathers*; Ballantine Books, New York, 1990

Russo, Gus: *Live by the Sword: The Secret War Against Castro and the Death of* JFK; Bancroft Press, Baltimore, 1998

——: *The Outfit: The Role of Chicago's Underworld in the Shaping of America*; Bloomsbury, New York, 2001

Ryan, Patrick J. and Rush, George E.: *Understanding Organized Crime*; Sage, California, 1997

Scheim, David: *The Mafia Killed President Kennedy*; W.H. Allen, London, 1988

Scott, Peter Dale: *Deep Politics and the Death of* JFK; University of California Press, Los Angeles, 1993

Shana, Alexander: *The Pizza Connection: Lawyers, Money, Drugs and the Mafia*; Weidenfeld, New York, 1988

Short, Martin: *Crime Inc*; Thames Mandarin, London, 1991

Sterling, Claire: *Thieves' World: The Threat of the New Global Network of Organized Crime*; Simon and Shuster, New York, 1994

——: *Octopus: The Long Reach of the International Sicilian Mafia*; Norton, New York, 1990

Strong, Simon: *Whitewash: Pablo Escobar and the Cocaine Wars*; Macmillan, London, 1995

Stewart, James B.: *Den of Thieves*; Simon and Schuster, London, 1992

Tanzi, Vito, ed.: *The Underground Economy in the United States and Abroad*; collected articles for the International Money Fund, Lexington Books, Lexington, Massachusetts, 1982

Theoharis, Athan and Cox, John Stewart: *The Boss*; Temple University Press, Philadelphia, 1988

Truell, Peter and Gurwin, Larry: *BCCI*; Bloomsbury, London, 1992

Tyler, Gus: *Organized Crime in America*; University of Michigan Press, Ann Arbor, 1962

Vaksberg, Arkady: *The Soviet Mafia*; Weidenfeld, London, 1991

Villa, John K.: *Banking Crimes: Fraud, Money Laundering and Embezzlement*; Clark Boardman, New York, 1987

Walter, Ingo: *Secret Money*; Unwin, London, 1989

Williams, B. Frederic and Whitney, Frank D.: *Federal Money Laundering: Crimes and Forfeitures*; Lexis Law Publishing, Virginia, 1999

Woods, Brett F.: *The Art And Science of Money Laundering: Inside the Commerce of the International Narcotics Traffickers*; Paladin Press, Colorado, 1998

Woodward, Bob: *Veil: The Secret Wars of the CIA*; Simon and Schuster, New York, 1987

Woodward, Bob and Bernstein, Carl: *All the President's Men*; Secker and Warburg, London, 1974

——: *The Final Days*; Avon Books, New York, 1976

NEWSPAPERS AND WIRE SERVICES

Agence France-Presse:
December 7, 2002: "Tax Haven Sails with Winds of Change"
June 3, 1999: "London Court Freezes Accounts of Late Nigerian Ruler"

Associated Press:
February 5, 2003: "Two Convicted, One Cleared in Miami Securities Fraud Sting"
January 14, 2003: Fowler, Jonathan – "Abacha's Shady Dealings Come Home to Roost"
December 9, 2002: Wilson, Catherine – "Judge in Miami Orders Man Charged with Tax Fraud Held without Bond"
December 6, 2002: Wilson, Catherine – "Insurance Helps Launder Drug Money"
December 5, 2002: Anderson, Curt – "Man Sought in Multinational Tax Evasion Case Extradited from Costa Rica"
November 5, 2002: "Worldcom Fraud May Top $7.68b"
August 16, 2002: Veiga, Alex – "Dozens Indicted on Fraud Charges"
May 14, 2002: "Former N.Y. Broker Charged with Fraud"
May 17, 2001: LaHay, Patricia – "Strip Club Tied to Mob in Testimony"
March 6, 2001: "IRS Raids Suspected Tax Evaders"
March 6, 2001: Gordon, Marcy – "Money-Laundering Proposals Denounced"
March 7, 2000: "13 Charged with $130 Million Metals Fraud Scheme"
December 22, 1999: "Fake Stock Brokers Bust Coke Ring"
November 8, 1999: Gordon, Marcy – "Citibank Didn't Question Deposits"

July 8, 1999: Maull, Samuel — "Former Broker Sentenced to Prison"

June 17, 1999: King, Jeanne — "British Lawyer Indicted in $17 Million Stock Fraud"

February 23, 1999: Nurse, E. — "Caribbean Drugs"

February 22, 1999: "Cayman Islands Economy — Tax Regimes Under Scrutiny"

November 16, 1998: "Three Sentenced in Insurance Scam Will Testify in Other Cases"

November 10, 1998: "Abacha Family Returns More Dollars"

November 2, 1998: "President of Gabon's Appeal against Account Block Rejected"

July 19, 1996: Gold, Jeffrey — "Industry Believes Undercover Probe Saved Operators More Than $100 Million"

June 26, 1998: "U.K. Police Quiz, Release Pair Over Alleged Fraud"

Atlanta Business Chronicle:

February 7, 2000: Rankin, Bill — "Nebraska Outfits Accused of Pirating Scientific-Atlanta Cable TV Boxes"

January 3, 1997: Murray, Brendan — "Wyoming Court Convicts Atlantan in Investor Scam"

Atlanta Journal and Constitution:

August 2, 2001: Rankin, Bill and Visser, Steve — "Plea Deal Could Give Gold Club to Feds $5 Million Fine, Prison Time Likely for Kaplan"

July 22, 2001: Rankin, Bill — "Witness Silence Imperils the Case"

July 20, 2001: Visser, Steve — "Video Kiss Tells Plenty, Prosecution Contends"

July 19, 2001: Rankin, Bill and Visser, Steve — "Defense Grills Key Witness"

July 14, 2001: Visser, Steve — "Defense Lawyer Says Witness Just Trying to Buy Less Jail Time"

July 13, 2001: Rankin, Bill — "This Time, Tapes Testify for Defense of Kaplan"

July 12, 2001: Visser, Steve — "Witness Details Mob-Style Justice"

July 11, 2001: Rankin, Bill and Visser, Steve — "Fraud Blamed on Renegade"

June 28, 2001: Visser, Steve — "Witness — Prosecution Relying on Serial Liars"

June 27, 2001: Visser, Steve — "Lawyer Has a Beef with Prosecutors After Testifying, Says Other Witnesses in Gold Club Trial Are Liars"

June 26, 2001: Visser, Steve — "Witness Links Kaplan to Mob"

June 26, 2001: Visser, Steve — "Witness Admits Contradicting Testimony"

Barron's:
   April 19, 1996: "Easy Money"

Bergen (New Jersey) *Record*:
   February 4, 2000: Voreacos, David – "Con Man's Plea Can't Assuage Victims"
   November 9, 1999: Lavelle, Louis – "2 in Brokerage Fraud Have to Repay $6.6m"
   June 19, 1997: Demarco, Jerry – "FBI Asks for Assets of Cable TV Thieves"
   June 28, 1996: Demarco, Jerry – "In FBI Sting, 14 Accused of Cable Television Piracy"

Bloomberg News:
   December 27, 2002: "Morgan Defends Enron Trades"
   November 21, 2002: Mumma, Christopher – "Lawyers Convicted of Helping Orchestrate Offshore Stock Swindle"
   May 4, 2001: "Finders, Keepers: Lawmen Get Meyers Pollock's Ill-Gotten Gains"
   July 27, 1995: "A.R. Baron, Officers to Pay $1.5 Million for Markups"

Canadian Press:
   January 18, 2003: Young, Gerard – "Bogus B.C. Cleric Ordered to Pay $37 Million U.S. for Bilking Polish Farmers"
   January 8, 2003: Erwin, Steve – "Valentine Breached Order: OSC Disgraced Broker Denies Violating Ban on Trading Complaint Says He Improperly Traded Futures Contracts"
   January 7, 2003: Erwin, Steve – "OSC Alleges Former Thomson Kernaghan Chair Broke Trading Ban Order"
   August 16, 2002: "High-Flying Canadian Stock Broker Mark Valentine Has Been Arrested in Germany on Charges Related to a Two-Year FBI Sting Operation into Stock Fraud and Money Laundering"

Chicago *Tribune*:
   May 21, 2000: Franklin, Stephen – "Cayman Thriving as Tax-Dodgers' Shangri-La, Is Under Scrutiny"

Christian Science Monitor:
   February 12, 2002: Kuzio, Taras – "Ukraine – Look into Arms Export"
   November 3, 1999: Tidwell, M. – "Fanning the Flame of Colombia's War"
   August 7, 1999: Richey, W. – "If Drug Smugglers Can, What About Terrorists?"

July 27, 1999: La Franchi, H. – "Drugs Pulling U.S. into Columbia's War"

July 9, 1999: Abel, D. – "Holes Open in U.S. Drug-fighting Net"

August 27, 1998: Baldauf, Scott – "Why It's So Hard for U.S. to Pick Terrorists' Pockets"

Dallas *Morning News*:

October 21, 2001: Robberson, Tod – "Investigators Hope Money Trail Is Path to Stopping Drug Flow Unlikely Helpers Aid Effort against Complex Global Transactions"

April 10, 1997: Lodge, Bill – "18 Months Added to Man's Sentence"

September 21, 1996: "Houston Man Reportedly Says He Led Phony Nation"

July 27, 1996: "Authorities Are Tracking Scam Artist"

April 10, 1996: Lodge, Bill – "Insurance Salesman Confesses in Fraud Case"

Edmonton Journal (Canada):

January 18, 2003: "Judge Orders Man to Pay \$37m U.S. for Flour Fraud – Man Said He Was a Minister Sending Aid Overseas"

European:

March 3, 1995: Parry, John and Patey, Tony – "King of Europe's Cash Bernie Cornfeld Dies"

Express (U.K.):

April 11, 2000: Connett, David and Gillard, Michael – "U.K. Lawyer Faces Extradition"

Financial Post:

November 13, 2002: Fitzpatrick, Peter – "Dirty Funds Haunt Small Exchanges OSC Comments About Money Laundering, Criminal Elements Earn Rebuke"

September 27, 2002: Brieger, Peter – "Brokerage Regulator Can't Be Sued by Investor Ruling on Suit Against IDA"

Financial Times:

September 24, 2002: Parker, Andrew, Burns, Jimmy and Peel, Michael – "Banks Set to Avoid Charges in Abacha Funds Case"

September 23, 2002: Parker, Andrew, Burns, Jimmy and Peel, Michael – "Sorry Tale of Efforts to Recover Abacha Loot to Repatriate Funds Stolen from the Country's Central Bank Now in Tatters, the Government Is Turning to the International Courts"

September 23, 2002: Parker, Andrew, Burns, Jimmy and Peel, Michael – "Nigeria Seeks to Recover Stolen Abacha $1bn"

March 23, 2002: Winer, Jonathan – "How to Clean Up Dirty Money"

February 13, 2002: "Caribbean Tax Haven Offers Assistance"

November 29, 2001: Willman, John – "Trail of Terrorist Dollars that Spans the World"

January 26, 2001: Mason, John and Parker, Andrew – "Government Drive to Seize Criminal's Assets"

October 30, 2000: "Banks Clean Up"

October 20, 2000: Willman, John – "Laundering Probe Targets London"

August 21, 2000: "Cyprus Tries to Shake Off Tax Haven Image"

May 12, 2000: "Islands Ask for Help on Offshore Rules"

July 23, 1999: "Nigeria Seeks Help in Tracing Billions 'Taken' by Former Military Leaders"

March 25, 1998: "Cartel Laundered Millions through Bank"

March 23, 1998: "Time to Take a Stand on Assets"

January 24, 1998: Graham, George and Wright, Robert – "Winds of Change on Treasure Islands"

February 17, 1998: "Panama to Capitalize on Clean Bank Image"

November 26, 1997: "Moves to Tame the Tiger"

October 31, 1997: "Secrecy Laws – Screen Has Been Drawn Back Briefly"

August 8, 1995: "Action Taken on Pyramid Scheme"

Gainsville Sun (Florida):

December 30, 1998: Fisher, Lise – "Drug Smuggler Sentenced to Life, Convict to Forfeit Millions"

Gannett News Service:

March 2, 2002: Scott, Katherine Hutt – "Antigua Bank Owner Was Largest Soft-Money Contributor to Daschle"

Globe and Mail (Canada):

March 26, 2003: Marron, Kevin – "Banks Investing in Systems to Bring Terrorists to Account"

February 4, 2003: Belford, Terrence – "Brokers Affected by Money-Laundering Legislation"

January 31, 2003: Stewart, Sinclair and Howlett, Karen – "Court Halts Tracking of Valentine"

December 10, 2002: McNish, Jacquie – "Trustee Slaps Former TK Staff with Suit Space"

October 23, 2002: McNish, Jacquie – "Valentine Sells Assets to Cover Defaulted Loan"

September 24, 2002: Alphonso Caroline – "Valentine Proclaims His Innocence Trader Freed on Bail, but Can't Leave Us"

September 23, 2002: Alphonso, Caroline – "Valentine Spends Weekend Behind Bars in Miami"

September 21, 2002: Alphonso Caroline and McNish, Jacquie – "Valentine Plans to Plead Not Guilty"

September 20, 2002: McNish, Jacquie and Dixon, Guy – "Lawyer in Sting Seeks Debt Relief, Man Charged by FBI Has Posh Lifestyle"

September 18, 2002: McNish, Jacquie and Freeman, Alan – "Valentine Sought German Brokerage Venture, Indicted Canadian Caught in FBI Sting Eyed Troubled Firm"

August 26, 2002: Saunders, John – "Greed Was the Bait for FBI Stock Sting"

August 18, 2002: "RCMP Expect Further Arrests from Bermuda Short Sting"

August 16, 2002: McFarland, Janet; Mckenna, Barrie and Kennedy, Peter – "FBI Arrests Star Canadian Trader"

July 8, 2002: McNish, Jacquie and Saunders, John – "The Rise and Fall of Broker Mark Valentine"

June 15, 2002: Oberman, Mira – "Pot Farms Conceal Deadly Risks"

Guardian:

March 7, 2003: Teather, David – "Enron Scams Fill 2,000 Pages, Second Report from Investigator Tells of Increasingly Desperate Efforts to Conceal Financial Disaster"

December 14, 2002: Levene, Tony – "An Elite Police Unit Is Using the Internet to Fight Back Against International Electronic Fraudsters"

May 18, 2000: Osborn, Andrew – "Nigerian Ex-Dictator's Stolen Millions in British Banks"

May 12, 1997: Plommer, L. – "Islands Link Drug Cartels to Economy"

Houston Business Journal:

October 22, 1999: Perin, Monica – "From Mexico to Antigua, R. Allen Stanford and Family Have Created a Financial Firm Catering to the Affluent"

Independent (U.K.):

June 28, 1998: Ricks, Michael – "International Fraud Squad Arrests London Lawyers"

Independent on Sunday (U.K.):
  January 28, 2001: Lashmar, Paul — "Banking Fugitive Woos Uganda"

International Herald Tribune:
  March 15, 2003: Sullivan, Aline — "World Watchdogs Make Life Unpleasant Offshore"
  May 12, 2001: Milbank, Dana — "U.S. Quits OECD's Drive to Rein in Tax Havens"
  December 4, 2000: Ignatius, David — "Getting Serious about Money Laundering"
  October 25, 2000: Buerkle, Tom — "Havens See Benefits in Tough New Rules"
  May 12, 2000: "Luxembourg Freezes Loot Abacha Took from Nigeria"
  November 27, 1997: Walsh, Sharon — "Mob Bust on Wall Street"

Irish Times:
  July 6, 2002: "Business and Political Figures Names in Ansbacher Report"
  July 5, 2002: "Walking Bank Who Financed Haughey's Secret Lifestyle"
  September 28, 2001: Cusack, Jim — "CAB to Lead Anti-terrorism Efforts"

Jerusalem Post:
  October 8, 1995: Rodan, Steve — "Home-Grown Terrorists May Return to Haunt the U.S."

Knight-Ridder:
  July 16, 2000: Ivanovich, David — "Houston Banker Tries to Create Caribbean Empire, Runs into Problems with Feds"

Los Angeles Times:
  December 22, 2002: Kristof, Kathy M. — "Author, Attorney Indicted in Offshore Account Case"
  November 5, 2002: Hiltzik, Michael and Weinstein, Henry — "Cigarettes Portrayed as Currency of Crime EU Suit Against R.J. Reynolds Describes a Worldwide System of Money Laundering"
  October 31, 2002: Weinstein, Henry and Levin, Myron — "EU Alleges Mob Ties to Tobacco"
  April 7, 2002: Meyer, Josh and Lichtblau, Eric — "Crackdown on Terror Funding Is Questioned"
  August 25, 1999: Leeds, Jeff — "Cayman Islands Lifts Veil of Bank Secrecy"
  May 17, 1994: "The Troubled Reign of Bhutto II"
  September 8, 1989: "Witness Tells of Mob Influence in Penny Stocks"

Mail (U.K.):

October 13, 2002: Beaton, Graeme – "Duo Face Jail in U.S. over £11 Million International Share Scam"

Mail on Sunday (U.K.):

September 16, 2001: Robinson, Jeffrey – "Following the Money"

December 1, 2002: Beaton, Graeme – "Ex-Magistrate Guilty in Huge Shares Sting Graeme Beaton"

Miami Herald:

August 16, 2002: Fields, Gregg – "Traders Charged in Fund Scheme Money Laundering and Kickbacks Alleged"

April 15, 2001: Fields, Gregg and Whitefield, Mimi – "Prosecutions Helping Lift the Veil of Secrecy from Offshore Banks"

February 21, 2001: Fields, Gregg and Whitefield, Mimi – "Offshore Governments Close Three Banks – Money Laundering Report Spurs Move"

October 27, 2000: Lebowitz, Larry – "19 from Crime Family Indicted"

Mobile Register (Alabama):

January 14, 1997, Wilson, Michael – "The Hollywood Guy"

January 13, 1997, Wilson, Michael – "The Informants"

January 12, 1997, Wilson, Michael – "Operation Skymaster – Undercover in Mobile"

Montreal *Gazette* (Canada):

February 14, 2003: Macdonald, Don – "Montreal Lawyer Sentenced for His Role in Stock Scheme – Harry Bloomfield Gets Five Years' Probation Plus Fine and 500 Hours Community Service"

November 26, 2002 – "Bloomfield Guilty of Conspiracy to Bilk Investors"

October 16, 2002: Hutchinson, Brian – "Disgraced Broker Had Bags of Loot – Witness at Montreal Philanthropist's New York Trial Says His Name Never Came Up"

Moscow News:

May 1, 1997: "Caribbean Havens for Money Launderers"

Naples Daily News (Florida):

November 9, 2001: Zollo, Cathy and Edwards, Gina – "Marchiano Gets 10–30 Years In Prison, Ordered To Pay $8m Restitution"

November 6, 2001: "Marchiano Negotiating Restitution Amount with Prosecutors"

June 4, 2001: Edwards, Gina – "Brother Testifies in A.S. Goldmen Case"

April 20, 2000: Edwards, Gina – "A.S. Goldmen – Broker Linked to Naples Firm Pleads Guilty to Corruption"

July 10, 1999: Edwards, Gina – "Marchiano Freed on $1 Million Bail"

October 24, 1998: Edwards, Gina – "Troubled Naples Brokerage Firm Trims Operations"

Nassau Guardian (Bahamas):

March 19, 2003: Thompson, Lindsay – "Clients' Job to Provide Credit Card Data to U.S. IRS"

National Post (Canada):

November 26, 2002: "Montreal Philanthropist Bloomfield Guilty of Conspiracy to Bilk Investors, Businessman and Partner Conspired in Criminal 'Pump-and-Dump' Stock Scheme"

October 19, 2002: Hutchinson, Brian – "Lawyer Used Envoy's ID, Court Told Liberian Diplomat Says He Helped Harry Bloomfield Send Money to Switzerland"

October 12, 2002: Hutchinson, Brian – "Bloomfield Drawn into Devious Scheme"

October 10, 2002: Hutchinson, Brian – "Letters Show Bloomfield Part of Sophisticated Fraud, Judge Told – Private Faxes and Correspondence Seized in U.K. Raid"

October 9, 2002: "Leading Montreal Lawyer Facing Fraud Charges Harry Bloomfield: Accused of Aiding in US$17m 'Pump And Dump' Scheme"

November 28, 1997: Tomkins, Richard – "Mob Linked to Pump and Dump Scheme"

Newsday (New York):

November 28, 2002: "Bank Admits Laundering $123M"

August 2, 2001: Harrigan, Susan – "Stratton Player Pleads Guilty/Ex-fashion Exec Was Last to Face Prosecution"

August 1, 2001: Harrigan, Susan – "Businessman Convicted in LI Brokerage Scheme"

July 10, 2001: Harrigan, Susan – "Views of Shuster's Role Are at Odds"

March 25, 2001: Harrigan, Susan – (Part Two) "Boom to Bust – How Authorities Turned 2 Crooked Brokers from High Rollers to Witnesses Against One of America's Top Shoe Designers"

March 24, 2001: Harrigan, Susan – (Part One) "Castles Made of Sand – Brokers Who Rode Fraud to Riches Now Federal Witnesses"

July 15, 1999: "S. Mazzeo, 41, Involved in Stock Fraud"

May 14, 1997: "13 Indicted in $75M Theft – Accused of Bilking Investors"

April 3, 1997: Hurtado, Patricia – "Stock Swindle/U.S. Alleges Millions Lost in Securities Scam, 18 Indicted"

New York *Daily News*:

October 15, 2001: Ross, Barbara – "Banks Back off Anti-Terror, Laundering Laws in Slow Spin Cycle"

September 10, 2000: Smith, Greg – "Mob Muscles in on Market"

May 3, 1997: Peterson, Helen – "Mafioso Held in Stock Fraud"

January 9, 1997: Ross, Barbara and Feiden, Douglas – "Sting Nets Bad Stock"

New York Times:

December 12, 2002: Johnston, David Cay – "10 Are Charged in Tax Evasion Case Said to Involve 2,000"

December 6, 2002: Lichtblau, Eric – "New Hiding Place for Drug Profits: Insurance Policies"

November 28, 2002: Worth, Robert F. – "Bank Failed to Question Huge Deposits"

November 16, 2002: Johnston, David Cay – "Two Plotters Are Sentenced in Big Tax Evasion Scheme"

November 12, 2002: Berkeley, Bill – "A Glimpse into a Recess of International Finance"

October 16, 2002: Gerth, Jeff and Miller, Judith – "Report Says Saudis Fail to Crack Down on Charities that Finance Terrorists"

October 8, 2002: "Plan to Stop Tax Evaders Hits Snag"

September 19, 2002: Andrews, Edmund L. – "U.S. Proposes Hedge Fund Rules to Prevent Terrorist Financing"

September 19, 2002: Frantz, Douglas – "Front Companies Said to Keep Financing Terrorists"

September 10, 2002: "Germany Probes Import-Export Firm"

June 28, 2002: Weiser, Benjamin – "Ex-Broker Helped to Launder Drug Money, Prosecutors Say"

June 26, 2002: Eichenwald, Kurt and Barboza, David – "Enron Criminal Investigation Is Said to Expand to Bankers"

June 15, 2002: Lambert, Bruce – "Four Admit Using Bank to Launder Money"

June 13, 2002: Weiser, Benjamin — "Officials Say Heroin Arrests Show New Supply Routes"

May 23, 2002: Sengupta, Somini — "UN Report Says Al Qaeda May Be Diversifying Its Finances"

May 15, 2002: Johnston, David Cay — "Nine Are Indicted in Investment Fraud Case"

April 24, 2002: Stevenson, Richard and Wayne, Leslie — "More Regulations to Thwart Money Laundering Are Imposed"

March 26, 2002: Johnston, David Cay — "IRS Says Offshore Tax Evasion Is Widespread"

February 25, 2002: Atlas, Riva — "Insurers Say J.P. Morgan Disguised Loans to Enron"

February 18, 2002: Eichenwald, Kurt — "Records Raise Questions Over Some Enron Gas Trades"

February 17, 2002: Holstein, William J. — "Hounds and Foxes Match Wits in Pursuit of Hidden Assets"

December 11, 2001: Wayne, Leslie — "Fight Against Money Laundering Widens"

December 11, 2001: Wayne, Leslie — "Wall St. Faces Rules on Money Laundering"

December 10, 2001: Eichenwald, Kurt — "Terror Money Hard to Block, Officials Find"

November 8, 2001: Sanger, David and Eichenwald, Kurt — "U.S. Moves to Cut 2 Financial Links for Terror Group"

October 14, 2001: Frantz, Douglas — "Pakistani Trader Denies He Ever Helped Bin Laden"

October 14, 2001: MacFarquhar, Neil — "Saudis Reject U.S. Accusation They Balked on Terror Money"

August 19, 2001: Schoenberger, Karl — "Regulators Check the New Economy's Books"

April 6, 2001: Morgenson, Gretchen — "2 Accused of Fraud Using Shell Companies"

March 6, 2001: Johnston, David Cay — "IRS Steps Up Tax-Evasion Raids"

February 11, 2001: Morgenson, Gretchen — "Striking a Blow for the Little Guy"

November 7, 2000: Daley, Suzanne — "Europeans Suing Big Tobacco in U.S."

October 20, 2000: Johnston, David Cay — "Taking Aim at Tax Havens, IRS Seeks Credit Card Slips"

October 10, 2000: Bergman, Lowell — "U.S. Companies Tangled in Web of Drug Dollars"

July 27, 2000: Brick, Michael – "D.H. Blair & Co Indicted for Racketeering"

April 21, 2000: "Former Bear Stearns Executive Barred from Securities Industry"

March 8, 2000: Finklestein, Katherine E. – "Banker Indicted in Metal Export Fraud Case"

November 19, 1999: Eaton, Leslie – "Penny-Stock Fraud Is Billion-Dollar Game"

November 2, 1999: Henriques, Diana – "A Brutal Turn in Stock Frauds"

August 6, 1999: Morgenson, Gretchen – "SEC Says Bear Stearns Subsidiary Had Central Role in Fraud"

August 3, 1999: Smothers, Ronald – "Banker Outlines Money Laundering in Caymans"

April 4, 1999: Navarro, M. – "An Outpost in the Banana and Marijuana Wars"

May 31, 1998: Navarro, M. – "Upgraded Drug Traffic Flourishes on Old Route"

April 23, 1997: Henriques, Diana and Truell, Peter – "Should a Clearinghouse Be Its Broker's Keeper?"

January 30, 1997: Rohter, L. – "Impact of NAFTA Pounds Economies of the Caribbean"

July 3, 1995: Anderson, J.R. – "Red Dogs' Battle Drugs in the Caribbean"

June 8, 1995: Cooper, Michael – "U.S. Indicts a Fugitive Over Drugs"

February 10, 1997: Raab, Selwyn – "Officials Say Mob Is Shifting Crimes to New Industries"

Observer (U.K.):

November 22, 1998: "How the Grand Lootocracy Beggared Nigeria's People"

Office of the United States Attorney, District of New Jersey

March 7, 2000: Press Release – "U.S. Bank Officials and Refining Firm Executives Indicted in Scheme to Defraud Argentinean Government of Export Incentives"

August 2, 1999: Press Release – "John M. Mathewson, former chairman of Cayman Island bank sentenced for nationwide, multi-million dollar offshore banking scheme"

April 20, 1999: Press Release – "William S. 'Trey' Prevost III, former fugitive sentenced to prison in connection with biggest cable TV piracy in U.S. history"

Office of the United States Attorney, Southern District of New York:
   August 14, 2000: Press Release, with sealed complaint against Oleg Zezov
      and sealed complaint against Igor Yarimaka in the matter of the extor-
      tion of Bloomberg L.P.

Ontario Securities Commission (Canada):
   July 31, 2002: "OSC Issues Reasons for Order Against Mark Valentine"

Ottawa Business Journal (Canada):
   February 17, 2003: "Valentine Trading Ban Extended"
   January 7, 2003: "Mark Valentine on the Hotseat Again"

Ottawa Citizen:
   March 25, 2003: Tibbetts, Janice – "Government Exempts Lawyers from
      Money Laundering Law"

Philadelphia *Inquirer*:
   December, 1, 2000: Webb, Robert – "Offshore Bank Accounts Are Not
      Secret to IRS"

Pittsburgh Post Gazette:
   January 28, 2001: "Offshore Tax Scam Unveiled by FBI"

Reuters:
   November 6, 2002: "Worldcom Sees $9 Billion Restatement"
   September 18, 2002: "U.S. to Propose Tougher Hedge-Fund Scrutiny"
   September 9, 2002: "Hong Kong Charges Eight in Massive Money
      Laundering Case"
   August 16, 2002: Clarke, Toni – "Sting Operation Could Be Tip of Iceberg"
   July 17, 2002: "U.S. Seeks Rule to Verify Bank Customer Identities"
   July 13, 2002: Wulfhorst, Ellen – "New York Jury Convicts Algerian in
      Millennium Plot"
   July 9, 2002: "U.S. Drops Three from Money Laundering List"
   April 17, 2002: "Nigeria to Get $1 Billion in Out-of-Court Deal"
   January 29, 2002: "Senate Sees Money Laundering Risk for U.S. Brokers"
   January 17, 2002: Loney, Jim – "Enron Benefited from Caribbean Tax
      Havens, Lax Law"
   January 8, 2002: "Atlanta Strip Club Owner Sentenced to 16 Months"
   July 10, 2001: "Schneider v IRS"

May 14, 2000: "More Arrests Seen in Liechtenstein Laundering Probe"

March 30, 2000: Loney, Jim – "Cayman Islands – Human Slave Traders Join Money-Laundering Flood"

October 14, 1999: "Swiss Freeze Accounts of Nigeria's Abacha"

September 23, 1999: Zengerle, Patricia – "Russian Report Unwanted Blow to Cayman Islands"

June 26, 1998: "U.K. Police Quiz, Release Pair Over Alleged Fraud"

San Francisco Chronicle:
   March 22, 1969: "British Plan Anguilla Troop Cut"
   March 22, 1969: Valencia, F. Scott – "The Anguilla Saga"
   March 21, 1969: "Anguilla May Face a Long Occupation"
   March 21, 1969: Valencia, F. Scott – "The Inside Story of the Anguilla Caper"
   March 20, 1969: "The British Quest of Anguilla"

Scotsman:
   November 28, 2002: Cox, David – "Briton on $2.7M Fraud Charge"

South China Morning Post:
   December 8, 1998: "Melchizedek Case Lawyer Seeks Deportation"
   November 28, 1998: "15 Banned in Passport Scam"

South Florida Business Journal:
   August 26, 2002: Fakler, John T. – "Securities Crackdown Hits Region"

St. Petersburg Times:
   February 4, 2002: Freedberg, Sydney P. – "Enron – The Offshore Ventures"

Sunday Express (U.K.):
   April 23, 2000: Connett, David and Gillard, Michael – "Solicitor Refuses to Hand Over £20M in Laundered Drugs Money"

Times (U.K.):
   October 11, 2001: Bremner, Charles and Doran, James – "Britain Denounced as Dirty Money Haven"
   October 11, 2001: Binyon, Michael – "Island Regimes Make It Easy for Smugglers to Clean Up"
   October 14, 1999: Lister, David – "Case of Brainy Don, the Bank and Money-Laundering Briefs"

September 25, 1999: Lister, David and Bone, James – "British Lawyers in Bank Inquiry"

August 8, 1993: "Plot Thickens in Phony Bank Scheme"

Times Colonist (Canada):

January 18, 2003: "Ripoff Artist Must Pay Millions to Polish Farmers"

Toronto Star:

August 20, 2002: Wells, Jennifer – "Stock Sting Has Quite a Cast of Characters"

July 11, 2002: "Canadian Court Decides against IRS in Tax Case"

February 27, 2002: "Survey of Brokerages Reveals 13,000 Accounts in Tax Havens"

Toronto *Sun*:

October 16, 2002: Lamberti, Rob – "Twist in Church-Fire Case – Ownership Linked to N.Y.C. Trial Figure"

February 27, 2002: Lewyckyj, Maryanna – "Investors Head Offshore – Accounts in Money Laundering Havens Worrisome"

United Press International:

September 5, 2001: "Funny Business – Honor amongst Fraudsters?"

United States Department of Justice:

August 2, 2001: Press Release – "Harry Schuster, Beverly Hills Businessman, Real Estate Investor and Film Producer Convicted of Money Laundering and Securities Fraud".

USA Today:

September 12, 2002: "Officials Accused of Using Tyco as Piggy Bank"

December 16, 1996: Fairley, Juliette – "Foreign Bank Accounts Offer Profit, Privacy, Protection"

Vancouver *Sun*:

January 18, 2003: Young, Gerard – "Victoria Man Fined $37m U.S. for Fraud Case: Plot Hurt Thousands of Polish Farmers"

July 11, 2001: Baines, David – "Regulator Cites Broker for Mob Link"

VOA News:

June 28, 2002: "Former U.S. Banker Indicted in Money Laundering Case"

Wall Street Journal:

February 8, 2003: Weinberg, Stuart – "Rogue Broker Suspended 10 Years"

July 23, 2002: Sapsford, Jathon and Beckett, Paul – "Called to Account-Citigroup, J.P. Morgan Marketed Enron-Type Deals to Other Firms"

February 28, 2001: Beckett, Paul – "J.P. Morgan Chase, Others Are Criticized Over Correspondent – Banking Standards"

February 29, 2000: Allen, Michael – "Grenada Banking Is Great, But Mr. Brink Is Off to Uganda Now, Ex-Head of Firm that Claims Staggering Profits Is Busy Fixing Congo's Currency"

April 6, 2000: "Secret Offshore Bank Accounts Not So Secret"

February 22, 2000: Beckett, Paul and Allen, Michael – "Bank of New York Investigation Widens to Include Swiss Financier Rappaport"

June 17, 1999: Schroeder, Michael – "Eighty-Five Brokers Are Charged with Allegedly Bilking Investors"

February 4, 1999: Gasparino, Charles – "SEC Staff Weighing Civil Fraud Charges Against Bear Stearns in A.R. Baron Case"

July 1, 1998: Jones, Roland – "British Lawyers Tied to A.R. Baron Investigation"

August 25, 1997: Alpert, Bill – "Buyer, Beware! Dizzying Deals Raise Questions about California's Fast-Growing Osicom Technologies"

May 12, 1997: Robichaux, Mark – "Cable Pirates Sought Plunder but Blundered into a Major FBI Sting"

March 16, 1990: "Gorbachev's Empire on the Cheap"

Washington Post:

October 3, 2002: "Fastow Charged with Fraud, Conspiracy in Enron Case"

August 15, 2002: Barbaro, Michael – "Rockville CEO among Dozens Accused in Stock-Fraud Sting"

June 3, 2002: O'Harrow, Robert, Jr. – "In Terror War, Privacy vs Security – Search for Illicit Activities Taps Confidential Data"

April 3, 2002: Samuelson, Robert J. – "Tax Haven, Anyone?"

August 29, 2000: DeYoung, Karen – "U.S., Colombia to Confront Lucrative Peso Exchange"

October 28, 1999: Hilzenrath, David – "Russians Use Tiny Island to Hide Billions"

February 3, 1999: "Banking with Big Brother"

October 7, 1996: Farah, Douglas – "Russian Crime Finds Haven in Caribbean"

November 5, 1995 – "The Ruse that Roared"

June 18, 1995: McGee, Jim – "From Respected Attorney to Suspected Racketeer – A Lawyer's Journey"

January 4, 1995: "Bagging a Bumbling Band of Alleged Money Launderers"

June 22, 1986: "Moscow's Shell Game – Soviet Bankers Use Our Money Against Us"

Washington *Times*:

December 6, 2002: Seper, Jerry – "Money-Laundering Scheme Squashed"

September 6, 2002: Rahn, Richard – "Nightmare on FATF Street"

August 9, 2002: "Worldcom Reveals Additional Fraud Worth $3.3 Billion"

MAGAZINES, JOURNALS, AND OTHER PERIODICALS

American Banker:

December 29, 1998: "Anti-Laundering Proposal Draws Flood of Complaints"

Art, Antiques and Law:

(Part I) December 1998, (Part II) March 1999: Snaith, Ian – "Art, Antiques and the Fruits of Crime-Laundering, Investigation and Confiscation"

Bulletin of Atomic Scientists:

May/June 2000: Woodard, Colin – "Offshore Banking – Clean Beaches, Dirty Money"

Business Crimes Bulletin:

August 2002: Mariani, Gilda – "Ungagging the Gatekeepers – Accountants' Sensitive Role in Probes"

Business Week:

February 2001: "Looks Like Every Day Is Money-Laundry Day"

November 2, 1998: Dwyer, Paula and Solomon, Steven – "The Citi that Slept?"

December 15, 1997: Weiss, Gary – "Investors Beware – Chop Stocks Are on the Rise"

June 1, 1998: "Tax-Haven Whiz or Rogue Banker? Marc Harris' Doings in Panama Are Raising Eyebrows"

Caribbean Affairs:

January 1990: Sanders, R. – "Narcotics, Corruption and Development – The Problems in the Smaller Islands"

October 1989: Pantin D. – "The Colombian Nightmare – Drugs and Structural Adjustment"

Caribbean Journal of Criminology and Social Psychology:
1999: de Albuquerque, K. and McElroy, J. – "A Longitudinal Study of Serious Crime in the Caribbean"

Dollars and Sense:
September-October 2001: Petras, James – "U.S. Banks and the Dirty Money Empire"

Economic Perspectives:
May 2000: Joseph, Lester – "Money Laundering Enforcement – Following the Money"

The Economist:
September 23, 2000: "Small States, Big Money Economist"
May 17, 1997: "Dirty Linen – Mexico"

Far Eastern Economic Review:
December 10, 1998: Lintner, Bertil – "Fantasy Island – Melchizedek Passport Scam Reveals How the Internet Can Take Fraud to New Frontiers"

FBI Law Enforcement Bulletin:
May 2001: Schroeder, William – "Money Laundering – A Global Threat and the International Community's Response"

Federal Reserve Bulletin:
September 1999: Houpt, James V. – "International Activities of U.S. Banks and in U.S. Banking Markets"

Foreign Policy:
May-June 2001: Morris-Cotterill, Nigel – "Think Again – Money Laundering"

Harper's Magazine:
February 1997: Schapiro, Mark – "Doing the Wash – Inside a Colombian Cartel's Money-Laundering Machine"

Jane's Intelligence Review:
    August 24, 2000: Galeotti, Dr. Mark – "Crimes of the New Millennium"

The Lawyers Weekly:
    January 25, 2002: Harloff, Glen – "Phony Financial Instruments Can Put
    Lawyers at Risk"

Maclean's:
    May 13, 2002: Geddes, John – "The Money Trail – Ottawa's Fight Against
    Laundering Is Going Slowly"

Mother Jones:
    November–December 2000: Silverstein, Ken – "Trillion-Dollar Hideaway"

The Nation:
    August 19, 2002: "Bubble Capitalism"

Newsweek:
    March 13, 2000: "The Lost Billions"
    March 29, 1999: Powell, Bill and Albats, Yevgenia – "Follow the Money –
    The Latest Kremlin Scandal Involves Billions of Dollars Moving Offshore
    Plus Sex and Videotape"

New York Times Sunday Magazine:
    December 10, 2000: Hitt, Jack – "The Billion-Dollar Shack"

New York University Law Review:
    October 1999: Bellwoar, John M. – "Bar Baron at the Gate – An Argument
    for Expanding the Liability of Securities Clearing Brokers for the Fraud
    of Introducing Brokers"

Playboy:
    January 2002: Robinson, Jeffrey – "Terror Dollars"

Security and Defense Studies Review:
    Summer 2002: Griffith, Ivelaw L. – "Security, Sovereignty and Public Order
    in the Caribbean"

Securities Reform Act Litigation Reporter:
    January 2002: Zweifach, Lawrence J. – "Current Developments and Issues
    in the Criminal Prosecution of Federal Securities Law Violations"

Securities Week:
   April 9, 2001: "New York D.A. Indicts Two in Wide Ranging Securities
   Fraud Case"

Tax Notes International:
   July 2002: Langer, Marshall J. – "The Outrageous History of Caribbean Tax
   Treaties with OECD Member States"

Time:
   June 10, 2002: Israely, Jeff – "Meet the Mob"
   October 22, 2001: Cohen, Adam – "Banking on Secrecy – Terrorists
   Oppose Scrutiny of Offshore Accounts – And So Do Many U.S. Bankers
   And Lawmakers"
   July 10, 2000: Wallace, Charles P. – "Funds in the Sun – Tax Havens Are
   Coming Under Increasing Pressure to Clean Up Money Laundering"
   April 24, 2000: Handelman, Stephen – "Confronting Cross-Border Crime –
   Law Enforcers Must Learn to Move Faster to Snare Global Lawbreakers"
   June 22, 1998: Walsh, James – "A World War on Bribery"
   February 26, 1996: Booth, Cathy – "Caribbean Blizzard – With Blissful
   Vacationers Unaware, Tons of Cocaine Flow through the Idyllic Islands,
   Thanks to Sharkish Drug Cartels"

U.S. News and World Report:
   June 22, 1987: Chesnoff, Richard Z. – "Liechtenstein – A Mouse that
   Roars"
   June 2, 1986: Zanker, Alfred and Scherschel, Patricia M. – "Why It's Getting
   Tougher to Hide Money"

Washington Monthly:
   July 2000: Dorgan, Byron – "Global Shell Games – How the Corporations
   Operate Tax Free"

World Policy Journal:
   Spring 2001: Malkin, Lawrence and Elizur, Yuval – "The Dilemma of Dirty
   Money"

SIGNIFICANT TESTIMONY AND SPEECHES

Bain, John S.: *Money Laundering – A Practical Analysis with Particular Reference to
   Bahamian and Caribbean Offshore Institutions*; submitted to the University of
   Wales and the Manchester Business School, Wales and England, 1998

Benn, Hilary: *Money Laundering as a Threat to International Development*; Money Laundering Conference, London, February 26, 2002

Gurule, James: *International Co-operation in the War on Terrorism*; delivered before the Commission on Security and Co-operation in Europe, Washington, D.C., May 8, 2002

Langer, Marshall J.: *Harmful Tax Competition – Who Are the Real Tax Havens?*; presented at a meeting of the International Tax Planning Association, New Orleans, November 20, 2000

Richards, Lori A., director, Office of Compliance Inspections and Examinations U.S. Securities & Exchange Commission: *Money Laundering: It's on the SEC's Radar Screen*; delivered at the Conference on Anti-Money Laundering Compliance for Broker-Dealers Securities Industry Association, Washington, D.C., May 8, 2001

Roth, Jean-Pierre, chairman of the governing board Swiss National Bank: *The Challenges of an International Financial Center – The Swiss Case*; delivered before the British-Swiss Chamber of Commerce, London, February 26, 2002

State of New Jersey, State Crime Commission: *Hearings on Money Laundering*; Trenton, December 9 and 14, 1993

Summers, Lawrence H., secretary of the Treasury: *Combatting International Money Laundering*; remarks to the American Bar Association, Washington, D.C., March 2, 2000

United Nations: *Attacking the Profits of Crime – Drugs, Money and Laundering*. A panel discussion, including: Ian Hamilton Fazey: *Setting the Context – Ten Years on from the 1988 Convention*; Pino Arlacchi: *The Need for a Global Attack on Money Laundering*; Jack Blum: *Financial Havens and Banking Secrecy*; Vito Tanzi: *Macro-Economic Aspects of Offshore Centers and the Importance of Money Laundering in Offshore Financial Flows*; Carla Del Ponte: *Practical and Legal Obstacles to International Judicial Co-operation in Financial Investigations*; N.K. Singh: *New Money Laundering Threats for Emerging Economies*; Timothy Donaldson: *Offshore Financial Business and Banking Regulation*; New York, June 10, 1998

United States House of Representatives – Committee on Banking and Financial Services: *Dismantling the Financial Infrastructure of Global Terrorism*; Washington, D.C., 2001

——: *Hearing on Money Laundering*; testimony of former money launderer Kenneth Rijock, March 9, 2000

——: *Russian Money Laundering*; Washington, D.C., 1999

——: *Money Laundering Deterrence Act of 1998 and H.R. 1756 – Money Laundering and Financial Crime Strategy Act of 1997*; Washington, D.C., 1998

———: *Money Laundering and Financial Crimes Strategy Act of 1998, Report to Accompany H.R. 1756*; Washington, D.C., 1998

———. *Efforts to Combat Money Laundering*; Jack Blum, June 11, 1998

United States House of Representatives – Committee on Commerce, Subcommittee on Finance and Hazardous Materials: *Organized Crime on Wall Street*; prepared statement of Richard H. Walker, director, Division of Enforcement Securities and Exchange Commission, September 13, 2000

———: *On Organized Crime*; statement and testimony by special agent Tom Fuentes, FBI, Washington, D.C., September 13, 2000

United States House of Representatives – Committee on Financial Services: *Cutting Off the Financial Life Blood of the Terrorists*; Dennis M. Lormel, chief, Financial Crimes Section, FBI, Washington, D.C., October 3, 2001

United States House of Representatives – Committee on Financial Services, Subcommittee on Financial Institutions and Consumer Credit: *Recovering Assets Stolen by Corrupt Foreign Leaders – Opening Statement*, Chairman Spencer Bachus; *Recovering Dictator's Plunder*, Jack Blum; *Social and Political Costs of Theft of Public Funds by African Dictators*, Michael Chege; *Recovering Dictator's Plunder*, John Conyngham; Washington, D.C., May 9, 2002

United States House of Representatives – Committee on Financial Services, Subcommittee on Oversight and Investigations: *Patriot Act Oversight – Investigating Patterns of Terrorist Financing*; Washington, D.C., February 12, 2002

———: *Preventing Identity Theft by Terrorists and Criminals*; joint hearing before the Subcommittee on Oversight and Investigations of the Committee on Financial Services and the Subcommittee on Social Security of the Committee on Ways and Means; Washington, D.C., November 8, 2001

United States House of Representatives – Committee on Government Reform, Subcommittee on Criminal Justice: *Drug Policy and Human Resources – Combating Money Laundering*; Washington, D.C., 2000

United States House of Representatives – Committee on International Relations: *International Organized Crime – The Larger Issues*; Jack Blum, Washington, D.C., October 1, 1997

United States House of Representatives – Committee on the Judiciary, Subcommittee on Crime: *2000 Money Laundering Crisis*; Washington, D.C., February 10, 2000

United States Senate – Committee on Banking, Housing, and Urban Affairs: *Prime Bank Schemes*; Herbert Biern, deputy associate director, Division of Banking Supervision and Regulation, Washington, D.C., July 17, 1996

United States Senate – Committee on Banking, Housing, and Urban Affairs, Subcommittee on International Trade and Finance: *The Role of Charities and*

Nongovernmental Organizations in Financing Terrorist Activities; Washington, D.C., August 1, 2002

United States Senate – Committee on Finance: *Tax Schemes, Scams and Cons*; Jack Blum, Washington, D.C., April 11, 2002

United States Senate – Committee on Governmental Affairs: *Crime and Secrecy – The Use of Offshore Banks and Companies*; a report to the Senate, Washington, D.C., August 1985

United States Senate – Committee on Governmental Affairs, Permanent Subcommittee on Investigations: *Offshore Tax Havens*; Robert M. Morgenthau, district attorney for the County of Manhattan, City of New York, Washington, D.C., July 18, 2001

——: *National Money Laundering Strategy*; Joseph M. Myers, acting deputy assistant secretary (enforcement policy), United States Department of the Treasury, Washington, D.C., March 6, 2001

——: *Law Enforcement Activities Related to Our Anti-Money Laundering Efforts and Correspondent Bank Relationships*; Mary Lee Warren, deputy assistant attorney general, Criminal Division, United States Department of Justice, Washington, D.C., March 6, 2001

——: *Money Laundering and Correspondent Banking*; testimony of Jack Blum, March 2, 2001; Robert Evans, March 2, 2001; statement of John M. Mathewson, March 1, 2001

——: *Hearing on Private Banking and Money Laundering: Abacha Sons – A Case Study of Opportunities and Vulnerabilities*; Washington, D.C., November 9, 1999

——: *Hearing on Micro-Cap Stock Fraud*; testimony of Arthur Levitt, chairman U.S. Commission; testimony of Barry R. Goldsmith, executive vice-president NASD Regulation; testimony of Joseph P. Borg, director, Alabama Securities Commission, Washington, D.C., September 22, 1997

United States Senate – Committee on the Judiciary, Subcommittee on Technology, Terrorism and Government Information: *Narco-Terror – The Worldwide Connection Between Drugs and Terror*; Rand Beers, assistant secretary for International Narcotics and Law Enforcement Affairs, and Francis X. Taylor, ambassador-at-large for counterterrorism, Washington, D.C., March 13, 2002

MAJOR REPORTS, COURT DOCUMENTS, AND DISSERTATIONS

Assemblée Nationale Française: *La Lutte Contre le Blanchiment des Capitaux en Suisse – Un Combat de Façade*; Paris, 2001

Australian Institute for Gambling Research: McMillen, Jan and Woolley, Richard – *Money Laundering In Australian Casinos*; Canberra, 2001

Beare, Margaret E.: *Critique of a Compliance-Driven Enforcement Strategy – Money Laundering and the Financial Sector*; draft working paper, Toronto, 2002

——: *Facts from Fiction – Tactics and Strategies of Addressing Organized Crime and Organized Criminals*; perspectives on organized crime in Canada for the Canadian Police College, Ottawa, 2000

Beare, Margaret E. and Naylor, R.T.: *Organized Crime within the Context of Economic Relationships*; Nathanson Centre for the Study of Organized Crime and Corruption, Toronto, 1999

Bell, Dr. R.E.: *Discretion and Decision-Making in Money Laundering Prosecutions*; from the office of the director of public prosecutions for Northern Ireland, writing in a personal capacity, undated

Bird, Graham and Rajan, Ramkishen: *Economic Globalization – How Far and How Much Further?*; Center for International Economic Studies, Adelaide, Australia, April 2001

Brookings Institute for Public Policy Education: Caux Roundtable – *Dirty Money – Nourishing Poverty and Terrorism*; remarks by Richard Newcomb, director, Office of Foreign Assets Control, U.S. Treasury Department, and Robert Morgenthau, district attorney, County of New York, Washington, D.C., 2002

Canadian Security Intelligence Service: *Counter-Terrorism*; Ottawa, 2002

Council on Foreign Relations: *Report of an Independent Task Force – Terrorist Financing*; New York, 2002

Executive Office of the President of the United States: The President's Commission on Organized Crime: *The Impact – Organized Crime Today*; Washington, D.C., 1986

——: *A Report to the President and the Attorney General of the United States – America's Habit – Drug Abuse, Drug Trafficking and Organized Crime*; Washington, D.C., 1986

——: *Cash Connection – The Interim Report on Organized Crime, Financial Institutions and Money Laundering*; Washington, D.C., 1984

Financial Action Task Force: *Report on Money Laundering Typologies*; Paris, 2003

——: *Review of the FATF Forty Recommendations*; Paris, May 30, 2002

Fraser, A. Gabriella: *Can the Sir Stafford Sands Model of the Bahamian Economy Survive Today's Global Economy?*; 33rd Conference of the Caribbean Center for Monetary Studies, Belize, November 2001

General Accounting Office: *Anti-Money-Laundering Efforts in the Securities Industry*; Washington, D.C., 2001

——: *Money Laundering – Oversight of Suspicious Activity Reporting at Bank-Affiliated Broker-Dealers*; Washington, D.C., 2001

——: *Money Laundering, Raul Salinas, Citibank, and Alleged Money Laundering*; Washington, D.C., 2001

——: *Money Laundering – Regulatory Oversight of Offshore Private Banking Activities*; Washington, D.C., 2001

——: *Suspicious Bank Activities – Possible Money Laundering by U.S. Corporations for Russian Entities*; Washington, D.C., 2000

——: *Money Laundering – Observations on Private Banking and Related Oversight of Selected Offshore Jurisdictions*; Washington, D.C., 1999

——: *Money Laundering – FinCEN's Law Enforcement Support Role Is Evolving*; Washington, D.C., 1998

——: *Money Laundering – FinCEN Needs to Better Communicate Regulatory Priorities and Timeliness*; Washington, D.C., 1998

——: *Report to the Chairman, Subcommittee on General Oversight and Investigations, Committee on Banking and Financial Services, House of Representatives: Money Laundering – Regulatory Oversight of Offshore Private Banking Activities*; Washington, D.C., 1998

Gillespie, Kate: *Smuggling and the Global Firm*; Third Annual International Business Forum, Temple University, Philadelphia, 2002

Goreux, Louis: *Conflict Diamonds*; World Bank, Africa Region Working Paper Series No. 13, Washington, D.C., March 2001

Government Accounting Office: *Extent of Money Laundering through Credit Cards Is Unknown*; Washington, D.C., 2002

Government of Canada: *Canada-U.S. Cross Border Crime and Security Co-operation*; Ottawa, September 2002

Government of Great Britain: *Report of Mr Rodney Gallagher of Coopers and Lybrand on the Survey of Offshore Financial Sectors in the Caribbean Dependent Territories*; London, 1990

Grand Court of the Cayman Islands: *Indictment – The Queen v Donald Stewart, Brian Cunha, Ivan Burges, Judith Donegan*; Georgetown, Cayman Islands, 2002

International Monetary Fund: *Governance, Corruption and Economic Performance; Corruption around the World – Causes, Consequences, Scope and Cures; Institutionalized Corruption and the Kleptocratic State; Corruption, Extortion and Evasion; Corruption, Structural Reforms and Economic Performance in the Transition Economies; Improving Governance and Fighting Corruption in the Baltic and CIS Countries – The Role of the IMF*; Washington, D.C., September 2002

——: *Caribbean Offshore Financial Centers – Past, Present and Possibilities for the Future*; a working paper prepared by Esther C. Suss, Oral H. Williams, and Chandima Mendis, Washington, D.C., May 2002

——: *Enhancing Contributions to Combating Money Laundering*; Washington, D.C., 2001

——: *Financial System Abuse, Financial Crime and Money Laundering*; Washington, D.C., 2001

——: *Offshore Financial Centers*; background paper, Washington, D.C., June 2000

——: *Offshore Banking – An Analysis of Micro- and Macro-Prudential Issues*; Errico, Luca and Musalem, Alberto, Washington, D.C., January 1999

——: *Money Laundering and the International Financial System*; Tanzi, Vito, Washington, D.C., 1996

——: *The Structure and Operation of the World Gold Market*; Washington, D.C., September 1993

Laidlow, Philip: *Shams*; Association of Corporate Trustees, July 2000

Library of Congress, Congressional Research Service: *The U.S.A. Patriot Act – A Legal Analysis*; Doyle, Charles, Washington, D.C., 2002

——: *The U.S.A. Patriot Act – A Sketch*; Doyle, Charles, Washington, D.C., 2002

Naylor, R.T.: *Follow-the-Money Methods in Crime Control Policy*; A study prepared for the Nathanson Centre for the Study of Organized Crime and Corruption, Toronto, 1999

Oxfam: *Tax Havens, Releasing the Hidden Billions for Poverty Eradication*; London, June 2000

Petras, James: *Dirty Money Foundation of U.S. Growth and Empire Size and Scope of Money Laundering by U.S. Banks*; report to the Center for Research on Globalization, Mexico, May 19, 2001

Phillips, Dion E.: *Another Look at the Royal Bahamas Defense Force*; Center for Hemispheric Defense Studies, University of the Virgin Islands, St. Thomas, August 2002

Public Citizen: *Congress Watch – Congressional Leaders' Soft Money Accounts Show Need for Campaign Finance Reform Bills*; Washington, D.C., February 2002

Robb Evans and Associates, LLC: *Various Reports of Receiver's Activities in the Matter of JK Publications, MJD Service Corp., et al.*; California, 2002

Santino, Umberto: *The Financial Mafia – The Illegal Accumulation of Wealth and the Financial-Industrial Complex*; private paper, 1986

Securities and Exchange Commission: *A.S. Goldmen and Co., Inc., and Employees Charged with Variety of Microcap-Related Violations*; Washington, D.C., 1999

Sirius, Francis J.: *Cubans in Miami – An Historic Perspective*; Division of Humanities, St. Thomas University, Miami, Florida. Prepared for delivery at the annual meeting of the Florida Historical Society, Miami, Florida, May 13, 1988

Supreme Court of the State of New York, County of New York: *The People of the State of New York against Harry Bloomfield and Stuart Creggy*; New York, 2002

Swiss Bankers Association: *Switzerland and the Fight against Money Laundering*; Basel, 2001

United Nations: *Report of the Policy Working Group on the United Nations and Terrorism*; New York, 2002

United Nations, Office for Drug Control and Crime Prevention, Global Program against Money-Laundering: *Financial Havens, Banking Secrecy and Money Laundering*; authored by Jack Blum, Michael Levi, R. Thomas Naylor, Phil Williams, New York, 1998

United Nations, Security Council: *Report of the Monitoring Group Established Pursuant to Security Council Resolution 1363 (2001) and Extended by Resolution 1390 (2002)*; New York, May 13, 2002

United States of America: *An Act to Deter and Punish Terrorist Acts in the United States and around the World, to Enhance Law Enforcement, Investigatory Tools, and for Other Purposes (Uniting and Strengthening America by Providing Appropriate Tools Required to Intercept and Obstruct Terrorism – U.S.A. Patriot Act)*; Washington, D.C., 2001

United States Court of Appeals for the District of Columbia Circuit: *Final Report of the Independent Counsel for Iran/Contra Matters*; Washington, D.C., 1993

United States Department of Justice, United States Attorney, Central District of California: *Malibu Man Pleads Guilty to $37 Million Internet Credit Card Fraud Scheme*; January 22, 2001

United States Department of Justice, United States Attorney, District of New Jersey: *Letter to Hon. Alfred J. Lechner, Jr., re: United States v John Mathewson*; July 29, 1999

——: *Plea Agreement with John Mathewson*; March 3, 1997

——: *Letter to Mr. William T. Walsh, U.S. district court clerk, re: Johnson and Dinan v United States of America: Brief of the United States in Opposition to the Petitioners' Motion for Return of Property; affidavit of special agent Sean W. McCarthy; declaration of James P. Springer*; Proposed Order, November 27, 1996

United States Department of State: Bureau for International Narcotics and Law Enforcement Affairs: *International Narcotics Control Strategy Report*; Washington, D.C., 2003, 2002, 2001, 2000

United States Department of the Treasury: *National Money Laundering Strategy Report*; Washington, D.C., 2002

——: *International Counter-Money Laundering Act of 2000, a Section by Section Analysis*; March 2000

——: *An Introduction to Electronic Money Issues*; staff paper for the conference Toward Electronic Money and Banking, Washington, D.C., 1996

United States District Court, District of New Jersey: *Amended Judgment in a Criminal Case, United States of America v John Mathewson, Attempt to Commit Tax Evasion*; Newark, 1999

——: *Amended Judgment in a Criminal Case, United States of America v John Mathewson, Conspiracy to Commit International Money Laundering*; Newark, 1999

——: *Indictment, United States of America v Francis Joseph Russo, Joann Russo, Joseph Russo, Frank Russo Jr, Joseph Olkowski, Daniel Zielinski, William S. Prevost III, Anthony Lee Marinacco, John Mathewson*; 1996

United States District Court, Eastern District of New York: *The European Community v RJR Nabisco, Inc, and others*

United States District Court, Southern District of New York: *Security and Exchange Commission v Invest Better 2001, Cole A. Bartiromo and John/Jane Does 1-10; Declaration of Craig S. Warkol in Support of Plaintiff's Motion for Summary Judgment and an Order of Preclusion; Exhibits to Declaration of Craig S. Warkol, Volumes 1-4*; 2002

United States General Accounting Office: *Report to the Chairman, Permanent Subcommittee on Investigations, Committee on Government Affairs, United States Senate – Anti-Money Laundering Efforts in the Securities Industry*; Washington, D.C., 2001

United States Senate: *Report to the Committee on Foreign Relations – The BCCI Affair*; Kerry, John and Brown, Hank, December 1992

United States Senate: Permanent Subcommittee on Investigations – *Report on Correspondent Banking: A Gateway to Money Laundering*; Minority Staff, Washington, D.C., February 2001

Wachtel, Howard M.: *Corporate Governance and Tax Distortion in the Global Economy*; InterDisciplinary Council on the Global Economy, Washington, D.C., 2000

——: *The Mosaic of Global Taxes*; Global Futures-Institute for Social Studies, Washington, D.C., 2000

White House Task Force: *International Crime Threat Assessment*; Washington, D.C., 2000

Winer, Jonathan M.: *Illicit Finance and Global Conflict – Economies of Conflict: Private Sector Activity in Armed Conflict*; Fafo Institute for Applied Social Science, Program for International Co-operation and Conflict Resolution, Oslo, 2002

Wriston, Walter B.: *Dumb Networks and Smart Capital*; Cato Institute, Annual Monetary Conference, New York, 1997

INDEX

OTHER BOOKS BY JEFFREY ROBINSON

FICTION

A True and Perfect Knight

The Monk's Disciples

The Margin of the Bulls

The Ginger Jar

Pietrov and Other Games

NON-FICTION

Prescription Games: Money, Ego, and Power
Inside the Global Pharmaceutical Industry

The Merger: How Organized Crime Is
Taking Over Canada and the World

The Manipulators

The Hotel

The Laundrymen

Bardot: Two Lives

The End of the American Century

The Risk Takers: Five Years On

Rainier and Grace

Yamani: The Inside Story

Minus Millionaires

The Risk Takers

Teamwork

Bette Davis